A SEA OF POSSIBILITIES

The Revolutionary Age

FRANCIS D. COGLIANO, CHRISTA BREAULT DIERKSHEIDE, ELIGA H. GOULD, AND PATRICK GRIFFIN, EDITORS

A Sea of Possibilities

THE REVOLUTIONARY ATLANTIC WORLD OF CAPTAIN THOMAS ALLEN

Kenneth J. Banks

UNIVERSITY OF VIRGINIA PRESS
Charlottesville and London

The University of Virginia Press is situated on the traditional lands of the Monacan Nation, and the Commonwealth of Virginia was and is home to many other Indigenous people. We pay our respect to all of them, past and present. We also honor the enslaved African and African American people who built the University of Virginia, and we recognize their descendants. We commit to fostering voices from these communities through our publications and to deepening our collective understanding of their histories and contributions.

University of Virginia Press

Printed in the United States of America on acid-free paper

First published 2026

1 3 5 7 9 8 6 4 2

LIBRARY OF CONGRESS CATALOGING-IN-PUBLICATION DATA
Names: Banks, Kenneth J., author
Title: A sea of possibilities : the revolutionary Atlantic World of Captain Thomas Allen / Kenneth J. Banks.
Description: Charlottesville : University of Virginia Press, 2026. | Series: The revolutionary age | Includes bibliographical references and index.
Identifiers: LCCN 2026003536 (print) | LCCN 2026003537 (ebook) | ISBN 9780813953939 hardback | ISBN 9780813953953 ebook
Subjects: LCSH: Allen, Thomas, 1728–1793 | Ship captains—United States | Merchants—United States | United States—History—Revolution, 1775–1783 | United States—Commerce—History—18th century | BISAC: HISTORY / United States / Revolutionary Period (1775–1800) | BIOGRAPHY & AUTOBIOGRAPHY / Aviation & Nautical | LCGFT: Biographies
Classification: LCC E467.1.A45 B36 2026 (print) | LCC E467.1.A45 (ebook)
LC record available at https://lccn.loc.gov/2026003536
LC ebook record available at https://lccn.loc.gov/2026003537

Maps by Nat Case, INCase, LLC.
Cover art: Painting of the sloop *Delancey,* L. F. Tantillo, 2016 (by permission of the artist); background, from engraving by Gustave Doré, scene from *The Rime of the Ancient Mariner* (duncan1980/iStock.com)
Cover design: Cecilia Sorochin

To Tracey

CONTENTS

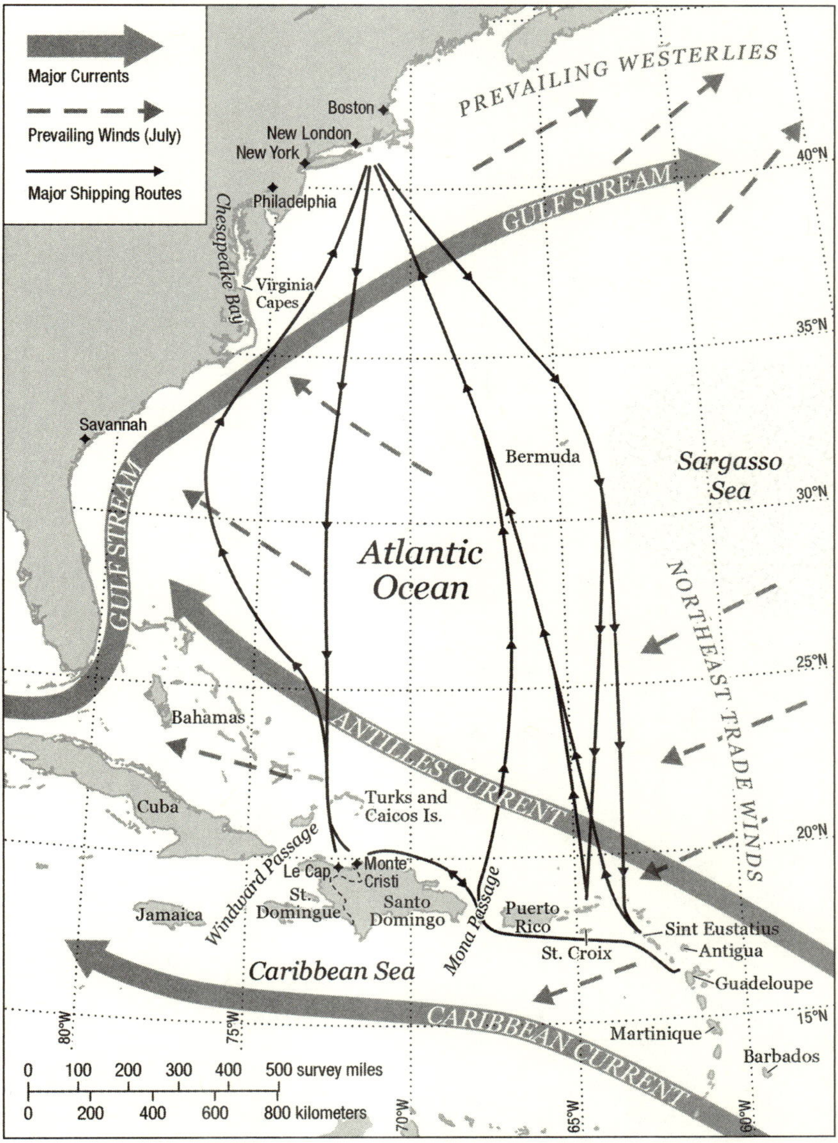

MAP 1. Sailing routes Connecticut–Caribbean Sea

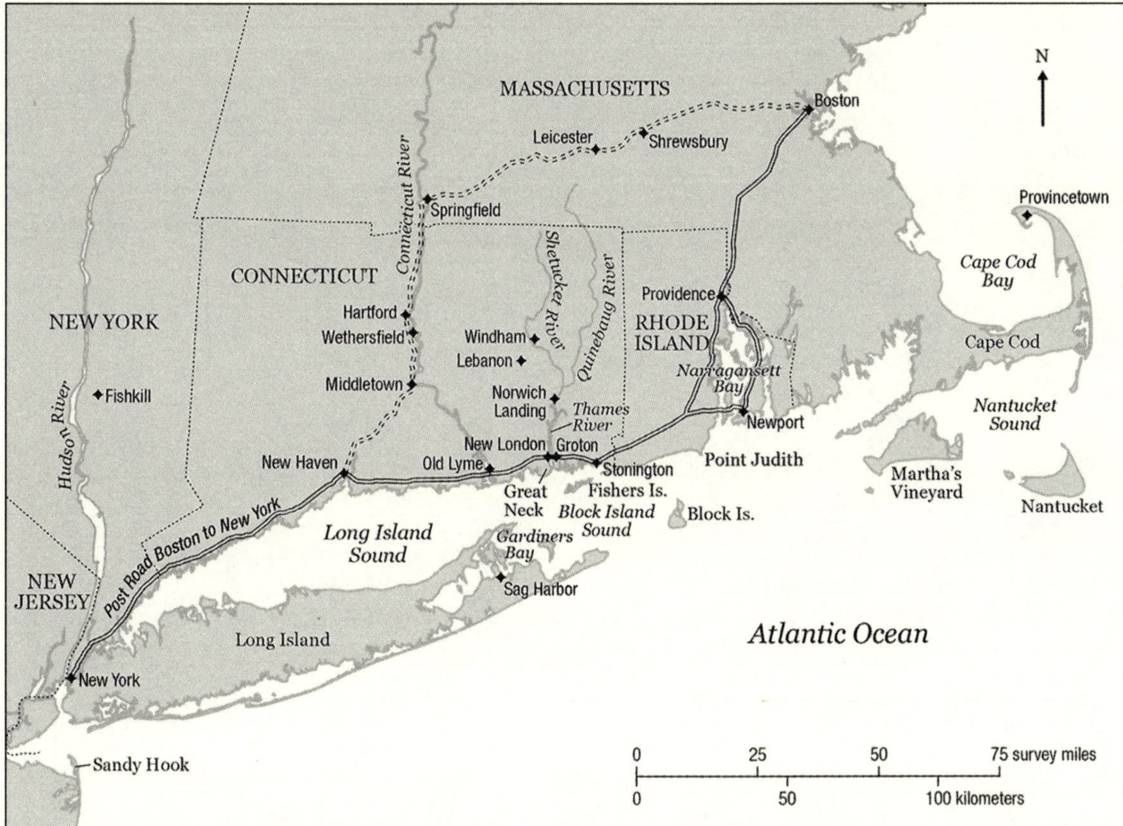

MAP 2. Thomas Allen's New England, ca. 1770

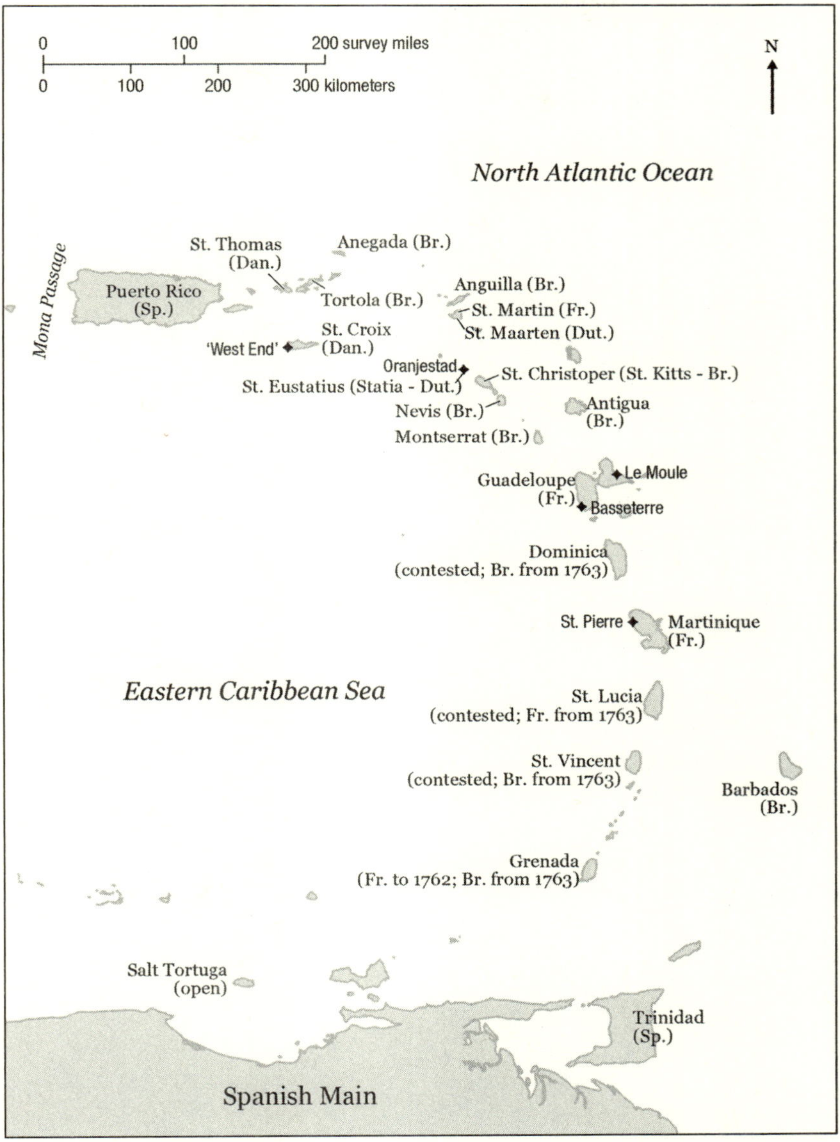

MAP 3. The eastern Caribbean with imperial claims, ca. 1770

Introduction

THE SEA PERVADED EARLY American and Revolutionary-era life. Yet the major histories of the era are largely turned toward the land, and the battles fought on it. Forest, field, and farm were undeniably important. But the deep blue sea, lapping an undulating coastline over a thousand miles long and rolling away to the eastern horizon, mattered greatly to all people who inhabited the mainland colonies. The Atlantic Ocean provided more than just livelihoods, or death from those livelihoods. It connected far-flung family, ferried new ideas and new people in exchanges between the Old World and the New, and offered a potential escape from oppression and poverty or, for many, entry into a new kind of hell. For some it became a pathway to self-discovery. The maritime world was a way of life, firmly written into the past in ways whose import has receded with time.

The influence of the Atlantic Ocean is written, for example, into the Declaration of Independence in ways that may not be immediately obvious. Many of the contributors were lawyers and landowners, plus one lobbyist and scientist (and former printer), Benjamin Franklin. Virginia delegate Thomas Jefferson, the primary composer of the Declaration, had little interest in seaborne trade or its connection to political values. He once remarked, "Agriculture [is] the surest road to affluence and the best preservative of morals." Only one member of the drafting committee, Massachusetts lawyer John Adams, had had close firsthand interactions with maritime merchants.[1] Yet the oceanic currents moved quietly beneath Jefferson's quill, reminding modern readers of the importance of the maritime context to the struggle for independence.

The seldom cited section on grievances, constituting over half the document, offers twenty-seven specific complaints of tyrannical misconduct by King George III. It submitted crucial evidence "to a candid world" of why American independence was necessary. The word "sea" appears in only three grievances, concerning the maritime issues of holding trials overseas, direct attacks on colonial towns by the British Royal Navy, and the highly contentious issue of impressing colonial American sailors into the Royal Navy during peacetime (nos. 19, 24, and 26, respectively).[2]

But issues emanating from royal control over maritime affairs provoked anger in more nuanced ways. Several charges addressed heavy-handed control by the Royal Navy over British American trading vessels or movement on sea lanes. These charges included the crown's restricting overseas migrants (no. 7), confining the seaborne trade of most colonies and ending access to the New England fisheries (no. 16), and outlawing all mainland seaborne trade in the Prohibitory Act of December 1775 (no. 23).[3]

The Declaration also listed transporting foreign troops across the Atlantic "to Compleat the works of death" against people settled on the mainland (no. 25). While this last charge might seem to be connected to the sea only marginally, most of these troops would be stationed at least initially in port towns. Jefferson sandwiched grievance 25 between charges against the Royal Navy of bombarding mainland ports and impressing sailors residing in North America into unwanted service in the Navy. Its placement likely was not arbitrary. Grievances 23, 24, and 25 seem to have cohered as a single logical argument in the minds of Jefferson and the other signers.

The erection of a much larger (and more efficient) customs bureaucracy to enforce taxation of seaborne trade in the eighty-nine officially designated ports in settler America prompted several of the most outraged charges. There were nine in all (nos. 8–14, 17, and 18). These charges included the crown's quartering of troops in major seaboard towns to enforce the king's law (especially to ensure prosecutions against ship customs violators), the king's direct payment of colonial judges, largely from customs receipts (thereby helping ensure customs duties enforcement), the inequitable taxation of shipped commodities such as tea, and the imposition of British Admiralty courts, which lacked juries.[4]

Three other charges touched indirectly on maritime affairs. They included the abdication of rule by royal governors, three of whom had retreated to British naval ships and left the countryside in chaos, and the disbanding of colonial assemblies for "opposing with manly firmness" the royal will, including restrictions imposed in the highly controversial Boston

Port Act (nos. 4 and 5).[5] Even charge number 20, "abolishing the free System of English Laws in a neighbouring Province," a direct reference to the Quebec Act of 1774, touched lightly on maritime issues. The act enraged American settlers because it assigned British control over the vast interior beyond the Appalachian Mountains to the single colony of Quebec and its majority French-speaking population while granting freedom of religion to French Catholics. Less well known is that it also transferred part of the Grand Banks fisheries and sealing grounds—long central to the livelihoods of New Englanders—to the "arbitrary" government of Quebec.[6]

At least sixteen and arguably nineteen of the twenty-seven grievances—or more than two-thirds—objected to direct or indirect royal control or use of the Atlantic Ocean, especially those parts integral to settler America's needs and identity. Yet no historian's analysis suggests that problems in settler ports, trade restrictions, the abuse of maritime merchants and mariners, the manner of exacting customs duties, and the imposition of Admiralty policing may have constituted the impetus that sent the Declaration into history. Historian Steven Pincus perhaps comes closest when he observes that the grievances "crystalliz[ed] deeply held Patriot beliefs . . . on both sides of the Atlantic" around the themes of suppression of a freer seaborne trade, limitations on transatlantic free migration, and British support for the oceanic trade in enslaved people (a charge that Congress expunged from the final version of the Declaration).[7]

Just as many of the Declaration's motivating grievances were steeped in seawater, the influences of the maritime world saturated much of early American and Revolutionary-era history. The American Revolution cannot be fully understood without grasping its maritime dimensions. The best method for exploring the ocean's influence, I believe, is to follow historian Michael Jarvis in viewing change "from the deck of a ship."[8]

The particular ship's deck from which this story is told belonged to an innovative and ambitious sea captain, Thomas Allen of New London, Connecticut. He and his family lived, prospered, and suffered during the long, turbulent era of the American Revolution. They survived death, disaster, and indebtedness by turning and returning to the vast reaches of the ocean, using it as a resource, a refuge, and a reservoir of hope. Their story illustrates how and why mariners and their coastal communities fitted themselves out with new ideas and practices to chart independent courses during the American Revolutionary era.[9] The Allen family's varied maritime experiences serve as a kind of compendium of possible choices, opportunities, and catastrophes for the free, and even a select few enslaved, settler peoples in what became a new republic.

Existing scholarship pieces together crucial parts of settler maritime culture from four distinct perspectives. Histories from below decks have shown how social mobility in shipboard environments shaped the opportunities and political choices of sailors, laying the groundwork for a revolutionary consciousness.[10] These mariners included Indigenous sailors and "Black Jacks," or freed African American mariners. Enslaved sailors "appropriated ships as conduits for dissent" to plunge into their own currents of revolutionary liberty.[11] A second line, largely taken by social historians of gender, has produced histories from the boarding house. These accounts underscore how shoreside women—daughters, partners, wives, and widows—not only managed homes and economies on behalf of their absent seagoing men but carved out independent lives of their own, often under harsh circumstances and without a genuine legal voice.[12] A third and very large area of study, histories from the counting house, has analyzed commerce conducted through British American ports and port merchants. These works trace the trajectories of specific commodities, the intricacies of mercantile networks, and the rise of mercantile capitalism, with the ocean a steady presence visible through the counting-house windows.[13] Finally, the view from the quarterdeck reflects the resurgence of interest in Patriot naval operations during the Revolution, and especially Patriot privateering, as captured in popular works.[14]

One goal of my biography of Thomas Allen and his family is to suggest how these separate historiographic courses merge to form a single tale.

An Atlantic World perspective is crucial to understanding the vast changes that helped shape the Revolutionary era. The Atlantic World geographically encompasses the Atlantic-oriented portions of Europe, Africa, and the Americas. It places mobility on the sea, and the sea itself, at the center of the story, tying together what have often been viewed as separate social, economic, and political events.[15] No part of the Atlantic World was arguably of greater consequence to the advent of the Revolution than the Caribbean Sea and the numerous plantation islands anchored in its vast waters. As Allen's and his family's story suggests, the direct roots of settler American wealth, and eventual settler hostility to new British imperial regimes, can be traced back directly to the spectacular rise of trade between the mainland colonies and the Caribbean from the mid-eighteenth century.[16] Trade and cultural exchange between the British mainland colonies and the non-British Caribbean islands were at least as crucial to the American revolutionary movement as the better-known conflicts over taxation, struggles for political autonomy, migration and social upheaval, or the rise of a market-driven consumer society. And the brokers of that trade and contact in revolutionary times were ship captains like Allen.

Historical work on sea captains occupies a foggy realm. Studies from the vantage point of common sailors as an emerging laboring class portray British Atlantic sea captains as vicious and arbitrary agents of an inexorable, eviscerating capitalist ethic.[17] There is much truth to this construct with respect to the longer transatlantic voyages. But the reverse could also be observed. For the New England–Caribbean run on smaller sloops, schooners, and brigantines of the kind that Allen and most of his fellow captains and merchants sailed, kinship bonds, existing community hierarchies, and the dangers of the sea often moderated spleen or wanton cruelty.[18] It took a community to sail and survive on vast oceanic expanses, and ship masters of smaller vessels from the secondary ports often worked with the crew rather than ruling as petty tyrants over them.

Oddly, sea captains are nearly invisible in most studies of ports and port merchants. When they are mentioned, it is in reference to their roles in managing the ships, such as "choosing and hiring a crew, making sure they were paid, stowing and unloading the cargo . . . handling the vessel at sea and serving as [the] business agent abroad." This last role of serving as overseas agents for merchants is the most important, for sea captains were the supercargoes of mercantile capitalism. They bought, sold, and arranged cargoes in an astonishing variety of overseas markets for port merchants back home.[19] Mainland merchant ship captains often controlled their own independent seaborne movements out of necessity long before "Independence" became a political rallying cry.

The great leeway in a ship master's instructions, along with easy access to cheap, non-British plantation commodities, combined to create a settler American culture of contraband. True, most colonial sea captains appeared to act quietly within the parameters of royal law and existing trade regulations. Yet contraband trade appears to have occurred on a large scale.[20] Historians believe that settler smuggling arose principally from a handful of causes: from long-standing, sloppy customs regulations enforcement that invited illicit activity, from patriotic fervor after 1765, or simply from greed. Others embrace Adam Smith's famous observation about an archetypical smuggler who "would have been, in every respect, an excellent citizen, had not the laws of his country made that a crime which nature never meant to be so."[21] But Allen's life suggests that a more subtle interplay of personality, economic realities, and evolving social conditions fostered illicit trade well before 1760, and helped it expand greatly after.

Minor merchants and ship captains strove mightily to improve their wealth and community standing, but always with an anxious glance over their shoulders at those pressing from behind. "Trade was a fickle master," one historian has noted, "and the instability of commerce and investment cast a mantle of anxious foreboding over the eighteenth-century middling classes."[22] People like Allen composed what might be called a "wary middling rank" of smaller merchants on the make who anxiously built their economic "interest," as they would have called it, in a wildly uncertain world. They formed a distinct group of people whom I refer to as "strivers." They were an eighteenth-century version of the self-made man, men and women in the mold of the original ambitious settler striver, Benjamin Franklin. They fashioned themselves into effective individuals to attain material and social success based on a highly personal, lifelong commitment to relentless self-improvement.[23]

Many strivers were largely honest. But in the rough-and-tumble world of Atlantic seaborne trade, several intelligent, educated ship masters and sailors became true rogues, who often used illicit means, and even violence, to take their seat at the captain's table. They were not mere scoundrels but more akin to a "self-fashioned gentleman . . . determined to 'make' himself through any means necessary."[24] As this biography makes clear, Allen and nearly all his many close associates and peers were cut from the same cloth. Several later became leading public leaders on the Patriot side during the Revolutionary era.

For many captains, their roles changed as they aged. Life did not simply end when they stowed their quadrants and retired. While some sank into destitution onshore, others sought a tranquil life as taverners or became proprietors of quiet country stores, as Allen's father did. But a select number of the more ambitious became merchants and used their connections, wealth, and sailing experience to become forceful community leaders. Among those who sailed early in life and later emerged as major Patriot leaders on land were Battle of Saratoga hero General Horatio Gates, South Carolina politician Christopher Gadsden, wartime financial wizard Robert Morris, General Francis Marion (the Swamp Fox), Back-to-Africa advocate Paul Cuffe, Declaration signer Carter Braxton, and American merchant, general, and enduring enigma Benedict Arnold.[25]

After his voyaging years ended, Allen lived through a variety of different pursuits and life stages. He was by turns a leading shipping magnate, destitute debtor, and innovative coffeehouse proprietor, among other pursuits. But he made his unique contribution to Revolutionary-era America by pioneering a popular newspaper column informed by Enlightenment ideals, his famous Marine List. With his quill, Allen crafted an opinion column championing a new, if racially exclusive, vision of the young republic as formed of "Brethren in Navigation."

For settler mariners and their families, economic independence, advancement based on merit, personal liberty, a free market, and the gentility born of cosmopolitan connections were not simply ideas. They were practical realities learned through difficult and often deadly experience acquired sailing on the wide Atlantic Ocean. Allen's tale is a chronicle of only one mariner's life. But his story, unfolding as it does on a vast oceanic stage, serves as a useful, fascinating, and provocative alternative to the well-trod pathways familiar from popular histories and even some scholarship. Allen's story helps us cut through romantic perspectives on the Revolutionary era and get at a deeper truth, often harsh, by interpolating the sea's role into the history of a new republic in the Americas.

A note on the use of "settler": throughout, I have adopted historian Alan Taylor's use of this word though without his more specific reference to backcountry migrants. Although authors have used various designations, "settler America" is used here to capture the diversity of people, free and unfree, who originally migrated or were forcibly migrated across the Atlantic and who remained for much of their existence in what became the British mainland colonies; in their origin stories and travels they were distinct from the Indigenous peoples, whom Europeans often referred to collectively as "Indians."[26] The term is not used here in the same way that "settler colonialism" is used in scholarship.[27] Readers are reminded that in the Revolutionary and subsequent eras, "free" does not connote social or legal equality with or between settlers of European origin.

Prologue

ONE EMPIRE TO RULE

WHATEVER GEORGIAN-ERA LONDON LOOKED, sounded, and smelled like, with its towering churches and rotting, refuse-strewn alleys, waves of rushing people and trotting horses, church bells and the shrill cries of hawkers, it was founded on the sea as much as on the land.[1] As the premier port of an emerging oceanic empire, London was permeated by the sea, even though it lay nearly fifty miles upriver from ocean currents. The city was arrayed roughly west to east, with bands of major thoroughfares forming a keel of sorts, along which most of the foundational institutions of imperial power could be found. In the 1730s it started its swift rise as the heart of an Atlantic empire, "Protestant, commercial, maritime, and free."[2]

On a chilly February morning in 1734, a single hackney carriage, carrying the Allen family, rumbled along the length of that keel. The carriage first passed through the fashionable western edge of London. This largely genteel district was also home to the government offices that guided the newly emerging empire. In the state offices clustered around the king's residence at St. James Palace, Westminster Hall, where Parliament met, and the busy inns and coffeehouses nearby, the various commissioners and officers who directed the king's overseas imperial affairs met to quaff sherry, browbeat underlings, and haggle over policies.[3]

The new imperial institutions consisted of the Admiralty Board, including the Navy; the Southern Department, which supervised the political rule of overseas colonies; the Treasury Office; and the Lords Commissioners for Trade and Plantations, or Board of Trade, which formulated all policies applicable to overseas merchant shipping and trade.[4] Discussions of state policy were "smothered in a cloud of private understandings among friendly antagonists." This meant that patronage often obscured the management of colonial problems and implementing regulations to promote and defend overseas trade.[5] Even so, this small cadre of administrators kept a wary eye on the tack taken by their counterparts in the four other major European Atlantic maritime powers, particularly France.[6] Only the year before, Parliament had passed a major act to curb the alarming rise in smuggling from the French Caribbean sugar islands to the British mainland colonies. Most colonists despised it as the Molasses Act.[7]

The hackney carriage halted on Portugal Street, under the sign of the White Bear Inn. Known informally in the 1730s as Piccadilly, after a famous lace collar sold to the city's elite, the area had become a terminus for passengers arriving from points further south and west of London.[8] Perhaps with a change of horses, the hackney moved slowly east toward London's center, known as the City. The coach first clattered down Fleet Street, passing near the offices of the Society for the Propagation of the Gospel in Foreign Parts, housed at Warwick Court. The Society sent missionaries to the Americas to help reinvigorate the Church of England's overseas presence. The coach then passed around the august dome of St. Paul's Church, which hovered with sublime solemnity over the waves of humanity jostling below. These pillars of the Anglican Church played a more subtle but no less important role in creating strong spiritual and cultural identities in the mainland colonies.[9]

As the street bent again and changed its name to Cornhill, the hackney's passengers would have caught a glimpse of the Bank of England sitting between two churches and looking oddly awkward and misplaced. Founded a mere forty years earlier, in its maze of busy offices clerks handled the innumerable government transactions that paid for crews and arranged the massive wartime loans that funded ships, which in turn projected growing British power around the Atlantic Basin.[10]

The coach then passed on toward the large, glass-windowed shops and open galleries of the Royal Exchange. One contemporary observer likened this part of the City to "a beehive, continually crouded, the passages being never empty."[11] Coffeehouses proliferated in the maze of streets around the Exchange. By the mid-1730s, there were about 550 in all of London, selling bowls of hot coffee and cheap meals. Each coffeehouse attracted a specific mix of clientele. Maritime merchants gathered at Lloyd's or Garraway's on nearby Lombard Street to set terms for insuring ships, while West India planters and major wholesalers in the Caribbean trades preferred the more opulent Jamaica coffeehouse, where they brought their enslaved Black men, dressed in livery of red trimmed with white, to wait on them. London merchants with mainland interests took seats in the New England Coffee House, exchanging gossip and reading newspapers from Boston, New York, or Philadelphia.[12]

Most of the city's major import and export businesses were located in neighboring streets and alleys. These formed "a Hotch-Potch of half-moon and serpentine Streets, close, dismal, long lanes, stinking Allies [alleys] . . . [and] suffocating Yards," as one merchant recalled.[13] Mercantile houses such as Lane and Caswell in St. Nicholas Lane supplied colonial merchants across the Atlantic Ocean with cloth, silverware, iron tools, nautical instruments, cut paper, and maps, among the many goods that maintained the empire's arterial reach. Snippets of French, Palatinate German, or Ashkenazi Yiddish could be heard among the voices. As the street changed its name again to become Leadenhall, the carriage passed near the new, manicured offices of the English East India Company.[14]

Leaving the eastern edge of the City, the hackney turned abruptly south on the Minories toward the River Thames. Here the passengers would have had their last glimpse of London Bridge, still crowded with residences, the Tower of London, and the massive Custom House. Merchants and mariners despised customs officers for their plodding ways, unfathomable amount of paperwork, and high rates. But customs officers collected the duties that, along with the internal (or excise) taxes, paid the lion's share of the cost of British sea power.[15]

The carriage's horses then slowed their pace to negotiate the narrower streets of Aldgate and Whitechapel before entering the dockside district of Wapping. More than 12,000 mariners and their families lived and worked in these districts of ramshackle wooden homes, taverns, and shops. Their number alone exceeded the populations of all British colonial cities save Boston. Reflecting Britain's imperial and commercial reach, people from across the seven seas had settled near the docks: French Huguenots, Dutch and Hessian émigrés, "Black Jacks" from the Americas, and a tiny but growing population of destitute *lascars,* or Indian sailors, mainly from Bengal. They all mingled and fraternized on the busy streets, shops, and taverns.[16]

Ships of all sizes unloaded crates, trunks, sacks, and barrels from every port imaginable—Surat to Surinam, Copenhagen to Kingston in Jamaica,

FIGURE 1. "A View of the Custom House, with part of the Tower, taken from ye River Thames, London," printed by Thomas Bowles, 1753. Engraving showing the density of the London waterfront and its busy seaborne traffic. The Custom House was sited just below London Bridge; the bridge hindered oceangoing vessels from moving further upriver. (Topographical Collection/Alamy Stock Photo, 2E9HH2J)

Amsterdam to faraway Alexandria in Egypt. They unloaded dark sugar, Dutch enamelware, bolts of dyed cloth in every color of the rainbow, fresh-cut timber from the Baltic Sea, and sweet Virginia tobacco, increasingly reexported from Glasgow by Scottish merchants. Much further down the River Thames, ships from the Indian Ocean tied up at their own docks at Blackwall or Rotherhithe, where stevedores unloaded heavy sacks of coffee or pepper, yard upon yard of bright cotton calicoes, chests of cinnamon, mace, and black and sweet green teas.[17] At the most visible point by the river's edge stood Execution Dock, with the decomposing corpses of mariners condemned by British maritime courts. The ill-fated Captain William Kidd had been strung up on its gibbet only thirty years before.[18]

All these elements—the imperial offices, the merchant shops and coffeehouses, the horse-drawn carts and coaches clattering on cobblestoned streets, the newspaper printers and hawkers, the quays teeming with a saltwater humanity—supplied the core of a British empire supported by the sea. They would also have been among the earliest memories of five-year-old Thomas Allen.

The hackney came to a halt before a large ship tied to the quay, bobbing up and down on the waves like an impatient horse tethered to a post. Thomas Allen and his brother Sam turned to wave to their older half-brother, Jolley. He would stay behind for now, apprenticed to a shopkeeper. The family slowly stepped up the boarding stairs onto the ship's deck. They were ready to cross the Atlantic, sailing on a vast sea of possibilities.

1

The Apprentice

On the deck of the swaying ship, Nathaniel Allen squinted, searching past the muffled shapes of islands in the mist for the thin spires of Boston's churches. He may have seen the port before—family lore imagined him, erroneously, as a Royal Mail Packet Service ship captain. On this voyage in 1734 his wife and sons, along with his widowed sister, Sarah Mann, were gathered around him. His two younger sons, Thomas and Sam, held hands as they peered over the deck rails to catch a glimpse of their new world.[1]

It is easy to imagine the Allen family as typical seaborne migrants in the 1730s, but they were not. The Allens were an anomaly, greatly outnumbered at this time by the swelling ranks of motley crews of convicts, the increasing numbers of impoverished and often indentured migrants known collectively as the Scots-Irish, and the tattered, largely German-speaking families escaping from the high-rent and famine-ravaged Rhineland, Switzerland, or Bohemia. The best estimates suggest that English families may have numbered at most two thousand people, many of whom likely joined kin or fellow villagers in New York, Pennsylvania, or the Chesapeake region—modern Virginia and Maryland.[2]

Altogether, roughly 40,000 European migrants reached American shores in the 1730s. They joined 51,300 men, women, and children from a range of different ethnolinguistic groups from across West Africa and the Western Sahel who were brutally forced across the Atlantic at the same time. The Allens, then, were among the happy few elite migrants who chose to leave England and could afford to do so, and who stayed on the coast instead of striking out for wilderness land deep in the backcountry.[3]

Even before the passengers cast their eyes on the city, they knew that Boston drew its life from the sea.[4] Faded green–, light blue–, or

FIGURE 2. "A South East View of the Great Town of Boston in New England in America," engraved by John Carwitham, ca. 1730. View from the sea showing the spires of the town's then eleven major churches, the Long Wharfe in the center jutting into the harbor, and at least three British Naval ships at anchor. Nathaniel Allen's shop was located just to the right of the Wharfe. (Andrew Fare/Alamy Stock Photo, KN9E4E)

orange-painted fishing smacks returning from the nine banks stretching northeastward to the Grand Banks followed the Allens' ship into harbor, as did a few bulkier whaling ships, their decks stained with blood, fresh from the frigid seas off southern Greenland. As the vessel picked its way through Massachusetts Bay, moving past the stone pillar lighthouse on Little Brewster Island, the bucking of the ship's bow became less pronounced. Running through a gauntlet of low islands, the ship glided past lobster shallops and around the low gray fort of Castle Island, the official residence of the colony's governor. Then Boston itself came into view.

There was no city in colonial America like Boston.[5] Rising up from streets angling away from the wharves, stout wooden buildings in hues of yellow ochre or slate blue with small, squinty windows frowned on people making their way down the cobbled lanes. At the Town Meeting House, near Dock Square, an English blacksmith might dodge an Irish merchant or a Scots-Irish peddler, while on the Long Wharf bonneted women in long green or purple skirts haggled with fishermen patting dark oak barrels filled with their catch. Professors from the country college of Harvard, in town for the day, browsed the new arrivals at bookshops like Henchman's and Hancock's, debating the finer points of Seneca's *De Officiis*.

Wandering the streets and markets were occasional Indigenous people, too: Nipmuc, Housatonic, and Wampanoag. Some were devout Christians seeking alms and a quiet place to pray, some worked as scullery maids in the fine brick houses. Still others, with arms tattooed, might be collecting their sailor's pay at the taverns. An occasional Abenaki or Mohawk delegation dressed in brightly colored English overcoats and leather trousers might march to the Town House to accost the gathering crowd with angry words about broken faith and forgotten promises while pale Bostonians looked on and scoffed. Enslaved African servants in scarlet livery from Barbados or Bermuda drove black chaises, while others nailed soles, forked horse manure into shabby carts, or did the mending while their young charges galloped about Rowe's Field.[6]

Sailors from across the Atlantic, fresh off their ships, congregated in the North End with old mates, unsteadily navigating the narrow, winding streets to reach dark taverns where they could sing, drink, and perhaps buy a painted Molly for the night. And everywhere were the merchants: always on the move, always meeting, always writing. On dark wintry afternoons they would emerge from their counting houses, heavily cloaked and tightly muffled, and head for their candlelit clubs, where they would immediately launch into arguments over paper money, poor relief, or the "mobs" leveling city markets.[7] Then came Sunday. From open church doors issued a medley of sermons, some delivered in a heavy brogue, others in French or with snippets of Latin, some high-pitched and fevered, all drifting back to the wharves where the ships, bobbing like stamping horses, awaited the next race to far-distant markets.

This was Boston when young Thomas Allen arrived. Nearly 16,000 people lived in the port by around 1740, about a third more than in New York or swiftly rising Philadelphia. Contemporaries likened the city favorably to London—a cosmopolitan city of bustle and commerce, of languages, learning, and debate; a city of conversation for those who could claim the right to be heard.[8] It was in this city that Thomas Allen sharpened his wit and imbibed a desire for social advancement.

No sooner had Thomas's father deposited his wife, sister, and two young sons in small lodgings than he sailed away, this time to Virginia. Nathaniel Allen was engaged in the burgeoning intercolonial trade that took advantage of the Chesapeake region as a rising exporter of wheat, corn, salted meat, and tobacco to other seaboard colonies. Beginning in April 1734, Nathaniel Allen conducted one long voyage or two shorter ones every year in the sloop *Three Brothers,* setting a pattern of long, roving absences from his family punctuated by brief, one- or two-month home stays.[9] Not surprisingly, Thomas Allen would first follow a similar sea-roving life as his often absent father before settling onshore as a merchant.

Nathaniel Allen returned to the sea just as Britain was renewing its imperial struggles with Spain from 1739. But when it became increasingly likely that France would enter the War of the Austrian Succession (known as King George's War in the colonies), Allen père shelved his quadrant and settled into the busy life of a Boston dry goods merchant. By late 1742 he had opened a shop on Union Street near the Town Dock, within shouting distance of Boston's Meeting House, marked by "the sign of the ship," perhaps a nod to his former livelihood.[10]

In the colonial Atlantic World, dress matched a person's grasp of civility, style, and the ability to command comfort. Nathaniel Allen tried to be a fashion provider to Boston's elites. His shelves offered up a veritable rainbow of cloth: bolts of blue, black, and scarlet shalloons, red cloaks, yellow camblets and crimson damasks (for bedding), glowing "taffetys" in gold and orange hues, white flannels, and green-and-white-checked linens, while drawers and baskets were filled to the brim with the luxuries of "gilt coat buttons" made of silver, gold, and brass, or black lace in prepackaged sets ("London styles nos. 18–26"). Another counter held delicate hose for both men and women, imported from the new spinning mills in northeastern France. Still, in Boston's drab climate, Nathaniel Allen wrote one supplier, "Dark Blues and Black most vendable." Grays, perhaps mirroring the often glum skies, seldom sold.[11]

Allen also distributed dry goods to regional merchants, probably using contacts forged from his sailing days. His own modest network reflected the "entangled networks of trans-Atlantic commercial relations" enjoyed by larger, cosmopolitan, and more geographically expansive Boston and other port merchants. While his customers included inland distributors as far as Concord, he preferred dealing with those in the ports south of Cape Cod, among them James Rogers in Newport, Nicholas Tillinghast in Providence, and, in New London, Nathaniel Shaw Sr. and the customs collector John Shackmaple.[12]

Although "buy low, sell dear" might be the traditional maxim, a more accurate one for colonial Boston's dry goods shops would have been "stock early and sell now." Despite the opulent shelves, Allen faced persistent frustration in stocking the exact range of products needed to stay competitive. Even though the Royal Navy had largely swept the seas of French and Spanish privateers by early 1747, he did not receive the regular shipments from his London suppliers that he counted on. He berated London merchant William Wellbank, for example, for botching his order, which "disappoint[d] severall ladies who counted on its coming, and hindr[d] me from selling many [other] things for want of it." "London Shalloons," he continued, "you have not sent me, which don't take well." By the spring of 1749 he was rhetorically asking another eminent London wholesaler, Thomas Lane, why Lane bothered sending him his order so late, "after my customers have already supply[d] themselves?"[13] Nathaniel Allen had found that the dry goods business was easy to dive into but difficult to remain afloat in.

As their father and mother built their shop's business, Thomas and his younger brother Sam (and later three more brothers born in Boston) watched and learned. Boston held a unique position in settler America for establishing public schools in the very first years of the city's founding. The five town schools in the seventeenth century taught reading and writing to boys as young as seven, and in the eighteenth century, increasingly to some young girls. Boston's merchants supported the schools, for literacy helped provide "practical knowledge for their earthly business" as their ships sailed ever farther across the Atlantic. Allen's sons attended one of Boston's schools, perhaps learning their alphabet using a hornbook, which was a small paddle printed on one side with lines such as "Who ne'er learns his ABC forever will a blockhead be." In later years they tackled simpler Latin texts, such as Cato's *Disticha* and Aesop's *Fables,* with the help of a composition by master instructor Ezekiel Cheevers, the *Accidence, A Short Introduction to the Latin Tongue.*[14]

Nathaniel Allen's sons clearly received solid training in writing and composition. All the brothers spelled words consistently, rarely by alliteration, and used complex, even witty phrasing to express subtle points, compared with many of their gruff and blunt merchant peers such as James Brown or Gerard Beekman. Thomas's efforts were lifelong: he practiced penmanship incessantly in the margins of rough drafts of letters, inside the covers of ledgers, even on the back of old promissory notes, with exaggerated flourishes for his signature.[15] His striving to improve his handwriting appeared to reflect his striving for social advancement in general.

While an elegant hand gained one entry into the parlors and men's clubs of the elite, basic skills in arithmetic earned money. Numeracy opened the door to a veritable cargo of invaluable skills: the ability to easily, swiftly, and accurately calculate currencies, plot land surveys, track statistics in the increasing demand for numerical measurements of a kingdom's resources, navigate ships, and record the taxes on products passing through customs houses. For a clerk apprentice, the art of recording and tracking complex business accounts, or bookkeeping, proved the most valuable. As his later correspondence showed, Thomas Allen had a knack for computation, scribbling on the back or in the margins of many of his business documents; his calculations were seldom wrong.[16]

Tracking a shop's transactions demanded grasping the concepts behind double-entry accounting "in the Italian style," first perfected by a Florentine monk in the High Renaissance. Bookkeeping authors, such as the famous Scots mathematician John Mair, who wrote the most widely used English accounting textbook of the eighteenth century, touted the benefits of bookkeeping for forging young, nimble minds. "The Theory of this Art or Science," he wrote, "is beautiful and curious, very fit for improving the Minds of Youth, exercising their Wit and Invention, and disposing them a close and accurate Way of Thinking." Other authors championed bookkeeping's "Beauties of Balance," upholding one of the key sensibilities of the emerging Enlightenment: balancing books became a method of discovering balance in nature through the natural logic of numbers.[17]

Of the three steps in the process of keeping accurate records, the most important was the second. This entailed posting transactions in a large book called a journal. The journal split every transaction into two accounts: one account became debtor to a second, and the second the creditor of its corresponding opposite. From this perspective, account books were manifestly Newtonian: literally every transaction had two equal and opposite aspects, an action and a corresponding reaction. The journal entries also served as a kind of currency in that they tracked verifiable "book debt" or pledges to pay or receive goods between merchants. Because of its centrality to profitable business, training in accounting emerged as a kind of international language, linking merchants and sea captains like Allen with their many counterparts across the seas, helping ease the language barrier.[18]

With an elegant hand, articulate phrasing, and accurate computations launched in letters that literally sailed the seas, settler merchants fashioned their own networks of exchange and opportunity. In a very real sense, bookkeeping and letters "articulated or created the self-in-markets." Bookkeeping endowed novice clerks, and hence future merchants, with honorable values, initiative, and gentility. For example, in seeking a new clerk, one of Allen's associates described the qualities he sought: "a young gentleman who writes a good hand & is acquainted with accounts—a steady, clever fellow is my aim—one that is obliging—free from selfishness—& acquainted with the Barter trade of our Country."[19]

The emphasis on "gentleman," "steady," and "clever" suggests the creation of a new persona that would combine refinement, lettered education, and industriousness—a "striver." These attributes were universal for aspiring young men during the Enlightenment and helped unify merchants from different backgrounds in promoting not only their own material interests but also the interests of their chosen countries.[20]

To be a merchant increasingly meant becoming a patriot of one's chosen country. Writing on the eclectic mix of merchants of French, Italian, Swiss, Levantine, and Jewish merchants in one French port, an observer in 1775 noted, "The trader . . . is the one who, superior by virtue of his views, his genius, and his enterprise, adds his fortune to the wealth of the state."[21] Merchants of different cultural backgrounds were especially dispersed in many of the non-Spanish ports of the colonial mainland and throughout the Caribbean Sea. Such merchant communities were both a sign of an expansive cosmopolitanism and exemplars of a more local and proud commercial patriotism at the same time.

Numeracy loaded Allen's intellectual bays with one other, and crucial, cargo: the skill of navigation. By 1750, settler ships already made up at least a fifth of the vast armada of oceangoing British merchant vessels, and the percentage increased dramatically over the next two decades. Coastal shipping could dispense with mathematics; within sight of land, ship masters still steered by visible landmarks and by observing animal and bird movements, or by studying wave action and the color and even the smell of seawater. But once out on the deep blue sea, with the lonely horizon the bounds of a vessel's world, settler navigators had to be able to work through a complex trigonometry to know where they were and where they were going.[22]

Navigation linked the twinned challenges of setting and maintaining a ship's course, or intended journey, under a vast array of oceanic conditions and determining a ship's position while keeping to that course. With an unimaginable number of razor-sharp reefs, shoals, and nearly invisible submerged islets scattered across the imperial Atlantic sea lanes—the Caribbean Basin alone has over seven thousand of these natural obstacles—the dangers of gales, drunkenness at the helm, or dry water casks meant little room for error in navigation.[23]

Mariners had to plot their theoretical position on a two-dimensional map but still adhere to the reality of the actual three dimensions of the earth's curvature. They did so by using a quadrant (or the more complex and accurate sextant) to measure the angle between the horizon and the sun, usually at noon, or the North Star on a clear night. This told them their latitude, or how far north or south of the equator they were.[24] Once trained, and with supportive skies and seas, they found it a routine operation to perform.

Measuring the distance east or west, or finding longitude, proved much harder. Most ships simply measured their speed on a given course, a process that left much to guessing. The British and French, among other maritime powers, sought to develop a ship's clock, or chronometer, that could keep accurate time at sea. An accurate clock would make it far easier to calculate the distance traveled, and therefore pinpoint longitude. In 1764 the Englishman John Harrison eventually won the race, inventing a clock that could be powered, in effect, by the rocking of the waves.[25] But mariners on smaller settler vessels could not afford such a luxury.

It is easy to see why ship captains, as young Thomas Allen would become, constantly strove to improve their skills in navigation, and the means of navigating as well. In effect, they embraced the early philosophical ideals emerging around the Atlantic Basin to "diffuse useful information" for the benefit of all. The practical contributions of sailors, sea captains, and maritime administrators created what might be called a "Deep Blue Enlightenment." This means a cooperative, pan-national movement among educated people excited by the practical possibilities of experimental science and careful record keeping to make ocean voyages shorter, more productive, and safe. This version of the Enlightenment was a seaborne cousin to what some historians have called the "Village Enlightenment," whereby ordinary people with a passion for the new sciences shared ideas and invented a plethora of new mechanical devices to improve the material life of humanity.[26]

Allen was no scientist, but his training in the classics and in two major forms of numeracy not only made him a better sailor but inculcated a secular, cosmopolitan perspective that championed self-betterment. Allen and many other mariners manifested this ethos by sharpening their skills and dipping into the wide world of knowledge about the ocean. They practiced sums and theoretical navigational problems in logbook margins, and, if successful enough, purchased and consulted updated mariner's guides. When captains kept ship's logs based on consistent, accurate observations, they were in effect guided by the Enlightenment ideal of self-improvement.[27] Mistakes made on one voyage could help them be safer and faster on the next—so long as they returned alive.

The theoretical mathematics of navigation could teach only so much; experience on the oceans taught much more. It is unclear when Allen first sailed. If his experience was at all typical of the age, he would have started young, probably in his early teens, sailing with his father on short voyages. After serving an apprenticeship lasting four to seven years, he would have graduated to the status of able-bodied seaman by the age of seventeen or eighteen, and to first mate shortly thereafter. Then, if he had a talent for elementary literacy and numeracy, he would have been offered command of his own ship in his early twenties. Mariners typically earned the title of captain on their first transatlantic command, although there was no set practice.[28] As the educated son of a respected mariner, Allen had obvious advantages—he was a shipmaster by the age of twenty-two, if not a year or so earlier. He used his new title frequently, for he referred to himself, or had others address him for most of his life, as Captain Thomas Allen.

Although earlier Puritan leaders had criticized mariners, likening shipboard life to "living among the dammed," by the time Allen became a captain, the New England social environment had changed completely. Sea captains, and mariners more generally, had earned a new public identity that denoted savvy experience, authority, and respect, powerful tools for a young man striving to improve his interest in the world. Mariners who obtained command of the larger, oceangoing vessels tended to have acquired at least some polish through classical literacy and to possess strong computational skills in both accounting and navigation.[29]

As Allen's later life suggests, such training created something entirely new, a broadly traveled person who accepted contact with others speaking different languages and attending different churches, expected promotion based on merit, and valued self-reliance in demanding circumstances. The experiential training that went into forming this set of attributes often exceeded in range and depth the traditional training of landed elites. Mariners could strive to better their lives materially by traveling and attaining commercial success anywhere in the world. Well before the turbulent 1760s, young, ambitious settler sea captains such as Allen were already marking out their own individual courses toward a practical independence underwritten by Enlightenment principles.

2

The Widow and the Young Captain

NATHANIEL ALLEN BECAME INCREASINGLY desperate toward the end of the War of the Austrian Succession (1744–48), despite some key British victories. Fighting had knocked the winds out of Boston's sails commercially and socially. French regular forces aided by Native Iroquois who had converted to Catholicism and Algonkian warriors attacked much of interior and northern coastal New England. French privateers sailing south from the fortress of Louisbourg, on the lobster claw of Cape Breton Island, had driven the fishing fleets from the Grand Banks in the first year of the war, halting the important trade in fish to the Spanish and Portuguese wine islands, especially Madeira. Nathaniel Allen's own fortunes paralleled those of his adopted city, for he lost heavily in three shipping ventures.[1]

Even though a combined British and New England force captured French Louisbourg in mid-1745, Boston benefited little. Economic uncertainty plagued the expected riches, and at the conclusion of the war, in early 1748, British peace negotiators handed Louisbourg right back to France. Allen was one of many incensed by what he saw as the betrayal of a marvelous economic opportunity, writing to one of his London suppliers, "Had Cape Briton not been Taken it would have been much better for this Town as it is given away again [and] we are all Sufferers for it." By the end of war his debts had mounted alarmingly, and he lamented to his young son Thomas that "Wee don't take money Enough to supplie the necessities of the familie."[2] Frustrated in his ventures and bleeding funds, Allen enlisted his son Thomas to help develop the family business in a subsidiary port on the rise. With additional backing from several

Boston merchants, Thomas Allen reluctantly settled in New London, in eastern Connecticut.

Sailing south from Boston around the great hook of Cape Cod, mariners entered a unique set of brisk and often adverse sailing conditions before they entered the slightly more sheltered sea of Long Island Sound. At the eastern end, the sound ended at the fishtail tip of Long Island and the entry to Narragansett Bay in Rhode Island. On the western edge lay the burgeoning port of New York. Although one disgruntled mariner remembered the waters as "invelop'd in those eternal Foggs that covers these Regions of Missery," the sea mimicked the sky's mood, changing from a sparkling blue to a dappled light green to a choppy, foreboding gray.[3]

Between Narragansett Bay and the Connecticut River, a short river had carved out a deep estuary. The Mohegan people usually referred to the area as Nameaug, "the fishing place." Captivated by the region, Puritan settlers, along with Indigenous groups that later became allies, such as the Uncas, had drenched the area in the blood of Pequot and other Mohegan peoples almost as soon as they had scouted it, claiming it for their own in the short but vicious Pequot War of 1636–37. Perhaps hoping that a bold renaming of the site might foster future greatness, the settlers eventually settled on the name "Thames"—in New England pronunciation, rhyming with "names"—for the river, and for the port, the idyllic "Faire Harbour." Within a few years the settlers had renamed the town New London. Nearly one hundred years later, young Captain Thomas Allen, fresh from his first transatlantic voyage, would heave his sea trunk onto his shoulders, walk up a gravely beach strewn with dried seaweed, and step into the town.[4] He would have been about twenty-one.

Farmland in New London's immediate area was similar to that of Boston's: stony, poor, the plots small, with crops subject to blight and the growing season short. The land for about ten miles on either side of the Thames estuary was little more than pasture and bog, believed by some locals to be "haunted by old Indians, deserters from English ships, witches, and tramps." The only decent farmland lay immediately southwest of town, in Great Neck, a jaw of land jutting into the sound. The largest expanses of farmland began some fifteen miles up the Thames River at Norwich, extending into the rolling hills and shallow valleys beyond.[5]

The town sat on a half-moon shelf of shore, behind which rose a few gentle hills. A triangular parade ground had been cleared at the center of town and fronting the harbor; around it were arrayed the newly built St. James Anglican Church, a small prison with stocks, and a clutch of taverns and shops.[6] A single dirt road led up the hill past the town hall and toward the Congregational church with its slender steeple. The steeple also doubled as a watchtower. From the parade ground north along the curving shore, a handful of small wharves lined Beach Street north toward the small Custom House, and just past a shallow cove on a hill behind stood the fine house of the original proprietor and colonial governor, John Winthrop Jr. South of the parade ground, another handful of wharves and piers lined Bank Street, ending at another cove, where laborers laid the keels of new vessels at William Coit's shipyard. Taverns and a few brick homes lined the beach area opposite the wharves. Up the slope, more houses of one or two stories, painted in shades of white, gray, or plum, fronted country roads; around the houses were scattered vegetable and herb gardens, sheds, and stables.

New London invited little admiration from travelers. Only five years before Thomas Allen arrived, Dr. Alexander Hamilton (no relation to the Revolutionary-era Hamilton) sailed into the port, describing it as "irregularly built along the water side, in length about a mile. There is in it one Presbyterian meeting [house] and one church [of England]. 'Tis just such another desolate, expensive town as Annapolis in Maryland [Hamilton's detested hometown], the houses being mostly of wood."[7]

Hamilton was not alone in his assessment. Elite members of settler society considered "the scruffy little port" a "mean, provincial backwater," inhabited by "rude & insolent people that will do what . . . notorious abuses they please under color of law & Justice." Given Thomas Allen's subsequent life, he would have fit right in. Still, even though it may have struck many as a ramshackle fishing village grafted to a country hamlet, some thought the port had potential. Anglican priest Matthew Stewart, who arrived about the same time as Allen, remarked that the town served as "the seat of his Majesty's custom-house, and so the port of greatest note in the colony . . . a city set upon a hill which cannot be hid."[8]

Coastal towns depended not only on "firm connections with the hinterland" but the full exploitation of local and regional marine environments, or *vorlands*. New London fit this description perfectly. A harbor of sheltered, deep, broad, and easily defended waters was itself a crucial resource in the age of sail.[9] The rocky, seaweed-strewn "beach" that ringed the harbor dropped away sharply, allowing very large ships to dock close enough that a sailor "may toss a biskitt on shoar," as one early settler recorded. A later royal memoir described the harbor as "about three Miles, the breadth about three-quarters of a Mile . . . entirely secure and commodious for large Ships." Even the fan shape of New London's shoreline naturally maximized the number of wharves and docks, increasing potential ships' berths by nearly 50 percent compared with a straighter shoreline's affordance.[10]

The estuary and the surrounding seas also offered an abundance of seafood, from striped bass and sturgeon to eels caught by torchlight, to hard-shell clams (quahogs) "as big as a penny white loaf," lobsters, oysters, and an "infinite store" of mussels. Such foods from the sea became daily fare in local diets and were staples in ship provisions, while shellfish also made prized gifts when captains voyaged overseas. Even dried seaweed could be used as fertilizer. But the port's location was perhaps its greatest single maritime asset. For ships passing northeast, southeast, or due south to the Caribbean, its snug harbor lay less than three days' sail from the major transatlantic shipping routes.[11] The importance of vorlands for settler ports cannot be overstated: the combination of physical siting and living resources dictated a port's sustainable future in the age of sail.

New London's expansive hinterland offered just as much. Dense and varied forests ran north into central Massachusetts, supplying a treasure trove of different trees crucial for different needs in building ships and crafting shipping barrels and casks. While grain could be grown profitably only far up the rivers, broad pastures fed livestock, which in turn were slaughtered, salted, and sold as ship's provisions or carried alive to ever-expanding Caribbean markets. As early as the 1670s, Connecticut sloops carried cargoes of salted beef, draft oxen, and horses to Barbados. Horses later came to dominate Thomas Allen's ventures to the Caribbean. Even the ubiquitous stones of New England were useful, for shipwrights spread the rounded ones in the keel of a ship as ballast.[12] It would be no exaggeration to say that New London's commercial fortunes were founded on buying and selling different modes of mobility.

Young Captain Thomas Allen must have liked what he saw, for he settled in New London and immediately opened his own small shop in late 1750. His father had advanced him stock worth £206 in colonial Massachusetts currency to begin operations, a kind of "float" loan. Thomas immediately became ensnared in two minor lawsuits, suing for nondelivery of goods (four slaughtered cattle) in one and for money owed him in the other. He quickly became a person of note in town, amassing an impressive £68 of property and contributing early and generously to St. James Church. He probably sailed on another transatlantic voyage during this time, captaining a ship known as the *Seaflower*—a common vessel name at the time—to Ireland, while a stray reference suggests he revisited his childhood home of London on his first voyage to visit his older half-brother, Jolley.[13]

One of the early trade contacts of Allen's father, John Shackmaple Jr., had been a merchant and customs collector for the port of New London. Shackmaple had died several years before Thomas Allen appeared, but the latter undoubtedly knew his widow, Elizabeth Christophers Shackmaple. In the custom of many widows, she may have rented a room to the young captain and helped him settle in the port. In any event, within a year or two after Allen's arrival, they began to look at each other very differently.

We know virtually nothing about Elizabeth Shackmaple's early life except that she was born September 13, 1714, and that her family connections were undoubtedly appealing to an ambitious young man. She was the granddaughter of the outspoken Puritan minister and governor Gurdon Saltonstall Sr., who was revered as one of Connecticut's greatest and most astute politicians. Ironically, perhaps, she married the son of one of her grandfather's most intractable enemies, the customs collector John Shackmaple. She and John Jr. were careful to defer marriage until both their warring patriarchs were dead. After exchanging vows in 1732, they had five children in short order, three girls, Sarah, Elizabeth, and Lydia, and then two boys, John and Richard. The couple's new house on Bradley Street, at the end of Towne Street, became an informal place of Anglican worship while builders finished St. James Church. The parishioners also elected her husband a vestryman.[14]

The 1730s were an exciting, busy time to raise a family. The colony's population as a whole grew nearly threefold between 1700 and 1740, with eastern Connecticut outstripping the central and western regions. New London emerged as an innovative and bustling port of entry for all Connecticut, broadening its religious and even racial tolerance by attracting small contingents of French Huguenots, some families of freed enslaved Africans, and possibly a Jewish family or two. In 1732 the port's merchants founded the first settler mercantile collective, initially named the New

London Society United for Trade and Commerce, in this way pioneering "Connecticut's first mortgage-backed public loan issue," a precedent that would later help finance the Revolution. The port also emerged as a focus of religious ferment during the New Light evangelical movement. Emotionally intense and outwardly directed, the New Lights challenged what they considered ossified Congregationalist theology, and even pried away several bored or disillusioned parishioners from the Anglican Church.[15]

For ten years the Shackmaple family prospered. Then, as swiftly as a knot slips, disaster struck. John Shackmaple died within two years after the birth of the couple's last child, possibly as a result of an epidemic spread by soldiers returning from Jamaica in the summer of 1742. People died at sea, but the sea also brought death and disease to land. Not yet thirty, Elizabeth suddenly faced a frightening future as a widow: an empty table and an empty bed, with five young mouths to feed.[16]

Widows were perhaps just as important a creation of the sea of possibilities as the wealth brought by sailing upon it. The high number of female heads of households and widows in seaports fostered strong female agency and legal authority in New England's otherwise traditionally staunch, patriarchal communities. With death always on deck for their mariner fathers, husbands, beaus, and brothers, women shouldered considerable economic and social responsibility in settler ports, not to mention dreary physical labor to support their families. Historians suggest that the proportion of widows in seaport towns was twice as high as in rural towns; and in neighboring Newport, Rhode Island, widows accounted for more than three-fourths of all female-headed households. They became "deputy husbands," a term developed and popularized by historian Laurel Thatcher Ulrich, and the bulk of the evidence used by her and other scholars is drawn from port towns.[17]

Many mariners' widows ran boarding houses or taverns or worked as seamstresses or launderers. They also served as midwives, sold produce and herbs from market gardens, and even painted interior walls. Most such occupations were extensions of domestic labor, and those who took them on infrequently encountered the litigation, or threat of it, that male merchant livelihoods entailed. Remarriage could pose further hurdles, both financial and emotional. In the port of Salem, four out of five middle-aged widows (thirty-five to forty-nine years old) never remarried. A widow at the end of her reproductive years held little attraction for prospective husbands, especially one without wealth.[18]

The widow Shackmaple is something of a ghost in terms of reliable documentation. She did not engage in court actions or cause trouble that would bring attention from the authorities, and her name is largely absent from church minutes. Only the slimmest documentary wisps hint at her life. Given her age when widowed and her sterling family connections, Elizabeth appears to have been not only emotionally strong enough to raise five small children but materially comfortable enough to not rush into a second marriage—no small feat in eighteenth-century New England. She owned her own home a block from the wharves, where boarding sea captains or voyaging merchants would have been easy and appealing generators of income. Owing to the accepted "rule of one-third," she certainly controlled at least that proportion of her late husband's property. Later correspondence suggests she enjoyed reading religious works. She also inherited her first husband's pew in St. James "in perpetuity." Widow Shackmaple does not appear in the local rate lists until 1751, when she was one of twenty-one women who paid taxes. The town's listers valued her taxable property at £18 in Connecticut currency, about a third lower than the average of £26 for all female taxpayers. This meant she was considerably poorer than the wealthiest woman (£130/2/6, or 130 pounds, two shillings, and six sixpence), but wealthier than the four women who had no rating at all, and evenly rated with the amount uniformly levied on the town's six "Free Negroes."[19]

It is plausible that the widow and the young captain may have engaged in a socially unacceptable liaison and hustled themselves into marriage to avoid church condemnation or even a rough charivari by a mob. They married, presumably in St. James, on October 29, 1753. Almost immediately, two events occurred. First, Elizabeth became pregnant. Second, and for the first time, she appeared in the legal records, sued for nonpayment of £30 by the Norwich merchant Joshua Appleton. The first ended tragically in a stillborn child the following July. This prompted Joshua Hempstead's only reference to her and Allen when he wrote, "Infant Still born of the Body of the Widow Eliza Shackmaple alias (as is hoped) the wife of Thomas allin a Bankrupt & gone of[f] to the west Indias." Hempstead clearly had no liking for the young captain. The lawsuit, by contrast, ended in Elizabeth's favor, for she pointed out to the court that the writ she had been served with had no date, and therefore was not legally binding.[20] Whoever she was, Elizabeth Shackmaple appeared to be at the very least a literate survivor, at most an educated, astute, strong-willed person not to be trifled with. She was indicative of the kind of independence and carving out of new public roles in religious and commercial life demanded by the harsh gales of misfortune that the assaulting sea invariably sent.

Back in Boston, Nathaniel Allen's financial situation deteriorated further. With the Louisbourg debacle and further trouble with his London suppliers, he could not pay his debts, and desperately sought a savior. Such an opportunity sailed into Boston in the summer of 1748.

Captain James Brown of Providence, Rhode Island, the eldest of five brothers, had inherited the family shipping business, pursuing the same currents as his mariner father, and quickly emerged as an able navigator in his own right. He partnered with his uncle, Obadiah Brown, and guided his four younger brothers into an early version of what would become a transatlantic entrepreneurial empire. He quickly became Nathaniel Allen's largest customer by far. Starting with a sizable purchase in August 1748 of £279 in Massachusetts currency in Allen's typical goods, Brown's debt had ballooned to the enormous sum of £5,278 (probably all in Massachusetts currency) by the time he died of fever off the Virginia coast in 1751. At his death, over £4,300, or about 80 percent, of his debt remained unpaid.[21] Nathaniel Allen apparently had no resources to demand payment from Captain Brown's brothers and now faced outright bankruptcy.

Allen turned to the best and only resources he had at his disposal—his three young sons and his firsthand knowledge of shipping to the Caribbean. At the wizened age of fifty-four, an ancient mariner by any measure, Nathaniel Allen shipped out to the West Indies, likely as a factor, since his name does not appear as captain in any customs clearances. At the same time, he enlisted the aid of his sons, Thomas in particular, to help shoulder the credit burden. As early as fall 1750, Nathaniel Allen attempted to unload a barrel of guilt in his son's mind. He wrote, "If you have any Regard for the Ease of your fathers Mind send Sumthing to fetch Money that I may be Able to Discharge those Debts here, that I may not be Dunnd to Death." Thomas acquiesced. How much of his father's burden Thomas accepted is unknown, but extant documents suggest at least £2,400, or about half his father's outstanding debt.[22]

Shortly after marrying Elizabeth, Thomas Allen shipped out on a short cruise to the Caribbean in early 1754. But as his father's and his own debts increased, he left New London again in early 1755, leaving Elizabeth once again pregnant. He remembered his exile with great bitterness, writing years later that he was "pusht abroad into a Strange Land by my Parents—to answer there purposes."[23] Leaving behind his creditors, his Boston family, and Elizabeth, Allen set his course to make his fortune upon a new sea of possibilities.

3

Partners of the Caribbean

MODERN MAPS SHOW THE direction of oceanic trade routes in firm, arching lines that imply an effortless passage over the waves. It looks so easy! Such depictions ignore the distinct segments of the New England–Caribbean voyage that added time to the journey, damage to cargo, and harm to the crew. How voyages actually worked, and the routes that ships took, had an impact on the captain's and crew's chances of survival on oceanic routes.

The distance from New London to what one ship master called "Sinchristophers" (St. Kitts) is 1,730 miles as a jet flies. For a ship plowing the waves and dodging storms, the course could easily be three or four hundred miles longer. Any seaworthy ship might cover as much as one hundred and fifty miles in twenty-four hours if blown by friendly winds. But these idyllic conditions were rare in the seas north of Bermuda. Winds shifted around the compass through the day and night; they might blow from the northeast at dawn, from the west by noon, and then from the southwest by dusk.[1]

Even worse, "running the westerlies" brought what one experienced master called "thick dark wather" at any time of year. Brisk winds easily grew to gales, forcing captains to "proced under Bare poals," which meant dropping sails completely, leaving the ship vulnerable to the pounding waves. As Captain Youngs Ledyard, one of Allen's associates, remarked of one stormy passage in 1755, "Chief of the time to the Northward of Bermuda . . . we met with hard gails and contrarys [winds] and the vessel was very leaquey weak and rotten[.] Upon the whole she is the miserablest thing that ever I saw Man to pretend to cross the Ocean."[2]

Once a ship left the Thames and neared Fishers Island or Block Island, the captain took the initial sightings, from which he calculated the rest of the course. The ship then sailed into what mariners called "the Horserace," or more often "the Race," a current that sped ships out of Block Island Sound into the wider Atlantic. This first segment of the voyage was the most fraught, for most shipboard losses occurred on the segment north of Bermuda, which often consumed up to two-thirds of the total sailing time. But as mariners neared the Tropic of Cancer, squalls and gales diminished considerably, outside the dangerous hurricane season. So long as vessels did not wander accidentally eastward into the midocean swamp of floating seaweed known as the Sargasso Sea, steady winds and friendlier waves brought mariners to the top of the hook of islands known as the Lesser Antilles, rimming the eastern Caribbean Sea.[3] (See map 1, showing the sailing routes.)

The first islands settler ships often sighted were the outposts of British Tortola, Anegada, and Anguilla. Such low islands were difficult to see, so mariners picked their way among them carefully. The islands offered easy anchorages in which to buy or collect wood, freshwater, and tropical fruits after a long toss on the seas; negotiate good prices from grateful locals, who were often ignored by the larger European vessels; and acquire advance news of markets from the major islands further south. The officials of these outlying islands also augmented their meager incomes by selling another prized island resource to settler shipmasters: forged papers.[4] Possession of such papers magically turned heavily taxed or prohibited French, Dutch, Danish, or Spanish Puerto Rican products into authorized British ones. On the return voyage such islets served as the marker for northbound nautical calculations, much as Fishers Island or Block Island served navigators leaving New England.

Once in Caribbean waters, all settler captains, like the young Thomas Allen, faced the same basic problem: "droging for sugar." First articulated by historian Frank Pittman to describe local interisland trade, this came to mean the challenge faced by shipmasters of tramping from island to island in search of plantation produce to buy at acceptable prices among the wildly fluctuating and easily saturated Caribbean island markets. British mercantile houses in London, Bristol, and Liverpool dominated trade on the larger British sugar islands such as Barbados, Antigua, and Jamaica. Access to cheap manufactures, deep investments in the Middle Passage ships hauling enslaved Africans, and a protected home market meant these larger merchants could withstand the vagaries of island trade.[5]

But settler merchants, with smaller capital, smaller cargoes of captives, and no real access to cheap manufactures, often remained marginalized.

Instead, they supplied niche or cheap commodities that literally fed, housed, cleansed, and transported plantation masters and their enslaved laborers. From fish to flour, livestock to lumber, from salted beef to unsalted butter, from candles to soap, settler captains from New Jersey to New Hampshire at this time supplied the basic materials that fed the maw of plantation production.[6]

Settler sea captains had known since the late seventeenth century that they could expand their markets and increase profits considerably by selling their cargoes directly to French, Spanish, and later Danish planters, or indirectly but still profitably to Dutch intermediaries. French plantation masters offered a broader array of tropical cargoes, including cocoa (for a time), indigo, coffee, silky island cotton, ginger, and even some low-grade tobacco, along with various grades of sugar. More important, many French planters undertook the first stages of processing their sugar on their island *habitations,* creating massive quantities of a dark sugary liquid, or molasses, as a by-product. They also distilled a somewhat coarse and slightly weaker version of rum known initially as *tafia* for limited use. Since French planting elites favored brandy from home over rum from their fields, and given the miniscule markets for sugar by-products, French plantation masters welcomed selling their enormous surplus of molasses to eager settler captains like Allen.[7]

Settlers also knew that French metropolitan merchants had seldom supplied the French Caribbean colonies adequately with European goods, basic foodstuffs, building supplies, or enslaved African laborers. The French Marine, the branch of the French Navy that managed the crown's overseas settlements, envisioned that the mainland colonies of New France and Louisiana would supply these basic supplies. They utterly failed. But ship captains from the British mainland could, and cheaply. Notoriously starved of goods and coerced labor but with cheap tropical produce ready to load, the French planters of Guadeloupe, Martinique, and later Saint-Domingue understood they had common economic interests with "Nor'ad" ("Northward") captains and merchants. Settler ship captains also knew that French customs officials in the Lesser Antilles were few and poorly paid, and that patrols by Customs cutters were spectacularly ineffective.[8]

By the time Allen first sailed southward, the Caribbean was functioning economically, and in many respects culturally, as a single "inter-imperial microregion" rooted in the rapacity and death of sugarcane production.[9]

FIGURE 3. "Shipping Sugar," William Clark, 1823. Enslaved men performed the heavy and often dangerous work of rolling massive sugar hogsheads onto lighters and then transferring them to small sloops. This image from early nineteenth-century Antigua would have been familiar anywhere in the Caribbean since the mid-seventeenth century. (The Picture Art Collection/Alamy Stock Photo, P01PFR)

The profitable cooperation between settler ship captains and foreign planters created a de facto merchants' Pax Caribbeana—an informal Caribbean common market, a peace among merchants bought with pieces of eight. Earnings from the Caribbean trade emerged as the key component that allowed mainland merchants to balance their deep debts to British merchants.[10] Exploited to the fullest by captains like Allen, this informal market had the potential to help the Nor'ad colonies become economically autonomous from Great Britain.

The French and British governments were well aware of the increasingly close trade relations among their colonies and sought to curtail or manage intercolonial exchange in various ways. The French acted first. After the signing of the Peace of Utrecht in 1713, the leading chambers of commerce in the Atlantic-facing French ports, particularly those in Bordeaux, Nantes, and La Rochelle, envisioned that tropical products, led by sugar, would be a key pillar of their postwar recovery. Their deputies quickly pressured the new regent, Philippe d'Orléans, to first "free" the French trade in enslaved

Africans in 1716—perhaps one of the most ironic trade policies ever devised—and then to proclaim two new policies designed to curtail *commerce étranger,* or smuggling. The second of these, the Letters Patent of October 1727, provided the basis for French colonial policy for the next forty years. Widely known as the *Exclusif,* the new law completely revamped French colonial trade. Its major clauses focused on eliminating Caribbean smuggling by imposing draconian measures on foreign ships and sea captains. Among other stipulations, it levied stiff fines amounting to a ship captain's yearly wages for the first smuggling offense, and a life sentence as a galley slave in the French Mediterranean for a third (and final) conviction.[11]

At the same time, Great Britain passed its own laws, supported by the powerful West India lobby. The most important was the May 1733 Act for the better Securing and Encouraging the Trade of His Majesty's Sugar Colonies in America, later dubbed the Molasses Act. Caribbean officials and planters heartily congratulated King George II for his commitment to "defend his People's Liberitie . . . [and] support and maintain them in all their just Rights and Privileges" by putting an end to "the unreasonable Advantages taken by the Northern Colonies."[12]

Mainland settler merchants, however, were deeply alarmed. The law slapped higher duties on foreign sugar, rum, and especially molasses. At six pennies per gallon on molasses, the duty may not have seemed steep. But it represented at least a 42–50 percent increase in the wholesale cost for a crucial staple, with retail prices therefore forced even higher. It would be easy to dismiss the Molasses Act as ineffective owing to lax enforcement in the mainland colonies.[13] But from the perspective of mainland merchants and sea captains at the time, the two sets of imperial regulations, if enforced, posed very real threats to the flow of riches of the growing "Pax Caribbeana."

Allen arrived at St. Kitts in late February 1755. He had originally intended to arrange shipping for his friend Nathan Allyn of nearby Groton, and would in fact send three cargoes to him by the spring of 1756. But even as he put quill to parchment to inform Allyn of their joint affairs in March 1755, Allen met Francis Goelet, and the two quickly formed a close and, for Allen, unusually long-lasting partnership.[14]

Goelet seemed to be something of an alter ego of Allen, even if he had been born in New York of Dutch or more likely Huguenot parents. Four years younger, Goelet had built a mill for making snuff tobacco in New Rochelle, outside Manhattan in the colony of New York. He was well traveled, cultured, educated, something of an artist, and open to the new ideas and social trends of the Enlightenment. In fact, Lord William Byron, Grand Master of the Grand Lodge of Freemasons in England, appointed Goelet to be the new grand master in his native New York. Like Allen, Goelet had incurred heavy debts, leading him to abandon *his* wife and young child and try his luck in the Caribbean "to improve his fortunes." For his part, Allen expressed himself delighted with his new partner, referring to Goelet as a "Gentl.^{mn} of Honor," and inviting Nathan Allyn to join them in the purchase of a fast Bermuda sloop.[15]

Goelet and Allen were among the pioneers of what one historian has called "the New Informal Empire" of British colonists settling in foreign Caribbean colonies. They joined other tiny communities of overseas Jewish, Dutch, Danish, and some French settlers who created interlacing webs of credit, trade, and fraternity. Whether marginalized religiously in their European homelands, hailing from smaller countries jostling with much larger states and economies, or simply on the lookout for a cozy opportunity, these merchants established a loose, shifting, informal, and highly profitable coalition of prosperity.[16] While they may not necessarily have possessed the striving character of Allen and Goelet, they were people who built their lives in the fluid seas between imperial jurisdictions. It took very little for Goelet to convince Allen to leave British St. Kitts and open a shop together on the nearby Dutch island of St. Eustatius, commonly referred to as Statia.

Though tiny and dry, Statia possessed a crucial resource in the age of sail: location. It lay near the top of the Lesser Antilles arc of islands, a mere three or four days' sail from most of them and an easy four- or five-day voyage eastward to the Greater Antilles islands. Originally settled to grow tobacco by the Dutch West India Company in the 1630s, Statia emerged during the wars of Louis XIV in the late seventeenth century as a convenient central warehouse among the contending imperial powers. By the late 1740s it was one of two Dutch centers of the *kleine vaart,* or regional transit trade, the other being Curaçao off the Spanish Main. By then, Dutch planters had abandoned any pretense of growing sugar on Statia, using their plantations as legal "fronts to feign production while the 'plantation owner' engaged in other activities."[17]

In the early 1750s, the new governor of the island, Jan de Windt, astutely cultivated close ties with officials in the nearby French islands. He also kept a spyglass keenly trained on passing British warships and made sure that customs duties stayed at a reasonable ad valorem tax of 2 percent. Most important, he welcomed non-Dutch merchants such as Allen and Goelet to join the cosmopolitan community in the island's only port, Oranjestad. De Windt's moves positioned the tiny island for long-term, explosive growth.[18]

Oranjestad's harbor consisted of a simple, open roadstead about three quarters of a mile long, with no docks or even natural protection from open water. But the town lay on the leeward side of the island, away from fierce Atlantic swells, so the island itself acted as a natural breakwater. An estimated 150 ships at a time, many of them small sloops, could anchor in aqua-stained-glass waters over a sandy shelf thirty to ninety feet deep. Rowboats and small shallops ferried people and goods to a narrow ledge of beach, which locals called the Benedenstad (Lower Town). This strip was crammed not only with warehouses but also with chandlery shops, kilns for firing simple ceramics, and even a slaughterhouse. Above the beach perched Upper Town, reached by a single, zig-zagging road that climbed a steep escarpment. Here most of the merchants lived and worked, attended their churches, or met privately with Governor de Windt at his residence.[19]

In the early 1750s the population stabilized at about 2,500 regular inhabitants, roughly one-third European, largely but by no means solely Dutch, with the other two-thirds enslaved African and Caribbean creoles. This forced labor ranged from laundrywomen to messengers, skilled coopers to apprentices in ship repair, performing the drudge labor that sent tropical cargoes from the Caribbean.[20] In addition, the many ships added a large, young, male, and undoubtedly boisterous temporary population of sailors, possibly six hundred to eight hundred at any one time—up to one-third of the town's usual population. Under de Windt's tutelage and trade-friendly approach, the rowdy, cosmopolitan port would soon be known throughout the Atlantic World as "the Golden Rock" (*de Gouden Rots*). By the time Allen and Goelet arrived, trade had already doubled from 1730 to 1750; it would double yet again between 1750 and 1775.[21]

Goelet used letters of introduction and credit obtained from the Freemason military commandant of Danish St. Thomas, Johannes Kronenberg, to help set up the business, with some of the capital apparently advanced by Low and Cole, one of London's overseas trading firms. At first the new partners simply joined their mainland contacts together to act as brokers for settler merchants in the Caribbean. They also introduced a unique niche business selling ship's provisions, such as kegs of ham, hardened ship's bread (hardtack), and casks of water, to passing settler captains. Unsatisfied, they quickly branched out to handle the cargoes of smaller, regional Caribbean merchants, such as "James Hammelton" of Nevis, likely the indifferent father of future American Revolutionary War icon Alexander Hamilton, as well as local Statian merchants. These also included the island's governor, de Windt.[22]

By May 1755 they had earned enough to purchase several pieces of mahogany furniture, including a table and armchair (for Goelet), fine Irish kenting for curtains, a cot, hammocks (unclear who slept in which), a small medicine chest, and pine boards for "Carpenders mak'ing ye compt house," a separate space to record and store the large leather-bound account books. By mid-June they had paid for a painted sign above the front door and had begun ordering large quantities of ink, quills, quires of fresh-cut paper, tanned leather account books, and "green candles," presumably for writing account entries when the sun dropped, promptly at six in the evening. In case of an intruder, or perhaps as a negotiating tactic, Allen also purchased a brace of pistols. With the goal of helping make connections in the nearby French islands, Allen wrote his younger brother Samuel in Boston to send him a French grammar book and "more French books if you have them as I purpose [propose] to make myself Master of the language."[23] He also sought a great map showing North America and the Caribbean, more likely as a decoration to enhance the cosmopolitan feel of their shop than as a tool to plot actual shipping operations.

As the shop expanded, the partners began investing in voyages beyond the hazy outline of nearby St. Kitts. Selling wholesale to other merchants was a relatively easy but passive approach and one with low profits. The real money could be made when risking their own cargoes on ships to seek out island planters directly. Starting in April 1755, Goelet & Allen launched at least fourteen voyages, labeled "Adventures" in Allen's accounts. At first the partners simply chartered space in the holds of small vessels. But as soon as possible, they purchased two used sloops, in late July 1755. While they sent ships to New York, Georgia, and nearby British Montserrat, they targeted a much richer prize: French Guadeloupe.[24]

Guadeloupe had long been the poor cousin of the wealthy and more populous island of Martinique, capital of the French Îles du Vent (Windward Islands). The colony consisted of two islands hinged together by a marshy, mangrove-covered ledge of land and surrounded by a convoy of eight smaller islands, most of which also grew sugar. The eastern island of Grand-Terre featured gently sloping land of rich volcanic soil carpeted with green-gold fields of sugarcane, rimmed by fine, white sandy beaches. The rugged, mountainous western island of Basse-Terre had just begun in the early 1750s to produce a new, lucrative crop: coffee. Best of all, from a planter's perspective, the island lay within a brisk twenty-four-hour sail from Dutch Statia.[25]

In their first "adventure," the partners sent the recently purchased *Charming Peggy*, with Allen sailing as supercargo, or agent for their partnership. They loaded hastily before the onslaught of the hurricane season. Allen reached the Moule, a small, protected estuary on Grand-Terre's rougher Atlantic side, and found an eager market. Their clients included a planter mentioned only as "Monsr Pointis," likely a grandson of the famed French admiral who had joined with French buccaneers to capture Spanish Cartagena in a spectacularly lucrative raid in 1697. Allen returned to Statia within a week, the small sloop laden with nearly six tons of various grades of sugar, 1,160 gallons of molasses (weighing at least another five and a half tons), and a case of fine French liqueurs.[26] They quickly arranged five more voyages to Guadeloupe, and another three to other French islands in the next ten months.

As the threat of war rattled rigging throughout the Caribbean, Allen's new cosmopolitan contacts with French planters and merchants in Guadeloupe ran aground on the virulently anti-French and anti-Catholic views of his New London neighbors back home. In August 1755, Allen arranged for two French merchants from the island to take ship to New England and examine the trade possibilities on the other side of the sea with their own eyes. Their arrival rankled so much that even Benjamin Franklin's old newspaper, the Pennsylvania *Gazette*, took note. In the midst of alarming news of British General Braddock's shocking loss to French forces in the Ohio country that summer, it printed a letter with the dateline New London:

> Captain Heath arrived here from the West Indies, in whom came two Frenchmen, gaily dressed; they visited the Town Battery; and entirely satisfying their Curiosity, as to our [military] Situation and Condition . . .

> read in several Newspapers an account of General Braddock's defeat, and drank a Health to the brave fellows that defeated him. This behavior at last, gave some Offence to the Magistrates, and they were put in Custody of a Constable Forty-eight hours, after which they appeared before a Court of Justices who, we hear, ordered them to depart the Place the very first Opportunity.[27]

Allen's business associate, Nathan Allyn, reported his own version to Allen. Local officials and townsfolk were so annoyed, he wrote, that "there was a talk of seizing the schooner when she first arrived," adding that the two French merchants were quickly "hald [hauled] befor the authority." After a few days, "the Court found nothing Against them[;] however suffered them not to stay but ordered them to returne Back to there own country . . . in the West Endia."[28] Allyn graciously (and profitably) arranged to purchase their entire cargo of molasses, and even gave them two horses as a parting gift. But he warned Allen never to encourage another such visit. The affair exposed the degree to which Allen's cosmopolitan views from the Caribbean clashed with those of less traveled folk, even in New England ports.

By May 1756, Allen had begun to receive major orders from Elizabeth's uncle, the distilling magnate Gurdon Saltonstall Jr. Saltonstall not only sent Allen the typical array of New England products but also ordered the sale of the ship that carried them, the newly built brigantine *Lyon*. As for the plantation products, he instructed Allen, "Lett the molasses be of the best Quality." This probably meant purchasing it mainly from French planters, who often sold the molasses derived from a higher level of refining that produced a higher quality of sugar (termed clayed sugar).[29]

Saltonstall also sent his own empty British-measure casks. This may at first seem curious—why use up valuable cargo space to send empty casks? But Saltonstall undoubtedly understood that, while customs inspectors could not tell the difference between British and French molasses, they certainly knew the difference between British- and French-built hogsheads. He needed to ensure that customs officers would pass French molasses in British casks. The profits from this single order filled Goelet & Allen's sails with nearly as many pieces of eight as they had earned in their first year of operation.[30]

Then, at the very height of their success, failed diplomacy back in Europe threatened their own small but rising Caribbean empire. Within two weeks of their sending Saltonstall's order in late June 1756, news arrived confirming the rumors of the past six months: Britain and France had declared war on each other.[31] The partners now faced a hard choice. They could return to their homes and incessant demands for repayment. Then again, they could stay put on Statia, in the eye of the spiraling hurricane of war, and profit from the carnage sure to come.

4

In the Shadow of Statia Rock

BETWEEN JUNE AND DECEMBER 1756, Allen seems to have vanished beyond the horizon. He suddenly reappeared in Statia, arriving from Holland with a hold filled with crates of European goods on December 3, 1756. By then, Great Britain and France had fully launched the Seven Years' War in Caribbean waters. At first, British officials displayed no interest in combating contraband, perhaps a holdover from the previous war. American southern customs Surveyor-General Robert Dinwiddie, for example, indifferently characterized British trade to non-British colonies in 1743 as merely the "residue vended to the French, Spanish and Dutch settlements in America."[1] The Seven Years' War would quickly change perceptions of smuggling as a result of the cunning innovations by merchants such as Thomas Allen during his nearly three-year sojourn in Dutch Statia.

Although documentation in the form of letters is sparse, Allen left a diary of sorts, a massive journal of accounts, started the year before open war began. In it he recorded in his own hand most of the important transactions of the partners from December 1756 to early 1758, just before he wound up operations in Statia. It is an astounding document, offering a unique perspective that helps later readers piece together how Allen actually operated as a smuggler during wartime in a precarious entrepôt.

The new entries open with several noticeable changes. First, Francis Goelet disappeared from the daily transactions. The reason why remains unclear. One of Allen's old acquaintances, writing decades later, asked what had happened to Goelet after he had been "stabbd by that negro on Statia." It may well be that the knifing forced Goelet into a long convalescence (we have no details on the fate of the enslaved person).[2] Goelet did become a silent partner, supplying some of the initial stock, and shortly after, he and Allen dissolved their partnership amicably. This allowed

Allen to form a new partnership. We know even less of his new partner, Richard Wait, except that he also hailed from Connecticut, possibly Saybrook, and had presumably established himself as a young merchant in New London trade circles at roughly the same time as Allen.

Allen also secured the services of a new, fifteen-year-old apprentice: his stepson, Richard Shackmaple. Richard had originally arrived in Statia on board the *Lyon*, the same ship that Gurdon Saltonstall had sent in June 1756. Seven months later, young Master Richard, as he would have been styled, had already lived through some exciting but deadly times. Shortly after setting foot on Statia, he fell ill with fever. Allen paid for a resident British American doctor, Charles Arding, to help Richard sweat the fever out for a month while recuperating in the home of a local merchant named Hermanus Erburgh. At some point, probably in early August, Richard took ship and left Statia for Amsterdam, possibly with Allen. Their travels are unknown, but Allen's accounts show that Richard returned to Statia on his own aboard another vessel arriving from Amsterdam in mid-January 1757.[3]

When Richard first climbed out of the rowboat, he might have walked up the escarpment into the town, shielding his eyes from the hot sun to find his stepfather's shop. It was a compact, one-and-a-half story building that merged showroom, warehouse, and accounts, on one of the town's short streets, probably not far from the small Anglican church. He stayed not only with his stepfather and Richard Wait, who had their own cots in an alcove, but also with the enslaved Jupiter, a young man who appeared to have been only four or five years older than Richard. Like most enslaved men of the era, Jupiter probably had a cot, or perhaps a hammock, among the barrels and firkins in the back of the shop or in the hot, stifling loft above. British American ship captains occasionally lodged and ate in the shop as well, a source of both income and undoubtedly some rum-laced sea tales told late at night through swirling pipe smoke.[4]

The first aspects of trade that young Master Richard would have needed to learn were the basic imperial and colonial regulations governing the movement of goods in the wartime Caribbean. Most casual readers, and indeed many historians, tend to think of smuggling as breaking only a single set of laws, running goods (or people) across a political jurisdiction from some faraway place to a single nation or colony.

However, settler captains needed to consider at the very least four different sets of imperial laws at any one time: the home colony's laws on

FIGURE 4. "The Bay and Island of St. Eustatius," based on a drawing originally by A. Nelson, 1774. View of the port of Oranjestad from the southeast. Ships, many of them single-masted Bermuda-rigged sloops, ride at anchor in the roadstead on the left. The warehouses of Lower Town crowd the beach in the middle. Up the escarpment on the right were located the various merchant shops, churches, inns, and the governor's home and fort (with flag) in Upper Town. (Horizons WWP/ Alamy Stock Photo, BC1TCX)

goods leaving, the foreign colony's laws on goods arriving, the foreign colony's laws on goods leaving, and, of course, the home colony's regulations on foreign goods entering. All these laws could be quite different. In addition, Customs regulations were product-specific: authorities allowed some commodities to enter freely, rendering smuggling unnecessary; they allowed others at various times and slapped a high duty on them; they forbade still other items entirely. Dutch trade regulations, such as those officially observed on Statia, added yet another layer of duties, although the 2 percent ad valorem tax ensured that taxes were low and easy to calculate.

Allen would have explained to young Shackmaple that each British mainland and Caribbean colony also passed its own restrictions, often as surcharges, modifications, or interpretations of imperial regulations. Richard would have needed to know these too. Massachusetts, for example, had already established the precedent that illegally shipping provisions from the colony during war in 1744 would be considered treasonous. New York and Connecticut later introduced similar legislation even before formal declarations of war in late 1755, while Massachusetts enacted a full embargo in December of that year. Even so, New England papers carried rumors that British (and not settler) sea captains evaded these new regulations, selling mainly English and especially Irish produce to French colonists.[5] Such news would spark increasingly shrill responses.

Allen might have further illustrated the nonsensical results of such regulations. For example, red onions grown in the farms surrounding Wethersfield (south of Hartford) and knotted into ropes (called skeins) of about eight to ten pounds each fetched high prices in the Caribbean. Imperial authorities in London considered onions provisions, a strategic part of the farm produce that fed troops in war, and therefore expressly forbade the exportation of *any* provisions unless the merchant had petitioned the colonial legislature for a license. Licenses were difficult to obtain except in the colony of Rhode Island.[6] Yet, when it came to selling ships, whether sloops or brigantines, Richard might have been surprised to learn that no British Navigation Act regulated colonial vessels, even though their sale earned far higher profits. So long as Allen sold a ship to a resident of a British or neutral island (primarily in the Caribbean), he broke no British law, even if that merchant then immediately resold the vessel to French buyers to be refitted with cannon to prey on British ships.

The wartime part of the journal opens on December 8, 1756, when Allen & Wait welcomed the first of two cargoes shipped to their new shop in Oranjestad. The first shipment arrived from Amsterdam on the brig *Marietta,* commanded by a Jewish Statian captain, Isaac Shano.[7] The partners received more than a hundred bolts of cloth in a range of bright colors, along with the kind of fine dress accessories that Allen's father had stocked back in Boston. However, this shipment of dry goods did not come from London but from the rising spinning mills in northeastern France, Holland, and central Germany. They had also obtained their stock largely on credit from the famous Amsterdam merchant firm of English ex-Patriot brothers Thomas and Adrian Hope, who also had long-standing accounts with major settler merchants such as Thomas Hancock in Boston and Philip Cuyler in New York. At the very back of the shop, Allen stored an entirely different type of European manufacture from the same shipment: four six-pounder Dutch-made cannons for ships.[8]

A second ship arrived barely two months later, also from Amsterdam. Along with Richard as a passenger, it carried a different array of manufactures: crates of expensive Dutch tableware and chests of smoky "Suchung" (Lapsang Souchong) and fresh "Heyson" (Hyson) teas, both originally harvested in South China. The vessel also disgorged ship supplies, including miles of tarred ship's rigging and ship's cables. Even the needs of babies were considered—Allen & Wait sold small batches of soft white diapers on a continuing basis, all to local residents.[9]

As Allen probably explained to Richard, selling European goods certainly contravened the Navigation Acts, but only if the partners sold them to other British subjects or French belligerents. No laws prevented the partners from conducting business with neutral nations. True, Allen recorded in April 1757 that he sold cloth worth 286 pieces of eight (abbreviated in his accounts as "pcs") on his "Adventure to Guardelope," one of the very few direct exchanges with the French islands recorded. But Allen might then point out that French planters and colonial officials, on the other hand, viewed the movement of goods in a decidedly more favorable light.[10]

Allen understood that at the start of the war, the French metropolitan government had already weighed the costs and accepted the inevitability of relying on neutral trade ships. By late 1757, the British Navy and British privateers had cleared the Atlantic of most French ships. On Saint-Domingue, for example, planters learned that of the fifty-seven ships sent from France prior to October 1757, British privateers had seized forty-five. Even more were captured the following year. Largely isolated from France itself, local French officials felt they had little choice but to accept neutral country trade ships. The French governor-general of Martinique, Maximin, Comte de Bompar, refrained from prosecuting British American sea captains, who arrived by the dozens, unless their behavior and movements aroused suspicions of spying.[11]

To conduct clandestine business, Allen and Wait swiftly inserted themselves into Statia's cosmopolitan community. The accounts refer to at least twenty-two merchants who resided on the island. At the pinnacle of the "resident" list was the island's wily governor, Jan de Windt, who traded not only sugar from his own estate but also gunpowder and some cannons. But the accounts show that Allen also cultivated a wide range of other merchants. Dutch land-owning families included Andrew (Anders?) Ravenie, Abraham Heyliger, and Docke Groebe (or "Ducky Groobie," as Allen wrote his name). Resident Statian merchants included the firm of (Jean-Pierre) Allier & (Anton) Pachaud (or Paccaut), and well-established Jewish merchants, such as Anton Kannegeiter (also written Cannegieter) and Loderwyck Aertsen. The latter's family originally hailed from Basse-Terre on French Guadeloupe. Allen and Wait also traded with several New England merchants. Among their numbers were fellow New Londoners

Thomas and William Packwood, who also resided permanently in Oranjestad, according to available census lists.[12]

The most intriguing of Allen's contacts was "Peter" (Pierre) Desmonts on the Franco-Dutch island of nearby Saint-Martin (Sint Maarten). Desmonts's life demonstrated the kind of profitable possibilities of living in the entangled imperialisms of the Lesser Antilles. Brought to England by his Huguenot parents as a child, he shipped out to Montserrat as a teenager, becoming an overseer on a plantation in his early twenties, then married the daughter of a prosperous island planter. Purchasing citizenship on the Dutch side of Saint-Martin, he then built up a large plantation on the French side (Habitation Saint-Jean). He further expanded operations by including marginalized islands, such as British Anguilla, ruled by the Gumbes family. Such contacts allowed him to easily move goods to all sides in any conflict. Desmonts was clearly a striver in his own way. He quickly became one of Allen & Wait's largest and most regular customers, trading in sugar, provisions, and small ships.[13]

Allen and Wait also counted some independent businesswomen among their local clients. Richard might have sold cloth by the bolt to people who were probably local seamstresses—linens to Rebekah Patterson or calicoes to Mary Blanchard. Three widows, at least two with English names, purchased small amounts of chinaware, Chinese tea, butter, and occasional barrels of beef, suggesting they ran taverns. Allen also counted some Afro-Caribbean people as his customers. He sold a barrel of pork "to a negroe" for 20 pcs, a rather large sum to a presumably "freed" man; a damaged barrel of flour for 14 pcs to one "Johaner, a negroe girl"; and a 155-pound barrel of coffee to "Negro Peggy."[14] Allen, Richard may have noted, sold all these goods at the same prices he charged his European customers, although it remains unclear whether they were acting on their or on a slaveholder's behalf. That Allen assigned women and either enslaved or free Afro-Caribbean people their own accounts is significant. It suggested to young Richard that while his stepfather clearly embraced patriarchy and supported African enslavement, he held clients and profits of any provenance in higher esteem.

Aside from introducing young Shackmaple into his circle, Allen would have introduced him to other aspects of life as an overseas merchant as well. Several intriguing and cryptic entries show that Allen paid for tutoring lessons and some clothes for Richard, including several pairs of new shoes. In addition to making him more comfortable, presenting the young man as a well-dressed apprentice undoubtedly aided Allen's own reputation on the island. He even gave or possibly loaned his stepson Richard a healthy chunk of money, at least 71 pcs, to do his own investing. Richard wisely followed his stepfather's lead and invested in French coffee, sending his cargo back to the sure markets of Amsterdam.[15]

Other items are more curious, and even ominous. Inserted into one folio is a note titled "Women & Gaming," with a list of what appear to be gambling debts running into the hundreds of St. Kitts pounds. Sitting at the card table were major merchants on Statia, including "John Devant," Allen's usual way of spelling Governor Jan de Windt's name. Other entries range from "Entertainment" on board the *Polly,* a ship that Allen had an interest in, to the copious amounts of pineapples consumed in April and May, to an expense account charge "pd for an anchor [anker] of wine," about ten gallons, of French arrack, or rum. Richard Wait, perhaps on a whim, once purchased a "parritt"; it somehow seems appropriate that roguish merchants anchored on a Caribbean island would have one. On a far more sobering note, one entry recorded an unusually large cash payment made to presumably English merchant Mary Barnard "pd for her negroe wench."[16] The wording may mean nothing more than money given to the enslaved women to settle a debt owed by Barnard. But it might also indicate the sexual abuse of enslaved women to fulfill settler men's carnal desires.

The partner's accounts are littered with references to the use of enslaved labor to move goods or, more rarely, to help with ship-related repairs. Allen sometimes rented an enslaved man named Cudjo (sometimes spelled Cudjoe), also from Mary Barnard, for just such a purpose. Later, when business boomed during war, he purchased a young teenage man named London as a house domestic in May 1757. Both probably rowed massive hogsheads to the Benedenstad, then rolled them up to the beach escarpment under the enervating Caribbean sun to the storehouse.[17]

Enslaved men might also simply carry other produce, such as individual sacks of coffee, which might weigh up to 110 pounds, on their backs. Aside from handling Desmonts's and the Gumbes' affairs, Allen sold the latter six enslaved people (two men, two girls, and two boys), though the entry is uncharacteristically incomplete. This is the only documented time during his sojourn that Allen sold enslaved people.[18] It is also probably where a young man such as Richard learned the behavior of how to be a "master" over other people.

Seaborne trade during war greatly increased, but also rearranged the possibilities for selling and winning profits. In certain respects, Allen & Wait participated in the conventional trade of the era, trading New England products of mainly salted meat and fish, staves, and board lumber for the plantation trinity of sugar, molasses, and rum (see table 1).

Richard learned from his stepfather the prime importance of the New England provisions trade. Even before the war, Allen was horrified to learn that the Connecticut Assembly had slapped a temporary embargo on New England foodstuffs. He wrote his friend Nathaniel Allyn in the summer of 1755 that "it's the General Opinion [in Statia] that Provisions Will Command as great a price as ever was known," and hoped for a quick end to the embargo. But until the actual declarations of war, Goelet & Allen never sold more than 1,100 pcs of New England food in a month, mainly as barrels of Newfoundland fish, salted beef, or thick Connecticut butter.[19]

Shortly after Richard's arrival in January 1757, however, the sale of provisions rose to 1,400 pcs. Then the volume shot up to 5,100 pcs by May. At that moment, merchants on Statia learned of the long-anticipated Flour Act, which prohibited export of mainland provisions (including onions) to any non-British islands. Thereafter, the value of New England foodstuffs remained steady at about 2,200 pcs in monthly sales.[20] Of course, Richard understood that selling provisions, down to the last sorry sack of flour or spoiled firkin of butter, remained strictly illegal for the duration of the war.

Return plantation cargoes also constituted a major part of the partners' trade, though not quite in the same proportion that classic studies would suggest. Sugar traditionally dominated exports—about 70 percent, according to one study—with much of this arriving from the French Lesser Antilles.[21] Molasses traditionally constituted far less of the cargoes, and rum less still.

Allen's accounts, however, tell a different story, at least during war. Sugar sales showed extreme swings, ranging from a miniscule 790 pounds in January 1757 to 33,987 pounds the very next month. Molasses and rum also had their own sales trajectories.[22] Overall, the partners exported the same percentage of sugar and molasses, while they sold a considerably larger amount of rum (27 percent by value) than traditional studies show. Richard's stepfather sold most of the rum to passing British ships.

TABLE 1. Net sales on Dutch Statia by Allen & Wait, December 1756–May 1758

ITEM	VOLUME/ UNIT[A]	NET SALES (PCS)[B]	ILLEGAL SALES (PCS)	ILLEGAL SALES (%)
Manufactures—cloth	Varies	7,213.3.3	6,342.3.5	87.9
Manufactures—tableware[c]	Varies	896.3.3	811.0.1	90.5
Imported ship supplies	Varies	1,510.6.1	1,483.6.1	98.2
Ship provisioning	Varies	3,041.3.2	3,041.2	100
Sloops[d]	4	9,650.2.4	?	?
New England provisions	Varies	27,075.4.1	27,075.4.1	100
Other New England products[e]	Varies	1,584.0.0	0	0
Sugar	85,917 lb	4,866.3.1	3,631.6.2	74.6
Molasses	23,773 ga	4,984.2.1	4,984.2.1	100
Rum	9,637 ga	3,646.1.3	?	?
Coffee	72,371 lb	10,386.0.4	7,993.3.1	77
Cocoa	10,627 lb	892.5.2	868.6.5	97.3
Tea	291 bt	474.1.0	421.6.0	88.9
Empty casks	346 hh	1,900.6.0	?	?
Total		**78,110.5.1**	**~55,109.3.5**	**~70.6**

Sources: American Antiquarian Society, Allen Family Collection, folio 5 (pp. 65–153), folio 6, and folio 7.

[a]Weights/measures: ga, gallon; lb, pound; hh, hogshead; bt, bottle (weight about 2 lbs each).

[b]Monetary denomination shown in format of pieces of eight (pieces, reales, stuivers/marevedis—a tripartite system). One piece of eight *del cambio* = 8 reales = 48 stuivers/marvedis.

[c]Includes china, glassware, and metal tableware.

[d]Tons burden of sloops unknown.

[e]Mainly lumber, fowl, candles, and tallow. Nearly all were sold locally or to passing ships.

Allen's records also show a trade in a unique settler commodity: swift sailing ships. By the spring of 1756, shortly before the declaration of war, Allen & Goelet had already sold three vessels. Within a year starting from January 1757, Allen & Wait acquired, cleaned, and refitted at least four more sloops, selling them at profits ranging from 31.8 percent to 41.5 percent. Three went to English merchants on St. Kitts, while the destination of the fourth remains unclear. As with Allen's other large sales, buyers often paid in bills of exchange, usually drawn on Amsterdam to be paid in London. Any outstanding amounts were settled up with a barrel of mackerel, a bolt of cloth, or perhaps a case of wine glasses. It is impossible to determine whether the purchasers in turn flipped the vessels to French buyers eager to use British-built ships.[23]

Master Richard might also have smelled the rich aroma of a new product handled by his stepfather: coffee. From December 1756, coffee was Allen & Wait's single most valuable Caribbean export. The partners loaded more coffee into New England ships than sugar and molasses combined. The raw coffee beans can be traced directly to the mountainous French Lesser Antilles islands, where enslaved people cultivated new coffee trees at a friendly elevation, impossible to do on the generally flatter British islands. While British planters in Jamaica's Blue Mountains had experimented with the bean since the mid-1730s, they found demand for sugar so vigorous and steady that coffee did not warrant much attention until after the end of the Seven Years' War. Spanish planters in eastern Cuba likewise developed coffee only in the 1760s, and not coincidentally after British occupation.[24]

French planters, however, had planted coffee groves on Martinique since the late 1720s and on Guadeloupe since the mid-1740s. By 1754, French Caribbean coffee exports accounted for a quarter of all colonial trade to the major French ports of Bordeaux and Rouen and about 10–15 percent of trade at several smaller ports. Martinique supplied the bulk of French exports, shipping just under 12 million pounds on the eve of the war.[25] Much like the sugar "revolution," rising coffee planting and consumption created its own revolution in trade and sociability. It would later play a crucial role in Thomas Allen's search for wealth and social acceptance.

As Richard finished the first stage of his apprenticeship in the smuggling business, he may have wondered how much his stepfather and Mr. Wait profited from their transactions. Most merchants in the Anglo-French Atlantic accepted "neat proceeds" (the term often used to describe net profit) of 8–10 percent from any single undertaking as quite satisfactory, while British and French planters, whether on Antigua or Saint-Domingue, closed their yearly accounts happily if they had wrung a yield of 15 percent from the sweat and blood of their enslaved laborers.[26]

Allen may have cited several examples from the big journal to illustrate to his stepson how smuggling paid off. The initial two shipments of goods from Holland, he might have noted, ranged between 14.5 and 19.7 percent, while the four sloops averaged about 35 percent. The partners' seven separate wartime "adventures" generated roughly 8–12 percent in neat proceeds. The selling price of individual commodities very seldom earned more than 25 percent. In the case of sugar, for example, they consistently acquired barrels of sugar at about 2⅔ stuivers per pound, selling them for 3⅓, a markup of about 20 percent. In the same way, bulk French coffee could be purchased during the war at 6¼ to 8 Dutch stuivers per pound and sold at 8 to 9, a markup of about 13 percent.[27] If a sharp clerk, Richard may have wondered why bother to risk so much for such paltry returns.

The answer, Allen might have patiently continued, rested on two basic truths that he had discovered in his early dealings. First, smuggling, especially during war, allowed business to continue when it might otherwise stay becalmed. In any event, profits on most goods were also roughly 50 percent higher than in peacetime. More subtle was the second point: the partners' business dealings during war *always* made *some* profit. In fact, the partners suffered hairline losses on only two documented major transactions, both involving sugar, which amounted in both cases to a mere one-half of 1 percent loss on the total invested. Not surprisingly, Allen & Wait quickly abandoned selling sugar. In an Atlantic World where losses were frequent, the key lay in generating incremental, consistent, and continual profits. Everything, or nearly everything, that Allen touched on Statia turned to silver—silver pieces of eight.[28] This was one crucial way in which the maritime contraband trades helped generate settler capital.

Even as Allen rebuilt his fortune under "Statia Hill" with his stepson's help, sharks in the form of French privateers were increasingly infesting the surrounding waters. In early January 1758, one of his close business associates in New London, none other than the king's New London customs official Joseph Chew, warned that sales in New London had dropped suddenly because the port's privateers were bringing in so much captured merchandise that "every day offers great Bargains in Prize goods." More ominously, Chew added, "Your affairs here have been since ordered." This meant that New London merchants were refusing Allen's bills of exchange and seeking court action to recover their money.[29] A second threat of bankruptcy could not be far behind.

In the wake of Chew's warnings, even worse news followed. British seizures of Dutch vessels had increased dramatically. The Connecticut port's freshly minted newspaper, the New London *Summary,* repeated news from other settler papers that the British crown seemed determined to end the Dutch neutral trade. They noted that the Royal Navy and British privateers had captured some sixty Dutch ships worth over nine million florins during the summer of 1758 alone. In addition, French privateers remained very dangerous. They captured a ship Allen had invested in, commanded by another young captain, Thomas Willson, hauling it into Saint-Pierre, Martinique, in early 1758. Willson and his crew sweated out at least four foul months before being exchanged.[30] Given the number of seizures by privateers on all sides, Allen may have decided it was time to cut his losses in the face of the increasing perils of wartime trade. He left Statia suddenly in June 1758, never to return.

But Allen's journal suggests a sadder reason why he chose to leave Statia at that moment. The entries by Richard cease in late March of that year, replaced by a few sporadic and confused entries in a squirrelly, unknown hand. Only in a document dated much later did the reason became clear. Young Richard Shackmaple had died, likely from another attack of fever, in April or May 1758.[31] He was not quite eighteen.

As the ship carrying Thomas Allen back to New London entered the Thames estuary in July 1758, Allen may have pondered why an endless gale of bankruptcy buffeted his life. Or perhaps he rehearsed the words he would have to say when he looked Elizabeth in the eye to explain why he had not returned with her son.

5

The "Fair Trader" and the "Deputy First Mate"

ALLEN'S RETURN TO NEW LONDON in the early summer of 1758 coincided with the first of Great Britain's major victories in the American part of the Seven Years' War. In early June of that year, British forces began their long siege of the French fortress port of Louisbourg in today's Nova Scotia. The elimination of Louisbourg not only opened the heart of New France to invasion, it also removed the swarm of French privateers that had used the port as a haven.[1] Now New England's ships could be unleashed to plunder French or neutral ships carrying French goods, from the Grand Banks to the Caribbean. Allen quickly joined the ranks of those looking for "Government Service," or privateering.

Privateers were merchant vessels, usually the size of a schooner or brig, armed with at least a dozen cannon and forty to one hundred men, sailing under a special royal commission (or letter of marque) issued by the king's representatives. Unlike piracy, perpetrated by "villains of all nations" who attacked merchant vessels indiscriminately, privateering operated by set rules and regulations. It was a business—trade by other means during war. As the Boston *Post-Boy* argued in reprinting a major London pamphlet, privateers were a positive social good. "Private ships of war," it noted, not only made enormous money but "trained up . . . his Majesty's fleets" by providing wartime experience for sailors. They also liberated "several thousands of his Majesty's subjects," weakened the French colonies, and were even a testament to the zeal of "public-spirited men" in defending the nation.[2]

Allen's sole foray into privateering proved to be wildly successful, and lucky. His rechristened brig the *Royal Defiance* captured a neutral Dutch ship off Martinique, *de Vrouw Ursula,* with a rich assortment of Caribbean cargo, including nearly forty tons of various grades of sugar, nearly fifteen tons of coffee, and 2,260 pounds of fine-grade sea island cotton. Allen's share from the nearly £10,000 prize came to £4,000. With the prize ruled legal by the local court the day before Louisbourg's surrender, Allen quickly paid off his remaining creditors of the 1753 Boston debts.[3] With his own coffers now filled to the gunwales, he invested heavily in two directions at once.

First, he and Elizabeth built on the land left by her first husband on the northern shorefront near the new customs house. Documents describe the small complex, completed in February 1759, as "large, commodious, and well-situated." In addition to the two-story home they built a combined shop and warehouse and, most important, a wharf, jutting well beyond the low-water mark into the Thames River.[4] The couple immediately filled their smart new home with the refined furnishings of the newly affluent. The parlor featured twelve gilt reproductions of the "Seasons," possibly variations on Antoine Watteau's well-known *The Four Seasons;* a cherry wood–topped tea table; some mahogany chairs; and likely Allen's mahogany work desk in one corner near the brick fireplace. Mahogany was an exotic luxury wood then gaining popularity in the Atlantic World. Wealthy guests would be served tea or coffee in "burnt soop" enameled cups and saucers from England, or perhaps imported dark red Madeira in "gold gilt glasses," before sitting down to play cards at a separate mahogany table. Upstairs, the various Allen family members slept on at least two feather beds (the two most expensive items in the house) and probably two or more straw ones. They would have had at least a half-dozen sets of formal coats, jackets, breeches, and blouses. Elizabeth had purchased several full gowns, which hung in at least three hulking wardrobes, and a four-foot-tall "gilt Black Walnut fram.[d] Looking Glass."

The parvenu wealth of the couple was reflected in the tax rates assessed by New London. In 1753 the Allens paid rates squarely in the middle. By 1760 they had climbed into the top twenty select families in town, owning at least £128/5/0 in taxable property. As part of the effects of a former sea captain fully immersed in the misery of the plantation trades, this "property" included at least two enslaved people.[5] Thanks to Allen's long self-imposed exile under Statia Rock and his lucky break in privateering, the rewards of commerce on the deep blue had brought his family a genteel level of comfort and community respect.

But Allen was not done. His new home had to match his aspirations of becoming a full-time settler maritime merchant. New London led

Connecticut's aggressive expansion of later wartime trade, and Allen became a key player. From October 1758 to the return of Allen's last ship in late April 1762, he invested in twenty-eight known shipping ventures. Nineteen were on his own vessels or those he chartered, and nine more were in the form of shares held in other voyages. At first he invested in a few voyages to supply his old friends in newly conquered French Guadeloupe, which had surrendered on May 2, 1759.[6] But losses from Martinique's privateers nudged him to reenter the shady world of contraband trade to Spanish Hispaniola.

Settler clandestine trade during the Seven Years' War operated in four basic ways. As the historian Thomas Truxes notes, these smuggling methods entailed the use of "Frenchified bottoms," or neutral intermediaries to transfer French cargoes; "flag-trucers," a practice dating from at least late medieval Europe in which ships sold cargoes as their fee for exchanging prisoners of war; and the smuggling of popular imagination, running a cargo into a desolate cove under cover of a moonless night. But Allen entered into the fourth and most profitable smuggling type of the era, the "Mountmen" trade. This meant settler ships calling at the Spanish free port of Monte Cristi on the island of Hispaniola to broker deals with Spanish merchants or French captains from nearby Le Cap, the major port on French Saint-Domingue, less than a day's sail away.[7]

Allen's entry into the Mountmen trade in 1759 coincided with a major change in perceptions of smuggling in settler America. At first, news reports and opinion pieces pitted an imagined law-abiding "fair trader" who earned an honest living against rogue merchants who cheated king and customs. Writers directed their ire at non-British merchants, specifically the neutral Dutch. They railed against the "pimps and underlings" who profited from trade by running neutral ships, "for by keeping a good look-out, they never wanted [for] good cheer, smuggling from the enemy's shore."[8]

However, newspapers were increasingly exposing the rise of smuggling closer to home, which unveiled the prominence of New England ships in the contraband trade. Investigations ordered by Rear-Admiral Thomas Cotes of the Royal Navy further suggested that settler ships not only helped the French Caribbean islands survive, they also posed severe logistical problems to provisioning military campaigns. Newspapers reported on this "iniquitous trade" and heartily applauded the forays made by the Royal Navy in late spring of 1759 into Monte Cristi to snatch any suspicious settler sloops. Selfish merchants who smuggled showed deep ingratitude to "our Mother Country . . . exhausted with Taxes for our Defence," and were "no less injurious to the fair Trader . . . who having paid high Duties . . . must be great Sufferers" from the illicit trade.[9]

But as smuggling increased, different settler voices began to rethink what it meant to be a fair trader. Samuel Green's New London *Summary* appears to have been among the first to offer a new, daring interpretation. In the late summer of 1759, his paper ran a short piece from a local source that hinted at the darkest collusion between the Royal Navy and Jamaican merchants. "The Monto Christi men seem to be the only object of their [the Royal Navy's] Pursuits and Jamaica's Resentment," the article read. The writer deplored Jamaica's "safe and advantageous trade with the French for Indio & sugars" carried on with the southern coast of French Saint-Domingue.[10]

Then, in early June 1760, Green printed a long and even more provocative two-page essay that supported clandestine settler trade to the French-owned islands in the Caribbean. The points are so cogent, and so firmly grounded in quantitative references, British law, and firsthand experience trading with the French islands, that only a select few settler merchants or sea captains could have possessed that knowledge. While there is no proof he wrote it, Allen was one of the few who could have.

The essay laid out a new, treasonous proposition: the various smuggling trades as practiced by settler sea captains had major advantages for American settlers in particular if viewed through a more objective lens. The author recast the debate by asking whether clandestine trade helped or hindered in bringing "an expansive war . . . to a happy conclusion." In effect, the author insisted that smuggling aided the war effort. To make the point, the essayist challenged three common misperceptions of settler-Caribbean contraband trade.[11]

First, contrary to popular belief, smuggling did not only supply French planters with necessities. Instead, the author accurately argued that settler smugglers not only helped British manufacturers by selling finished British goods to French planters but also reexported French sugar obtained in the trade to the rest of Europe. In effect, British merchants were undercutting French merchants in Continental markets by selling French-grown sugar. This had in fact begun to happen. Second, settler smugglers did not supply the French islands with provisions that fed their own privateers.

Instead, the author noted that Martinique's infamous marauders were launched from an island with little trade and desperate for food, whereas Saint-Domingue's unofficial embrace of settler trade made privateering superfluous. As the author summarized, where the smuggling trade grew fat, privateering starved.[12]

For his third and last point, the author challenged a long-standing mercantilist assumption: smuggling did not drain British bullion reserves. Instead, the essayist again accurately showed that French planters paid for the vast majority of their imports (about 90 percent), either by direct barter or with bills of exchange on neutral Dutch Amsterdam; actual gold and silver specie were seldom used. This antimercantilist argument predated the appearance of Adam Smith's groundbreaking work, *The Wealth of Nations,* by sixteen years. The author concluded by pointing a marlin spike directly at an unnamed Royal Navy commander, likely Rear-Admiral Cotes himself, who had "converted a court of justice . . . into a sanctuary for piracy and robbery" by siding with Jamaican planters. The end destination was clear: from the deck of economic rationality, American mainland merchants and sea captains charted a course completely different from that of British merchants and major planters, or Royal Navy admirals.

Within three months of publication of the essay, papers in the larger settler mainland ports had begun to recast their blanket condemnation of smuggling. The "freer trade"–oriented New York *Gazette,* for example, echoed the *Summary* essayist's last point. The author argued against

> the severe and cruel hardships [the Provisions Act of 1757] laid upon his majesty's loyal subjects in America, who were prevented from exporting their staple commodities, while their fellow subjects in Great Britain and Ireland, enjoyed the Privilege of sending every kind of provisions to Monte Christo, and every other neutral Port in Europe and America . . . at the time when our men of war and privateers from Jamaica, Providence, and some other places, where [were] distressing the Trade of these colonies to a degree very little different from Robbery and Piracies.[13]

In December 1761, an outraged writer in the Boston *Gazette* pounded out this conclusion: "We want nothing but to be as free as others are, or others should be restrained as well as we." He signed his piece "A Fair Trader." The meaning of "fair trader" for settlers had by now become the exact opposite of what it had meant barely three years before. This piece appeared in the immediate aftermath of the famous Writs of Assistance case. Hired by a group of shady Boston merchants, James Otis Jr. had argued against the legality of universalized search warrants to catch smugglers. This shift in the perception of overseas trade by mainland merchants was arguably revolutionary in itself. Witnessing the Writs of Assistance trial as a young man, John Adams later famously recalled that "then and there the child Independence was born." But had Adams been a merchant, he might have traced the birth a bit further back, to an essay in the New London *Summary,* or even further still, to the bay of Monte Cristi.[14] The "child Independence" was very plausibly born at sea on a smuggler's ship.

Ironically, even as New London's *Summary* began to defend settler smuggling to the Caribbean, Allen began to lose by it. His returns on his 1759 and early 1760 voyages were hit by a hurricane of misfortune. French privateers captured several of Allen's ships, including the *Triumph,* again commanded by young Captain Thomas Willson. The French again locked him and his crew in a fetid prison in Saint-Pierre, Martinique, for at least two months. Willson never forgot or forgave the French. All told, Allen's first six shipping adventures lost money, slapping losses of £1,683/17/3 on him before his new store and wharf were even a year old.[15]

As the losses mounted, Thomas and Elizabeth again had to confront a rising tide of debt. Creditors began to besiege their new house, dunning Allen, which meant pounding on his door and windows to try to coax him out of his house so that they could hand him court orders demanding payment. The pressure rattled Allen to the point that he took to drinking and carousing. On one cold afternoon in late winter of 1759, he and the young Nathaniel Shaw Jr., "making hadious noise and Uttering horrid Expressions," disrupted a Town House meeting by carousing and yelling outside. Constables tried to arrest the pair as they shouted "thay had a hell of their own, and call[d] for assistance to make it more so, Damning the Grand Jury."[16] The two were each let go with stiff fines and court costs of £5/4/0. But Allen's situation only worsened.

Allen spent the next year flopping around greater New England like a fish out of water. He first tossed up in nearby Newport, Rhode Island, which provided him with a good haven: a busy port with many merchants to connive with, but close enough to sneak back into New London to see his family. He then jumped over to New York to arrange more cargoes and to buy three enslaved people—Tom, aged forty, Jupiter, aged twenty-two, and a teenage girl named Juno—to transfer to Captain Willson, in an

FIGURE 5. *Sea Captains Carousing in Surinam,* John Greenwood, ca. 1755–58. Carousing captains in a colonial tavern, drinking, smoking, playing cards, puking, dancing, even sleeping around tables, served by two African males. At upper right a younger man, perhaps a first mate, lights the way to the beds upstairs. (Courtesy of the St. Louis Art Museum)

apparent attempt to raise cash. Allen may have visited Boston, then definitely returned to Newport, fretting over how to pay the bills. He may have journeyed back to New London to see his wife and young son, Thomas Jr., at Christmas.[17]

At this same time, Allen learned of the capture of the *Loyalty* by Martinique's marauders. This hit Allen with his greatest single loss yet—over £800. Allen then ventured back to the Caribbean, this time to Monte Cristi to see the Mountmen trade for himself. But fever quickly gripped him, and his words voiced only grief. "To live here to please Creditors," he wrote Elizabeth, "I shall not, & Sacrifice the prime of Life & be Absent from you & family which is all I Esteem . . . in this Transitory World."[18] Once recovered, he sailed immediately back to Newport.

Allen's frantic tacking in every direction around Greater New England and the Caribbean made waves beyond New London. Freed from debt with Allen's considerable help, his parents were able to purchase a country store in quiet Shrewsbury by 1757. That left his younger brother Sam in Boston, struggling to piece together his own career as a merchant. Sam had arranged for the insurance on at least two of Allen's failed ventures and had invested his own money in several more. But his brother's disasters dragged him into a maelstrom of debt, reaching nearly £5,000 in Massachusetts currency by mid-1759. As Sam ran low on money by that

October, his annoyance quickly turned to bitterness. "Oh, Cruel Brother," Sam wrote their father, "that has never remitted me on[e] Shilling . . . notwithstanding his many promises," adding that if he could only get £300 from Thomas, he'd be able to weather the immediate crisis and then would be entirely "done with him." By Christmas, Sam had somehow righted his financial ship. He may have been aided by his older half-brother, Jolley, who had moved his family from Old England to Boston at the start of the war and hung out his own shop sign, initially as a baker. But Sam soon suffered his own reverses from French privateers. He never had the chance to rebuild his business, for he died suddenly in 1760, likely from a smallpox epidemic then ravaging Boston.[19]

As Allen scurried from port to port, Elizabeth managed the mess her husband had left behind. Sources for Elizabeth's life during this fraught period are few. But the Allen Papers contain a remarkable string of some twenty-one "Dearest Elizabeth" letters he wrote his wife from late 1760 to early 1762. While her role can only be viewed through the lens of her husband's ink, they nevertheless offer some striking details on Elizabeth's role as a business partner, especially as a "deputy husband," in which capacity mariners' wives acted as merchants, ship-owners, shopkeepers, bookkeepers, and overseers of small processing businesses in the absence of their husbands.[20] She ran their small store, raised their son, Thomas Jr., being sure to supervise his schooling, and helped her eldest daughter, Sarah (Sally to the family), raise her own family. Sarah had married Captain Willson shortly after his release from prison in Martinique, and the couple now had an infant daughter and a son on the way.

Much of Allen's directives to Elizabeth pertained to keeping other trusted captains or merchants aware of his plans and movements or to ensuring that bills of sale or credit instruments were delivered properly and on time. She also directly handled several practical business affairs. For example, in March 1761, Allen shipped "sundry bales, boxes, and Trunks, etc. of goods" for her to store in their warehouse, along with some forty small bills of credit totaling £50/8/0 in New York currency for her to "dispose of to those most needy and deserving" of their creditors. Two months later, he asked Elizabeth to personally deal with several urgent business affairs, including arranging with five other local merchants the loading of a ship with water, fodder for livestock, wood staves, and other miscellaneous cargo.[21]

Allen very seldom provided details on sailing experiences to other merchants unless they were ship captains. Yet he shared nautical news frequently with Elizabeth, who clearly understood the risks and dangers of the sea. In one letter, he reported that "Johnny [Capt. John Deshon of the *Fox*] has mett wth a flash of Lightning & thunder[,] Tore his mast to pieces & sett fire to his vessel. However, got in here again, & is fishing his mast [out of the sea]. . . . Came via the Race at same time as Harding, who made it down in 13 days, all well."[22] In this context, Elizabeth might also be considered a kind of "deputy first mate," a sympathetic listener who understood the "dangers of the sea" and would also pass information on to other local families.

All of Allen's directives to Elizabeth offer at least the semblance of long-distance emotional support and his desire to "Remove all Grievances when i git home." In a letter penned while waiting out a storm in Long Island Sound before leaving for his first Monte Christi voyage, Allen's emotions rose above the usual business details. "D.^{se} [desire] youll keep a good Heart, and all things surest to yourself until Please God wee mett," he wrote, then added, rather poetically, "Be not unmindful of your affectionate Friend—base & naked is the journey southward; Hurry me Relief (which will hurry me to your Dear Arms)." Allen punctuated this letter, as he did all his longer ones, insisting on his integrity: "you know my Intentions, to do every One Justice."[23] Such assurances may have been aimed at addressing Elizabeth's own anxieties, frustrations, and undoubtedly annoyance as much as to trumpet his own self-vindication. Yet the letters underscore the crucial contribution of women's economic labor and emotional support offered to their absent mariner partners.

By July 1761, Allen had run out of room. One of his New York creditors, William Cobham, had begun pursuing him relentlessly, attaching Allen's cargoes and forcing him to begin the arduous process of negotiating with his many creditors for debt relief. Allen first signed the titles of his—meaning Elizabeth's and her children's—property over to a group of creditors headed by Gabriel Ludlow & Company of New York. Yet the family's situation only deteriorated. By October they had sold their remaining household possessions to her eldest surviving son, Captain John Shackmaple, with a guarantee signed by Elizabeth's in-law, Groton merchant Thomas Mumford. This arrangement satisfied a group of local creditors headed by Sheriff Christopher Christophers, another distant relation of Elizabeth.[24] Keeping the possessions within the extended family may have been a publicly acceptable way to preserve Elizabeth's security and respectability while probably inviting snide asides about her husband's reckless deals.

With their property temporarily secured, Allen gambled on a desperate scheme in November 1761. He returned to the Caribbean on a "flag-truce" voyage to Monte Cristi, taking a berth as supercargo on the brigantine *Hawk,* captained by his younger brother William. Sailing with him was the young enslaved Jupiter. Fending off a French privateer with Jupiter's help, Allen arrived at Monte Cristi. He reported to Elizabeth "the trade her[e] quite open, & believe Business may be done to great advantage; I am kindly rec'd by the Governors Secretary [Mr.] Nicholas, etc."[25] But Allen's real destination lay barely a day's sail westward: the thriving French port of Le Cap François.

"The Cape," as many English newspapers called it, excited Allen's enterprising and aesthetic sensibilities more than any other Caribbean port he had visited. The city served as the outlet for French Saint-Domingue's North Province, which included the expansive Plaine du Nord, or great North Plain. This region stretched nearly to the Spanish frontier to the east and gradually became lost in the craggy hills to the south and west, covering at least 720 square miles, more than four times the size of Grand-Terre on Guadeloupe. At least two-thirds of Le Cap's population consisted of enslaved Africans, mainly Fon, Igbo, and Kongolese people, or Creoles born in the Americas. They labored under not only a small number of white French overseers, but also a dynamic and swiftly growing community of *affranchis,* or freed people of color. Many of the *affranchis* read and wrote French, worshipped in their own Catholic churches, and were astute and cultivated businessmen and -women in their own right.[26]

Allen stayed for nearly a week. After his first day navigating its humid, choked streets, he reported to Elizabeth, "I find here a very fine town and Civil, well-dispos'd People for trade." Details of his time in Le Cap are few. Allen likely visited different parts of town of interest to a New England merchant. One possible destination was the Marché des Blancs (Market of the Whites), where "Every Sunday merchants hawked, along the whole length of the avenue from the Rue du Conseil to the Rue Chastenoye, all sorts of dry goods and jarred foods from all parts of France; wrought iron products, fine pottery, earthenware, assorted notions. . . . One finds also jewelry and fine chains, shoes, hats, wigs, monkeys, virtually anything one could possibly sell in le Cap." Allen even bumped into several familiar New London mariners, including one of his old Statia clients, Captain William Packwood.[27]

The enterprising glow afforded by Le Cap did not endure. A severe fever gripped Allen shortly after his return to Monte Cristi, laying him low for nearly three weeks, sweating and barely conscious in the small cabin on board the *Hawk*. Allen thought he was near death; "physicks" on shore bled him twice with brown leeches to alleviate the disease, which only weakened him further. He later wrote to Elizabeth that he wouldn't have been surprised if reports of his death had reached her by then. When able to sit up, he scrawled to her, "Oh, I hope it may Please Almighty God of his Infinite Goodness & Mercy to restore me . . . to the Happy sight of you, my Loved Wife and Childr^{n}." As the fever subsided, he sailed back to New London in January 1762, knowing that his sortie to Hispaniola had been a complete debacle. Toting up the balance sheets, Allen realized that the *Hawk*'s disaster had capsized his finances with a loss of an additional £1,100.[28]

Upon his return, Allen took the extraordinary step of urging the Connecticut Assembly in June 1762 to allow him to declare bankruptcy. He provided a portrait of himself as an honest fair trader smashed by angry forces beyond his control. "Your Memorialist," his petition began, "for several years past carried on Trade & Navigation in said port to the great Benefit of the Subjects of this Colony," but "having my Interest taken by ye Enemy, Bad Voyages, and Disappointments," he had become "a bankrupt." His creditors, he claimed, had disregarded his reasonable solicitations, with "each one inclined rather to confine me in a Dark and Loathsome Gaol."[29] Despite the plea, the Assembly dismissed his petition. Crushed, Allen believed his only hope lay in one last desperate gamble at the very bottom of the Lesser Antilles. He quickly set sail for the newly conquered island of Grenada, only a few leagues ahead of his creditors.

6

The Insolvent Debtor

DECEMBER 21, 1765, A Saturday, dawned cold but bright. Outside New York's New Gaol, the remaining snow from the recent storm had left dirty white mounds. The Provincial Assembly had built the New Gaol on the outskirts of town, in what had been a scattering of farms only a decade before. The Assembly had just finished its round of lawmaking the week before, ushering in the start of the festivities for the winter social season. And this Christmas season would be even more special. The new provincial governor, Sir Henry Moore, had just arrived with his family from England. As if to offer a gift to the people, Moore carried full confirmation of the end of the widely despised Stamp Act.[1]

On the second floor of the prison, a motley crew of five men were housed in one cell. They included Samuel Stitt, a squat, square-shouldered sailor, his hair tied back in a ponytail; Robert John Livingston, with a "thin visage, long light-color'd hair," his face pockmarked with "carabuncles" from a youthful disease; and lean, one-eyed Tunis de Klerke. He must have been brought low from a more privileged past, for he still sported "a piss-burnt wig." In the corner at a makeshift desk sat the last inmate in the cell: "Thomas Allen, of New London, about 5 feet 9 inches high, thin visage, streight grey hair."[2] They spoke quietly and anxiously, for they had agreed on a plan of escape.

As the guard made the late rounds at supper, Allen knocked him down, seized the keys, and opened the doors. The inmates quickly raced downstairs, through a back door, and into the freedom of the frosty night. Once safely away, Allen may even have paused to catch his breath, cast a backward glance at the jail, and wondered: How had it come to this?

After returning from Le Cap in early 1762, Allen had evaded his creditors in New London by signing on as supercargo aboard the aptly name brigantine *Hope,* headed for Grenada, the furthest south of the Lesser Antilles. The French island, recently captured by British forces, offered a wonderful opportunity for a merchant who spoke French.[3] Allen spent a year and a half trading in Grenada, partnering with another emigrant merchant, William Kingdon, in selling the island's coffee and sugar. But Kingdon died in November 1763, and Allen himself again fell ill, this time with yellow fever, shortly after. His exile strengthened his resolve to "quit this sad, Sickly place," as he wrote his father.[4]

But then he saw an opportunity. Allen took on a large consignment of tropical produce from a young and self-admittedly naïve would-be emigrant planter from New Hampshire named John Evans. If Allen could not make money through legal trade, he would do so by smuggling; and if not by smuggling, then by outright theft. As Evans bitterly recalled in a letter to Allen twenty-five years later, "When you quitted Grenada in the Year Sixty Four I found the next morning an empty store. . . . My only consolation was a sheet of paper . . . containing an Account of sales of a Large Quantity of Goods, a considerable part of which I understood you embarked on the same bottom [ship] yourself."[5]

Once on a ship headed back to the mainland, Allen reviewed his situation. He had few options, none good. In all the Nor'ad, or northern sea ports, where he had connections, he owed money; where he owed little or no money, he had no connections. Therefore, he headed back to Newport, Rhode Island, where he owed the least amount of money and would be close to Elizabeth in New London. The colony of Rhode Island also offered one other singular advantage to Allen. Its laws offered relief for insolvents debtors, even if it meant the colony was "routinely denounced as a notorious debtor's haven."[6]

On first returning to the settler mainland in December 1764, Allen found himself in a stricken, rancorous land. The folk of Newport were in an ugly mood. Only a few months before his arrival, merchants in Rhode Island had voiced their anger against the Royal Navy. Two years previously His Majesty's Navy had diligently protected Rhode Island's ships from Spanish and French privateers. Now, their aid of customs patrols seemed to besiege the port. Governor Samuel Ward alerted London that, compared to wartime prosperity, "the demand for the produce of the country, employ for laborers and other kinds of business, are all proportionately decreased. . . . The lands within this colony, have also sunk nearly or quite one half their value."[7]

From Nova Scotia to the Chesapeake capes, the cries of hardship, scarcity, or outright ruin resounded with a depressing familiarity. In the north, the new naval base at Halifax, no longer needed against French Louisbourg, suffered from severe postwar cutbacks. Boston, already stumbling through economic and population stagnation since the end of 1748, had been hit by the twin horrors of fire and an influenza epidemic. The first left the town looking "like a frightful skeleton," while the second killed more than three hundred people in one month and halted seagoing traffic. Many other mainland colonies fared little better. Jonathan Trumbull Jr., son of Connecticut's future wartime governor, returned home from England in late 1763 to find the colony a "Strange Scene of Bankruptcy and ruins." In nearby New York, one merchant wrote that "trade in this part of the world is come to so wretched a pass that you would imagine the plague had been here." The economic outlook for Philadelphia's waterfront was equally glum and seemingly endless.[8]

Even the planters of the previously wealthy Chesapeake region were experiencing trying economic times. High wartime tobacco prices abruptly tumbled by nearly 50 percent after 1760, leading a young son of the Virginia gentry, the future Patriot leader Arthur Lee, to claim that the tobacco trade was so "oppressed with such intolerable exactions, that it yields to the laboring planter scarce one-tenth of its original value." Settler merchants were clear in their minds who had caused the economic malaise: Parliament, by introducing the Revenue Act of 1764 and ignoring the economic downturn building since the end of war in North America.[9]

Allen undoubtedly understood that the Rhode Island Assembly had been the first mainland colony to emulate the bankruptcy reforms of British law, begun in 1754. Merchants were in effect free to pursue a second chance in trade if they had the stomach to do so. He filed his own petition to the Rhode Island Assembly February 20, 1765, one of at least fourteen filed in the colony that year. Yet no sooner had he done so than he withdrew it. He had learned that the Connecticut Assembly would shortly introduce its own version of Rhode Island's laws, which would give him a far stronger opportunity to settle his debts. The new laws were "tolerant, lenient, and friendly rather than harsh, grasping, and litigious."[10] Allen scurried back to New London in May 1765.

The new Connecticut law reflected the pervasive spirit of gain that had embedded itself in the settler colonies. The propertied ranks of

FIGURE 6. "The Power of Justice," George Morland, ca. 1788. This poignant, ironic painting shows a poor weaver taking leave of his wife and two children as a sheriff hustles him off to debtors' prison. The horror of such prisons and the destitution of families became an increasingly powerful motif supporting change to debt laws from the mid-eighteenth century onward. (Heritage Image Partnership Ltd./Alamy Stock Photo, 2X22DB8)

Connecticut colonists had slowly altered their view of debtor-creditor relations in the generation before the economic depression of the 1760s. Distinctions between honest and dishonest bankrupts date back at least to laws introduced in sixteenth-century England and continued to inform the attitudes of British settlers into the eighteenth century. New England minister Samuel Moody characterized the new perceptions when he distinguished between those "Diminished and brought Low by the Holy Providence of God" and therefore "the Proper Objects of Charity" from those who "made themselves Poor by hearkening to Satans Temptations . . . living in Pride and Luxury . . . without Care or Conscience how they should get out."[11]

The spectacular rise of English maritime trade from the early seventeenth century sharpened this distinction. As English trade expanded, playwrights and pamphlet writers such as Thomas Dekker urged that "the infortunate Marchant, whose estate is swallowed up by the merciless Seas . . . Deserve[s] to be pitied an[d] relieved." New England merchants, developing their own routes of overseas trade nearly a century later, came to similar conclusions. By 1762, an anonymous New England pamphlet writer could plead that for merchants in oceanic commerce, "So many unforeseen Accidents happen, so many Casualties are we subject to under the Sun [that] it is Folly in us to be unable to bear Disappointments, and cruel in us to make no Allowance for them in others."[12]

Overseas trade had helped spur a revolution in debt management, socially legitimizing an important part of what had previously been considered irresponsible conduct. The Connecticut Insolvency Law of May 1765 provided a prime example of the new support granted risk-taking, fast-talking, ever-rebuilding overseas venturers like Allen. The charge to reform debt laws began with a former evangelical minister, country shopkeeper, and later governor, Jonathan Trumbull. He introduced the first bill revising bankruptcy in the colony and pressed for its adoption. As is now known, Trumbull had secretly and nimbly avoided his own impending personal bankruptcy by relentless reelection to office.[13]

Regardless of Trumbull's personal motivations, his views combined with the worsening economic depression convinced the Connecticut Assembly to eventually adopt his bill. The major argument given was the "great inequality and injustice [among creditors that] has been occasioned, and law suits . . . greatly multiplied" in the courts from the winter of 1764. The law passed in the spring of 1765 had several new features that rewarded the rationality of both debtor and creditor—"enlightened" debt restructuring. For example, men or women who initiated debt proceedings and who expressed a suitable humility could not be imprisoned, or if already imprisoned could petition for release. But the Assembly limited the law to two years, not only to clear the backlog of suits but undoubtedly also to help carry the colony over the sharp shoals of the depression.[14]

In writing his own petition, Allen drew up five neat sets of inventories in early July 1765 to explain his situation. Most of his creditors were New York merchants, to whom he owed the princely sum of £4,260/10 in New York currency, three times what he owed in all of New England. The most poignant part of his petition came at the end, where Allen listed what the law allowed his family to keep in half a page. Court officials allowed him to retain the tools of his trade, "Nautical Implm^{ts}," including a quadrant, and "1 sword and a p^{r} of Pistols." The rest was sparse: a few pots and pans, a single set of old tableware, a couple of chairs, two old mattresses, and "wearing Apparel for my Self Wife and Son. And No More."[15] In less than three years, Allen and Elizabeth had tumbled from enameled China to cracked pewter.

As draconian as the law might seem today, Allen had to act quickly in order to take advantage of it. As stipulated by the law, he would first need to visit New York, where the largest number and the most truculent of his creditors resided. Reaching out to them would satisfy the transparency and humility demanded by the law, and he might even be able to arrange good terms. He arrived in New York in the sweaty days of late July 1765, just as anger over the new Stamp Act was beginning to fester and build into a furious swell along the eastern seaboard.

After sailing into New York's double-bay harbor, Allen stepped off a sloop into a beehive of activity. Even with the slowdown in overseas trade, New York probably felt like an enchanted market to him. As one recent visitor noted, "This pleasant City . . . Enjoy[ed] the most delicious Climate in the world [and] was inhabited by an hospitable cheerfull social people living by their extensive Fortune Landed & Commercial." As Allen walked, he undoubtedly saw through the shop windows of bookseller Hugh Gaine the freshly printed copies of "An Act for Granting and Applying certain STAMP DUTIES, and other Duties, in the British Colonies and Plantations in America," priced at one shilling.[16] The cost of the pamphlet was about the same as the cost of the official stamp when the law became effective later that November.

But two constables cut Allen's freedom short. On July 29, they thrust a sealed parchment into his hands, signed on its cover by Sheriff John Roberts. It was a summons for payment by Allen's second largest creditor, Thomas Doughty. Allen had just been arrested for debt. They marched him through the streets to the outskirts of town, where a cell awaited him at the city's New Gaol. Later inmates referred to the prison as an "unhappy mansion," a "human slaughter house," and a "dismal cage."[17] Once stripped of his more valuable belongings and confined, Allen quickly set to work writing letters to his creditors.

Being arrested in New York meant that Allen now came under that colony's insolvency laws. Following more lenient Dutch precedents, and predating even Rhode Island's generous acts, New York offered the first "full bankruptcy system" in the British overseas colonies. Some viewed the laws as far too forgiving. One of Allen's creditors, Gerard Beekman, firmly believed that the law "made a damd many Great Rogues," and called the lawyers who urged filing for bankruptcy "Great Villains." However, unlike many other colonies, New York's Assembly upheld the incarceration of debtors with over £50. Allen was one. At first, he possessed enough credit and goodwill to purchase some decent food and comforts, such as a small desk and chair, ink, and parchment.[18] He also undoubtedly had access to newspapers describing the growing turmoil on the mainland over the Stamp Act.

Throughout August and early September, anger up and down the seaboard increased. The Providence *Gazette,* for example, spouted venom directed toward the "men of war, cutters, marines with their bayonets fixed, judges of admiralty, collectors, comptrollers, searchers, tidewaiters, landwaiters, with a whole catalog of pimps, [who] are sent hither, not to protect our trade, but to distress it." Even if the Stamp Act was an older law grudgingly observed in England, many free settlers then, and many Americans since, have viewed the Stamp Act as an obvious attempt to control the growing economic power of the mainland colonies. Yet the challenges of fair customs collection had a severe impact on both sides of the pond. For example, Lord Grenville devoted much energy to an even thornier target, the revestment of the smuggling dukedom of the Isle of Man, anchored in the Irish Sea. This tiny island cost English customs an estimated £100,000 sterling a year, only slightly less than the amount expected from all the mainland colonies combined.[19]

While the stamps were bothersome for every free settler, they were particularly onerous for merchants. Ship's papers in the Caribbean trade, for example, often numbered fifteen or twenty separate forms and copies of documents. Each single form or document required its own stamp. True, the tax amounted to only £2 or £3 sterling for ship's papers, but it sliced off typically 10–15 percent of the earnings from a small, modestly successful voyage's profits, tilting a mediocre venture into a wash, or even a marginally costly one. It also added from three days to a week to crucial departure times as overburdened customs clerks laboriously handled the extra paperwork.[20] Coming in the wake of the Revenue Act and the depression, the Stamp Act seemed especially punishing, and therefore incendiary.

News of further unrest filtered into the New Gaol as fall succeeded summer. Following Boston's lead, ugly mobs harassed stamp tax collectors, their families, and administrative supporters. In Newport, which Allen had left only a few months before, an enraged mob torched the homes of the stamp distributor and His Majesty's customs collector, Dr.

Thomas Moffat. Mortified by the attacks, Moffat soon relocated to New London, where he was rewarded with another appointment as a customs official. New York's own prospective stamp tax collector, local merchant James McEvers, resigned his post in late August, hoping to avoid "Disagreeable and Dangerous Consequences" at the hands of an enraged mob. By October 23, the sea captains Isaac Sears and John Lamb (the latter of whom may have dealt with Allen at Statia in the 1750s) were leading other "rough men of the Waterfront" to denounce the stamp duty and the self-righteous, unpopular lieutenant governor, Cadwallader Colden.[21]

As the Stamp Act storm erupted, Allen's situation deteriorated. Elizabeth could no longer send any aid, and he ate and kept warm only by the grace of public charity. He scribbled furiously with his remaining ink to make a new proposal to his creditors, completing a new set of inventories to sway them. On the same evening that he wrote, All Hallows' Eve, October 31, Stamp Act rioters began shattering windows and launching attacks on supporters. The next morning Allen would have seen people converging on the open ground near the goal. An estimated two thousand protestors—a fifth of the city—assembled on the open ground near the New Gaol to denounce the Stamp Act and plan an attack on the Assembly.[22] Hasty negotiation brokered a deal to ease the mob's anger, but the port remained very tense.

Many of the same merchants who helped negotiate the easing of tensions were also Allen's largest contingent of creditors. They represented merchant rogues and strivers of the first order—smart, educated, and determined wartime flag-truce smugglers, army contract gougers, and immigrant sons on the make. Two of Allen's largest creditors, Doughty and William Cobham (the latter of whom who had first brought suit against Allen in 1761), were both dry goods merchants. They likely dabbled in wartime profiteering and smuggling.[23]

Several of Allen's other creditors also sprang from the financially precarious British "wary middling ranks" who had left behind the Old Country to chisel out fortunes in the New. Hugh Wallace, for example, had shipped in from southern Ireland a few years before the war and become a prominent "vendue master," the contemporary term for a public auctioneer. He used his position and connections to advance from "middling stature to prominence" by the war's end, successfully investing in army contracting and marine insurance. He had married into New York's elite and sat on the Governor's Council by the time the stamps arrived. Theophylact Bache had also migrated to New York on the eve of war to learn the dry goods importing business from a relative. Once the fighting began, Bache quickly shifted to selling shirts and shoes to the army, flag-truce trading, issuing marine insurance, and making property investments in the city. His younger brother, Richard, joined him at war's end, relocated to Philadelphia, and eventually married Sally Franklin, daughter of Benjamin Franklin and Deborah Read. Allen owed smaller amounts to other notable New York merchants. These included Jacobus Van Zandt, "a veteran of every phase of wartime trade with the French," according to one historian, and the radical free-trade supporter, future Patriot leader, and Declaration signer Philip Livingston Jr.[24] The small amounts held by the last two suggest they did not know Allen personally.

Of the twenty-two New Yorkers' names on Allen's list, the most intriguing is the man to whom he owed by far the most money: famed future Patriot printer Samuel Loudon. Loudon and Allen were shadows of each other, contemporaries whose business relationship lasted nearly thirty years, their lives coiling around each other to intersect at crucial points for both. According to Loudon's most thorough biographer, the printer lived "life on the run," much as Allen did. Unlike Allen, he became a "shrewd, opportunistic businessman who always seemed to be in the right place at the right time."[25]

Much of Loudon's early life remains conjecture. Probably born in Aberdeen, Scotland, about 1727, a year before Allen, he migrated to New York in 1753, about the time when Allen settled in New London. From the few ads and faint letters his biographers have discovered, Loudon opened first a general store, then a ship chandlery with "the LOWEST PRICES" at Hunter's Quay in early 1757. He rented rooms above his shop to ship captains, branched out to trade in West Indies products, such as muscovado sugar, by 1762, then acted as something of a ship broker by early 1764, all the while entering into ventures with other minor merchants, including privateering, as Allen did.[26]

Loudon may have learned of Allen from fellow New York merchant Gerard Beekman, or more likely from his brother-in-law, the prominent Norwich merchant and lawyer Elijah Backus. Regardless of how they connected, Allen's correspondence provides new details on Loudon's investments in several of Allen's failed shipping ventures beginning in mid-1758. By the time Allen entered the New Gaol, he owed Loudon the "supposed" amount, by Allen's reckoning, of £1,012 sterling. This was more than twice the money Allen owed his next highest creditor.[27]

By Thanksgiving, an uneasy truce and shivering snow had both claimed the streets of New York. Allen penned a short letter to circulate among his creditors. Acknowledging he owed the massive amount of £5,354/1/7, he proposed a precise process for repayment: his two principal creditors would manage his estate while he operated with a "Letter of License" signed by all his major creditors allowing him to reenter trade for a "Reasonable Time." Allen pledged "to use all my Endeavours abroad to collect on interest . . . which [I] will Chearfully do." His proposal followed several aspects governing Chapter 11 bankruptcy for businesses in the United States today.[28]

Receiving no immediate response, Allen wrote to Doughty directly. "I Intreat of you to come into the same measures wth my other Creditors," Allen wrote, pleading with Doughty not to "Distress the Distressed." Doughty's response is unknown, but his actions clearly are: Allen remained in the New Gaol. Allen was incensed. For him, debtors' prison was the antithesis of mercantile efficiency. As one early English anti-debtor prison pamphleteer concisely observed, "A Prison can pay no Debts."[29] Allen's few words to his creditors, in his petitions or in marginalia in his inventories, all suggest he viewed them as irrational and cruel.

As snow dusted the ground outside the New Gaol in early December, Allen became ill and even more desperate. Then came the worst news: the colony's Assembly had passed the remaining legislation for the year, including removing the possibility of debtors reaching personal, and undetected, arrangements with specific creditors.[30] It's possible that Allen had such an understanding of repayment with Loudon; if so, the implementation of the new law might help explain the timing of Allen's prison break.

Whatever the trigger, Allen participated in, and likely planned, the escape from the New Gaol on a cold Manhattan night on December 21. He was identified as the one who punched a guard, allowing the inmates to seize the cell keys. Where Allen went next remains a mystery. A scribbled letter more than two decades later may hold a clue. In 1789, an old business associate named Jonathan Bull, a small merchant on Long Island, wrote Allen asking for repayment on an ancient debt. "You undoubtedly remember the time when I assisted you in New York," Bull wrote. "Certainly you cannot forget it." It is possible that Allen, either with Loudon's surreptitious help or on his own, found refuge with Bull.[31]

By February 1766, Allen had snuck back into New London, where Sam Loudon's letters finally caught up with him. Loudon struck a friendly tone, urging Allen to return to New York. "The Sheriff (John Roberts) assures me you will not be touched," he wrote, "til April [court sessions] & prob^{y} not then." Loudon was of course self-interested, very worried he would face the "blame by your going from hence in the manner you did." He also counseled Allen to keep working. "I don't care whither you go, to West Indies or else-where," he wrote, "but I fear if something can't be done by way of settlement with y^{r} Cred^{ts} before you go abroad, twill be attended with bad consequences."[32]

The bad consequences came quickly. Receiving menacing threats from one of his New London creditors, Allen finally accepted his fate. He wrote the County Court Judge in August 1766, offering to surrender himself and his assets. Once reassured of his legal rights, he signed away his and Elizabeth's assets. By October 1766, the ordeal of running and shame that had begun in mid-1761 had finally ended.[33] He still owed money, but he had regained his freedom and mobility. In late 1766, he once again waved goodbye to Elizabeth and Thomas Jr., now entering puberty, and set out again on a new sea of possibilities to seek yet another fortune in the plantation Caribbean trades.

7

The Smuggler

IMPORTANT AS THE POLITICAL wrangling over parliamentary acts was in the mainland colonies from 1764 to 1774, in Thomas Allen's world the Caribbean Sea loomed much larger. When he returned in late 1766, he sailed into a very different region from the one he had known nearly ten years before during the Seven Years' War. The stunning triumph of British arms had accelerated changes already well underway before the war erupted. In many ways, the varied reshaping of the plantation Caribbean, often subtle and sometimes violent, was as politically convulsing, even revolutionary, as those on the settler mainland at the very same time.[1]

From the early 1760s, the Caribbean experienced explosive economic growth. Enslaved laborers cleared the ground for new plantations or greatly expanded many existing ones. Much of the expansion occurred on Spanish Cuba and Puerto Rico, and on the Ceded Islands—those officially transferred by the Peace of Paris in 1763 from French to British control. These islands included Dominica, St. Vincent, Tobago, and Grenada. But of all the plantation islands, the growth of French Saint-Domingue soared above the rest. Within ten years of defeat in 1763, the remaining French Caribbean colonies, led by Saint-Domingue, astoundingly *doubled* the value of their plantation exports over the prewar levels. The French colonies collectively outpaced even the massive surge in exports of British-grown sugar. Exports of other products throughout the Caribbean Basin, such as rum, cotton, cocoa, and coffee, and of hardwoods, such as mahogany, also rose to new heights. The acreage for new foodstuffs such as cassava and bananas also increased. Such foods provided enslaved families with new crops largely under their control and with some added nutrition, while potentially lowering food and medical costs for planters.[2]

New groups of people arrived, too, through either free or forced migration. The Atlantic trade in enslaved peoples jumped to new levels, adding two new, major African ethnolinguistic groups, the Igbo and Kongolese peoples. Many of them or their progeny would later become revolutionary agents in their own right. Entirely new, self-consciously aware communities claimed their place before the mast, such as freed people of color (or *gens de couleur*) and French emigrants "of modest means" in Saint-Domingue, Scots in the Ceded Islands, and the Maroon towns in the interior of Jamaica, who fought against repeated British planter forays. The expansion of enslavement and opposition to it in turn helped nurture two radical new concepts: easing the hardships faced by enslaved peoples, or amelioration, and, of far greater impact, the abolition of slavery itself, following the lead of Anthony Benezet's 1760 *Observations on the inslaving . . . of Negroes*. The abolition of enslavement could potentially be just as radical as settler demands for a republic to replace the monarchy.[3]

Both economic and human forces in turn invited new ideas that translated into reform policies supporting freer colonial trade. Disagreement over the pace and direction of reforms often turned violent as colonists challenged new metropolitan regulations. Concurrent with protests on the settler mainland, and well before the start of the Haitian Revolution in 1791, the newly Spanish Louisiana, French Saint-Domingue, and the Afro-Carib–dominated island of British St. Vincent were all were rocked by violence within two years of each other in the late 1760s.[4] In short, the forces of change in the Caribbean Basin during the postwar period were arguably as powerful as those operating on the settler mainland.

To survive, and eventually profit, merchants like Allen first had to grasp the new Caribbean trade regulations sweeping the Caribbean. The changes began with a small but sharp dispute over smuggling between the new British governor of Dominica and his French counterpart in Guadeloupe in 1763. The dispute erupted into a major issue within a year and forced imperial regimes to grudgingly accept ideals of freer trade in the Caribbean. A major reason for the change lay in the decision by the secretary for the French Marine, the Duc de Choiseul, to enlist Enlightened philosopher and Martinique planter Jean-Baptiste Dubuc to become, in effect, the deputy minister responsible for all the French Atlantic colonies. For the first time, the French Creole plantation plutocracy now possessed a firm, intelligent advocate in the heart of the newly revamped French imperial system.[5]

Dubuc moved quickly to restructure French colonial trade regulations to better suit the realities of Caribbean trade. In July 1767 he unveiled three new *arrêts* (formal legal pronouncements signed by the King) collectively known as the *Exclusif mitigé*—loosely, "modified mercantilism." While the new customs duties and free ports may in retrospect seem timid and marginal, they had the practical effect of signaling to local officials they could be far less restrictive in the larger ports such as Basse-Terre, Saint-Pierre, Port-au-Prince, and Le Cap.[6] It acknowledged what Dubuc and the French planter elites had long understood: French plantations needed the settler seaboard, from Pennsylvania to Newfoundland, in order to prosper.

Aware of Dubuc's moves, the British Parliament under the brief first ministry of the Marquess of Rockingham pursued its own attempts at freer trade. Rockingham introduced a trident of new customs rules: relaxing British trade with the Danish Caribbean islands, lowering the duties on French molasses from three pennies per gallon to just one penny (the Revenue Act of 1766), and allowing the reexport of sugar, coffee, and cocoa by mainland merchants to foreign markets. Parliament also passed the Free Port Act in May 1766, opening four smaller ports on Jamaica and two on Dominica. British hopes were high. The act's preamble confidently predicted that Dominica would emerge as "the great Mart and Magazine for the Merchandize . . . of that part of the world," stealing the commerce of the French Îles du Vent.[7] While aiding Jamaica, it did little for Dominica. However, the act did have the unintended benefit of allowing settler captains to claim the island as a legitimate sailing destination, disguising their real destination to non-British islands.

Settler merchants eagerly followed the rumors and news on free ports right from the signing of the Treaty of Paris. It is easy to see why. Free ports were sites of geographic "dispatch," potentially quickening the mobility of goods and money, and offered hope for reenergizing commerce in a period of economic malaise. The end of the Seven Years' War ushered in a brief era of "free port mania," at least as far as settler newspapers were concerned. Rumors identified, among other locations, Spanish Monte Cristi, Bermuda, St. John's in Newfoundland, Pensacola in British West Florida, all of French Saint-Domingue, and (correctly) Dominica as new free ports.[8]

But some settler merchants guessed that free port winds might becalm their ships instead of filling their sails. The Boston *Evening Post*, for example, complained that "cunning North-American smugglers . . . alone will be the gainers. . . . An English free port amongst the French, Dutch, and Danish islands, will operate in all shapes against *us*, and for *them*." Others questioned the value of the Revenue Act of 1766, noting that North American commerce was "so clogged and restricted . . . as to afford a melancholy presage of its Destruction."[9] Free ports appeared to favor British imperial merchants everywhere except in settler America, heaping more coals on the smoldering seaboard discontent.

Allen first headed to his old haunt of the Moule on French Guadeloupe, but business was sluggish. Setting out on a new voyage on a snowy January day in 1767, he charted a new direction. Officially cleared for the new free ports of Dominica, he sailed instead for Danish St. Croix, not far from his old haunt of Statia. The Danish crown had founded or purchased colonies on a triangle of islands early in the eighteenth century. From a merchant's perspective, the largest, St. Croix, combined the best features of the Caribbean: plantations, convenient location, and two safe anchorages. By 1767, St. Croix had become a de facto British economic colony, ruled by a Danish administration but accepting all European inhabitants; even a few Jewish merchants settled without apparent hostility.[10]

While anchored off the West End (today's Frederiksted) of St. Croix in early 1768, Allen appeared to have an epiphany on how to rebuild his fortune. Nearing forty, with at least £3,000 in debt still to pay, plagued by recurring stomach pains and coughing fits, and with a head of frosted gray hair, Allen likely found little appeal in the physically rigorous, lonely existence of seafaring at his stage of life.[11] He needed a new life back on shore. While he left no written plan, his actions over the next seven years appear to have been so consistently and deliberately undertaken as to constitute a vision of an innovative form of overseas trade based on St. Croix. This voyage marked the end of his long-distance voyages. Once he returned to New London in May 1768, Allen never again sailed the seas.

While most merchants were content with one or possibly two voyages a year, Allen's business plan was based on keeping three ships in motion at any given time. One ship loaded cargo in New London, a second loaded a return cargo on a Caribbean island under the supervision of a resident factor, while a third sailed the open Atlantic between the two ports. In effect, Allen juggled his ships like a busker with three batons, having one in the air at any given moment.[12] It sped up operations, allowing at least three and sometimes four complete voyages in a single twelve-month period. The quick turnaround also meant he enjoyed up-to-date information, which in turn helped him arrange more attractive return cargoes. But for the plan to work, Allen needed a tough, dependable, discreet factor to be his partner on St. Croix. He knew just the man.

Like foam floating on the waves, Captain Thomas Willson has left little behind of his existence. He may have been born into a family of sailmakers of the same name and particular spelling who had migrated from New York to eastern Connecticut during the Seven Years' War. Probably six to ten years younger than Allen, he first came to the latter's notice as a young but capable first mate just before the start of the war. Willson later suffered capture and imprisonment on French Martinique twice while commanding Allen's adventures. He married Elizabeth's eldest daughter, Sarah, in about 1758 or 1759, judging by the ages of their three children, thereby becoming Thomas Allen's son-in-law.[13]

Captain Willson had some formal schooling. Though he frequently wrote in a flowing hand, he also used alliterative spelling and inconsistent grammar. He rarely employed punctuation. His letters were sprinkled with delightfully salty phrasing. In one passage describing adverse sailing, he wrote, "The *Sally* was Verry Crank with me oute [and] Sloop *hector* Was throud on her Bum Ends in her pasage"—meaning the second ship had nearly capsized. He was close to Allen—they often signed their letters "your afecc^{t} Friend"—but he frequently referred to many of his fellow mariners as "raskells" or "D—d roges." Unlike Allen, he had the more typical New England mistrust of the era for anything and anyone French, likely prompted by his incarcerations on Martinique. He also did not seem to share Allen's powerful ambition for social climbing. More ominously, merchants and other captains later confided to Allen that his son-in-law seemed to have a drinking problem, causing him to be rough to his crew.[14] Undeterred, Allen sought out Willson and his ship, the *Sally,* for help.

Allen and Willson partnered for the first time in November 1768. They split the cargo space, with three quarters for Willson and one quarter for Allen, but with Allen advancing Willson the capital. He convinced the younger captain to return to St. Croix as a resident factor, much as Allen had been on Statia during the Seven Years' War. Securing Willson's agreement was no easy task. Willson despised St. Croix, writing Allen at one point, "I Intend to quit trading to this Dam^{d} plaese [place] the next Voyag and Wash my hand[s] clear of it[,] for old Debts is as Bad as old sores."[15]

FIGURE 7. *The Sloop Delancey navigates a rolling sea, ca. 1765,* L. F. Tantillo, 2016. An accurate painting depicting the type of sturdy, heavily laden New England sloop that sailed to the Caribbean. "Horse jockey" vessels used by Thomas Allen would have had an additional tarp affixed to the lower boom pole of the gaff sail to help shield horses tethered on deck from the elements. (Courtesy of L. F. Tantillo)

The first vessel named *Sally*—here designated *Sally I*—sailed as a typical "horse jockey," a Connecticut term for ships ferrying horses to the Caribbean. The trade had begun in a miniscule way in the mid-seventeenth century, largely to Barbados, even when horses were still relatively rare in early New England.[16] While West Indies planters avidly snapped up all livestock, they chose horses with particular care, normally paying the equivalent of £15–£20 in New York currency for good draft horses and up to £35 for a handsome steed.

Horses had many uses. The heavier ones were often yoked to the stone mill wheels turning the drums that crushed cane and extracted the juice, or they were used to pull creaking carts when donkeys were scarce. But planters purchased the finest horses—Allen referred to them as "saddle horses"—as status symbols for liveried carriages or to make social calls on neighbors. Of course, horses were also crucial to the mobility of plantation overseers and of officers tracking maroons who took refuge in the hilly interiors of islands. As in the Chesapeake region, betting on horses became an obsessive pastime for many planters. Regardless of their use, "Horses is Sure mony when landed," as Allen once reminded Willson.[17]

The horse trade assumed a huge importance after 1763. Connecticut's exports of horses leapt from about two hundred per year during the Seven Years' War to over 4,300 on the eve of the Revolutionary War, or about three quarters of all mainland American-raised horses sent to the West Indies. Assuming conservative selling prices and the probable numbers actually landed, the legal horse export trade to the West Indies alone generated perhaps £62,000 sterling every year, roughly the same as New England's total exports of wood or whale products and almost the same as the Chesapeake's legal exports of food to the Caribbean. No wonder the *Connecticut Journal* pondered rhetorically, "Who would not kill all their sheep to enable them to raise horses?"[18]

The exports of livestock transformed ships into floating barnyards, with very specific demands. Large animals had to be coaxed up narrow gangplanks or hoisted one at a time by ropes and pulleys strung from the mast or boom and lowered into the ship's hold, mooing or neighing in terror as they were suspended in air. In addition, ships loaded live pigs, sheep, and lambs and makeshift cages of geese, chickens, ducks, and turkeys. Fodder, maize, and seed had to be stored onboard for the voyage to feed the animals; both horses and cows consumed at least fifteen to eighteen pounds each of hay, oats, and rye every day, even when cooped up on a tossing ship.[19]

Once under sail, managing large animals in the hold or on deck under sail awnings, called "housing," posed difficult challenges. Cows still needed to be milked on heaving decks, and the stench from the daily piles of dung clung to the ship's boards even after the crew had shoveled the refuse into the ocean. Losses in heavy seas could be frightful. Drawing on Dutch records, one historian found that more than a third of the horses destined for the colony of Surinam died in transit. Allen's own correspondence is littered with accounts of livestock injury and death. In one instance, Willson reported that six horses were severely lamed by the terrified kicks of others during a storm.[20] Thinking in terms of simple numbers transported makes it easy to forget that the horse jockey voyages were also killers of animals, as cruel as they were profitable.

With thirty-five shivering horses on board, the *Sally I* pounded into the heavy swells of the Race in early December 1768, just as "weather beg[a]n to sett in Severe, Snow & Cold."[21] Once it left, Allen then turned his attention to loading a second ship. He encountered problems immediately.

The original contract of this second ship, designated here the *Sally II,* split the loading evenly between the ship's owner and master, a Captain Zadock Brewster of Boston, and Allen. But Brewster disappeared for a long time, only later informing Allen he had retreated to a remote farm outside Hartford to avoid creditors. Allen was forced to assume the whole charter for the ship and hire his own master. Fortunately, he found Samuel Champlin Jr., a seasoned and respected captain, just days before the crew finished loading.[22]

Allen filled the *Sally II* with a more varied cargo than the *Sally I.* Along with the usual livestock, barrels of fish or pork, and packs of hoops and staves, Allen loaded new Connecticut manufactures: six thousand bricks, a water pump presumably built with English metal parts ordered by a St. Croix planter, a fine hand-tooled horse bridle, and thirty-nine collapsed hogsheads. The bricks, pump, and bridle represented a new range of simple manufactured goods that very rarely appear in scholarly studies of New England–Caribbean exchange. Such settler products escaped the restrictions on colonial manufacturing specified in the Navigation Acts, providing ambitious settler merchants with enough capital earned from the maritime trade to diversify into new enterprises on land. The collapsed hogsheads were an innovation suggested by Willson. Since plantations always needed new barrels, and since they were as cheap as they were bulky, shipping new but empty containers presented an expensive and wasteful logistical problem. Instead, Allen hired a Norwich cooper's apprentice to travel to St. Croix and assemble the staves, hoops, and tops into hogsheads on the island.[23]

The *Sally II*'s manifest also reveals another little-known aspect of transatlantic trade, the private cargo loaded by the ship's crew. These were called "privileges," which meant that Captain Champlin, his first mate, and the ship's six sailors all had the right to load trade items and animals to sell on their own, a kind of supplementary pay. Regular duties did not seem to apply to these items, though their volume and value could be significant. For example, the first mate could load up to one chicken coop, twelve turkeys, seven sheep, six pigs, and four barrels of provisions to sell. Common sailors had smaller but no less profitable privileges. As the captain, Champlin was also allowed a horse plus a disassembled cart with four wheels, another settler-manufactured product. As wet snow clung to the black lines of the rigging in early January 1769, the heavily laden *Sally II* cleared New London customs, heading for British Anguilla. But Allen's real orders directed Champlin to meet Willson on Danish St. Croix.[24]

As soon as the *Sally II* sailed, disturbing reports began to filter back from Bermuda about the *Sally I*. In late February the Connecticut *Gazette* alerted readers that the "Sloop Sally [*Sally I*], Thomas Willson master . . . was lately drove on the Rocks on the S.W. Part of Bermuda, in a violent gale of wind S.S.W., which obliged him to throw overboard 38 Horses." The fate of the crew was not mentioned.[25] As always when a seaborne disaster struck and scant tidings presaged disaster, maritime folk looked out on the relentless waves, wondering whether their own had perished.

Allen sweated out the next two weeks. Finally he received a letter in Willson's own hand in early March explaining *Sally I*'s disaster. As it sought shelter from a storm off Bermuda, the heavy swells had carried the vessel toward the reefs on the island's north end. Already angry with his first mate, Stephen Tinker, and his "little backbiting way," Willson blamed him for causing the wreck. Tinker had panicked, ordering all the livestock, some goods, and even the cabin doors tossed overboard to lighten the unwieldy vessel. The horses, cows, and sheep all drowned in the surging waves or were gashed to death on the ragged rocks. The sloop itself sustained about £140 in damage. Willson "discharged that D—d Raskel Tinker." After making minimal repairs, he continued on to the West End of St. Croix, there to await further orders from Allen.[26]

Upon receiving Willson's letters, relayed by two different New London sea captains, the usually hard-nosed Allen softened. He wrote his son-in-law, "Joy, gladness & thankfull heart over flows, when I again see your hand Writing in Saifty." He offered Willson advice, urging him to take "One Leaf out of my Book . . . as I know you are not so anur[d] to Meeting with Losses as I am; Keep up your Spirits, and that Noble fortitude which it please God to Give you." Willson later expressed great relief that Allen had taken the hard news so well.[27] He may have suspected that Willson's poor report of Tinker smudged an uglier truth: Willson may have been drunk during the catastrophe.

Despite the *Sally I*'s disaster, the partners decided to keep largely to the original plan. Champlin had navigated the *Sally II* safely to St. Croix in mid-February. This early arrival meant a profit could still be made. Willson quickly ordered the *Sally II*'s cargo unloaded and the horses and livestock stabled, and set the apprentice cooper to work on shore assembling the hogsheads. Three of Allen's horses sold quickly for £24 each; but four others had been injured, and it took five weeks to nurse them back to health.[28]

As Willson readied the ships in St. Croix, back in New London Allen wrote to warn him of a new danger haunting the waters of Long Island Sound. The acts of Parliament since 1764 had ushered in stronger and more widespread customs patrols, and captains could no longer be as nonchalant about their papers, nor onshore customs officials so forgiving. Allen warned Willson of the arrival of a new customs officer from Scotland, Duncan Stewart, along with a soon to be notorious naval ship. He advised Willson that "the New Waiter[,] Ga[u]ger etc. etc. is here on Duty and very Sharpe, also the Schooner *Gaspee* Cutter, billethead painted Red Black & Yellow, the crew of which Searches Vessels very Closely." Allen advised Willson to first stop at Fishers Island, just off the entrance to New London's harbor, to obtain a letter with further orders.[29]

But then Allen suddenly thought of a new plan. He recommended that both *Sally I* and *Sally II* "Gett a Clearance from Tortola . . . for Eight hhd Rum or 10, if it be Latin. Let it Read Eighty in English, for depend on it there will be now [no] Quarters wither by Sea or Land at that time, from the Present Appearances of Military Gents." By this Allen apparently meant a simple ruse to avoid completely losing ship and cargo. By bribing the officials at British Tortola to register eight to ten casks legally using Latin numbers ("VIII") but keeping the actual number ("Eighty in English") in the manifest, the master could claim that an ignorant official at Tortola did not know how to fill out the forms properly, shifting fault to him.[30] Depending on the mood or financial need of the new customs officials at New London, some or even all of the casks would still be liable to duty, but at the lower British rate. Obscuring the records this way at least avoided the outright confiscation of ship and cargo. This form of under- or misreporting cargoes was another tool in the smuggler's trade.

In March, Allen reminded Willson that customs patrols still prowled Long Island Sound: "The *Gaspee* cutter thay say is gone off to Boston[,] But another Devill will Come Doubtless." Back in St. Croix, Willson fretted over what to do once the cargoes were ready, writing Allen in late April, "I am at my wits end End to know How to manage ab^{t} Getting clear of those 2 wolves of Cutters as We have a Sad acc^{t} here of them."[31] But the British official in Tortola wrote the clearances without any fuss. Both ships were back in St. Croix by early April 1769, in time to load the first cargoes of sugar and rum.

Champlin again took command of the *Sally II* and sailed home first, arriving in mid-May. He dutifully obtained Allen's instructions at Fishers Island. These directed him to nearby Stonington, where nine men unloaded the sloop's cargo, including fifteen hogsheads of foreign sugar. According to the *Sally II*'s accounts, the landing men were paid three shillings each, received some rum, and enjoyed a hot meal as well. Allen then sold the sugar to six different customers and sent three hogsheads to his own stores to sell locally, netting £324/13 just for the sugar. Overall, the voyage cleared a profit of £147/7/6. Despite the death of the thirty-eight horses, the partners had made back much of their investment, inching closer to paying off all their debts. One can almost hear Willson exhaling in relief when he wrote Allen, "I never was better swetted in my Life then this Voyage," adding, "I hope to get soon Clear of them D—d Robers of the world."[32]

The adventures of the two *Sallys*, along with the ad hoc sending of cargo on a third ship, established the basic parameters of Allen's business model. Between December 1768 and November 1770, Allen and Willson collaborated in sending seven different vessels on twelve adventures, staggering departures every six to ten weeks. Of the twelve, eight were known to have been clandestine in some way; the others likely were as well.[33] As successful as they were, and like so many other mainland merchants, Allen and Willson were just getting started.

By early 1770, Thomas Allen and Elizabeth were able to resume the genteel life that had been eviscerated by personal loss, captured ships, and bankruptcy ten years earlier. They built a new wharf with a small store nearby on the shoreside land Elizabeth still owned and leased a nearby rambling house "on the Bank," close to the Custom House. Allen thought the property looked worn and dilapidated but pledged to his landlord to undertake repairs for the reduced rent of £60 per year. His landlord was none other than Customs Inspector Duncan Stewart himself, acting on behalf of his father-in-law, Boston merchant George Erving. Allen assured Stewart there would be no irreputable use of the building, for he planned to open something entirely new that Connecticut had never seen. "I purpose," he wrote, "to Keep a Genteel Coffee House for Gentlemen and boarders, which will bring custom for the Wharfe."[34]

Even as Allen negotiated the terms of the lease, new political gales had begun to swarm the settler seaboard. Focused on running Caribbean cargoes past customs to repay his remaining debts, Allen did not seem overly concerned with news from other colonies of settler anger over parliamentary insistence on dictating all colonial laws, eloquent "Letters from a Farmer" objecting to unjust taxation, or the billeting of British royal troops in settler ports. Then somber news arrived in New London. On the very day that Allen signed the lease for his new coffeehouse, March 16, 1770, the *Gazette* printed accounts of a "fatal manouevre" that ended with the shooting deaths of three on the streets of Boston. Some accounts even called it a massacre.[35]

8

The Rogue Merchants

IN THE LATE SPRING OF 1773, Eleazer Fitch, the sheriff of the quiet inland farming community of Windham, wrote Thomas Allen in a panic. The garrulous Fitch was typical of Allen's business cronies. In addition to his office as sheriff, he was also a tavern keeper, Harvard graduate, respected colonel in the Seven Years' War, rum distiller, descendant of one of Connecticut's most illustrious families, and a long-time investor in Caribbean shipping.[1]

Fitch had just received a letter that one of his ships, commanded by a Captain Whiting, was about to depart from French Saint-Domingue and Dutch Statia. Whiting had loaded the sloop with a cargo "that if detected they"—meaning His Majesty's Customs—"must infallibly Seize him." "I must desire you," Fitch continued, "to send a Boat Immediately to be on the lookout for him, for unless he is advised of the Danger, he is gone. . . . I know not who or what kind of a Beast or prey is in Search to devour him." His postscript was even more exasperated. "Damnation Seize the Robbers," he added, "why don't you continue to blow up the Scoundrels!"[2]

Fitch's frustrations with Customs, and the reference to the fiery red-and-black inferno that destroyed His Majesty's Customs schooner *Gaspée* near Providence, Rhode Island, the summer before, can be seen as strangely prophetic.[3] The "devouring beast" that Fitch feared was a new British naval vessel that had recently assumed its station patrolling Long Island Sound. Its name, *Sloop of War,* and its refitting as a fast schooner, commanded by a Captain Howe, clearly announced its purpose in the minds of Connecticut merchants.[4]

Fitch was representative of the kind of rogue strivers with whom Allen collaborated. His letter encapsulates several broad aspects of the settler trade world at this time: the reach of seaborne trade far into the countryside and the brisk and expanding trade with French merchants in Saint-Domingue. Most important, Fitch's letter suggests angry and increasingly violent encounters with customs officials. This last issue emerged as a proxy war over taxation and increasing settler control over their part of seaborne trade in the decade before the Battles of Lexington and Concord. Fitch's plea shows how the now shorebound Allen had engineered a new system, and even new personae, to aid his cronies while profiting himself. He accomplished this through his most singular contribution to the early Enlightened culture of his colony: the London Coffee House, the first in Connecticut.

The New London where Thomas Allen opened his coffeehouse in April 1770 no longer resembled the scraggly town he had first sailed into some twenty years before. The Seven Years' War had changed much, and the desperate postwar depression years even more. By 1775, New London's shipping clearances had tripled from their previous wartime high. Well over two hundred ships called at the port every year on the eve of rebellion. Livestock continued to be Connecticut's largest and most lucrative single export, with the colony sending at least two-thirds of all North American animals to the West Indies.[5]

Because New London had emerged as a major trade destination serving the Caribbean, it was less reliant on the financial woes back in Britain. For example, Connecticut merchants largely escaped the shock of the Anglo-Scottish financial crisis of 1772–73 that forced many British and some settler merchants into bankruptcy. Of greater importance, it also meant that New London merchants were more insulated from the crises of the mainland nonimportation movement. Many American histories emphasize the pervasive and unifying aspects of the Nonimportation protest movement in creating a "consumer public sphere" of protest. But in Allen's world of largely Caribbean trade, the boycott of imported English-manufactured goods barely interfered with the port's growing commerce.[6]

As New London's trade grew, so did its population. By 1774 a census ordered by the crown counted nearly 5,900 residents in the town proper and its immediate areas, more than twice the population of the pre-1756 town. It had become a sizable city of the era. The census number included an estimated African American population of about 650 or about 11 percent, both free and unfree. The expansion of seaborne traffic in turn invited improvements in marine infrastructure, including a new custom house (1760), a new lighthouse (1763), and the doubling of major wharves to more than fifteen. Not surprisingly, the number of taverns in New London town also nearly doubled, from fourteen to twenty-five, including two owned by women, although this was a relatively tame showing compared with the roaring docksides of many other settler ports. New businesses sprouted up and down King Street, including printer Tim Green's *Gazette*, launched in 1763, three large general stores, two of which were managed by recent British immigrants, and the renovated St. James Church dominating the parade square near the shore. The town even acquired a cartable fire pump, purchased by Allen's old carousing partner, Nathaniel Shaw, who conveniently stored it near his own house just off Banks Street.[7]

Allen and Elizabeth opened the doors of their new establishment on the north shore of the port near the Custom House. Wishing to paint his establishment with a fresh coat of respectability, Allen named his tavern the "London Coffee House," perhaps a tribute to his birthplace, or possibly to a famous Boston coffeehouse he and his father may have dined at. To attract an extended clientele, Allen did something even more unusual: he advertised his new establishment in newspapers from Boston to Philadelphia.[8]

FIGURE 8. "Figures in a Tavern or Coffee House," attributed to Joseph Highmore, ca. 1750. Male patrons, probably seated at "club," gather around a punchbowl in a small London coffeehouse. Newspapers and pipes are scattered on the table. One male patron accosts a female server on the left, while a fire on the right warms the room. (Courtesy Yale Center for British Art, B2001.2.86)

By 1760, coffee had emerged as a major transatlantic business, and coffeehouses as a crucial cultural phenomenon of sociability and political debate. Allen's establishment became the first true coffeehouse, as opposed to a tavern or inn that sold coffee, in Connecticut. His establishment "pitched the new language of gentility and respectability then sweeping the Atlantic World," functioning as a "a commercial venture . . . [that] satisfied the functions of mailroom, boardroom, desk space, and, of course, cafeteria."[9] In effect, coffeehouses such as Allen's were in the business of creating business.

Allen planned his London Coffee House as the focal point of a one-stop enterprise catering to passing sea captains and visiting maritime merchants. For a shilling per day, masters could tie up their brigs, schooners, or sloops at any one of Allen's four wharf berths.[10] Captains, sometimes with their mates or supercargoes, then trudged the short distance to the coffeehouse.

The spacious house featured two larger public rooms of polished oak and whitewashed walls for customers downstairs, each with its own small fireplace, along with a kitchen with a larger hearth opening onto a pantry. Hanging their tricorn hats on a peg, guests would sit down to sup and sip, usually from a communal set of bowls holding the hot meal of the day. Their mugs might be filled with coffee—Allen even roasted and ground his own beans. Like all coffeehouse proprietors, he also sold copious amounts of wine, ale, and alcohol, especially a variety of rum-based drinks.[11]

Most of Allen's patrons sat "at club." These were set times during a week when patrons, exclusively men, gathered in groups of usually five to eight (but as many as twenty), to dine, drink, socialize, and address pressing issues, usually in a separate alcove or room. Allen offered three types: a "dancing club," occasional "turtle clubs," inspired by the barbeque feasts in the Caribbean, and a special "fiddle club" to celebrate New Year's Day.[12]

Later, as dusk gave way to drowsy night, captains would trudge upstairs to one of four small rooms to sleep, or possibly sleep it off. The next morning the captain could rent horses from Allen's stable, galloping north or west to seek payment for old debts and contracts for new cargoes. Should the ship need any supplies—shovels or buckets, new rigging, a new tin night lantern, a brace of used pistols—Allen obligingly sold whatever could be needed on short order and decent condition in the chandlery shop.[13]

Ship captains and traveling merchants made up by far the largest proportion of guests. In 1772, for example, of Allen's thirty-two guests who enjoyed more than one meal or stayed overnight, at least twenty-three came from beyond New London—ten sea captains, six settler merchants, and seven French Caribbean *négociants,* or long-distance merchants. By catering to merchants and captains from all across eastern Connecticut, Allen's coffeehouse opened a hatchway between two worlds. He connected rural towns and hamlets raising horses to gruesome Caribbean plantations, which used the horses to power the mills that refined the raw sugarcane grown by enslaved African laborers. Ships then returned home with sugar and molasses to be distributed far inland to those same towns and hamlets. As Voltaire understood, the system functioned as a single, seamless chain of delightful delicacies and sweated misery.[14]

As innovative as Allen's London Coffee House was, its everyday operations hid deeper clandestine currents. Under Allen's proprietorship, the coffeehouse played a small but decisive role in forging a loose-knit settler "culture of contraband." It operated as the discreet nexus of like-minded Connecticut and foreign merchants who finessed suspicious cargoes past His Majesty's Customs.

The New London customs office was probably typical in most respects of those operating in the second-tier settler ports. Allen's landlord, the customs collector Duncan Stewart, had been part of the wave of new British officials that washed into settler ports after the war. Stewart took up his post in September 1763 and quickly became a respectable community leader, including appointment as warden at the St. James Church, where Allen and Elizabeth also heard services. Aside from three minor recorded seizures of clandestine goods, he kept the helm of the port's commerce on a sure course by interfering with it as little as possible. Dr. Thomas Moffatt, a Scots physician who had trained in Edinburgh and been forced out of Newport by mobs during the Stamp Act crisis, served under Stewart as the controller, or keeper of accounts and records. He also attended St. James. Allen clearly used his comfortable familiarity with the two to spin "charm and yarn" stories to help his close-knit Connecticut business contacts gain lawful entry for their shady cargoes; or, as his crony Willaim Coit wrote with winking eye, "Doo the needfull with an oppen Sincert Heart" at the customs office.[15]

Allen drew his business contacts in a great arc of the eastern half of Connecticut. Of the nearly eighty known Connecticut merchants who stayed at the inn or corresponded with Allen in the chaotic years before

1775, only thirteen were steady contacts, with most signing their letters as "friend." These cronies were clustered in three regions: Groton, across the Thames, the base for the Mumford family; Norwich and its outlying farming regions, which fanned out from Pomfret to Lebanon and Windham (where Eleazer Fitch resided); and the Connecticut River towns of Hartford, Wethersfield, and Middletown.[16]

Allen's contacts were seldom the most prominent or richest merchants. Rather, they belonged to a second tier of upstart, middling men striving to establish themselves. Several blended their trade investments with other ventures, such as running taverns, distilling rum, operating dry goods shops, or acting as agents for colonial lotteries. Two of them arranged marine insurance: Richard Alsop of Middletown, and Barnabas Deane of Wethersfield, the latter the brother of infamous schemer (and striver) Patriot Silas Deane. Several supported innovative navigation improvements to coax greater maritime trade, such as attempting to cut a channel through the sand bar at the mouth of the Connecticut River that blocked larger ships from sailing upriver.[17]

Judging from their correspondence, they were very similar in character and background to Allen. All were well educated, wrote with an elegant hand and consistent spelling, occasionally indulged in witty turns of phrase, and were well versed in numeracy. Fitch, Jabez Huntington, Comfort Sage, and the brothers Barnabas and Silas Deane all had college training and had read some of the classical Latin authors. Like Allen, at least six had sailed as sea captains, while all the others had close family members—brothers or sons—who sailed as ship masters. Sage, like Allen, also owned enslaved people at some point, though it is likely that some of Allen's other friends did as well. About half of Allen's correspondents became Freemasons, a fraternity always popular among settler merchants with commercial connections. These included Samuel Olcott, Joseph Webb, Comfort Sage, and Richard Alsop.[18]

There was one major difference between Allen and his colleagues. Unlike Allen, several had strong political aspirations. Many served in the Connecticut Colonial Assembly or joining the Governor's Council. William Coit also helped lead, along with future Patriot General Israel Putnam, a company of "military adventurers" of "disbanded and discarded" Connecticut soldiers, who successfully won a land grant in the Mississippi Valley from the king in 1772. Seven of Allen's friends later occupied prominent positions on local Patriot Committees of Inspection.[19] Allen's coffeehouse thus served as a kind of command center for these aspiring merchant princes, helping them clear both legal and clandestine cargoes. His guests formed a rogues' gallery of ambitious, well-traveled, locally prominent and cultured men who entered seaborne trade to improve their social standing and "interest." For them, as for Allen, improving their interest often meant by any means necessary.

A telling example of Allen's role in the landing of illicit cargo is provided by a strikingly complete account of the introduction of Madeira wine made by Allen's friend John Chenevard of Hartford in October 1772. The Portuguese island of Madeira, and the Atlantic islands more generally, had by the 1760s become a prime destination for settler captains, second to the Caribbean as a foreign trading partner. These islands sold wines that were highly-prized by the upper ranks of Mainland society. Chenevard, the son of a Protestant refugee from Switzerland, had been a captain in the Caribbean trade and at least once had also commanded a slave ship to West Africa. He later settled in Hartford after the Seven Years' War, eventually opening his own tavern and adjacent wharf in Hartford's small but busy riverside harbor.[20]

In October 1772, Chenevard hastily wrote Allen asking help guiding a first mate, Benjamin Bigelow, to enter the ship *Abigail* at New London customs. He explained that Bigleow "was Indorsed on the Register in Madeira, as Capt. Deming was Sick and not able to do the business, which you will Put in its true light at the Custom House." This would appear to be completely legal, even if the phrasing is rather odd. What followed was very unusual for entering a very small and commonplace cargo like Madeira wine. First, Chenevard urged Allen to "procure a Good gauger to come to the sloop." Since the customs office assigned weighmasters, and not the merchants, Chenevard counted on Allen's discretion to try to enlist a friendly official. Second, Chenevard expressed great concern about weighing and entering what could only have been a miniscule amount of an average sloop's capacity, barely 8 percent of the total. Chenevard then continued,

> If they [Customs] should insist on Sending one [a gauger], we Shall be Ready to receive *him* but the Quantity being so small as Twelve quarter casks,

> should think they might compute the duty very Easy—our Voyage turns out very Light, not one article being dispos[d] of when they left the island . . . ad to this that the merchants [in Madeira] informed us that the Wine was not to be got [inserted above: 'owing to the shortness of last years vintage'] . . . youll excuse . . . the freedom taken in giving you this trouble.[21]

Chenevard's words were in fact instructions to Allen on how to explain the nearly empty vessel to customs officer Stewart. Given the inexperienced new captain (due to illness of the original captain), the surprisingly tiny volume of return cargo carried (a result of the previous year's poor vintage), and Allen's reasonable tone explaining how such voyages could turn sour, Chenevard clearly hoped that a small duty on what amounted to a mere three hogsheads of wine might be imposed, and the bond on the ship still redeemed.

But Chenevard provided far more intriguing information on the reverse side of the letter. He listed five anchorages on either side of the Connecticut–Rhode Island boundary, with the names of five men, three of them known former ship captains and two of those with stores in the area. He also listed a series of numbers designated for each place, totaling forty. If the ship had in fact carried forty-three hogsheads of Madeira wine—forty hogsheads plus the twelve quarter casks, a likely load for a sloop—but landed forty of the hogsheads *before* the captain filed the ship's papers with customs, then Chenevard paid duties on just three hogsheads, saving him nearly £120 in New York currency in duties—mainly all profit. Chenevard cleared the bond, and received no trouble; in return, he assured Allen, "hope I may in some measure make retaliation," which in eighteenth-century phrasing meant recompense. The ruse proved so successful that Chenevard repeated the exercise a year later almost to the day.[22] This is but one example of how mainland smuggling actually operated.

Allen received similar requests for help entering ships at customs, along with some pledge of recompense, usually in the guise of a hogshead or three from the cargo. The myriad cases in which Allen performed "the needful" at the New London Custom House form a crucial yet overlooked dimension of settler clandestine trade in the decade before Lexington and Concord.[23] Remote landings, bribes, camouflaged cargoes—all were means of entering goods illegally. To these traditional ploys may be added the "charm and yarn" tactics of merchants like Allen to underreport or misrepresent the true value of cargoes. While illegal, it kept the settler economy humming and profitable. These smuggling operations by Allen and his peers reached their logical conclusion, upending the imperially sanctioned traditions of British Atlantic commerce. As one English polemicist angrily wrote, the "Fair Trader . . . must now sell his Goods dearer than the Smuggler and be stiled an Enemy to his Country for paying the Duty."[24]

Allen's command of French and his earlier experience sailing to the French Caribbean islands allowed him to develop friendly relations with a completely new set of contacts: merchants from the French colony of Saint-Domingue. Striking up friendships and developing contacts with any French or Catholic people still riled local Protestant animosities. Suspicions of Catholicism filled news opinion pieces in New England papers, animated anti–Catholic Pope's Day parades, and prompted settler outrage over the Quebec Act of 1774. The act was in large measure an act of toleration that guaranteed freedom of religion to French Catholics in the colony of Quebec.[25] But many xenophobic settlers still suspected popish conspiracies to destroy the rights of Englishmen.

How and why avowedly and virulently Protestant settlers eventually embraced aid from France, *the* major Catholic power since at least Louis XIV's time, is often answered as a matter of political and military pragmatism, perhaps coupled with an Enlightened "widening vision of legitimate religion . . . brought to the new nation." Others note that some select sons of settler elites, including the Catholic Carrol family of Maryland, studied in French-speaking cities before the war, learned from French tutors, or, more rarely, studied French in college. Still others confine their views to the visits of naturalists, celebrated officers who fought later in the Revolution, or high-profile refugees during the French Revolution.[26]

But French-speaking people had long held a crucial social and economic position in the settler mainland. French Protestants, or Huguenots, had escaped religious persecution in Louis XIV's France in the seventeenth century. They settled largely in seaport towns such as Boston, New York, and Charleston. During Allen's lifetime, nearly seven thousand Catholic French speakers had been forcibly settled throughout the settler seaboard during the Acadian Deportation of 1755–57. Their new settler neighbors perceived them as "malnourished and 'Full of Vermin.'" Yet they remained, adopting English in public while quietly rebuilding their francophone families.[27]

In the decade before the Revolution, several mainland merchants engineered mundane but very practical connections with their French and Catholic counterparts throughout the world. They had been trading for years with Catholic regions such as Madeira, Lisbon, and Cork, or supping and bartering with French, Spanish, and Irish Catholic ship masters and merchants throughout the plantation Caribbean. On the mainland, French people were seldom free of suspicion, but they were free to move, to sip wine or hot coffee, and plan business ventures with their English-speaking colleagues.[28] One of those who pioneered such connections was Thomas Allen.

At least fourteen French sea captains and merchants, most presumably from Saint-Domingue, stayed at Allen's coffeehouse from mid-1771 to early spring 1773. Allen always applied the title "Monsieur" in referring to them, as if proud to have such exotic guests, making them easy to spy in his inn accounts. The French were generally gracious, paid their bills fully and punctually (unlike some of Allen's other customers), lodged with Allen for two or three weeks, and—*bien sûr!*—drank a lot of wine. None appeared to have arrived in their own ships, and none were identifiable as planters or major merchants in any of the French islands. Their absence as *grands blancs* in the French islands suggests they were among the many *nouveaux émigrants* of resourceful but resource-poor French-born men who descended on the French Caribbean to carve out their own fortunes in the colonies, especially after 1763.[29]

Judging from Allen's accounts, the French merchants mixed easily with their New London counterparts. At one "turtle club" in October 1771, for example, the twenty guests included four French merchants, an "Old Frenchman," the powerful Shaw brothers Nathaniel and Thomas, regular local Allen business associates William Coit and Samuel Latimer, and at least five local ship captains. Nathaniel Shaw paid for two of the French guests' dinners. Shaw himself invested heavily in both French and Spanish Caribbean ventures and later employed a Spanish ship captain, Gabriel Sistare, apparently convincing him and his teenage son to settle permanently in New London.[30]

Allen may have liked his French contacts because they shared many of the same values. Schooled by necessity and opportunity in nearly twenty years of war, the French Creoles of Saint-Domingue increasingly stitched together their own sails of political and economic autonomy. Even before the Seven Years' War, one horrified metropolitan French noble observed that the white Saint-Domingue Creoles were "rich, republican, and ready to ally with the English at any moment."[31] The friendships forged over plates of steamed oysters and glasses of brandy in 1771 translated into profitable exchanges within the year. Perhaps remembering his visit in 1761, Allen switched many of his ship destinations to Le Cap. They visited the port right up to the abrupt cessation of shipping in the fall of 1775.

Allen directed his partner Captain Willson to sail the shorter and more efficient Le Cap–Philadelphia trade route. Willson despised anyone French, but even he had to admit that his local contacts in Le Cap upheld their promises. He landed his cargoes of illicit French molasses below Philadelphia on the silted muck of Reedy Island (in the colony of Delaware), working with the rising merchant family of John Biddle, whose son Clement would soon become a Patriot leader and army quartermaster.[32] In short, as the political situation on the mainland deteriorated, some of the more cosmopolitan ranks of settler society may have already altered their biased perceptions of the French. In the Seven Years' War the French were an intractable enemy; after years of cozy business relations, they had graduated to the role of a palatable, perhaps even desirable, ally in the war to come.

Within eight years, Thomas and Elizabeth had climbed out of bankruptcy and into the top ranks of society. Based on tax assessments, they were again comfortably lodged among the top 15 percent of New London's ratepayers.[33] Given their increased wealth and stability, the town awarded Allen more public community responsibility. He had been elected one of five inspectors of "cording of wood" in 1771—a mundane but essential post of public trust in winter-worn New England—advancing to the highly visible post of juryman for New London County Court just two years later. His zeal for tinkering and innovation earned him "the Liberty at his own expense to erect a Hay Engine . . . for weighing of Hay brought to market," and the right to charge a shilling per load. For a port that specialized in exporting livestock, the sheer number of animals turned pennies into pounds, a very lucrative side venture.[34]

Allen made other civic contributions. Under the guidance of the ministry of Mathew Graves, the vestry of St. James voted Allen a junior church warden in April 1770, working with tax collector Duncan Stewart. He then attained the post of moderator of the vestrymen by May 1775. Allen's other major civic contribution lay in helping expand New London's educational horizons. He served on the committee that founded a local school to instruct young boys and some girls in advanced arithmetic, the Latin classics, and elegant penmanship. Meeting at the Coffee House over the course of a year, Allen and the Committee drafted a charter for the new Union School and debated on the right candidate to be the first preceptor. They found the right mix in a young, recent graduate of Yale who impressed them with his dynamic spirit as much as with his talent for reading Cicero and Tacitus. His name: Nathan Hale, the future Patriot martyr.[35]

As early as December 1771, Allen felt socially and financially secure enough to launch what would become his single most innovative contribution to improving the public good: a weekly marine list. Marine lists were announcements of ship movements that appeared in local newspapers, usually inserted right below the official Custom House reports. Customs reports, however, listed only entries and departures according to officially stamped documents. Marine lists instead relied on the immediate news from captains and merchants reporting actual captains' names, departures, arrivals, destinations, cargoes, and sometimes news exchanged by ships hailing each other on the deep blue. The accuracy of information is the major reason why marine lists emerged as the key resource for arranging marine insurance. Allen's list at first served only New London. But as the port's traffic grew, and as Allen included more salty observations promoting maritime trade and decrying British patrols, his column was reprinted on a regular basis in other New England newspapers.[36] It ran without interruption until September 1775.

Allen's contribution to his family's wealth and public stature, and to New London, reached its height just as the first British Empire began to break apart from the constant battering from political storms and the crashing waves of parliamentary acts. On the early evening of December 16, 1773, a defiant mix of artisans and merchants, many dressed in grotesque "Indian" costumes, boarded three English East India ships tied up at Griffin's Wharf in South Boston and tossed legal shipments of tea into the harbor while a mob on the wharf cheered them on.[37]

Already alarmed by the shocking rise of smuggling violence throughout Great Britain itself, Lord North on March 31 easily pushed through a draconian act in Parliament to close the port of Boston, effective that June. For the first time since the medieval Hundred Years' War, the now preeminent nation of global commerce openly forbade the trade of its own people. For good measure, it quickly adopted three other acts, essentially smothering the Massachusetts colony in martial law until Boston's people repaid the English East India Company for the destroyed tea.[38] The Boston Port Bill set in motion events that would once again sink the prosperous life that Allen and Elizabeth had so painstakingly rebuilt over the preceding ten years.

9

The Inimical

THE CLOSING OF BOSTON'S port sent New England into a downward spiral of fear and suspicion at the same moment that many merchants in the region had, like Allen, increased their trade to new levels of prosperity with the non-British Caribbean. It is easy to see how the two could be linked in the minds of settler merchants and sea captains. Parliament, long engaged in fighting customs battles in the British Home islands in addition to the settler mainland, created the Port Bill to function in effect as an antismuggling act. This time it also supplied an effective set of naval patrols to exact a menacing compliance. Boston suddenly became "a city under siege, seemingly alone and facing a doubtful political future" within the empire.[1]

From late 1774, the British Atlantic no longer existed as an amorphous, entangled ocean of cooperation and clandestine noncompliance. Instead, the ocean became a contested space, a "battlesea" between settlers and the British Parliament and crown over political autonomy and economic independence. From this moment, Allen's and his family's story shows how mariners revised the use of the ocean as refuge, resource, and provider of security under the duress of suspicion, acts of violence, and war. While mainland communities swiftly divided into opposing camps of suspicion and vilification, the coast in particular became the dividing line between a largely Patriot-controlled countryside and a largely British- and Loyalist-controlled set of select ports and sea lanes.

In the summer of 1774, white settlers feverishly separated themselves into "Whigs" and "Tories" in response to the Boston Port Bill and the other retaliatory parliamentary acts. The more radical Whigs, or Patriots, were initially inspired from across the Atlantic by professional political pufferfish and "friend of America" John Wilkes. The Tories, also known at this time as Loyalists, included a wide range of settlers who supported a mix of traditional institutions and laws, even if grudgingly, and who engaged in a variety of different artisanal and maritime trades. Many were unified by their fear of the breakdown of law and order far more than most Patriots. Allen left no overt clue as to his own beliefs. However, as a devout Anglican and sly opponent of the king's customs, Allen paid little heed to acts of Parliament so long as they did not interfere with his own schemes. He might be considered a lukewarm Loyalist, proceeding with caution under shifting political winds, discreetly hoisting the king's flag until financial prudence dictated otherwise.[2]

In a world where accepted authority suddenly seemed uncertain, to threaten or be threatened created its own rationale for seeking security from one side or another. Violence increasingly replaced passionate debate between neighbors. In Connecticut, radical young and self-proclaimed Patriot men began to harass the outspoken upholders of law and those who criticized the use of violence by such groups as the reinvigorated Sons of Liberty. They heckled the services of prominent Anglican minister Dr. Samuel Peters and brutally beat or tortured four members of his church. After preaching against sedition directed toward the king in early September, another group of young men forcibly dragged Peters from St. Peter's Church in Hebron, just off the central cart road near Colchester, and threatened to mutilate him if he did not immediately disavow his sermon. He did so, then hastily departed for the relative safety of Boston, which was then under martial law. It may be this event that Joseph Webb noted in September when he wrote Allen that the local Sons of Liberty "have been Alarm'd but the affair now Subsides intirely—None Dead."[3]

The measured response by royally sanctioned Governor Jonathan Trumbull to the attacks became itself a cause to further sharpen division. Trumbull had called on the local justices of the peace to "quiet the Minds of the People" and "lead them to learn their Mistake, that while they contend for Liberty they do not destroy it, and by causing divisions to hurt their own designs." To be on the safe side, always the governor's strategy, he also separately urged the people of Connecticut to remain loyal to the king. Trumbull had not actually condemned the violence or ordered sheriffs to seek the perpetrators. This incensed pious Anglicans even more, while at the same time apparently encouraging young radical Patriot men to greater heights of violence. By late fall of 1774, formerly peaceful neighbors ostracized, withheld help, or even occasionally attacked each other in many Connecticut communities, such as Fitch's home in Windham.[4]

True, the lower ranks of Patriot-leaning settler society—"Plowmen and Leather Aprons"—nobly sought "elementary political rights and social justice" and were "fully capable of understanding political affairs" to challenge wealthy elites. It is also clear that many of these same fervent Patriots also held xenophobic views about foreigners, despised Catholics, advocated public shaming and torture for those who dared to hold ideas different from their own, firmly believed in keeping enslaved people shackled, and held a murderous rage for Indigenous people when not seeking their outright extermination.[5] The two sides of Patriotism are not so easily separated. The Patriot desire for political independence quickly translated into a loss of liberties for anyone not overtly joining the cause.

Allen, trying to sniff out which way the wind was blowing, had to be careful which scent to trust. By September 1774, town meetings in eastern Connecticut were supporting more stringent nonimportation measures, threatening to isolate the "mercenary Wretches, whose Avarice seek Gratification in the Distress and Ruin of their Country." At the same time, Patriots took the lead in forming new local committees to handle donations to gather and transport supplies to feed and warm Boston's people. New London's Aid Committee, formed somewhat later than many in January 1775, included the core Patriots and richest merchants of the town, such as Captain Guy Richards, Judge Richard Law, and the mercantile brothers Thomas and Nathaniel Shaw Jr.[6]

With shipping slowed to a trickle, the now suspiciously named London Coffee House had evidently lost customers. Allen and Elizabeth took the advice of their Patriot in-law, Thomas Mumford, to retire to the obscurity of the countryside. They moved to the outskirts of town and temporarily rented a farm as early as March 1775. They eventually leased a larger farmhouse with outbuildings, which they idyllically christened Mt. Pleasant, in the Great Neck parish, about three country miles southwest of the harbor.[7] Here they evidently hoped to quietly ride out the increasingly menacing storm of open rebellion.

As reflected in his Marine List, Allen tried at first to ignore the growing division, reporting only ship movements and the occasional patrols by the Royal Navy. At the same time, he caused a stir among local Patriots by lodging Philip Dumaresq, one of the major Boston merchants to publicly

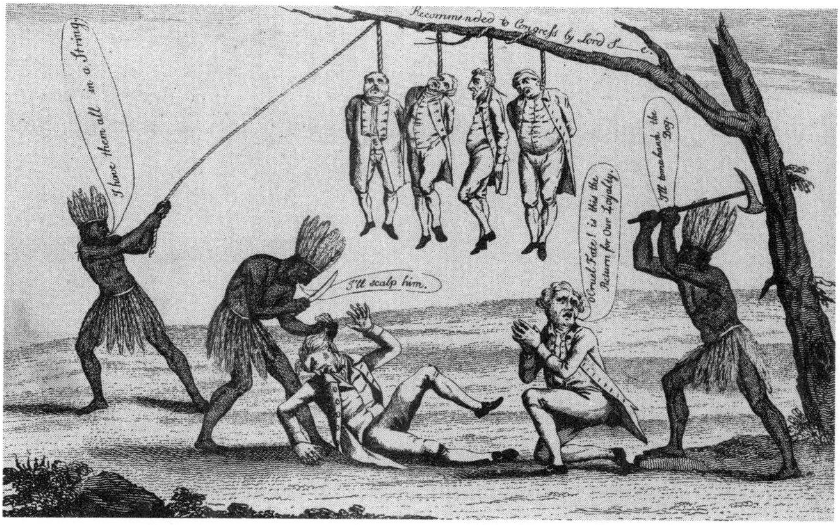

FIGURE 9. "The Savages Let Loose, or The Cruel Fate of the Loyalists," cartoon by William Humphrey, ca. 1780. British cartoon warning of the atrocities awaiting Loyalists if the British were to abandon the war in North America. American Patriots are depicted as gleefully vicious Native Americans, a common trope of the time. (Library of Congress, Prints and Photographs Division, LC-DIG-ppmsca-37324)

support Massachusetts Governor Thomas Hutchinson, when Dumaresq visited New London. As Green's *Gazette* reported, Dumaresq arrived "last evening and put up at Mr. Thomas Allen's, Innholder:—Thereupon we waited on said Mr. *Dumaresq* at 9 o'Clock A.M. and informed him that it would be disagreeable to the inhabitants . . . to continue long in said New London." The local Committee of Correspondence forced Dumaresq to issue a short apology, which he hoped would "reinstate me in the Favor of all true Friends of the Constitutions of both Countries."[8] This recanting was soon to set a pattern that would be enshrined in Patriot law.

Meanwhile, in Allen's preferred smuggling port of Philadelphia, white settlers convened the first pan-seaboard answer to Parliament, a Continental Congress. The attendees directed long-standing anger over commercial injustices, taxation, and fears over parliamentary legislative belligerence into articulating a broader framework for increasing political power, removing corrupt officials, and adopting an Enlightenment-infused concept of natural rights. As one historian phrased it, "Base economic metal was transformed into constitutional gold." In this way, "dispatch" for trade in 1760 had come to mean dispatching with parliamentary authority.[9]

At the same time, Allen was bowed under by the emerging problems from his Caribbean trade winds. A few blocks away from Carpenters' Hall in Philadelphia, where the First Continental Congress would later meet, Thomas Willson set quill to parchment to complain about the myriad problems he faced landing poor-quality cargoes from Saint-Domingue and the unreasonable charges for a shallop damaged when he landed the illicit hogsheads at Reedy Island on the Delaware River below the port. Closer to home, the return from Scotland of now ennobled customs officer Duncan Stewart forced Allen to wave one of his New London–bound ships to New Haven in order to land seventy hogsheads of illegal molasses. His agent there, Noble Hinman, botched the landing, forcing Allen to pay full duties and take a loss on the voyage. Through the winter of 1774–75, British patrols increased, poking into every cove and estuary. Referring to a new customs inspector at Hartford, Barnabas Deane sourly wrote Allen that he had been forced to pay "a new Devil that they have Bro^{t} in to Plunder the Trader."[10] By the spring of 1775, the placid marine-based prosperity enjoyed since 1768 had foundered on the rocks of political belligerence.

Meanwhile, Allen's family was haunted by death and divided by rancor at this time. Elizabeth's youngest son, Richard, Thomas's younger brother Sam, and Elizabeth's eldest son, John, had all died within eight years of each other in different parts of the West Indies. In Shrewsbury, patriarch Nathaniel Allen had managed to pass away peaceably at his large home on November 1, 1770. Although he had been investigated earlier by Boston's Non-Importation Committee, it had cleared him. His passing rated a gentle obituary for a beloved community stalwart "universally respected for his Integrity and Uprightness of his dealings, as well as for his Charity and Benevolence."[11] But after leaving Boston in 1757, Nathaniel Allen had greatly augmented his wealth, leaving an enviable total estate estimated at £9,000 in Massachusetts currency to his heirs. His last will locked the family into a festering inheritance dispute.

As was standard practice, Nathaniel Allen left one-third of his real estate—the widow's third, as it was commonly called—and all of his personal property to his wife, Dorcas Allen. However, the other two-thirds of the estate were divided into unusual shares. The eldest heir, Jolley, Thomas's older half-brother, would normally have been considered the main beneficiary. He had built a dry goods business since emigrating to Boston in the mid-1750s, specializing in toys. But the nonimportation movement undermined his shop, preventing him from selling teas, a profitable sideline. His father left him a mere five shillings. With finances already tottering due to the credit crisis, he was forced into bankruptcy in late 1772.[12]

In the case of William, the third eldest behind Thomas and the deceased Sam, such callousness would be irrelevant. As Lewis, the youngest brother, observed to Thomas in 1772, William had "never heard of the Death of Fath^r^, but supposes the Old Folks is dead [and] wants no favours." That left Thomas Allen as next in line. Like Jolley, he received a mere five shillings. An equal portion with his brothers beyond the widow's third would have helped Allen pay off most of his remaining debts. Of greater importance, it would undoubtedly be recognition by the father for his son's steadfast aid in the 1750s when he needed it most, and the many struggles to rebuild his fortunes that supporting his parents had cost Thomas Allen. When his mother died five years later, the five shillings were still waiting for him and Jolley at Shrewsbury, to be paid "when they respectively come for it."[13]

Instead, Nathaniel Allen left a full one-third of his real estate to each of the two youngest sons, the second youngest, Caleb, and the youngest, Lewis. In the case of Lewis, the money could be seen as a sound family investment. A goldsmith by trade and something of a gentleman farmer, Lewis proved to be cautious and devoted to the comfort of his elderly mother. She stayed in the rambling house on Shrewsbury Road with Lewis and his new bride, Mary Adams, likely the daughter of one of Nathaniel Allen's regular customers. But the second youngest son, Caleb, drifted in and out of jobs on both sea and land and wasted much of his share drinking heavily in taverns. He died at the age of just twenty-seven. Probably worse from Allen's perspective, Caleb still owed him £60 in Connecticut money, slightly more than a simple sailor's yearly wages.[14]

Given his two decades of suffering shame and bankruptcy on his father's behalf, Thomas Allen interpreted the token inheritance as more than a sharp slap in the face. It was a betrayal. His intense rage festered until it came pouring out in several later letters. In one rare surviving document written nearly ten years later, Allen directed his anger mainly at Lewis. "This Youth by his low artifices & Connivances," Allen wrote, "Perswades ye old Parents to make a will to Intirely Disinherit there old

Slaves Son Thomas . . . Exil'd from his Family 4 or 5 yr^s to Toil and Sweat . . . [and] Collect an Interest out of Noth^g."[15] The sense of betrayal of his elusive inheritance reset Thomas Allen's compass. He increasingly steered by his hurt and righteous outrage for the next fifteen years.

Allen did have one solace. His son with Elizabeth, Thomas Jr., had begun an apprenticeship with the growing New York chandlery and shipping firm of James and Alexander Stewart. The elder brother, James, had long been a personal friend of Allen's. Having already sailed the Caribbean, Tom Jr. lived with the Stewarts from the fall of 1772, to train in the clerking side of shipping. He had just turned seventeen. Two years later he impressed the Stewarts as a bright and very capable young man. "Your Good and Dutifull son Tom," the partners wrote his father, "has so farr merrited our good Oppinion and Esteem."[16]

Thomas Jr.'s early letters to his father suggest a remarkably self-possessed young man, one with a clear sense of propriety but who ultimately cared deeply for his family. For example, one letter began, "Sir, Your kind favor by Capt. Tinker I received with an order on Mr. Vandervoort," but ended with gifts of apples for the family and books for his mother, and ended with the sweet sign-off, "My Love to Mama and the Children," the latter referring to his young nephew and niece, Thomas Willson's children. Thomas Jr., however, expressed horror on learning that his father had actually *paid* the Stewarts for his room and board. He wrote in November 1774 that spending such money "goes Against my principle for I am sure you are not willing to throw away so much money Every year for nought[,] for it is but Little I have learnt here."[17] The time had come for Thomas Jr. to move on.

Back in Massachusetts, the sullen fall of 1774 turned into a deep winter of resentment and smoldering suspicion. Former neighbors moved from shouting insults to physically attacking each other. A courtroom conflict descended suddenly into insurrection in central Massachusetts. Just two days before the Battles of Lexington and Concord, Rhode Island Patriots from Bristol sent a posse after former Seven Years' War hero and now avowed Loyalist commander Thomas Gilbert in nearby Freetown, Massachusetts. Gilbert not only had the audacity to oppose Patriot ideals of liberty but, far more frightening to Bristol's men, had armed several formerly enslaved African American men, offering to help them preserve their own hard-won liberty. Something of an early abolitionist, his actions echoed the threats voiced by the royal governor of Virginia, Lord Dunmore, of enlisting enslaved African settlers to rebel against those rebelling.[18]

The tense winter in New England ended suddenly on April 19, 1775. British General Thomas Gage launched an ill-advised foray into the Boston countryside to seize suspected arms caches. After the shooting in the confused skirmishes in and around the farming communities of Lexington and Concord, the British retreated to fortify their shaky hold on Boston. By early May, the rivulets of young Patriot men had grown into a swollen river as they converged on the rain-swept roads to the port. The Second Continental Congress, already gathering in Philadelphia when news of the fighting arrived by breathless couriers, quickly embraced the disaffected Connecticut war hero Ethan Allen for commandeering cannon from the old fort of Ticonderoga. Shortly after, the Continental Congress gratefully accepted the offer from the former royal officer and current Virginia plantation master George Washington to organize and discipline the hodgepodge, eager groups of young Patriot men gathering before Boston.[19]

By mid-August, the British garrison under the command of General Gage of nearly five thousand men, a formidable number by eighteenth-century standards, was besieged by a vast, angry mob of nearly 14,000 young American men. Already the geographic fault lines of the emerging conflict had emerged. The British held Boston and controlled coastal waterways only by the power and mobility of the Royal Navy while arming Loyalists who moved gingerly thorough select parts of the countryside. By contrast, militias of Patriots moved openly and with little hindrance through much of the countryside but controlled only select parts of the coast.[20]

Patriots all along the seaboard quickly instigated hunts to expose and force into submission those living among them with suspect sympathies or ideals. In Connecticut, darker portrayals of Loyalists in news columns rapidly invaded the pages of Patriot-controlled newspapers in campaigns of vilification. Tim Green's *Gazette* particularly delighted in casting "Tories" as base, animalistic conspirators. In applauding the Continental Congress's call to police Loyalist activities, he printed a piece by "A Son of liberty," who demanded harsher measures, warning that "Tories are subtle and malicious beyond measure. . . . You will need . . . a Thousand Eyes to espy all their secret Machinations and lurking places. A Tory is a sort of Amphibious Beast, that can practice his Monkey Tricks either by Land or Water." Shortly after, the New Haven *Journal* reported that General

Gage had recruited the very dregs of society for Loyalist regiments, composed of "*some head* Tories, a few negroes, and some Scotch rebels and convicts."[21] The servile coalition and its inability to comprehend true liberty seemed to be the unifying element in that writer's mind.

Fear mixed with loathing dominated community relations. Patriot newspapers also began to move beyond the loose use of "Tory" to apply the legal term of "Inimical" or, more precisely, "persons inimical to the Liberties of this State." Originally used during a contentious meeting at Faneuil Hall in Boston on May 17, 1773, the term was increasingly applied to those who actively and vocally opposed Patriot initiatives and the work of local committees, or of the Congress itself. The first legal use of "inimical" in Connecticut appeared in a Norwich town ordinance in May, 1775; the Connecticut Assembly first used the term later in the year.[22]

In New London, the euphoria of the Lexington Spring dissipated through the summer of 1775. The port appears to have been more ideologically divided than its later nineteenth- and twentieth-century chroniclers might have cared to acknowledge. Earlier estimates placed the number of Loyalists in Connecticut at around 2,500, a seemingly miniscule 6.5 percent of the male heads of households. But the bare number obscures a more divided reality. The findings reflect only committed Loyalists who took a public stand or raised their rifles in defense of the king's law. Missing is a measure of their social influence on vulnerable nonvoting poorer folk, their families and neighbors, apprentices, and enslaved people. This number also would not account for the far larger number of lukewarm Loyalists who, like Allen, kept their eyes down and their mouths shut in the face of Patriot threats.[23] The surge in vilification, neighbors turning in neighbors, and forced silence erased any middle ground for "Moderate Men." While few American readers may have read Rousseau's *Social Contract*, Patriot communities had begun to install a version of his "General Will" as the political reality of Connecticut life.

Although the number of New London's Loyalists remains conjecture, the complex Patriot–Loyalist social landscape can be surmised from Green's *Gazette* in various ways. In one example, three ships of a British naval squadron cruising Long Island Sound entered New London harbor to buy supplies in August 1775. They encountered no problems, paid in full, and cast off without incident. Green, evidently touchy about the town's commitment to the Patriot cause, published a long disclaimer on how little the British captains actually bought. While the *Gazette* consistently emphasized the rapacious nature of the British patrols, especially at the smugglers' rendezvous of Fishers Island, it also admitted that naval captains paid for their supplies most of the time along coastal Connecticut. In his Marine Lists printed after the Battle of Lexington, Allen himself confined his negative reports to movements of customs vessels, such as noting at one point, "No Appearance of Men-of-War, Tenders, or Cruisers within the Limits of this Port—but keep a good Look-Out a-fore there!" But he never once questioned British authority or attacked Loyalists, nor did he overtly champion Patriot ideas.[24]

Allen published his last Marine List on September 15, 1775, reporting that only four ships were set to sail, with no papers stamped at Customs; no ships had entered. Throughout the summer, his correspondents had weighed in with rumors of port closings. But Governor Trumbull had already instituted an embargo on the crucial provisions trade in order to keep provisions handy to help Boston and feed people locally. Regardless of which side a merchant might support, both Patriot and king's governments had effectively suffocated long-distance legal trade by late summer. John Adams voiced the concern that many undoubtedly felt: "Shall We be able to maintain the War, wholly without Trade?"[25]

At the very same moment, New York threw itself into frenzied activity, fearing an imminent shutting up of the port. But young Thomas Jr. apparently paid no attention to the alarming news swirling around him. Having completed his apprenticeship, he eagerly awaited sailing to the "Streights," or Mediterranean Spain. His father took quill in hand to advise his son and grapple with his own sense of losing a maturing child, tinged perhaps with envy that the old can feel for the blossoming young. "You are now Launching out into a Wide & Large Field," his father wrote, "to enter a New Country of Language Religion, & Customs quite & Intire^{y} Foreign & new to any Scenes yet appear^{g} before you." Then, with sudden pride, Allen Sr. added, "I've the honor to be Father of an Aspire^{g} Genius."[26] The elder Thomas also loaded his son with several pouches of gold "Joes," silver pieces of eight, and a hundred pounds of fine yellowed beeswax to start his own trade venture.

Allen Sr. had not simply given his son the money but rather had advanced it based apparently on collateral for two enslaved people that his son officially had inherited, "Chloe and child Juno." These two, his father advised, should be deeded to his mother, should death befall Thomas Jr. on the voyage. With his affairs ordered and the enslaved people assigned and laboring for the family, Thomas Jr. waited to sail. But he barely sailed, for a fierce gale struck the ship shortly after embarking, forcing it back to New York.[27]

Young Thomas hoped to ship out again in a couple of months. But by then Parliament had formulated its answer to John Adams: it replaced the Boston Port Act with the more draconian Prohibitory Act in December 1775. Leaving no leeway for interpreting its intentions, Parliament ordered all settler ships to be regarded as enemy vessels, and therefore vulnerable to seizure by the Royal Navy.[28] It effectively closed all American ports. The rebellion had now entered the vast, heavy seas of an Atlantic war.

In Boston, General William Howe replaced an exhausted Gage as commander in October 1775. But he quickly confirmed his predecessor's assessment: Boston could not be held much longer. He determined to abandon exposed Boston, taking as many of the "King's Friends" as possible, and regroup to the north in the secure waters of the great Royal Navy base at Halifax. He planned the evacuation for March 1776. The evacuation order set in motion a frenzy of packing and low selling among the town's remaining loyal subjects. Among those were Thomas's older half-brother, Jolley Allen, and his extensive family.

Jolley's outspoken stand had so enraged local Patriots that even John Adams referred to him as "Black Jolly Allen."[29] Through the winter of 1776, Jolley and his wife, Elizabeth Warren, and their four daughters and three sons scrambled to sell his stock and shop, pack dozens of boxes and chests, and secure a vessel to sail them out of Boston along with the British squadron. Jolley finally secured passage on a ship on March 11. Dangerously overloaded with other families aside from Jolley's, the ship finally sailed from Boston harbor on the morning of March 28, 1776, trying to catch up with the rest of the British evacuation convoy. "Without either a Captain, a Mate . . . or even a Boy who had been a week at sea," Jolley recorded, the vessel floundered, when suddenly a late winter squall barreled into the brigantine.[30] It ran aground on the beach just north of Provincetown, Massachusetts.

When the survivors waded ashore, the local council, composed entirely of ardent Patriots and seasoned wreckers, lost no time looting the ship. They dispersed the other passengers but placed Jolley Allen and his family under arrest. As he waited to hear their sentence in the county court, Jolley's wife took ill and died, he and "her seven children round her Breathless Corps all in Tears," on April 22. Unsure how to proceed, the court granted Jolley and his eldest son, Jolley Jr., a pass to take his wife's corpse back to Boston, and, while there, to present his case to the Massachusetts General Court, then still sitting at nearby Watertown.[31] The remaining children stayed in Provincetown under the care of seventeen-year-old Eleanor, semistarved and essentially hostages.

Jolley and his son hurried to Boston, "insulted on the Road in a most barbarous manner all the way." He visited his old house, only to find his barber of fourteen years had broken the door down and taken possession. Once arrived at Watertown where the Patriot General Court still sat, Jolley and his son waited for two weeks, running low on food, rebuffed, and graphically threatened with torture and hanging. Only the sudden intervention of his half-brother Lewis Allen and his offer to pay for Jolley and his family moved the court to dismiss Jolley as a viable threat.[32]

Jolley and his son settled in with Lewis, Mary, and Lewis's aged mother, Dorcas, now near ninety, in Shrewsbury. They spent what would become Independence Day fearing for their lives. Every day, an increasingly ugly crowd gathered in front of Lewis Allen's porch to scream threats and hurl abuse at the Allen family. At night, after the Patriot crowd had sullenly drifted off, Jolley recorded that some "Three Friends of Government," or local Loyalists, would slip onto the grounds, bringing fresh produce and local rumors, including ideas of the crowd's next moves. From them, Jolley and Lewis learned that the mob's leaders planned to burn Lewis's house on the night of July 8. In Jolley's telling, he defeated their plan by boldly wading into the surprised crowd the next morning, demanding that two of their representatives take him to the local General Court representative, the respected Patriot leader Deacon Jonas Stone.[33]

Pushing Jolley forward as their prisoner, they reached Stone's farm near Northborough. He brokered a deal to keep Jolley under guard in his house, allowing tensions to dissipate, and return him under bond to his brother's house within a week. But when Jolley left a week later, a mob quickly gathered and followed him as he walked to Lewis's house. Upon reaching the house's front door, two Patriot men knocked Lewis down, and "forc'ing there way thro' it, braking every thing before them," cuffed Jolley and hustled him back to Stone's farm for judgment and hopefully a hanging. They found their representative quietly weeding his fields.[34]

In a scene that might be culled straight from Cicero, Jolley described in his memoir what happened next. Stone calmly heard the crowd's various shouted demands for Jolley to answer for his crime as a traitor. When the yelling had subsided, Stone said in a clear voice, "I have heard you plainly," then, professing himself "thoroughly Tired," invited the crowd to sit down right there in his fields with him, leaving Jolley standing. When all were seated, Stone continued. "I now understand your conversation right well. You want to send this Man who is standing up amongst us to Water Town, Thirtyone miles because . . . you had not the Satisfaction of Murdering him eight days back."[35]

Stone then slowly turned in a circle, looking straight into every pair of eyes fixed on him. He continued,

> Now you are all sitting calmly with me, I have this to say to you. You are the Transgressors, not only upon me, but this Man who you have made a Prisoner. . . . You are the people I ought to send to the General Court, for disobeying the General Court's orders, and not this man, who, by your own confession, has nothing to lay to his charge . . . you even say he has not brook [broken] his confinement. . . . You all say you are the True Friends to the United States and to the Thirteen Strip[e]s; I say now, you are the People that want to Pull Down the United States, and Teare the Thirteen Strip[e]s to Pieces. [36]

Stone offered his resignation as their representative right then and there.

Stunned, the mob broke into groups to discuss his words, while Jolley waited to see if he would be hanged or not. Eventually, the mob agreed not to harm Jolley if he renewed his oath and signed a bond to remain rooted to his brother's home, on pain of receiving five hundred lashes—a death sentence. Jolley signed, and the mob slowly broke up. By mid-September, with a court-issued pass, Jolley journeyed to rescue his remaining children from Cape Cod.[37] They had received no news of him or their now dead elder brother, confined as they were to living in filthy cellars, dressed in shredded cloth and living off scraps and occasional sympathetic meals.

By fall 1776, the angry crowds near Shrewsbury had reformed, looking for any sign of an impending escape on Jolley's part. Jolley took a perverse pleasure in their excited state by "playing at bopeep," vanishing from view for a week at a time, only to reappear when the crowd seemed on the verge of storming his brother's front door. Jolley waited and waited. Then came the stunning news of the Patriot victory at Princeton in mid-January 1777. With the ugly mood of the Patriot mobs more relaxed, Jolley sensed his moment had come. Since the crowds were now used to his disappearing act, he determined to disappear again, but this time to leave North America behind for good. His account is vague and hurried at this juncture. He noted only that "three friends of Government" from New London appeared February 7, 1777, and spirited him away from his brother's house just after midnight on February 8. The foursome rode on horseback southeast for eighty miles through the wintry, skeletal forests, reaching New London at two the following morning.[38]

What happened next remains even more a mystery. Thomas Allen, in a later official deposition, recorded merely that he had received word on the night of February 9 that Jolley had suddenly appeared near his farm, having found shelter with the family of Thomas Jr.'s fiancée, Amelia Taber.[39] The Tabers and Allens were close neighbors, and Pardon Taber, the family patriarch, had a reputation as a tough Seven Years' War veteran, a contentious and formidable man—and a strong critic of Patriot violence.

Jolley wished to speak to his half-brother one last time before departing. But Thomas refused, having "fallen out over business matters & etc." more than a decade before, as he later recounted. According to official court records, one of Taber's sons stated that, unaware of who Jolley really was, he had accepted a small wage to row him through driving sleet into the sound. Here on the choppy waves they encountered His Majesty's Royal Navy frigate *Amazon,* commanded by a Captain Jacobson. According to Jolley's account, Jacobson received him like a long-lost brother, turning over his own "apartment" on board the ship to Jolley while showering him with "every kindness." Jolley asked Jacobson to land him across the water on Long Island near Montauk. Jolley then walked about 120 miles across the icy ravines and shivering grasses stretching the length of the island to the safety of the British army then in control of New York City. General Howe himself welcomed Jolley to safety.[40]

Relieved of Jolley's drama, Thomas Allen turned to other brewing concerns. He had been forced to suspend all his shipping operations, so he shifted his energy to building stock for his farm and trudging into town to keep the coffeehouse open as best he could. His brother Lewis's precarious position in Patriot Shrewsbury would be untenable, and there remained the problem of how to care for the six children Jolley had left behind. They began to argue over the burden of Jolley's children.[41]

Meanwhile, Allen's trusted partner and son-in-law, Thomas Willson, had suddenly vanished, apparently escaping by rowboat to Loyalist Long Island. He had abandoned his wife Sarah and their two teenage children, and, perhaps of greater concern to Allen, still owed him more than £522. Willson's disappearance, along with the spreading war and anxious retreat to the farm, also exacted a toll on Elizabeth's health. Fourteen years Allen's senior when they married, she was now sixty-two, and her health was brittle. Surveying his shrunken world, Allen knew he had much to plan, and more to decide.[42]

Then, a few days later, at noon on February 17, there came an abrupt pounding on Allen's door. As he undoubtedly had many years before when hiding from public view as a bankrupt, he peeked covertly from behind the curtains. Outside, a squad of Patriot militia surrounded his house, their rifles raised.[43]

10

The Prisoner and the Privateer Port

UPON ALLEN'S OPENING THE door, the militiamen rushed in, seized hold of him, and demanded his name. When Allen confirmed his identity, their commander, Sam Worthington, declared, "You are one of the men we are in pursuit of." Allen pleaded extra time to finish his noonday meal; the soldiers, evidently hungry, readily agreed, and sat right down to eat with the family. As the detachment left for Allen's neighbors, the Taber family, two remaining young guards, whom Allen did not recognize, with long bayonets fixed to their rifles, walked Allen three miles to Fort Trumbull in the frosty air.[1]

Other prisoners trickled into the neighboring cells. Allen correctly guessed they were his son and several members of Taber's family. As the faint sun gave way to a low, remote moon, the young soldiers marched them through the darkened dirt streets to the same Union School that Thomas Allen had helped build and staff only three years before. There, General Sam Parsons sat behind Nathan Hale's old wooden desk, looking like a dour headmaster. He interviewed each prisoner separately, calling for Allen last. He had just two questions for him: Did Allen and Elizabeth visit Pardon Taber's on Sunday evening, the night of Jolley's escape? Yes, answered Allen. Parsons noted his response, then asked whether he saw Jolley Allen there? Allen gingerly replied only that while he was surprised to find Jolley there, he "had not seen him on the turf in eighteen years." Parsons immediately sent Allen out to join the other prisoners, instructing the guards to "run them though" with their bayonets if they dared even whisper to each other.[2]

Coughing and hacking, Allen was hustled back to his cell. The following morning he somehow cajoled one of the guards into bringing him syrupy ink and ragged paper to write a note of protest to the fort's commander,

Colonel Dyar Throop. "As an Englishman and a subject to this state," Allen demanded "the Right of being Heard (and for Redress)." Throop did not respond. Despairing, Allen wrote another note the next day. This time Throop sent a note of apology, apparently unaware that Allen was still locked in a cell. But Allen stayed put. He began to panic, realizing that he could swing from a gibbet for treason.[3]

After six numbing days, Allen finally received word. He would not be hanged—yet. Instead, General Parsons ordered him transported immediately to an inland market town, there to be exiled as an "Inimical to this State" for the duration of the war. Allen later learned from visitors that Parsons, something of a rogue West Indies merchant himself, thought Allen "rather too Cunning a Person to Live so near the Seaside."[4]

The trail of rich documents in the prewar era dries up beginning with Allen's incarceration in mid-February 1777. Did some disaster scatter or incinerate the documents? Or did later generations purge them? And if they did, what embarrassment or shame did they hope to hide from curious eyes?

Yet there is enough to make a sketch of his and New London's world in the desperate depths of war. Though sparse, the records touch on three crucial aspects that indicate the altered uses of the deep blue wrought by war. First, Allen's incarceration is indicative of a larger removal to the security of the interior countryside by Patriot politicians and entrepreneurs. In this way the war marked the beginning of a distinct shift away from the seas as the nexus of trade and ports as the homes of an entrepreneurial aristocracy to the growing fields of manufactured prosperity, powered by drudge labor in an expanding democracy. Second, privateering not only kept ports awash in desperately needed supplies but also, and more subtly, appeared to accelerate interstate maritime cooperation pioneered by merchants, in parallel with the political and military integration of institutions such as the Continental Congress or the Continental Army. Third, ports proved to be transit centers not only for goods and people but for information as well. The ebb and flow of reports and rumors was constant, from all quarters, and often confusing. Focusing on some of the news in the *Gazette,* and some of the letters Allen received in a typical month, provides insight into the harrowing daily life of a privateer port such as New London.

After the British occupied New York City and large swaths of Long Island in the late summer of 1776, Long Island Sound emerged as perhaps the most bitterly and continuously contested body of saltwater. By December 1776, the noose had tightened as a squadron of the Royal Navy made its berth at Newport. Cross-sound raids by "lousy Tories" quickly multiplied. At the same moment that the local Patriot militia arrested Allen, his old friend Nathaniel Shaw, now the Connecticut State naval agent, warned Congressman Robert Morris of New London's precarious position. "His Majestys Friggates have intirrely shut up this Harbour," he wrote, "its impossible to git out without falling into their hands."[5] The sea of possibilities, previously a space of hope, commerce, and reinvention, had become a watery prison for the Patriots.

Fear of British and Loyalist raids from Long Island prompted the early organization of a Connecticut coastal militia. It also prompted anxious state Committees of Safety to send suspect Inimicals like Thomas Allen inland. He was not alone. Loyalist prisoners of high station or the middling ranks were removed inland. William Franklin, son of Benjamin and the last royal governor of New Jersey, endured imprisonment in three Connecticut inland towns over two years. Many others were sentenced to the old copper mine at Simsbury, nearly twenty miles northwest of Hartford. Here, Patriots confined up to a hundred male Loyalist prisoners at a time at the bottom of a shaft nearly eighty feet underground in dripping caverns hewn from old, unstable mine shafts. Most labored twelve hours most days pounding iron into nails. Prisons were among the first institutions spearheading the many institutions and enterprises removed by the Patriots to the safety of Connecticut's interior.[6]

Parsons first sent Allen to the interior town of Lebanon. As the home of Governor Trumbull and his clan, Lebanon served as the unofficial "wartime" capital of the new state. He arrived under armed guard on March 3, taking a small room at the tavern of Elizabeth Alden, the widow of a former sea captain. Yet within a week, and for reasons unknown, the state ordered Allen transferred to the nearby market town of Windham, home of his old friend Eleazer Fitch. Fitch had also been confined by local Patriots and would be exiled shortly. As a well-known Inimical, and with his own case balancing on the edge of a noose, Allen would have studiously avoided his old friend. Since Allen had not yet faced sentencing for any crime—he had been condemned but not charged—he had the freedom to walk within the town limits, attend church services, down a glass at local taverns, and even entertain select visitors in his rooms.[7]

While Windham served as a genteel prison for Loyalists, it also quickly emerged as a new center for crafting and repairing rifles used by the Continental Army. Other inland Connecticut towns contributed to the war effort according to their location or immediate resources and traditions of production. As one historian has noted, "For some types of manufacture, unparalleled [wartime] demand afforded a fine opportunity . . . for high production and large profits." By early 1777, new shops and small mills had sprouted up in many country or riverside market towns. Norwich turned out socks; Farmington, rough woolen coats; Middletown, clunky shoes; East Hartford, paper; and inland Yantic forged iron ship's anchors. The large Salisbury foundry in the northwestern part of the new state switched production from iron bars before the war to smooth-bore cannons in the early months of fighting. It eventually forged the majority of American-made cannon. Connecticut's Assembly chose to build the frigate *Trumbull,* its contribution to a nascent Continental Navy, not in one of the established seaports but nearly twenty-five miles up the Connecticut River in the far more secure haven of Chatham (now part of East Hampton), near a foundry famed for crafting ships' iron fittings. Even a few of Allen's former business friends, on the run from the British, also decamped inland. Former hardware merchant Pieter Vandervoort, for example, fled British New York to bake hardtack bread in Hartford for marching soldiers and congressional navy ships.[8]

Of all the Connecticut towns, Hartford quickly emerged as the central inland Patriot stronghold of the new state. Situated nearly midway on the major road between Boston and the Patriot-controlled towns of the Hudson River Valley above New York, it channeled the increasing movement of men, supplies, and especially the livestock and foodstuffs that earned Connecticut renown as the "provisions state" for the war effort. Trumbull's commissary agents, for example, used Hartford as the staging area for the great Connecticut cattle drives that saved Washington's army from starvation at Valley Forge in February 1778. Three years later, some four thousand crack French troops under the Comte de Rochambeau left their base at Newport, safely and largely undetected by the British, by marching inland along the roads through and around Hartford, eventually to join Washington's Continental Army and ensure victory at Yorktown.[9]

Allen even glimpsed the shift of industry inland with his own eyes. On one of the few days when he felt stronger, he received permission from the Windham Committee to ride in a chaise under the eye of another old merchant friend, Captain Brewster of the old *Sally II* days, to visit a new gunpowder factory. Powder had remained in notoriously short supply in the first two years of the war. Connecticut's Assembly responded by authorizing and partly supporting six new gunpowder mills. Allen did not record its name, but it was very likely a local mill that began production in April 1776.[10] Allen might have seen the approval for the visit as an encouraging sign: surely officials would never allow an enemy of liberty to visit the place manufacturing Liberty's gunpowder!

But as the days of March trudged forward, Allen, still uneasy over possible execution and growing more ill by the week, tried to calm his mind. He read and wrote constantly. Instead of reading scripture, he sought solace in a popular translation of the stoic Seneca. He took notes, penning short quotes such as "the Foundation of True Joy is the Conscience" or "Philosophy only Makes the mind Invincible & places us out of the Reach of Fortune so that all her arrows fall short of us." True to his training, in other writing he visited and revisited the charges of betraying his country by recording them as if writing in an accounting journal. "As Mme Fame has spread her Acco^{ts} open (all *debts*) to the World against me," Allen summarized, "it's quite Necessary for me by fair Law and Evidence to Support my credits."[11] Allen's writings during his exile stand as the most eloquent melding of the practical mercantile and popular Enlightenment thinking that guided his life. In true Stoic tradition, he seemed resigned to his fate. Escape never entered his mind, or at least his diary.

Still, Allen grew weaker, more forlorn, more bitter. Then a sudden visit from his in-law Thomas Mumford near the end of March changed everything. Mumford, now a major figure in Trumbull's government, promised to do what he could to obtain Allen's freedom. He urged Allen to pen several copies of a certificate attesting to his good conduct that his supporters could sign. In words echoing Daniel Defoe's *Robinson Crusoe,* Allen began, "Had I been Half the Space of Time from you on a Desolate Island, either in the Character of an unfortunate Merch^{t} or Sojourner I'd found some means to have communicat^{d} my Ideas of the Clime[,] Revolution, etc. . . . But alas!," he continued, "on Reflection find myself doom^{d} to banishment from my Family, Friends & etc." [12]

Several of Allen's old cronies, many of them Patriots, quickly signed the certificates. The greatest prize undoubtedly was the certificate signed by General Sam Parsons himself, attesting to Allen's honorable conduct following the Battles of Lexington and Concord. Allen must have felt personally vindicated. At eight o'clock on the evening of April 3, a clerk from the local council arrived with news. "I was at Liberty to go and come as I please," Allen wrote as the very last sentence in his journal.[13] The next day he left Windham for good.

As Allen scrambled to revive the coffeehouse and make what trades he could to earn income, two major events turned the war in a completely new direction. First, and spectacularly, Patriot forces under General Horatio Gates, aided by General Benedict Arnold, routed the largest British invasion force ever launched in the Americas in two running battles near Saratoga, New York, in September and October 1777. When news reached the French court at Versailles, the minister of the French Navy, Charles Gravier, the Comte de Vergennes, immediately invited the small American delegation headed by Benjamin Franklin and Connecticut merchant Silas Deane to negotiate a treaty pledging France's considerable support.[14]

On the debit side of the ledger, British forces under General William Howe attacked and occupied the fledgling capital of Philadelphia at about the same time. The attack forced Congress to flee inland to the market town of York. Unable to halt the British advance, and badly mauled in two battles, General Washington's ragged forces grimly retreated to the west of the city, digging into the high terrain above deep ravines known as Valley Forge, there to face winter's vicious onslaught. The "glorious" early years of Minutemen, *Common Sense,* and the Declaration were over. After the icy midnight of Valley Forge, "the northern public grew weary of financial and bloody burdens of the struggle." Folks in ports adjusted to increasing poverty as best they could.[15] Only the sudden, heartening appearance of privateer prizes punctured the gloom. Nowhere was this more evident than in New London.

As Connecticut's main window on the Atlantic, New London had one distinct wartime advantage—it served as an ideal base for privateers. Connecticut had authorized letters of marque for the state as early as December 1775, but it took two directives by the Continental Congress, enacted the following March and April 1776, to establish the legal basis to launch Patriot privateering. These laws turned privateer crews and ships from mere "Villains of All Nations" into a legitimate force of war. A major product of the congressional acts was the creation of regional Admiralty courts to judge whether the captured ships, or prizes, were legitimate. These courts were arguably the first national institution to be created by Congress, predating even the Declaration, and functioned relatively smoothly throughout the early confederation period of government.[16]

In the same month that the Continental Congress issued privateer commissions, it also appointed Allen's old crony Nathaniel Shaw Jr. the Continental Navy's agent for prizes captured by naval ships. Connecticut followed by appointing Shaw agent for the state navy in July. Shaw had long been a committed Patriot, clandestinely smuggling gunpowder and ammunition from the French Caribbean islands for the Patriot cause before Lexington and Concord. He served briefly on the early "Secret Committee" of Congress, helping plan and supply the ships that raided the Bahamas for munitions in September 1776. His trusted younger brother Thomas served as the new state's deputy commissioner of prisoners, effectively meaning that he handled all accounts for prisoner care and flag-of-truce exchanges.[17] In short, no Patriot ship sailed in southern New England waters without the Shaw brothers hearing the hoisting of its sails or the dropping of its anchor.

In addition to their considerable naval duties, the Shaw brothers also managed their own successful fleet of New London–based privateers. In fact, they were instrumental in launching New London's bold entry into deep blue privateering with the early construction and first cruise of the *General Putnam* in the spring of 1778. The ship and its first venture are a striking example of how privateering could foster interstate mercantile integration even as Congress pioneered interstate political cooperation.

As is well known, building ships for the new Continental Navy proved to be a laborious, long process. By contrast, building and refitting privateer ships could be accomplished much faster because all parties involved understood they would likely be paid for work and supplies after the first voyage. Shaw tapped his far-flung contacts in eastern Connecticut and Rhode Island to procure the materials necessary to construct a sleek, twenty-gun privateer in a mere six months. Based on the strong recommendation of Philadelphia merchant and Continental Navy commander Nicholas Biddle, he hired Captain Thomas Allon of North Carolina—not Captain Thomas Allen of New London, as some historians have assumed—to oversee final construction and be its first commander. Captain

Allon left his wife and plantation in Hanover County (near Wilmington) to oversee construction of the *Putnam* in late October 1777. Six months later, in late April 1778, he tested the new ship on a trial sea run, announcing excitedly to Shaw that "she exceeded my sanguine expectations."[18]

Captain Allon first bolstered his crew of 150 sailors by recruiting thirty-one more hardy whaling mariners from Nantucket in Massachusetts. He then steered the *General Putnam* well out into the North Atlantic. Unlike most Patriot hunters, which sought British merchant vessels along the American seaboard or chased British sloops in the Caribbean Sea, Captain Allon was among the first to sail two-thirds of the way across the Atlantic into European waters. He quickly snatched six prizes, although a British privateer later recaptured one. An unexpected mishap forced the first prize, the *Princess Royale,* bound for Newfoundland, to seek haven at Portsmouth, New Hampshire. But the others landed where Shaw had instructed Allon to send them: Boston, the largest port and the one with the best prices. There, Shaw's agent, Josiah Waters, arranged the auctions, or vendues, of the goods for sale, as well as the purchasing of supplies and tools—such as munitions, quadrants, maps, and naval flags—useful for the Continental Navy or the Connecticut state navy.[19]

The role Captain Thomas Allen of New London played in the *General Putnam*'s first cruise was a minor one. But it also indicated the problems of investing in privateering ventures. Isaac Sears, one of the two major Stamp Act riot leaders in New York and later a prominent Boston privateer financier, had invested in the *General Putnam* and in other of Shaw's ventures. Investors of any social station could buy shares as small as one-128th of a single venture; Sears owned a full one-eighth of the *Putnam.* However, the vendue of the first prize in New Hampshire, combined with Nathaniel Shaw's transport of goods from the more lucrative Boston market overland to New London, spurred a complex legal case. Sears rightly complained that the rewards would have been higher had all the prizes been sold in Boston. But he eventually lost in court, and grudgingly offered the massive sum of £31,968, which he owed Shaw as his part for building the *General Putnam,* along with other ventures. Sears offered to pay only the equivalent in the dollars of Continental currency and loan certificates. An affronted Shaw "refused receiving the same as . . . it was no good Tendry," possibly hoping for either hard currency or bills of exchange in pounds sterling payable in a French port or on the Amsterdam market.[20]

Shaw needed a legal witness of good character to confirm that the Continental funds would not be acceptable. This could only be seen as a stoutly disingenuous position for a state naval agent. Nevertheless, he posed the question to Allen in front of witnesses: "What is the value of Continental Money at his time?" Understanding the performance desired, Allen responded, "Of very little, if any. Just sinking into Oblivion." It is unknown whether Allen owed Shaw a favor or expected payment; Shaw's own accounts show that he owed Allen money for unnamed reasons at this time. It is clear that an enraged Sears rejected the affidavit and sued Shaw. The case dragged on well after Shaw died, and well after the war had ended.[21]

That privateering could be a highly lucrative business is well known, nor would it be unusual for two merchants to clash over such a large sum of money. But this small episode of financial wrangling that Allen participated in reveals two little-known aspects of privateering. First, it demonstrates just how easily, if uncomfortably, public and private interests merged for the elites who commanded positions of Patriot public trust during the Revolution. Second, the fruits of privateering spread throughout small port communities in minor and often unexpected ways, well beyond the selling of captured goods at vendues.

Whatever shortcomings privateering posed—a drain on manpower, the redirection of resources away from naval ships, and greed-based profiteering—it helped integrate the old colonial seaboard into the new republic-to-be. The *General Putnam*'s construction and successful first voyage depended on the cooperation of many players along the eastern seaboard. A Pennsylvania merchant recommended a North Carolinian captain, who oversaw the construction of a ship in Connecticut. Its construction drew on the resources of both eastern Connecticut and a part of Rhode Island, and its crew hailed from those states and Massachusetts. The captured ships and cargoes were sold largely in New Hampshire and Massachusetts. If it took a community to send a ship to sea in peace, it could take half of a new nation to send a privateer to war on the deep blue.

By the time of the *General Putnam*'s second successful voyage in early spring 1779, New London's mariners had launched their largest assault yet on British shipping, capturing forty-six ships that year.[22] But the business of privateering and the many works on battles at sea and life onboard do not capture how Allen's family, and folk in ports generally, fared during the gaunt years of the Revolution. Since Allen's own records are relatively sparse, this part of the story must be bolstered with another source, newspapers. Unlike the countryside, where terror erupted when battles were close and dissipated to some degree when armies moved on, ports were awash in a constant influx of war information and activity. The incessant reports arguably created a different atmosphere for people in ports like New London. The port was inundated with war reports and rumors at all times, and this magnified and deepened both the hardships and the joys of life. A small taste of the information flows in New London can be had by examining a typical month, May 1779.[23]

In that month, Tim Green's *Gazette* carried the usual, sometimes dated smattering of overseas news: Parliament was expected to launch attacks on Boston and Charleston by the following spring; British spies reported a French conspiracy to attack the British naval base at Plymouth; anti-Catholic violence had erupted in Scotland; and a rumor circulated that France had sent a squadron of naval ships to the Caribbean, evidently hoping to lure the Royal Navy away from North America. Green also alerted readers to seaboard events, such as the recent British attack on Augusta (information received via French Martinique), which caused the greatest alarm. News closer to home or in bordering states yielded a potpourri of other items: a Loyalist attack on Bedford, Massachusetts; the announcement of a Connecticut census to ascertain the exact quantities of "grain, flour, and meal . . . to make Provision for an immediate Supply of Bread for the Army," to be made under oath. He even printed a column listing the degrees conferred at Yale College, which had somehow doggedly held classes during the war.[24] These reports did not necessarily affect all mariners and their families directly. But because of the port's reach into the Atlantic, all of them could, and usually did, have maritime repercussions.

In the spring of 1779, New London had just started to recover from a major pandemic that had ravaged the port that winter. Smallpox had infiltrated the eastern seaboard, the disease spread by returning privateers and sickly sailors who had suffered imprisonment by the British. It struck New London particularly hard. In explaining the problems of victualing and repairing naval ships, Nathaniel Shaw explained to the Marine Committee that "We are in such a wretched state in this town by reason of the Smallpox, Fever, and Famine . . . I cannot carry [on] my bussiness & am laying my own [privateer] Vessells as fast as they come in."[25] Shaw's letter is a sober reminder that the Four Horsemen took ship at least as much as they rode on land.

Despite or more likely because of the grim news, Green also sprinkled some wit into his paper. He had tucked into the opinion section what appeared to be a typical ad searching for a lost horse. It read:

LOST or STRAYED

> Thirteen Colonies, situated in America, with all their appendages thereto belonging
>
> A most valuable and well-established Commerce, worth at least two millions
>
> About sixteen thousand good, disciplined soldiers. . . . The Honesty of our Ministries . . .
>
> Whomever may be able to restore . . . the Above articles to the Proper Owners, may receive the PROMISE of being handsomely rewarded.

Green had lifted the language and style of the "ad" from the *London Packet,* a newspaper critical of Lord North's prosecution of the war.[26] Such small pieces not only won quick smiles from readers but reminded them that even across the sea and deep within the heart of empire, Patriots had supporters and potential allies.

Of course, no regional or local news was of greater interest to maritime folk than the fate of its mariners in the navy or on privateers. Triumph and tragedy shared the columns. Numerous American privateers in the West Indies and those operating off the coasts of Atlantic Europe, from the English Channel to the southern coasts of Portugal, all seem to have taken at least three prizes each; liberated American sailors seemed to arrive nearly every other day under flags of truce, sailing into Charleston and Philadelphia. But alongside these buoyant stories the *Gazette* also carried the sad news of Captain Edward Conkling, late commander of the swift-sailing *Eagle.* Conkling had been hailed in New London as an exceptionally "humane and worthy man, and brave commander." He had won wide local renown by scouring eastern Long Island Sound clean of dangerous British and Loyalist privateer predators earlier in 1779.[27]

In Conkling's and his crew's greatest triumph, they took the lead in capturing the hated Loyalist privateer *Ranger,* sailing it and its shackled crew into New London to loud cheers. But disaster stuck on its very next voyage. The *Eagle* captured a British ship, locking its large crew below decks. But at some unguarded moment, the British sailors "fell upon, and murdered the whole of the sloop's crew, except two boys; many of them were mangled in a most savage manner after they had surrendered." This and other stories became chilling memorials: for every dashing privateer captain, another shared the grim fate of Edward Conkling and his crew.[28]

Newspaper advertisements during this time also provide a poignant glimpse into the desperate movement of Loyalists at this stage of the war. For example, by 1779, farms or shops owned by escaped Loyalists, known as Refugees, began to be seized by the state. Notices of the auction of these estates increasingly populated the back pages of newspapers. One of these concerned the Windham lot of Allen's longtime business associate Charles Ward Apthorp, who, like Allen, had been "Judged Inimical to the independence and Liberties of these United states" and had had his property seized.[29]

Green also published news of the departure of two notable Loyalists who had been central to Allen's life. New London's longtime customs collector and Allen's nemesis, the nobleman Ducan Stewart, and his family had earlier left New London, in June 1777. The Committee of Safety not only allowed Stewart to take all his goods and furniture but also a "milch cow for the benefit of his children on their passage" back to London. He caused a minor stir by unloading a rather large number of goods to pay for his impending departure, having "purchased sundry articles of goods in New York for sundry persons" in New London, prompting the local committee to later disallow such clandestine transactions.[30] Stewart's generous treatment may be explained by the fact that it occurred earlier in the war, and perhaps as a mark of gratitude for supporting the prewar maritime commerce that built New London, by the committee turning an eyepatch to illicit cargoes.

By contrast, the beleaguered Reverend Matthew Graves, with whom Allen had served as a church warden, caused a small riot when he dared to offer blessings for the royal family in a sermon in November 1778. The committee ordered the church closed for the remainder of the war. Graves quietly left in August 1779, only to die shortly after in British New York.[31] These two departures, then, summarize the two extremities between which New London handled noncombatant Loyalists. Both Stewart and Graves were allowed to leave, the first lauded and with his wealth intact, the second shunned, shamed, and penniless.

Some people on the Patriot side of the ledger were also eager to leave New London. Green regularly printed ads for deserters and escaping enslaved men. One advertisement offered $10 for each arrest of five deserters from Colonel Johnson's Sixth Connecticut Battalion, while another offered $20 for each of nine sailors who had recently deserted the Connecticut naval ship *Oliver Cromwell.* The sailors may have been part of the nearly fifty men recently pressed into service against their will.[32]

Advertisements for escaped enslaved people mentioned young men. They often escaped individually, and rated the higher bounties of up to $100 each. Pomp, for example, was "23 years old, 5 feet 9 or 10 inches high, well built, very black, small round Head, flat nose, talks good English"; he had carried off from his former master "a Butternut colour'd Great Coat . . . with a yellow Button on his Hat, and a quantity of other clothes." None of the escaping enslaved had departed from New London or Norwich but had instead left from inland towns to seek passage out. No wonder so many newspaper advertisements for them carried the warning "All Masters of Vessels are hereby forbid harbouring or carrying off said Negro"![33] Such ads indicated the degree to which the Atlantic Ocean and its adjacent seas still presented the last, best hope for the self-interested, the scared, and the unfree.

News articles were not the only source of information circulating in ports. Ships also brought correspondence from other Patriot ports, or less often from overseas. The businesses that published newspapers often earned additional income by acting as post offices, as Benjamin Franklin's original print shop did. Although Thomas Allen and Elizabeth had closed the coffeehouse and retreated to their farm, they made weekly forays to shop, trade news and rumors, and pick up their mail. For Allen, business associates sent the few letters he appeared to have received at this time. Most demanded that Allen pay an outstanding bill, excused their inability to pay him, or sometimes both at the same time.[34]

But a few hinted at more clandestine arrangements. One small run of letters in May 1779 concerned business ventures Allen had arranged with Major John Bigelow, a state Assembly member and in-law of Continental Commissary Jeremiah Wadsworth. Earlier, Allen had planned and directed two separate droves of several hundred sheep, defying state embargoes to send them to his brother Lewis in Massachusetts. Now Allen had struck up a seemingly clandestine partnership with Bigelow. The details are murky, but they arranged at least one small cargo of finished goods and several bushels of corn to be carried by whaleboat to contacts in British-held Long Island. If accurate, such ventures would have added a few dollars to Allen's meager earnings, reflecting the increasing return to smuggling during the desperate stages of the war.[35]

Mail from the British home islands or any mainland port they held accompanied exchanged prisoners on truce ships. In New London, the Committee of Safety had its own clerks who opened such suspicious letters and scanned them for treasonous doings. If they contained nothing worth reporting, the clerks then clumsily resealed them with a quick smear of bright red wax. Allen intermittently received several such letters from Jolley, who by then had returned to England. The fact that Allen was never again arrested, and even held a post of public trust as the town's vendue master, meant that the committee found nothing treasonous to lay on Allen's shoulders. Even so, he and Lewis remained deeply worried about the content of Jolley's letters. They angrily pointed out to him more than once that "there's Many thousand things you write would as well be left out[;] no Letter's comes without being Inspected," and insisted he include only family news.[36]

The lag in correspondence caused by relying on truce ships and the requirements of censorship created moments of painful irony. As the war ground on, Thomas Allen retrieved two letters from the post office in mid-December 1779. Jolley had written them in July and they had arrived surprisingly swiftly. As always, one of the Committee of Safety's clerks had opened them, as indicated by the smudged red seal and a barely perceptible penciled *X* in the top right corner of the envelope. Jolley had sent one to Allen and a longer one to his beloved eldest daughter, nineteen-year-old Eleanor. Allen may have opened Eleanor's first, since she would never see it. It began:

> You must be sensible that it will give great delight to hear from my Dear Children in these times of public Distress. I understand you are about changeing your Situation. . . . I beg to know the person's name, and wether in Circumstance to maintain you. . . . At present, a dark cloud hangs over us, but I hope the time is not far off, when I shall have the pleasure of seeing all my Dear children around me as in former happy days.[37]

How could Thomas Allen tell his brother that young Eleanor had died of consumption—now called tuberculosis—on May 12 in that same spring of 1779? The letter is a sad memorial to the reality faced by port folk, that bitter irony, sudden death, and tears haunted the sea of possibilities perhaps even more than privateers.

11

"Unhappy New London"

By late 1779, the war had turned desperate for the Patriots. In the mid-Atlantic region, the Continental Army, commanded by General Washington, remained sequestered in camps and forts strung out in a ring around British New York, from northern New Jersey to western Connecticut. Washington's soldiers shivered and stamped their feet through another severe winter in 1780. Many of the foot soldiers not only lacked consistent supplies of food and warm clothing but watched as the value of their pay in Continental certificates evaporated. Some began drifting away when their enlistment terms expired; others took collective action and mutinied against their sometimes heavy-handed officers.[1]

Unbeknownst to Washington and his staff, General Benedict Arnold, the soon-to-be appointed commander of the strategic citadel of West Point on the Hudson River, had already begun to plot handing over the fort to British General Henry Clinton. Far to the south, the British foiled a combined Franco-American siege of Savannah. Worse for the Patriots, the British had developed a new strategy sure to end the war. Lord George Germain's plans for a new Southern Campaign called for liberating the wealthy plantation states first, and then rejoining the attack on the Middle Atlantic states and eventually New England. By May 1780, Charleston had fallen, and British forces moved inland with devastating efficiency.

Germain based his new strategy largely on one major assumption. He had conducted numerous interviews with American Loyalist refugees who had arrived in London. Already by early 1777, over three thousand largely genteel Loyalist refugees had sailed for the safety of England. Many assured Germain what he himself believed: that there lived many, many more Loyal subjects in America in the southern colonies, awaiting only bold action by their king to escape "Congressional tyranny."[2]

One of those whom Germain interviewed was none other than Jolley Allen.

Jolley Allen left American shores on February 19, 1777, with heavy bundles of fresh clothes and goods gifted by several British officers. Exactly one month and a day later, he stepped off a naval ship to board a carriage that took him into the heart of his native London. He passed small congregations of men in black tricorn hats, gray powdered wigs, and smart powder blue or forest green waistcoats shouting to be heard over the clacking of cartwheels. Beside them chatted smartly dressed women in freshly pressed petticoats, some faces painted white in the latest fashion.[3]

As in a Baroque painting, soot and mud encrusted the bottom of their skirts, but they draped their heads in angelic, pastel-colored bonnets of light blue, pale yellow, or faded scarlet. Darting around and sometimes between them were burly men carrying bags or bundles and broad-shouldered, grizzled, pipe-smoking women hawking broadsheets, crisp apples, or fortune cards, ringing their hand bells as if beating their customers. London had grown in the twenty years since Jolley had emigrated, but its streets felt as chaotic as ever.

Within the first two days of his arrival, Jolley experienced two horrifying shocks. The sister-in-law he had hoped to lodge with, Mrs. Lewington, had been locked up in the new insane asylum of Bedlam. She had been crying uncontrollably that her sister (Jolley's wife, Elizabeth) and her entire family had been "all Sacrifice[d] to the Barbarity of the Americans" and was convinced they had been eaten alive by cannibalistic Patriots. Jolley next visited his banker, only to find that the funds he had left had all been protested. He stepped back out onto the street with barely enough money to last him for a week. "I was almost as great a Stranger," he recalled, "as those who had never seen the place. . . . My friends and acquaintances was Dead and Gone Away." "Had I not gone to the New England Coffee House," he added, "where I saw many Boston and New England Gentleman, I don't know what would have become of me."[4]

Sympathetic compatriots urged him to seek out Sir William Pepperell, adopted grandson of the famous Louisbourg hero and the only American-born holder of a hereditary title. He offered Jolley a letter of introduction to secure a visit to Lord Germain. Several newspapers viewed Germain as a "proud, conceited, and supercilious man, fully convinced of his own importance." Yet his uncompromising handling of the early part of the American war had won praise from the king, grudging support in Parliament, and limited criticism in London newspapers—the last no mean feat.[5]

Jolley applied for an audience, and to his surprise, Germain's secretary arranged for a private audience the very next day. Lord Germain not only courteously welcomed Jolley but, taking him by the arm, "did me the honor to cause me to sit down by him." Germain then ordered his secretary to read selections of a manuscript Jolley had written, a "Memorial" of his hardships, listening intently without saying a word. When finished, Germain, evidently greatly moved, asked detailed questions, motioning to his secretary to keep notes. After hearing his story, Germain wrote out a note on the King's Treasury, guaranteeing Allen a stipend of £50 sterling every three months, the limit of funding for non-nobles. Jolley Allen left Germain's office spilling compliments on the carpet.[6]

Jolley Allen had landed in London at a propitious moment in the early spring of 1777. Even though the Massachusetts insurrection had already advanced from a rebellious breeze into a fully formed storm of war, from the vantage point of London the conflict still appeared relatively confined and winnable. Jolley Allen represented the second wave of humbler, largely New England folk who had suffered through the first year and a half of active Patriot attacks and humiliations. These mainland Refugees, as they were called, had initially received a rousing and sympathetic welcome. By the time Allen arrived, their numbers had multiplied fast as poorer, more desperate American Loyalist families were forced by Patriots from their homes in New England and the Middle Atlantic colonies.[7] They created a growing strain on British resources.

The imperial capital awed many of the Refugees. As New Englander Jonathan Sewall remarked, in London "everything is upon a scale so much above what I have ever seen, that my mind seems to be lost & confounded in infinity." They visited, often for the first time, the city's many famous monuments: St. Paul's Cathedral, the old Tower of London, the new hospitals at Chelsea or further afield at Greenwich, a new zoological garden, or the world of curious artifacts in new glass cases at the British Museum, which had opened its doors in 1759. In the afternoons they might view "tumbling" performances and magic shows, and in the evenings they could take their wives or mistresses in a chaise to catch a stage or opera performance at Drury Lane or Covent Garden.[8]

Above all, Refugees spent their time visiting other Refugees. They took tea with each other's families, attended Loyalist clubs at taverns or coffeehouses, or graced soirées at the homes or offices of noted London merchants who had extensive colonial dealings, such as Lane, Son, & Fraser. But many more undoubtedly confided their sorrows over their lost homes to alcohol. As Allen's younger brother William, who lived in London with Jolley when not sailing with the British Navy, astutely observed, "The Americans in London seem to take their pleasure & be contented with their little Salery[;] I hear none of them talking about returning home [for] London is a fine place if plenty Casks to sport with."[9] The Refugees had been reduced to living in an angry present colored by past betrayals by former friends and neighbors, with little of a future to comfort them.

Perhaps most galling of all to the Refugees, the London press increasingly praised Patriot General George Washington. Enlightenment newspapers and magazines imagined the American commander as "Fabius" Washington, after the Roman statesman who stopped the Phoenician Hannibal's massive invasion of the Roman Republic. The London *Chronicle* ran a portrait of the Patriot general in which British readers learned that "Washington . . . is strict, just, vigilant, and generous; an affectionate husband, a faithful friend, a father to the deserving soldier. . . . No man ever united in his own person a more perfect alliance of the virtues of a philosopher, with the talents of a general."[10] Along with the entry of France into the war, Washington's press popularity appeared to undermine support for British arms in Parliament and the English public generally by late 1779.

Wracked with grief over leaving his family, Jolley buried himself in the accumulation of material goods and dreamed of reuniting with his remaining six children. He wrote to his brothers Thomas and Lewis to learn whatever he could. He confided to Thomas that "I had more happiness in being with my family & children in America for one week than ever I had since [I] left them." He filled his few extant letters to his children with promises that he would unfailingly send "gold and silver" for them to afford the passage to England, plans always in the making but never made. In the meantime, he advised his children to keep "a tender Eye over your Brother & Sister & do everything in your power to help each other whilst you live in this troublesome World." With the death of his eldest son and then his daughter Eleanor, he shut himself in, wearing only black the few times he ventured from his paltry lodgings. He spent much of his time after late 1779 preparing his written "Sufferings" for publication, which he thought would "shew the depravity of Nature, and how cruel Mankind can be to their fellow Creature, when divested of Parental Affection and true Religion, which is the case of a great part of the Americans at this Time."[11] Despite the shopping, occasional visits, and work on his manuscript, life in London offered little to him. Shut in, he perhaps began to realize that he had merely replaced a physical exile with a prison of mental grief and isolation.

On the other side of the ocean, New London increased its privateering war. From the port's perspective, the Atlantic had become a massive, watery green chessboard. By the last days of August 1781, upward of thirty ships were anchored in the Thames, on par with the number of trading ships in the port just before war erupted six long years earlier. Even New London Captain Dudley Saltonstall, who had been disgraced by his ignominious defeat in the failed Penobscot Expedition in Maine (July–August 1779), briefly turned his fortunes about by capturing the *Hannah* in July 1781. It was one of the richest British prizes of the entire conflict. Its hold was crammed with Indian calicos and heavy European woolens, bags of silver, and crates of ammunition, valued at nearly £80,000.[12] Basking in the glow of their privateering success, the townsfolk in New London appeared to pay little heed to their inviting vulnerability.

But the British, stowed away in New York, watched the port very carefully. If the British ever attacked, it would be by sea. England had long carved out overseas territories by controlling them by sea routes, such as the coastal lowlands of the Irish Pale, originally carved out from farmland surrounding fifteenth-century Dublin. The British had developed a genius for mounting amphibious landings in what were known as "joint operations." Early in the conflict, one British military observer who advocated that the Patriots be "thoroughly punish'd and be made to smart" doubted "whether either can be done *by land,* without an endless and ruinous expence now and hereafter: whereas their destruction by sea is certain and easy."[13]

Despite some early setbacks in 1776, British forces had launched several successful amphibious attacks, seizing New York, Newport, Philadelphia, and Charleston, among other ports. Benedict Arnold, the former Patriot turned British general, in particular seemed to relish the challenge of such attacks. In January 1781 he sailed partway up the serpentine James River in Virginia and captured the wartime capital at Richmond, forcing Governor Thomas Jefferson and most of his legislature to flee further inland. Arnold's forces then pillaged the town and extorted a ransom of nearly £30,000 worth of tobacco from the region's Patriot planters. By comparison, Patriot and French forces had so far failed in the few similar operations they attempted.[14]

In New York, the commander of British forces in North America, General Henry Clinton, fretted over General Washington's moves by land. But he feared the French forces under General Rochambeau and the naval squadron anchored in recaptured Newport even more. Clinton watched the squadron closely, almost obsessively. "Could the Rhode Island squadron be fortunately destroyed," he wrote in early 1781, "I had no doubt but every hope and expectation of the enemy must be effectually frustrated." Washington also understood the value of sea operations, writing, "No land force can act decisively unless accompanied by a maritime superiority."[15] Coordinating with the French fleet was by no means easy or certain. Still, if the Continental Army could devise a plan to capture New York with the support of French naval ships, Clinton knew it would certainly mean a swift, inglorious British defeat.

In the midst of planning, Clinton received increasingly shrill dispatches over the summer of 1781 from Lord Charles Cornwallis. His beleaguered army in the Chesapeake region would need reinforcements or evacuation back to New York. Clinton therefore devised a two-pronged strategy. He firmly believed that the British must destroy both French naval and Patriot privateering ships, not just raid the ports. Burning the ships in both ports simultaneously would remove the threat to New York and also aid Cornwallis.[16] He targeted the French naval ships at Newport and the Patriot privateers of New London.

But on the eve of his force's departure, Clinton suddenly received word that the French ships had already vacated Newport, racing for the Virginia coast, probably to help block any British attempt to evacuate Cornwallis by sea. Giving up on Newport, Clinton ordered the Royal Navy to pursue the French. But he evidently decided to proceed as planned with the second objective against New London.[17] He had the perfect commander for the operation: a native son of the area, still fresh from his success at Richmond.

At his Great Neck farm, Allen and his family slept on the night of September 5, 1781. On the same night, General Benedict Arnold's fleet came to anchor in the soft waves off Gardiner's Bay, at the very eastern tail of Long Island. Some small boats from New London reported the ghostly outline of ships far off, but most assumed they were Loyalist vessels launching yet another sleepy, sheep-snatching foray.[18]

The next morning dawned fair and bright, with trees wrapped in the first crimson veils of early fall. The British landed in waves, crunching ashore on the gravel and organizing themselves on beaches on both sides of the Thames River. The New London detachment would burn the ships, wharves, and docks only, while the Groton detachment would capture Fort Griswold, with orders to unleash its cannon on any escaping ships in the harbor below, before razing the walls with the fort's own gunpowder. But Arnold had misjudged several parts of the plan. To begin with, the breezes were not as strong as he had remembered, and the tides were contrary. This meant that the last wave of soldiers assembled on the beach only by ten o'clock in the morning.[19] His surprise had utterly failed; Arnold had lost three crucial hours.

Once warned, New Londoners jumped into frenzied action. They tossed goods and children into carts while sailors jumped aboard any nearby ship to hastily push off for safety upriver. Militiamen vainly sought their officers. The *Gazette*'s publication suggested the depth of confusion. The masthead displayed publication as if it had appeared as usual Friday morning. In fact, it appeared the following Monday, with an apology on page 3 the only clue to the disruption: "We had prepared our paper thus far for publication," he explained, "when at about daybreak on Thursday morning last twenty-four sail of the enemy's shipping appeared to the westward."[20]

Passing Fort Trumbull, the same fort that had temporarily housed Thomas Allen in early 1777, the British marched quickly north, following the shoreline. As morning approached noon, they reached the northern end of the town at the Custom House. They wheeled around and, with burning torches in hand, touched flame to tar barrels, woodsheds, and rope coils. They moved systematically back south through the heart of the harbor front. One of the first buildings they ignited was Tom and Sarah Willson's old chandlery store. Ships tied up at wharves were set alight, burning like massive daylight bonfires mixing bright red flames and writhing black smoke. At some point a warehouse filled with gunpowder ignited, sending huge flames from the docks into town. People panicked. British soldiers and local "many evil-minded persons" plundered amid the scarlet flames and billowing smoke.[21] Alarmed that he had not received any signals from Fort Griswold, and now losing control of his own soldiers, an anxious Arnold ordered a return to the transports.

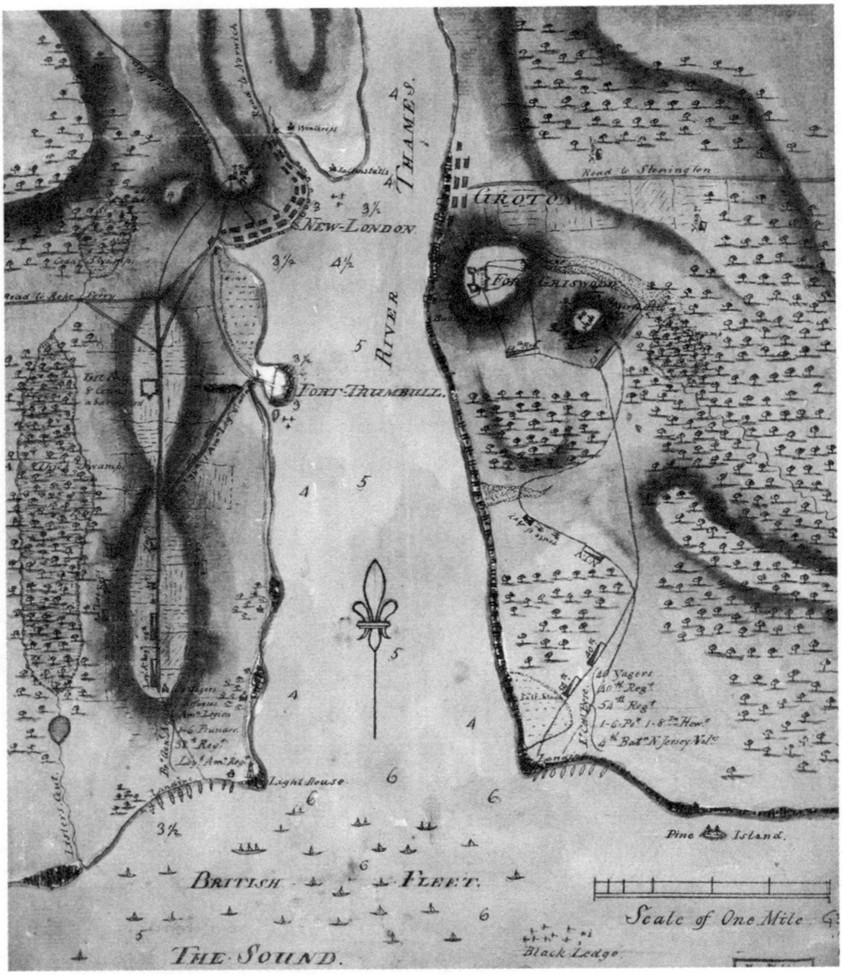

FIGURE 10. "A Sketch of New London & Groton with the attacks made on Forts Trumbull & Griswold by the British Troops under the command of Brig$^{r.}$ Gen$^{l.}$ Arnold, Sept. 6th 1781," map by Captain David Lyman, 1781. Contemporary map by an American Loyalist showing the troop regiments, beach landing, river depths in fathoms, and movement of Arnold's soldiers. During the war, Allen and his family lived near the Rope Ferry Road just off the map (*center left*), and he was briefly imprisoned in Fort Trumbull. Thomas Willson's chandlery shop was located in New London opposite and slightly south of the house marked "Saltonstalls." (Library of Congress, Geography and Map Division, LC Maps of North America, 1750–1789, 1027)

Meanwhile, the easy capture of Fort Griswold anticipated by Arnold had devolved into a bloodbath. The Patriot defenders were unexpectedly fierce and determined, fending off waves of British attacks until nearly the last Patriot soldier standing. According to Patriot accounts, when the British finally entered, they massacred any survivors. The British reports simply stated that they left the Patriots to bleed while spending much of the early afternoon burying sixty-one of their own dead on the hillside. As they moved back to their ships, the British and Loyalists made sure to set alight the small Groton waterfront and the home of Patriot politician Thomas Mumford.[22]

Despite his upbeat report, Arnold could not hide the truth from General Clinton and his staff that the New London raid had largely failed. In his account, carried in London's major magazines and newspapers, Clinton proclaimed the attack a mixed success. While applauding the brave efforts of the soldiers, he also stated, "It gives me concern that . . . the tow^{n} was unavoidably burnt." Officers on Clinton's staff mumbled behind Arnold's back that "the British could not afford any more such victories."[23] Benedict Arnold may have burned New London, but the attack scorched Arnold's career nearly as thoroughly. He never again received command, though not through lack of trying.

News of the fiery devastation of New London sped overland by horse through the colonies. A sense of overwhelming confusion over the pointless destruction weighed on these news stories, often printed a page after the stirring and exciting events of the allied American and French siege of Cornwallis in Virginia. Some in the Patriot press even called for retribution. The *Freeman's Journal* of Philadelphia, for example, urged Congress to "turn the current of vengeance upon the head of the destroyer; there are many wealthy towns on the British coasts which might be destroyed by a single privateer with the utmost facility." Writing to her husband John, Abigail Adams mixed outrage with sorrow, decrying the debasement of the empire's lofty ideals while identifying the attack as a war atrocity. "Haughty Britain," she wrote, "sheath your sword in pitty to yourselves. Let not an other village be added to the long list of your depredations. The Nations around you shudder at your crimes. Unhappy New London Named after your capital—may she close the devastation."[24]

In the aftermath of the burning, shock shrouded the town in grief and stillness. Teenage militia private Jonathan Rathbun vividly remembered entering the desolation the day after the attack. What had once been a lively port was now a smoldering cemetery, with blackened chimneys like burnt headstones. He recounted that

> though the city was destroyed, it was far from being deserted. Numerous companies of militia from the neighborhood were pouring into the town[,] the inhabitants . . . returning to gaze with anguish on the worthless remains of their property. Women were seen walking with consternation and despair. . . . Some were inquiring with the deepest distress for the mangled bodies of their friends, while others were seen following the carts which bore their murdered fathers, husbands or brothers to the grave. [25]

One *Gazette* account printed the names of the destroyed buildings, arranged like a list of the fallen in battle. British torches had gutted the growing commercial and artisanal center of New London. Public causalities included the town meeting hall, the courthouse, and St. James, Allen's church. Gone were at least twenty-two shops: several chandleries, a distillery, two slaughterhouses, three tanneries, three cooper's shops, several smithies, at least one shipyard (William Coit's), and James Tilley's rope works. About a third of the town had suffered severe damage, representing losses then estimated at a shocking £500,000 sterling. The town had also lost people. Aside from the death toll at Fort Griswold, nearly two hundred men had been taken prisoner. Nearly half never returned, and those who did were emaciated and ill from confinement in the festering British prison hulks anchored opposite New York in nearby Brooklyn.[26]

Despite the destruction, or more likely because of it, New London's privateers quickly resumed prowling the seas. Within a week of the raid, some charred stores partially reopened to sell captured goods. By mid-October, at least three prizes had been brought in, while another three privateers prepared to sail. By late November, the *Royal Gazette* in British New York was again complaining of the "New London reptiles . . . [who are] very mischievous in enterprises against the British trade." After the raid, New London's privateers captured twenty-nine more vessels by the end of the war.[27]

Nevertheless, New London recovered slowly. The anticipated trade between the new nation and France remained "chaotic and irrational" and stumbled through ups and downs with the non-British Caribbean colonies and the flotilla of Atlantic islands governed by Spain or Portugal. After the 1781 burning, New London began to fall behind the growing and far more secure interior cities such as Hartford, Norwich, and Litchfield. Following literally in the footsteps of marching Patriot and French soldiers, the interior roads and workshops of nascent industry, so hastily built or expanded during the Revolution, became the new postwar turnpikes and future factories of an enlarged internal market between the new states.[28]

The burning of New London also accelerated the return of an extensive seaborne contraband trade. In the early part of the war, cross-sound traffic between the rocky coves of Patriot Connecticut and the pebbly inlets of British-held Long Island appeared to be sporadic, involving relatively small amounts, perhaps because of intense public policing on both sides. But as congressional paper slid further in value, British specie and manufactured goods flowed across the sound from New York to Connecticut in exchange for basic provisions, livestock, and lumber, reminiscent of the previous clandestine New England–French Caribbean trade. As early as August 1780, Governor Jonathan Trumbull advocated for the free trade of goods by land with its neighboring state allies to snuff out seaborne contraband trade. By late 1782 the new state had reverted to old habits, having "clearly become the center of the traffic with British-occupied New York."[29]

From the burning of the port to the signing of the peace treaty, notices of libels for contraband in New London County outstripped those for privateer prizes by three to one, as reported in the Connecticut *Gazette*. In April 1782, for example, the Maritime County Court libeled four prize ships—a decent catch for the month—but separately gave notice for thirteen seizures of "illicit trade" goods or animals. Intriguingly, it appeared that the people involved in late wartime smuggling in Connecticut also changed, from formerly long-distance merchants like Allen to farmers, fishermen, and small artisans conducting shorter cross-sound exchanges from the fall of 1781. Wartime smuggling began to resemble the ubiquitous "cottage and cove" smuggling that developed across the English Channel in the late Middle Ages. Even officials such as General Sam Parsons and Governor Trumbull were implicated.[30] Such incidents show that the morality of smuggling had again reemerged as an explosive and emotionally charged issue, harking back to the fair trade debates of the late 1750s.

Although it might be expected that lukewarm Loyalists like Allen would immediately be singled out for a savage retribution, the records do not show this. If anything, the devastation of the coastal part of the state thrust everyone into the same miserable hold. Rebuilding cost money, and many quiet Loyalists still possessed useful capital, or access to it.[31] For those thinking ahead, Loyalists who had not openly aided British forces or shouldered British weapons could prove useful after the war.

For Allen, the devastation marked a slow reintegration into the community as a whole. He not only retained his post as the town vendue master but also earned extra income auctioning the cargoes of privateers. By December 1781, town records were naming Allen as one of two road surveyors, a critical post requiring tact and public trust. His crusty neighbor and in-law, Pardon Taber, reopened a country store in the Great Neck, possibly in partnership with Thomas Jr. But the war had exacted a toll on Elizabeth, now sixty-seven and an elderly grandmother. Her health had been declining for some years, and by the time Arnold gutted New London, she had contracted what Allen called "the palsy." She was no longer capable of reading. In the bleak winter that followed, she began a noticeable decline.[32]

Allen shrewdly looked toward the future of his son. In February 1782, Allen Sr. officially gifted all seven parcels of land purchased in the hectic winter and spring of 1778–79 to his son Thomas and his growing family. Allen probably made the transfers as a means of guarding the land from any state seizures. Connecticut, following the lead of Massachusetts, had officially forfeited the land of convicted Inimicals in May 1778, but then moved slowly, establishing probate only in October 1780 and actually auctioning lands only from July 1781. Allen may have felt too vulnerable to keep the land in his name. He may also have decided it was time to start the professed retirement he had once written Jolley about.[33]

In the meantime, Thomas Allen kept up a low-level war of charge and countercharge with his brother Lewis over the upkeep of Jolley's children. During the tough years after 1780, Lewis lodged escaping Loyalists, which greatly alarmed Allen over the children's safety. At one point, Lewis harbored "13 lads of Crowne" in one week, all heading from Massachusetts to reach the safety of the British-held positions in New York. One of them reported news from a man recently returned from London who had met with Jolley. Jolley, the man said, had fretted over whether any of his daughters had become a "Common girl" in Boston—a euphemism for prostitute—prompting Lewis to observe, "Thus much for his Great Doings for his Child^{n}." Lewis's attitude incensed Allen even further.[34]

Then Lewis died suddenly. In early November 1782, Allen received a letter from the Reverend Thomas Waight, a longtime family friend, from Leicester. Lewis and his wife, Mary, had escaped the belligerence of Patriot Shrewsbury for the more discreet nearby town of Leicester. Waight informed Allen that his brother Lewis had died, at the young age of thirty-four. His death had left his wife and Jolley's remaining two children in shock. Venturing into the study, the reverend found still worse news. On Lewis's desk, among his account books, Waight discovered a letter announcing the death of Jolley Allen the previous May 31.[35]

Thomas Allen later learned that Jolley's belongings fetched barely £51 sterling at a poorhouse auction. Lewis had been heavily indebted; like Allen, he had anticipated Jolley reimbursing him for the nearly £700 in Massachusetts currency Jolley owed for his children's care. It was clear that Jolley's death meant that Allen would never see a penny of the money he had hoped for. He realized that the only chance of recapturing at least some of his "lost" inheritance lay in taking charge of settling Lewis's estate. This meant convincing his brother's widow, Mary, to cede at least some of her rights to him.[36]

There was much for Allen to gain. Whatever his shortcomings in making seaborne deals, his father, Nathaniel Allen, had left Lewis an impressive legacy in land. The appraisal showed that the country seat of Mt. Pleasant held everything an aspiring New England family might covet. All told, widow Mary Allen stood between Thomas Allen and the whale's share of at least £1,786 in goods, furnishings, and livestock alone, along with an undetermined amount for the house and land.[37]

Allen had never dealt much with Mary. He addressed her stiffly as "Sister," and certainly never used the familiar or affectionate name Polly (or Polley). He clearly saw her as a conniving accomplice to his younger brother. Allen contacted a lawyer, Elijah Dix, to be his eyes and ears at the estate in Leicester. Dix reported back that Mary Allen had other ideas about handling the estate, choosing to use her in-law uncle, Nathan Patch, as her "advisor and Concile," and balked at having an appraisal of the assets. As Allen well knew, every day delaying the appraisal meant one more day to hide valuable silverware, clothing, or furnishings, or time to alter Lewis's will surreptitiously. Allen urged Dix to threaten legal action to force her compliance. But in the midst of the proceedings, Mary fell ill. Allen, perhaps realizing he must act quickly, left his ailing Elizabeth in the care of their son, determined to confront Mary and convince her of his right, or take what he could from her by court action.[38]

Allen finally journeyed to Leicester on the last day of May 1783, ready to duel with Mary. They had at least agreed by letter that upon his arrival, she would journey to court sessions at Worcester while he stayed at Leicester to gauge his brother's estate. But for some reason she tarried at the house for a couple of days after Allen arrived. When she finally left, Allen stayed on, examining the books. When Mary did not immediately return from county court, Allen prepared to leave. He had his own pressing court sessions in New London. Before departing, he left her this note:

> My Dearst Polley,
>
> This with the most tender feelings of affection toward you and witho^{t} further Display (than Silence) must realy confirm to you my Great Disappointment in not meeting you here. . . . I'm greatly mortifyd most Certainly as have many matters to unBosom to you wh^{h} I trust wod be agreeable & of mutual advantage to us, . . . I have . . . for you two pieces Nankeen to make a Riding Habit, which is all ye top Fashion with us.

He added as a postscript, "I have had the pleas^{r} to enjoy your Sweet Bed one night, but no body now to Speak to (yet Patience I ever had—& may it continue)."[39]

Their own negotiations had taken a completely unexpected and decidedly amorous turn. Allen rode back to New London, to his court sessions, and to his dying Elizabeth, his mind now preoccupied with a new sea of possibilities.

12

The Born-Again Yankee

ON THE FROSTY, CLEAR morning of January 14, 1785, Thomas Allen stepped back onto the frozen ruts of the newly named State Street in New London to survey a freshly painted sign hanging over the door to his house. His sign may have sported a picture, perhaps a simple, rustic view of a colonial harbor, with green lettering—Allen seemed to like the color. It proclaimed "The City Coffee House" in large letters, and in smaller, curlicue lettering underneath, "Thomas Allen, Prop." No sooner had he stepped out to take in his new triumph than two men greeted him. He waved them in. Thomas Allen was back in business.[1]

Only two years before, the new United States and the now defunct First British Empire had wrangled over the future of territory and power in eastern North America. The Americans deftly demonstrated their own savvy grasp of diplomacy by jettisoning their French allies from negotiations and congratulating themselves on winning a surprisingly generous formal peace, signed in September 1783.[2] Like his newly independent country, Allen embraced peace, eager to start anew.

With the "Unnatural Contest" now over and "so Happy as to see the Independen^{ce} of his Country established," Allen had applied to the Common Council of the newly created City of New London to reopen his old coffeehouse cum tavern in October 1784. Allen appeared to believe, as did many other new Americans, that the time for sacrifice had ended. Now came the time for rebuilding personal fortunes and, in so doing, those of a republican future. "You may have the firmest relyance," he assured local officials, "on my strict Observan^{ce} of the Laws and Customs Prescrib'd . . . to serve Gentl^{n} in a reasonable way."[3] The war years had transformed Allen into a thoroughgoing champion of the republic, a rechristened Yankee.

Or so it would seem.

In the remaining decade of Allen's life, the role and meaning of his Atlantic World shifted once again as New London and the coastal mainland rebuilt. Even as Congress launched the young republic on a new sea of possibilities, many dangers lurked beneath the sparkling waves. Prewar debts in ports and on plantations, stemming largely from overseas trade, became enmeshed with unresolved wartime disputes over privateer prizes. Postwar British and French maritime trade regimes complicated American commerce. And there remained the divisive problem of the Loyalists. Some returned from overseas to the new republic, some used the sea to escape it, and still others saw new opportunities provided by the shift in the currents of trade. All these themes loomed large in Allen's postwar life, as they did for most of his generation of new Americans.

With the arrival of his own winter years, Allen surveyed the potential. He and his new wife Polly, his brother Lewis's widow, had married in Leicester in the summer of 1784, less than a year after Elizabeth's death. Judging by the generous blessings and compliments to Mary in letters from friends and business associates, especially for her domestic prowess in crafting suppers for the coffeehouse, Allen appears to have been rejuvenated and happy. The new couple were buoyed by their gaining full title to Lewis's home, for the State of Massachusetts did not seize it. It may well be that the money from its sale helped Allen relaunch his coffeehouse, and even expand it a year later.[4] He advertised the opening in select port newspapers from Boston to Baltimore. His first ad emphasized its utility for all "genteel customers . . . By Land or Sea," and boldly proclaimed:

> *DRINK* for the *thirsty*
> *FOOD* for the *hungry*
> *LODGING* for the *weary*
> *Good* stabling for *horses*[5]

The future was also looking brighter for Jolley's three surviving children. While Allen remained estranged from his niece Sarah (Sally), Mary Allen corresponded with her. Sally later moved with her husband, Thomas Waight, to the mid-Hudson River Valley at Kinderhook, south of the new state capital of Albany. She wrote alliteratively, "I am in helth At prassont and I hop . . . You in the same," urging Mary to convince her uncle to visit. Her husband, she wrote, "was a Goin to the hiho [Ohio] but . . . we hav heard th^t it is vary dagrens [dangerous] tharfore I think th^t we warnt go."[6]

Allen had groomed his brother's two surviving sons, Jolley Jr. and Nathaniel, for the sea. Young Jolley stayed employed in coastal shipping. But Nathaniel appeared to be temperamentally unsuited to the calling. "I am discouraged of ever making Nat a sailor," wrote the Providence firm of Berry & Sage, one of Allen's minor suppliers, in 1787. "His indefren^{ce} and inattention has caused Mr. Brown to refuse him wages," the writer continued, referring to magnate John Brown, senior partner of Brown and Francis. Shaking their heads in dismay with their words, they added that Nathaniel "has no gratitude . . . and wishes to slouch himself about the Market with a Low class of people." Their assessment proved premature, for serving on the deep blue would transform him. Just three years later, Nathaniel Allen shipped out as first mate on the brig *Warren,* launched by Brown and Francis as one of the first wave of American voyages to "Calcutter" in India.[7] Peace on the sea offered the first young man security and the second the excitement and the opportunity for a second chance to find his sea legs.

The end of the war years also reintroduced a familiar struggle over debt, one that dominated the rest of Allen's life. The vigorous printing of congressional money, whatever its wartime uses, had lit a bonfire under inflation, furthering distress especially among poor seaport laboring families and small inland farmers. Both groups included many former Patriot sailors and soldiers who had sold their congressional promises of pay for whatever port merchants or country store owners might care to give them. To survive the lean years, lawsuits to recover old debts erupted in the immediate aftermath of the Yorktown victory. In such a hothouse of legal action, many naturally connected freedom from debt with political freedom. An old crony of Allen's, for example, excused bringing a lawsuit against him by pleading "so that as the States were freed from England, so I May be freed from Execution," that is, his own debt suits in county court. Getting and guarding funds, or convertible resources of any kind, became an intense concern of nearly everyone.[8]

Allen was no different. His new financial troubles began with a series of lawsuits with his former partner, confidant, and son-in-law, Captain Thomas Willson. When Willson sailed away to Loyalist Long Island, he seemed to have taken with him any remaining good will. On the eve of the Battles of Lexington and Concord in 1775, Willson already owed Allen £275 Connecticut currency, an amount that could easily tide Allen over for three years. After his release from incarceration, Allen found that the amount had grown to the small fortune of £522. Still, he let the suit with Willson lie dormant for the next several years.[9] But as newspapers reported the peace talks, Thomas Willson reappeared. His arrival immediately inflamed the smoldering animosity.

At stake was the contentious issue of exactly who owned the increasingly valuable harborfront land that Elizabeth's first husband, John Shackmaple, had left her. When she died, Allen and Willson tangled for the claim. Once again, General Sam Parsons played a key role in Allen's fortunes. Parsons headed the New London County Court, which reviewed ownership of the land and, after several postponements, released its decision in March 1783. The court under Parsons ruled that upon Elizabeth's death, all the valuable land should descend to the one inheritor "of the Whole Blood," meaning her only surviving daughter, Sarah. As her husband and the male head of household, Captain Willson legally administered the property, even if the couple was separated.[10] Allen would have none of that.

Suit followed countersuit for the next several years, reflecting in many ways the chaotic national finances of the new, postwar United States. The backlog of debt-recovery cases, impending bankruptcies, and postwar anger, which in central Massachusetts exploded into Shays's Rebellion, forced yet more postponements. At one point the New London County Court even reversed the suit entirely, ruling that Allen owed Willson £534. The two reached a reluctant settlement only several years later, their agreement coinciding with the crafting of a proposed national constitution in September 1787.[11]

Throughout the acrimonious wrangling, Allen kept alive "Affection & Tenderness" for Willson. Only when Allen had fully lost did he apparently hear one last time from Willson, in a letter sent from nearby Mystic. Willson wrote that he had been "laying on his oars," waiting for his sloop to finish loading. While he had no good words for his former wife—"I ave no inclination to see any part of her hear after"—Willson wished to part with some kind of friendship. "God Bless y^{r} Fam^{y}," he wrote, "and Take my part against all y^{t} [that] wod defame me unriteusly and by so doing oul Oblige an Old Acquantance that may do sum good yet."[12] Willson sailed off into his own new sea of possibilities, never to be heard from again, at least as far as the known sources show.

Allen at first tried to rebuild the mercantile world he had lost. But he lacked the capital, and could not collect on the many of the lingering debts owed him by West Indies merchants. Instead, he chose to pursue opportunities in trade as they arose, cobbling together income that augmented the steady but modest livelihood of the City Coffee House. Between the fall of 1783 and the summer of 1786, Allen supplied at least fourteen departing vessels with small cargoes—a handful of animals, a hundred bushels of hay, perhaps a thousand board feet of lumber, or a dozen barrels of meat at a time. Molasses, sugar, and coffee had largely disappeared from his sporadic accounts; instead, Allen speculated in a few bales of sea-island cotton, barrels of limes, or casks of Madeira wine. He also advertised and presumably acted as an agent for a few ships, using the coffeehouse as his office.[13]

In the hard times of the postwar Atlantic, Allen took on whatever cargoes he could. In one case, he sent a ton of ebony wood to a New York merchant, who eventually reported that musical instrument makers in the city rejected the wood as inferior for their purposes. He also received friendly requests to send special products or local produce to those who had moved away from New London. For example, a homesick Captain Nathan Sage pleaded with Allen to send him at least four hundred pounds of local cheeses, a dozen kegs of pickled oysters, and as many pots of "cranbarry sauce or what you may call it" to remind him of New London, and to stock for sale.[14]

Allen also received a very different kind of request at least once. In April 1789, Oliver Bowen contacted Allen "In Confidence" to help him find a New London ship suitable to transport enslaved people from West Africa. Bowen had been a slave-ship captain before moving to Georgia to take up a vast plantation near Savanah, where he had fought on the Patriot side. Temporarily back in Providence, Bowen sought a ship "one hundred fifty tons burden . . . well-sheathed [in copper], high between decks, and sail fast" that could take its human cargo to his new home. Bowen believed that enslavement would shortly become illegal in the new republic, probably referring to gradual emancipation laws passed in 1784 in both states. He need not have been so secretive, for provisions in the ratified Constitution in effect allowed the African trade in enslaved people to continue until January 1, 1808. In fact, Bowen participated in a voyage from Rhode Island to West Africa within a year of his request to Allen. It is unknown whether Allen supplied the ship, or how many other such inquiries he received. But ports in Greater New England from New York to New Hampshire did send out nearly sixty more voyages to forcibly transport enslaved Africans to the Americas before the official end to the trade on January 1, 1808.[15]

In the summer of 1786, Allen's small ventures came to a sudden halt. As the savvy American politician Tench Coxe observed in the understated language of the day, the new United States "had fallen into a very disagreeable condition by the year 1786."[16] The misfortunes of Allen and his son Thomas Jr. at this precarious economic moment show how national and overseas imperial decisions could decide the range of possibilities dockside and on ship's deck. The roots of the problem can be traced across the Atlantic to London.

At the time of impending peace in early 1783, Parliament adopted Orders-in-Council restricting American ships entry to British ports on July 2, 1783. These actions temporarily chased away the many American ships that had suddenly crowded the wharves of London and other British ports even before the formal peace agreement had been signed. But it remained poorly enforced. After a temporary slowing of exchange, American shipping grew over the next three years, especially in the British Caribbean islands. This suited both British planters and American port merchants just fine. The Norwich *Packet,* for example, carried a typical letter from a Barbados merchant in mid-1784 who predicted that the "prohibitory act will be done away with," hoping "that this intelligence might prove true, and acceptable to our American friends."[17] However, direct trade with Great Britain slowed.

As factions in Britain jostled for a coherent policy after 1783, members of Parliament were shocked to discover the high number of American ships calling at British colonial ports, even accounting for emergency supplies received in the aftermath of hurricanes. The governor of Barbados, for example, reported that eighty-eight American vessels visited the island in the single customs year of 1784–85. A Royal Navy captain stationed in Antigua, the young Horatio Nelson, observed with evident disgust that "to see the American ships and vessels with their colours flying in defiance of the Laws, and by permission of the officer of the customs, landing and unloading in our ports was too much for a British Officer."[18] The Royal Navy and staunch anti-American ministers found common cause in expelling American ships from contact with the British plantation islands once and for all.

At the same time, France had launched into another thorough revision of its colonial trades. Versailles became riven by contending parties with differing philosophies on how to promote economic progress, especially in light of the massive debt contracted in supplying aid to the United States. The crown first restored the old *Exclusif* policies in January 1783, then reversed the laws in May, in part to coax American ships to bring enslaved West Africans. After a few more twists, the court settled on the policy known as the *Exclusif mitigé* of August 1784, which allowed American ships access to the French Islands, particularly Saint-Domingue. But problems persisted. French merchants were very reluctant to extend long-term credit when there was "far too little good faith on the part of the Americans" to pay up. The constantly shifting laws, uncertain applications by local officials, and challenges to securing favorable credit terms limited the entry of American ships to France and the French Caribbean.[19] In short, for the first three years after the Peace of 1783, trade with the British was predictably illegal, and trade with the French was legally unpredictable.

Back in New London, Thomas's son and his son's new wife, Amelia, had built up a productive farm during the lean war years after 1780. The couple had a kind of genius for the quiet, calculated nurturing that successful coastal market farming demanded. They coaxed steady returns from all parts of farm life, including through renting out pastures, carts, and their own cattle for breeding, and slowly expanded their land holdings.[20] They seemed to epitomize the happy, prosperous yeoman farming family of the new republic.

Yet the deep blue called Thomas Allen Jr. once again. Through his contacts with the New York merchant James Stewart, with whom he had apprenticed before the war, he supervised the building of a new sloop. The timing of the sloop's construction is important, for the New York firm laid the keel at the crest of activity and profits for resurgent American shipping in the British Atlantic. The firm was so pleased with Allen Jr.'s work that it hired him as captain for a voyage to Madeira in late summer of 1785, then for a second voyage that fall.[21]

The following May, Stewart offered Thomas Jr. another command for the same sloop, but this time for a London voyage. With his scribbled hand and words suggesting his excitement, Thomas wrote his father for advice. Thomas Sr., seeing also a chance to inquire into Jolley's dormant affairs with Sir William Pepperell, responded by the next day's post: take the offer. "You are sencible how I and the family at Large have sufferd . . . to support Jolley's Family," he wrote, then urged, "Don't be Bashful in matters." He also sent his son warm clothing and his old quadrant. By the time Thomas Jr. received the package, however, in late May, reports of an ominous new "American Trade Bill" before Parliament had made their way into seaboard newspapers.[22]

The British had decided there could be no place, at least not legally, for American trade. In early June 1786, Parliament passed the "Increase and Encouragement of Shipping and Navigation Act." It allowed only registered, British-built vessels, fully owned only by British subjects, commanded by British captains, and with crews of whom three-fourths were British sailors, to dock anywhere in the reconfigured empire. To ensure there could be no mistaking the law's intent, the act specified that "no Ship or Vessel built in any of the Colonies of North America, now called 'The United states of *America*' . . . nor any Ship or Vessel which was owned by, or belonged to the Subjects of the said United States . . . shall be entitled to be registered under this present act, or to enjoy any of the Privileges or Advantages of a British-built Ship." Anticipating the act, British customs officials immediately began seizing American ships in the larger British West Indian ports, to the annoyance of many British planters.[23] As intended, British trade gains would come at the cost of substantial American losses.

Back in New York, the firm of Randall, Son, & Stewart evidently decided to postpone the voyage when they learned of the new act. As the hot, humid summer weeks dragged on, they agonized over what to do. By late July, the partners thought they had discovered a loophole. They changed the destination to Dublin, since Ireland required its own navigation act, then under heated debate in Parliament. The sloop sailed, but Thomas Jr. apparently made it only as far as Boston.[24] Knowing that the ship itself would never pass muster as a British vessel, the firm had apparently decided at the last moment to replace Thomas with a British-born ship captain and crew, probably from Nova Scotia, to finesse compliance. The ploy did not help. Stewart later wrote Thomas Sr. that the ship had been turned away from every British port. With the pedigree of American vessels now of crucial concern, Stewart lamented, "The American trade is completely done with in American bottoms."[25]

The new, belligerent British trade act, along with Spanish blocking of navigation on the Mississippi River and cantankerous jostling over tariffs, prompted delegates from five of the new republics to convene in Annapolis, Maryland, in September 1786. Their goal was to craft an integrated, cooperative, national commercial policy. Frustrated by poor attendance and horrified by Shays's Rebellion, which erupted just as they gathered at the table, the crises over trade at Annapolis in turn spurred a larger conference, a Constitutional Convention, to open the following May of 1787.[26]

Back in New London, the new British law pushed Thomas Jr. to turn away from the sea permanently and search for more stable possibilities on land. He even galloped off with two friends later in June 1792 to survey farming tracts opening in the Mohawk River Valley. He found "a good township of land but very dear," and "almost froze to Death" during the short summer nights.[27] The farmlands of upstate New York were not for him. Instead, Thomas Jr. looked more closely at the nearby pastures on the old smugglers' haunt of Fishers Island.

War had invited or forced migrations within the settler seaboard. With peace came a second wave of resettlement. When the remaining white Loyalists in New York—estimated at 32,000—endured their final evacuation from the city by November 25, 1783, they left behind their own crushed vision of settler America in addition to carts of furniture and sheds of goods. Many white settlers took ship and dispersed around the swiftly reshaping British Empire from London to Jamaica to Calcutta. According to one historian, these Refugees "personally conveyed American things and ideas into the Empire," including a sharp "discourse of grievance against imperial authority" in new environments. Meanwhile, Black Loyalists, who had enlisted to fight for the king, left with their families, seeking refuge within an empire that largely did not want them. Nearly 1,200 eventually left Nova Scotia for the first "repatriation" to the coast of Sierra Leone in West Africa. But the majority of Loyalists migrated to raw communities in the remaining North American British colonies. For example, Allen's old crony Eleazer Fitch eventually migrated with his family to British Lower Canada (now Quebec) in the region later known as the Eastern Townships.[28]

Although historians of Connecticut have often imagined the new state as a bulwark of Patriot fervor, it became a haven for the "rehabilitation" of Loyalists immediately after the war.[29] New London in particular emerged as a kind of safe transit hub, and Thomas Allen appears to have been at the center of a loose network of support and temporary lodging. Whether they were Loyalists escaping republicanism, Loyalist opportunists returning despite republicanism, or people simply looking for a quiet corner to get on with life in the new republic, all found a seat in Allen's coffeehouse.

Requests for refuge in the port of New London began even as the war was ending. As the British prepared to evacuate New York, Dr. Charles Arding, one of Allen's associates from his Statia days, wrote Allen on behalf of several Loyalist families. "Would be Glad to [k]now," he inquired, "if it is, as we hear, that New London is an Asylum for those attacht to the British Constitution. If it should be So, I think it would be A great Advantage to that place." Arding clarified: "I have my fears, tho' I do not come under the Description of Any Penal laws of this State, or Any other[;] but Some of My Friends Do, & therefore Would Wish to know how they would be Receved in N. London. . . . Be Very Candid in the Matter." Arding decided to stay in New York, but several of his friends did not. Over the next year, he thanked Allen for his help in temporarily housing and feeding at least three Loyalist families on their way to other imperial destinations.[30]

Two other early members that Allen shepherded into a new life were the merchant partners Levi Thayer and Philip Jarvis. Thayer hailed originally from a successful but not socially prominent Boston Loyalist-leaning merchant family. He left Boston at the same time as Jolley Allen, joined the exodus to Halifax, then later in the war sailed to British-occupied New York, supplying provisions to the sprouting Loyalist settlements in the Maritime Provinces. Jarvis apparently belonged to the extensive Jarvis clan of Huntington, Long Island, led by Anglican pastor Abraham Jarvis. Several members of the family had taken an oath of allegiance to Loyalist New York Governor William Tryon in 1778. By early 1783, Thayer and Jarvis had joined in a partnership in New York, then left to open a shop in postwar New London, where they met Allen. Dogged by debt, and with the prospect of free land, they departed New London for the deep-cut, black-forested coves of Nova Scotia in March 1786. They settled into the instant Loyalist town of Port Roseway, which British officials had rechristened Shelburne. They apparently envisioned establishing their own version of a triangular trade managed from their new Nova Scotia base, reaching contacts in the British West Indies and using Allen as their agent to handle the New England angle of the trade.[31]

Even though committed subjects of the king, they ran into trouble at the same time as Thomas Jr. did in 1786, and for similar reasons: the new British trade act. In the messy world of the early peace, customs officials were increasingly tough. Thayer and Jarvis advised their captain that once in Jamaica, he must confirm "wether a Brittish Vessel can go to an English Island after loading at [an] American Port. You recollect there is an act against it. . . . [A] number has been juried Lately." Worse, when the new British Navigation Act did come into force, they realized they had no way to prove that their brig, the *Dolphin,* had been constructed in a British yard. The partnership could not weather this type of close customs scrutiny; they dissolved their fledgling empire that same August.[32]

Allen's brief connections to Nova Scotia included a strong Church of England connection. Vocal Anglican priest and Loyalist poet Roger Viets, for example, stayed with Allen on his way to Nova Scotia. Originally born in Simsbury, Connecticut, he graduated from Yale in 1758 and eventually returned as a minister to his hometown before the war. The Patriots jailed him briefly on suspicion of aiding escaping British officers. Lacking firm evidence, the state eventually authorized him to return to his church. In December 1785 he accepted an offer to be the new minister at the growing Loyalist agricultural town of Digby, Nova Scotia. Viets stayed with Allen's family over part of the winter of 1786. He just missed the arrival of another famous boarder at Allen's inn. The newly ordained Episcopalian bishop Samuel Seabury, whose father had preached at St. James, had returned to Connecticut in June 1785. Seabury first stayed with Allen while workers readied the old parsonage, which had escaped Arnold's burning. Seabury oversaw the rebuilding of the Anglican Church network based on the now more acceptable Episcopalian (Scottish Rites) model. He later consecrated the rebuilt St. James in September 1787.[33]

For these and other Loyalists scattered along the western Atlantic from Nova Scotia to Barbados, Allen functioned as a kind of transit broker, safe enough for both formerly antagonistic sides to interact with each other. The fate of Thayer & Jarvis, Viets, and Seabury is a reminder that the ocean of human intercourse within the anglophone world had utterly changed. Their Atlantic World would no longer be defined by the same bonds within a single, shared empire. After the Revolution, the old sea of possibilities would be divided into two: two new seaborne empires, running on parallel courses and intersecting at many, but not all, compass points.

13

"Brethren in Navigation"

MARY BUIESSON HAD A problem: her husband had gone missing at sea. As winter tightened its grip on New England in late November 1789, she contacted Thomas Allen, seeking his help. "Altho a stranger," she wrote in an elegant hand, "I Have the Presumption to believe you will oblige me . . . from the excellent character which you bear." Her husband, Captain Buiesson, owner of the Bermuda-built brig *Joseph and Maria,* had last written her from Guadeloupe on September 15, announcing his intention of returning shortly to New York, but the brig had not arrived. Desperate, she found in Allen's Marine List of September 4 that a ship captain had just returned from Guadeloupe. Could Allen locate him and ask on her behalf for any news of her husband? "Your kindness," she added, "will, I hope, expel the gloom."[1]

We do not know how Allen responded, or whether Mrs. Buiesson ever located her husband. But this poignant search reveals one facet of the human dimension behind what became Thomas Allen's most singular contribution to the early republic: resurrecting his old Marine List for the benefit of an imagined community of "Brethren in Navigation." In his own small way, Allen rode the waves of a new Enlightenment ethos, optimistic for all humanity, yet self-congratulatory on the achievements of European thinkers and ideals.

Allen's ideas, reflecting the concerns of many contemporary maritime scientists, explorers, and administrators, centered on the ocean—a particular ethos termed here the "Deep Blue Enlightenment." As one historian has cogently argued, "The most ambitious [Enlightenment] reforms, and the most creative, involved European states with 'ultramarine' empires,'" for they had most to gain or lose in the contest for overseas trade and colonies.[2] He humbly envisioned his Marine List as a kind of public utility, dispensing timely advice, morsels of salty wit, and keen weather observations, all while helping mariners rebuild trade. Through the Marine List, Allen turned to the sea, but this time in print to help an expansive fraternity of mariners and boost republican maritime expansion. If he derived some income from providing this public service, then so much the better. For him, it was a new form of trade.

Connecticut *Gazette* printer Tim Green inserted Allen's column into his newspaper at a propitious moment in American news media development. On the eve of the Battles of Lexington and Concord, American printers were setting type for thirty-five newspapers in eighteen colonial towns, all but two hugging the seaboard from Georgia to New Hampshire. The numerous interruptions, occupations, and migrations of printers during the war led to half of those papers falling silent. But new printers founded new papers, and in just ten years the new republic could boast forty-seven newspapers in twenty-seven towns. Printed news not only reached the new (and then independent) country of Vermont but also crept inland into market and upriver towns such as Litchfield, Connecticut; Trenton, New Jersey; and Alexandria, Virginia.[3] News printing spread even faster after 1785. Spurred in part by the intense interest in the hotly contested ratification debates over the new Constitution and the revolution erupting in France, the number of newspapers doubled to just over one hundred in the next five years. Circulations were also increasing—according to one estimate, the basic print run of a major paper was six hundred copies per issue before the war; by 1790 it had more than tripled, to at least two thousand copies.[4] Not only were there many more readers, there was a sharp increase in the number of white women and freed people of color who sought out newspapers.

The nature of what news meant and how to present it evolved quickly and dynamically in the second half of the Enlightenment century. American newspapers not only informed an expanding literate public but helped mold public ideals, and did so according to a new range of emerging values. News editors promoted a genteel discourse that emphasized "rational speculation" built on evidence and logic and less on biblical authority and traditional assumptions of social deference. For those with the privilege of sharing a classical training, the Enlightenment replaced the tattered sails of fear with the fresh canvas of progress.[5] Allen's revitalized Marine List championed these ideals by promoting an idealized, universal fraternity of brethren in navigation that shared his belief in the value of nautical science and freer markets across the ocean, and conferred its own form of honor and integrity.

To create the Marine List, Allen tapped into the existing ad hoc gossip network of mariners, creating in effect a network of captains as corresponding stringers. A letter from a longtime associate, Captain Nathaniel Gardiner of Sag Harbor on Long Island, shows how this worked. Gardiner wrote to Allen in May 1786 of the return of the brig *Lucy*, under Captain George McKey, which reached home after sailing the coasts of Brazil hunting whales. Gardiner sent copies of parts of McKey's logbook to Allen, thinking it might be of interest. In the logbook, McKey reported meeting the brig *America* off Brazil in January, then another American whaler from Nantucket in mid-March. This ship in turn had spoken to a third whaler. On the homeward voyage, McKey stopped at British Dominica and spoke with yet a fourth American vessel, which then mentioned a fifth, also from Nantucket. The crews on all five ships had crammed the holds with high-grade whale oil, obtained relatively more easily off the bright Brazilian coast than in the frigid northern seas.[6]

Receiving the logbook, Allen was clearly impressed with the mariners' haul from the Atlantic whale commons. In his next Marine List, he not only succinctly summarized McKey's news of "all well" from all the ships mentioned in McKey's logbook but urged his readers to rethink old trade patterns: "Now, my Horse Jockies, beat your horses and cattle into spears, lances, harpoons, and whaling geer, and let us all strike out!—many Spouts a-head!—Whales plenty, you have them for catching!"[7]

Allen's readers would have easily recognized his play on Joel 3:10—"Beat your plowshares into swords, and your pruning-hooks into spears: let the weak say, I am strong." But his promotion of whaling came exactly with the first whisperings of the new British Navigation Act in 1786. Some New London merchants clearly weighed his thoughts about expanding their commercial horizons beyond simply ferrying horses to the West Indies. While the port's first whaling voyage had departed in 1784, New London remained a minor player during Allen's time. Only later did the port emerge as one of the three major centers of the nineteenth-century whaling industry, making Allen arguably something of a commercial prophet.[8]

Allen's renewed Marine List offered little at first. The inaugural column appeared in the *Gazette* of January 14, 1785, within two weeks of the coffeehouse's reopening. It ran only six short lines and mentioned only two ships. But it also contained an aphorism that quickly became the most distinguishing feature of Allen's column. At the end, he added, "Steady Jack, mind your Helm—the Ship is by the Wind." Puzzling to landlubbers, mariners would have picked up his pithy observation immediately. "Jack" referred to a jack-tar or the common, universalized idea of a sailor; the helm that steered a ship symbolized Congress; the ship signified the American ship of state; and "by the wind" meant a ship sailing almost directly into a fierce, oncoming wind, which was risky and could endanger the crew.[9] It was a slight sniff of political commentary but also wry, thoughtful, and lively.

Within a few months, Allen had added more varied comments to his Marine List: notable people traveling by packet boat, weekly wind and weather reports (measuring and predicting weather patterns emerged as a major Enlightenment preoccupation), short price lists, ship sightings on the open Atlantic, and more salty observations and aphorisms. By June the list had assumed its full form, and Green's *Gazette* published forty-eight to fifty pieces a year for the next nine years.

Allen's mind roamed widely, but he returned to three themes repeatedly. The year 1789 is typical. First, Allen had become fascinated with the nautical heirs of Captains Cook and Bougainville and the enthusiasm for maritime exploration, particularly if it pointed toward new trade destinations. Green supported Allen's mild scientific bent as the *Gazette,* like many newspapers in the early republic, printed a steady stream of articles on practical improvements or potentially new and beneficial processes.[10]

One such occasion presented itself when Captain Peter Macchet of the brig *Enterprize* docked in New London in April 1789. The captain stayed overnight with Allen at the City Coffee House on his way back to New York. Macchet had just completed a voyage to Cape Horn at the very southern tip of South America, apparently scouting new whaling grounds. While exploring, the *Enterprize* had touched at the Falkland Islands, where Macchet's sailors found "tuck'd into a wall a letter, giving an account of the ship *Hope,* and sloop *Washington,* having touch'd there from Boston . . . and proceeded a round the world." The story fired enough maritime imaginations that at least eleven different newspapers reprinted Allen's brief story verbatim, citing his Marine List. These papers ranged from the business-focused Pennsylvania *Packet* to the general-readership New York *Daily Gazette* and the short-lived, erudite Berkshire *Chronicle* in Pittsfield, Massachusetts.[11]

A second theme was support for what Allen presumed would be the centralizing power of the new Constitution. As he had since 1785, Allen sometimes celebrated patriotic events at the City Coffee House, such as Washington's birthday or Independence Day. Even with such events, he might offer an observation on political economy. For example, when the British Shipping Act became known in early July 1786, Allen muted his celebration of Declaration Day by ending his column "INDEPENDENCE *revis'd—DEPENDENCE!!*" But in his second most repeated column from 1789, Allen celebrated the new set of federal customs laws, among the first five pieces of legislation passed under the new Constitution, in his Marine List for July 31. Tim Green prefaced Allen's column by printing a precise list of the ninety-four new customs officials, praising Congress in a signed opinion piece (unusual for Green) for their "wisdom, impartiality, and independency" in choosing customs officials of sterling character.[12]

Ironically, the old smuggler Allen celebrated the enactment of the new customs regulations, and even urged full compliance. He underscored his views with an eye-catching graphic showing a ship's anchor and the slogan "The Anchor Hope." Beneath it, Allen wrote a kind of short manifesto of his ideals. In his extended metaphor, Constitutional Hope now stabilized the ship of state in each port. If all brethren in navigation fulfilled their patriotic duty by not cheating customs (his mention of "slip o'er platforms" referred to sailing furtively past the sandbar at the mouth of the Connecticut River to evade declaring cargoes), then the new Constitution would create a new era of prosperity. Eight newspapers from Philadelphia to Boston reprinted the "Anchor Hope" column within two weeks of its initial appearance, giving Allen credit, though only half included the anchor graphic itself.[13]

Allen's enthusiasm for the new customs regulations should not be surprising. The Constitution in effect reinstated a republican version of the centralized, stable British trade regulations that had been tossed overboard with independence. Calls for a unified, national customs service began even before the British passed their menacing Shipping Act of 1786. Some politicians, such as John Adams, viewed national regulation of the economy as a matter of virtue "to ensure that fair value was always exchanged for fair value." But diplomat John Jay argued more practically in Federalist no. 4 that if European monarchies "see that our national government is efficient and well administered, our trade prudently regulated . . . [and] our resources and finances discretely managed . . . they

FIGURE 11. "The Looking Glass for 1787. A house divided against itself cannot stand. Mat. Chap. 12th verse 26," attributed to Amos Doolittle, 1787. This satirical cartoon depicts issues and personalities in Connecticut pertaining to the constitutional debates in the summer of 1787. At top, a wagon labeled "Connecticut" and weighed down with debts is being pulled one way by the Federalists (*left*) and in the opposite direction by the Anti-Federalists (*right*). At center right, Allen's old trade crony, Samuel Holden Parsons ("S-H-P"), appears to be defecating in the direction of another Connecticut politician, William Williams; at the bottom, Connecticut ships sail to New York, where they pay annual customs dues of £40,000 to that state instead of to their home state. Thomas Allen keenly supported the Constitution, believing that a national customs union would revive and expand overseas trade. (Library of Congress, Prints and Photographs Division, LC-LC-DIG-ppmsca-17522)

will be much more disposed to cultivate our friendship than provoke our resentment."[14] For merchants and maritime boosters such as Thomas Allen, the value of the Constitution did not lie in ideals of freedom, equality, or sovereignty of the people, salutary as those might be. Instead, they viewed a national constitution as a balanced, inclusive force promoting global trade—a cohesive, regulated, *American* trade around the globe.

Allen devoted most of his Marine List commentary to a third theme: supporting high-seas humanitarianism. It is in these entries that his concept of a loose-knit, masculine, unified fraternity of deep blue mariners is best articulated—his idealized brethren in navigation. Allen set the tone for the year by noting in late January the help rendered to the damaged *Clarissa,* under Jared Tracey of Norwich, by a Captain Cunningham, returning to Ireland from New York. "Like a true generous hearted Hibernian," Allen wrote warmly, Cunningham "supplied Capt. Tracey with such necessaries that they were much distressed for—*May every American seaman's heart thus feel, and be also generous to all in need.*"[15]

Allen also reported disturbing, *Mary Celeste*–like discoveries at sea that might help anxious family members searching, like Mary Buiesson, for lost family. In one story, Captain Curtis, commanding the sloop *Polly,* spied on his homeward run an abandoned wreck in the open Atlantic. He supplied the coordinates and found "her mast, bowsprit, and all spars gone, quarter deck and bows out of water, her waist appeared stove in—water running a-cross her decks—about 70 tons burthen." Other newspapers supported Allen by widely reprinting this and other similar reports. Other stories over the year involved aid to a disabled ship in the Bay of Honduras, also freely given by an Irish captain; the rescue of a New London ship off Saint-Domingue; and the wreck of a New York ship in the Turks Islands, which the crew somehow survived. "*Sailors, keep a good look-out forward!—Alas, and so we go again!*" Allen wrote, mixing admonishment with a nod to the fates of the sea.[16]

Regional sea captains and maritime merchants understood that by helping Allen, they helped themselves. Captains writing to Allen often opened their reports by thanking Allen, as Captain Jabez Perkins did when he wrote, "As you are so obleaging to the Publick as to keep a marine list . . . Gratis." Some simply grunted a simple "my estem[d] thanks," while others readily adopted Allen's terminology and addressed him as a fellow "friend and brother in Navigation." Through the power of easily transportable print, Allen's Marine List apparently even sailed on New England ships down to the Caribbean, where the major Bridgetown merchant house of Le Gay & Evans complimented Allen's efforts, "well knowing the truth and regularity of your Information."[17] Captain Amos Palmer succinctly summarized what many of the brethren undoubtedly felt when he wrote Allen,

> By the Inteligence of your Marine List[,] Number of owners, Fathers, Mothers, Brothers, etc etc Hear from their Interest and Friends which Certainty gives Satisfaction to all sorts of People and as you are so kind to do the whole Gratis, I look upon it a duty incumbent upon all Masters [of]

> Vessels, etc to Give you What inteligence in their Power. . . . Please select . . . what you think will be of service to the Publick.[18]

Later, one of Allen's old cronies, Captain Jabez Lord, even celebrated Allen and the City Coffee House in verse. Appearing first in New York, the piece provided a portrait of "honest Tom" as a federalist Bacchus crowned with "the hoary harvest of a length in years." Thundering "Gale Town hears his cry," it gave Allen perhaps more notoriety than he himself might have claimed:

> Who knows *not* Tom? His glories and his name,
> Are weekly sounded from the trump[et] of fame;
> O'er all Columbia *Allen's* humors spread,
> And his marine remarks in evr'y clime are read.

It is striking that in his winter years, Allen had traded his identity as captain for that of a sage and witty tavern landlord. The piece became another popular post, reprinted in seven papers from New York to New Hampshire.[19]

Other readers were not so charitable. Some were irritated by inaccuracies, angered by personal attacks, or, in at least one case, demanded repayment of old debts. John Evans, the young merchant whose goods Allen had stolen ("decamped with") from Grenada in 1764, located Allen twenty-five years later by reading his Marine List. He demanded that Allen "send me something now, be it more or less[;] I shall be glad to receive it."[20] Evans did not seem as interested in money as he was in some kind of apology. Neither man recorded the outcome.

To one crucial and growing group of sailors, or humanity more broadly, Allen never extended his concept of brethren: people of African descent. Many "Black Jacks" had sailed on privateers during the war, and their numbers increased with peacetime shipping. While many made excellent sailors, very few could advance to positions of command unless they owned or had freedom to pilot their own small vessel.[21] The British Shipping Act of 1786, however, may have offered a back-hatch ladder for a select few by encouraging American merchants to employ Black Loyalist mariners to man ships for trade to imperial ports. Such a crew may well have arrived in New London when Hartford merchant William Bull advised Allen to help load a ship bound for the Bahamas. "You will know when she is at New London," Bull wrote, "by the appearance of Suden darkness, as the Vessells' [crew] and Master is black & all are black."[22]

Emerging genteel republican society north of Virginia began to view enslavement as a "national evil" even as the war engulfed the seaboard. But Allen clearly did not agree with the abolitionist wind that began to blow with force after 1783. This should not be surprising; freed people of color in Connecticut were met with wide indifference at best, and more often with deep hostility. Tim Green's *Gazette* set the ambiguous tone by printing some gentle abolitionist pieces in the very same issues in which he carried notices advertising the sale of enslaved women and children. Further, Allen reported maritime disasters affecting "slave ships" with concern for the white crew but none for the Black "cargo."[23]

Allen's comments in the Marine List on the rebellion by enslaved laborers in the hills south of French Le Cap in August 1791—the start of the Haitian Revolution—may well sum up his perspective. Allen was among the first to alert settler Americans to the uprising in Saint-Domingue in mid-September. After the initial reports of violence, many merchants expected the rebellion to be quashed by the French. But the French did not, and indeed could not, beset by their own revolutionary turbulence. In early February 1792, Allen noted almost plaintively: "Markets dull, and negroes still burning—no canes growing, and no troops arrived from France; they are coming to come—but when, Jack?"[24]

For reasons that remain unknown but that undoubtedly sprang from years of collaboration and perhaps friendship, Allen insisted that his Marine List first appear in Tim Green's local *Gazette*. His insistence limited other opportunities. While Allen may have harbored hopes that the List would earn an income, only after the first three years did he consider seriously selling it as a commodity. Every time he met with the same set of problems. For example, in the spring of 1788, Elisha Babcock of the upstart *American Mercury* of Hartford wrote Allen with a proposal. "I have been informed that Mr. Green gave you nothing for it, not even the paper to write it on," Babcock wrote, noting that if "true, I am sure it cannot be an object worth[y of] his attention." In exchange for the privilege of being the first to publish it, Babcock offered a probationary amount of twenty-one shillings a year, paper, and expenses for sending it. At the end of that time, if Babcock found it useful, he would consider a higher payment.[25]

Allen demurred, apparently hoping to prompt a bidding war. He contacted Babcock's rival, George Goodwin, senior partner of the Hartford

Courant. When he found out, Babcock, understandably testy, wrote to Allen again in September, demanding to know whether he or Goodwin would have the privilege of printing it first. Babcock reiterated his offer but sweetened it by sending five quires of paper, offering to forward Allen any newspaper from "the Continent" that Babcock could lay hold of.[26] Others, however, rebuffed Allen's inquiries outright. Woodward and Green, the Middletown printers of the newly established Middlesex *Gazette,* wrote him, "As long as your marine list is first published in the New London paper, we shall not thank you for it, because we can have it gratis . . . [with] the least trouble, attention, or concern." They then offered something of a backhanded compliment to the Marine List's success: "Indeed, it is at present a disadvantage to us, as people concerned in Navigation will naturally take the paper where the List is first published, that they may have the latest intelligence."[27]

While this statement begs the question of why the partners did not therefore jump at the "privilege" of being first to print the List, the Middletown newspaper's rejection identified the problem of ubiquitous print piracy. The efficiency of the early republic's postal service, coupled with the lack of accepted standards of authorship backed by a national copyright law (passed only in May 1790, and not applicable to newspapers), seemed to conspire against Allen. He tried to broaden his geographic appeal, writing to his old smuggling colleague Clement Biddle in Philadelphia. Biddle agreed to post a notice in a local coffeehouse but warned Allen, "I have little hopes of the application."[28]

Navigating a paper's finances proved exceptionally tricky. Allen succeeded in selling his List to only one editor, John Trumbull, the publisher of the nearby Norwich *Packet,* and their brief correspondence sheds light on the practical finances of early newspapers. Trumbull and Allen reached a one-year agreement in October 1788 to allow the *Packet* to carry the full Marine List. According to Trumbull, he printed the list "at the request of several Gentleman Merchants & others of this City," charging his subscribing customers $15 year extra for access. He then paid Allen "by the piece," as if he were a cottage worker stitching together a pair of breeches.[29] If the list failed to appear by overnight post, Allen received nothing.

When it came time for Allen's contract to be renewed, however, the Norwich merchants all balked at paying the higher subscription price, citing economic hardship. Reluctantly, Trumbull did not renew his agreement with Allen. Worse, reflecting the printer's own economic straits—"times here hard, my employers Small Farmers, etc., cash not to be had"—he begged Allen to be patient as he foraged for money owed from the previous year. Instead of cash, Trumbull could only promise "produce of some kind . . . from my Country Customers."[30]

Realizing that he could not sell the List as a commodity, Allen appealed to the charity of American mariners. One New Haven captain recognized the List's "usefulness" and offered to take up a collection among returning ship captains to help out a brother mariner. A few months later, in answer to an entreaty, a merchant friend of Thomas Mumford's promised he would talk up Allen's "Morean List" among potential subscribers in Hartford. Clearly, neither had any success. By August 1789, Allen was using his own column to make his case. Addressing his "Brethren," he appealed for their support. "BEHOLD I have toil'd one year more," he wrote, lamenting that "I have caught little or nothing—still I have a generous heart and spirit, to preserve in well doing . . . the laborer is worthy of his hire, I humbly submit the matter to the considerate and concern'd."[31] There is no record in Allen's accounts or correspondence that this or any other appeal convinced merchants or his fellow mariners to open their purses.

Only after Allen began working with marine insurance broker George Philips of Middletown did he seem to grasp that marine insurers, not publishers, offered the best chance for selling the List. In April 1790, Captain Jacob Sebor, who had relocated to New York, notified Allen of the interest expressed by an informal consortium of his contacts. They offered to pay Allen \$30–\$40 per year if they were sent the list by post on a weekly basis. For reasons that remain unclear, Allen never fully pursued this option. Now in his sixties, it may have been a case of too little, too late. At the same time, *Gazette* printer Green changed his tactics and began soliciting business for competing marine lists.[32] Allen's difficulty in making a living from his labor of love offered two abject lessons on life in the early republic. The first reflected the stuttering of seaborne commerce even in the glow of the new Constitution. It would take new gales of war to fill the economic sails of American ships. The second concerned human nature. Many applauded Allen's grand fraternity of brethren in navigation but few were willing to bear the private cost.

Allen died suddenly at his City Coffee House on November 19 or 20. In May he had published an extended and rather jovial account of his voyage "thro' the Cramp Gulph into the Cholice Sea." Although he listed "cholic," which was normally a short, sharp, usually abdominal pain, the affliction may have been a minor heart attack. He published his last Marine List on September 14 and notified the public that the City Coffee House had moved on September 26. After this date, he appears to have been too weak to continue writing.[33]

The news of his death had a life of its own. Like a pebble thrown into a pond, Allen's obituary was published in concentric circles emanating from the epicenter of his demise in New London. It first reached nearby papers in Connecticut and Rhode Island, next the major newspapers of New York, Boston, Salem, and Philadelphia, and finally reached a few smaller inland papers in the course of several weeks. A total of nineteen newspapers carried the obituary. Its author remains a mystery, but it may well have been a fellow merchant, Thomas Pool, who presumably had helped Allen before his death and continued the Marine List under his own name afterward.[34] In a fitting tribute to Allen's news persona, the obituary read:

Conclusion of T. Allen's Marine List

—

Founder'd last week on the *reef* of
MORTALITY, in *lat.* 65, Capt. THO-
MAS ALLEN, of New-London;
where his *timbers* still lie in one *fathom*
water, to rot and be eaten by worms.
And so we go, Jack ! !

Although Allen had foundered on the reef of mortality, his debts sailed easily right past it. At his death, Allen owed thirty-nine creditors more than £800, enough to fund a comfortable living for at least eight years. Most of this he owed to his son and to his second wife, Polly. To help pay the debts, Thomas Allen Jr. became the administrator of his father's estate. It took an unusually long time to sell off the estate and placate his deceased father's many creditors. Two dozen other people owed Allen's estate minor amounts of money; but since the debts were so small and the debtors were largely located overseas, his executors "thought not worth carrying out" the effort to pursue them.[35] In a sense, the sea provided them with a protecting barrier, defeating any meaningful collection.

The only hope to pay off the debts rested in Thomas Jr. selling his father's estate. But when three appraisers poked through the City Coffee House in mid-January 1794, they discovered only dilapidated possessions.

The inventory is punctuated with a long list of sorry items: an "Ancient brown silk coat," "one Hair Trunk—old," "1 Small Eight square mehogany table—broken," "one crack'd coffee pot"—the list goes on. It appeared that Allen had given up trying to improve his "interest" and had simply hung on for the last year until death. The vendue fetched only £278, barely a third of the amount owed.[36] Allen's dreams for material independence and saltwater fraternity had turned out to be another lost venture on his own vast sea of possibilities—a sea, it turned out, of debt and withered dreams, not one of wealth and a merited respect.

Epilogue

TWO WORLDS TO CONQUER

IN THE SUMMER BEFORE his father's death, Thomas Allen Jr. ferried his wife, Amelia, and their six children, a half dozen tenant farming families, and thirty cows, oxen, and other livestock to Fishers Island. He had leased the whole island in April 1793 from New York magnate Francis Bayard Winthrop, a descendant of first Massachusetts Governor John Winthrop, in effect becoming a vassal lord.

Under Thomas Jr., every square foot of the island seemingly became a source of income: the remaining stands of trees were chopped into firewood or sawn into fine lumber for ship's planking, furniture, or saddle trees for horse saddles. He raised cattle for Winthrop and churned the milk from cows into cream and butter, pastured mules and horses for others, and provided stud services for livestock. He even sold the heavy stones of the island as ballast for ships and foundations for homes and barns in the growing towns on either side of Long Island Sound. As he and his tenants cleared the land of trees, he seeded pastures for a far more profitable endeavor: raising sheep. But instead of slaughtering them for exported meat, as his father might have purchased, he sold their wool to feed the growing demand by New England mills for manufacturing wool cloth.[1]

No longer constrained by British laws, and lacking a steady supply of basic English goods after 1783, American entrepreneurs began manufacturing a variety of goods, initially for regional markets. Taking advantage of natural fast-flowing rivers or building races to channel water to turn massive wheels, they built small textile mills for weaving wool, linen, or increasingly cotton throughout southern New England, northeastern New Jersey, southeastern Pennsylvania, and along the fall line of Maryland, where rapids divided the Tidewater from the hillier country. The mills depended heavily on outwork, or the preprocessing of yarn by women and often children in farm families during the slower winter months. In 1775 there were perhaps thirteen such mills in all the colonies. By 1790 their number had doubled, and grew much faster thereafter.[2]

Supplied with wool by extended industrial farms like Thomas Jr.'s, these mills in turn became the champions of a new range of American industries. They dressed everyone from genteel New Englanders to enslaved African Americans as plantations expanded ever westward. Clearly impressed with Allen's industry, Winthrop offered him a seven-year lease. By 1800, Allen's domain on Fishers Island was thriving. Now adding the suffix "Esquire" to his signature on letters, he had built his own community and, in the family tradition, of which his father would have heartily approved, had founded a school for his tenants' sons and daughters.[3] Surveying his own rising empire, Thomas Allen Jr. may have drawn deep satisfaction from having found the secret to steady wealth and community respect that had eluded his seafaring father. The secret lay not on the waves but in exploiting every square inch of the land to the fullest extent conceivable.

At the same moment, halfway across the globe in Madras (Chenai), India, Nathaniel Allen, one of Jolley Allen's two surviving sons, put quill to paper to write his uncle, Thomas Allen Sr. Less than seven years previously one of his uncle's mercantile contacts had sadly despaired of "ever making Nat a sailor." Now, Nathaniel could proudly inform his uncle that "by my own industry and frugality" he was well on his way to "geting an independence." Not only had he advanced to the rank of captain, he was now owner of a 250-ton ship engaged in the American trade to the Indian subcontinent.[4]

Young Captain Nathaniel Allen's course represented an entirely different direction for citizens of the new American republic. Within months of American representatives in Paris signing a peace treaty ending the war, New York investors in 1784 sent the *Empress of China* to Canton (Guangzhou) in south China, launching American trade to the far Pacific Ocean. Salem and Providence ships quickly waded in, expanding ancillary trades to the Indian subcontinent and to the northwest American coast for furs, and later hunting for whales, using the mid-oceanic Kingdom of Hawai'i as their base. At first, barely a handful of American ships made the long and arduous voyage to the ill-defined "East Indies" every year. But Nathaniel Allen's first voyage on the *Warren* in 1788 signaled a sudden sixfold leap in American shipping to Asia.[5]

Americans in the India trade relied heavily on the French Indian Ocean colony of Mauritius (*Île de France*) as a base. Many American mariners, probably including Captain Nathaniel Allen, carved out a role in the "country trade" between Mauritius and the major European-controlled ports of India. American merchants were uncertain what might sell, so they sent varied cargoes ranging from American-grown ginseng to dairy products, Madeira wine, and leather saddles. Ships returned with a vast assortment of what newspaper ads labeled "NEW GOODS, which would not generally be known by their Names." These usually consisted of cloth and spices that American consumers saw as new, exotic, and exciting. Early ventures often generated profits of 40 percent or more, nearly double the average realized by his uncle in the prerevolutionary smuggling voyages to the West Indies.[6]

There was only one request that Captain Nathaniel Allen wished to trouble his uncle with. In a private letter for his uncle's eyes only, he revealed that he had fathered a "Natural Child, a fine blossmin'g boy the very picture of me." Nathaniel Allen wished to send his son back to Connecticut to be schooled and raised, either by his uncle or perhaps by another recently retired Connecticut sea captain that he knew. He assured his uncle that he could pay all the child's expenses and more.[7] Sadly for young Captain Nathaniel Allen, his proud and joyful letters would never be read by his uncle, for they reached New London nearly eighteen months after Thomas Allen had died. The fates of Captain Nathaniel Allen and his child remain unknown.

In 1857, on the verge of what would become a convulsing civil war, Hiram Holt gifted the majority of the Allen Family Papers to the American Antiquarian Society. Sizing up Thomas Allen, and the generation of the Revolution more broadly, Holt wrote, "He was several times rich and as often poor—a result rather common to great adventures of modern days."[8]

Holt's observation made a simple but no less powerful point. The crests and troughs of Allen's fortunes mirrored the deep blue on which he and like settler mariners sailed and on which their families and communities depended. Many self-interested, striving rogues from the mainland colonies who sailed in the seaborne trades rose through their own merit and the scrappy experience of free trade to positions of community influence. They openly went to war against existing, largely English institutions and traditions of governance, law, and commercial relations from the 1770s.

Those striving rogues who survived in turn created a republic in their own image, one often as turbulent as the restless ocean waves.[9]

By 1790, with revolutions in Europe filling the sails of a robust American overseas trade and a new, voracious, intertwined expansion of industrialization and enslaved plantation agriculture domestically, the successors of the Revolutionary generation went further. From 1804 they launched a two-taloned imperial tradition: one by land in a drive to the Pacific shore, a second by sea to commandeer trade around the globe.[10] This striving tradition, guided by the same ardent desire for improving one's self-interest, dismissed if not disrespected political traditions, established laws, and often virtuous conduct in commercial relations. It animates American society still, a hidden legacy of a revolutionary sea of possibilities.

ACKNOWLEDGMENTS

I have not written a biography so much as been a party to piecing together a massive jigsaw puzzle that portrays an obscure man and his family in the eighteenth century.

Many, many people helped with this puzzle. The then Curator of Manuscripts at the American Antiquarian Society, Tom Knowles, first suggested I look at the Allen Family Collection. Disheartened by this vast collection, I had conversations with Richard Wightman Fox, poet Tess Taylor, and Joe Cullon, among others, that helped me see what the overall finished puzzle could look like. From that initial NEH fellowship in 2006 through several return visits, the good folks at the AAS, including Ashley Cataldo, Kimberly Toney, and Dan Boudreau, helped me in every way possible to track down usable pieces.

I am very grateful to Wofford College, which supported summer research trips to New England in 2012, 2018, and 2023. These allowed me to pursue further research at the AAS, Yale University's Manuscripts Division, the New London County Historical Society, the Connecticut Museum of Culture and History, and the Connecticut State Library and Archives, where the indefatigable Mel Smith helped uncover a veritable treasure trove of hidden pieces. Wim Klooster, Steven Bullock, and David Hancock shared their usual penetrating insights during this time, and a roundtable at the AHA in 2011 with Michael Kwass, Jesse Cromwell, and Thomas Truxes proved crucial in broadening my initial perspective.

The hard work of expanded research and crafting the first manuscript began when I held the Marie L. and William R. Hartland Fellowship at the John Carter Brown Library in 2016. I am grateful for the enormous help and advice of Director Neil Safier, Kimberly Nusco, Val Andrews, and Allison Rich, among so many others. Discussions with many fellows, especially Rebecca Earle, Anne Ruderman, Johnhenry Gonzalez, and once again, the amazing Bertrand van Ruymbeke, were essential to crafting a first draft. I shared an early draft of chapter 4 at an Omohundro Colloquia in 2021, receiving invaluable commentary.

At Wofford, my colleagues Tracy Revels, Anne Rodrick, and Mark Byrnes discussed and critiqued portions of that manuscript. Students in my History 309 classes read and critiqued some early chapters, helping me reach out to a new generation of readers. I cannot forget the dedicated efforts of Wofford's Inter-Library Loan staff, who collectively obtained for me more than six hundred monographs and articles.

Collecting, sorting, and placing the pieces is not enough. At the University of Virginia Press, Nadine Zimmerli patiently and perceptively steered me toward a shorter, sharper, and more colorful final version of the completed puzzle. I also owe a huge debt to Nadine's excellent colleagues, including Ellen Satrom and Kirsten Stewart, and copyeditor Marjorie Pannell. I am very grateful for the insightful suggestions of peer review readers Christian Koot, Eliga Gould (who also first urged me to contact the University of Virginia Press), and an anonymous reader.

Piecing together the puzzle of Allen and his family became an undertaking for *my* family. In New England, my late brother Andy and his wife, Diane, provided good cheer and many kindnesses that I cannot now ever repay. My sister, Mikie, and older brother, Joel, read through an embarrassingly cumbersome second draft. Alex Rizzo-Banks spent many hours deciphering Allen's account entries, which proved essential for chapter 4. My other now adult children—Dylan, Morgan, Donner, and Emile—all fitted pieces into the emerging picture over the years. Above all, my partner and colleague Tracey Rizzo shared her keen insights on the project over two decades. Through discussions concrete and theoretical, she helped me explore alternate dimensions, shared her vast knowledge and wisdom on history, and provided loving support through many frustrations.

Thank you all. I gratefully acknowledge that any missing puzzle pieces are my fault alone.

Spartanburg, February 2026

NOTES

Abbreviations

ADLA	Archives Départementales de Loire-Atlantique
AFC	Allen Family Collection, American Antiquarian Society
ANB	American National Biography
ANOM	Archives Nationales d'Outre-mers
APDC	Adams Papers Digital Collection, Massachusetts Historical Society
BFBR	Brown Family Business Records, John Carter Brown Library
BNF	Bibibliothèque Nationale de France
CCR	*Public Records of the Colony of Connecticut* (*Connecticut Colonial Records*) (Hoadly, ed.)
CSR	*Public Records of the State of Connecticut* (*Connecticut State Records*) (Hoadly, ed., vols. 1–3; Labareee, ed., vols. 4–6)
CSL	Connecticut State Library and Archives
CSRNC	Colonial and State Records of North Carolina (online)
DCB	Dictionary of Canadian Biography
EEB	Early English Books Online (Proquest)
FGD	Francis Goelet Diary
JCB	John Carter Brown Library
JCC	Journals of the Continental Congress
NDAR	Naval Documents of the American Revolution
NLCC	New London County Court (in CSL)
NLCHS	New London County Historical Society
NLTC	New London Town Clerk's Office
NTSP	Nathaniel and Thomas Shaw Papers, Yale University
RIHS	Rhode Island Historical Society

B refers to box, F refers to folder, L refers to ledger, and q. refers to quotation.

Introduction

1. General works: Fisher, "The Twenty-Eight Charges Against the King in the Declaration of Independence"; Becker, *The Declaration of Independence;* Pencak, "The Declaration of Independence," esp. 231–33; Maier, *American Scripture;* Armitage, *The Declaration of Independence;* Anastaplo, *Reflections on Constitutional Law,* chap. 3; Pincus, *The Heart of the Declaration;* Law, *The Founder's Revolution,* chaps. 3–5. Jefferson cited in Wood, *Empire of Liberty,* q. on 625.
2. Grievances 19, 24, and 26: Lemisch, "Jack Tar in the Streets"; Magra, *Poseidon's Curse,* 2–3 and chaps. 9–10; Gilje, *Free Trade and Sailors' Rights,* chap. 5; Brunsman, *The Evil Necessity,* esp. 241–45.
3. Grievances 7, 16, and 23: Grievance 16 refers to the New England Trade and Fisheries Act, 15 George III, cap. 10, Mar. 30, 1775, and the act curbing colonial trade south of New England, 15 George III, cap. 18, Apr. 13, 1775; see also Magra, *The Fisherman's Cause,* chap. 7. Grievance 23: 15 George III, cap. 3, "An Act to Prohibit All Trade . . . with the Colonies . . ."; Lynd and Waldstreicher, "Free Trade, Sovereignty, and Slavery," 609–15.
4. Grievances 8–14 and 17–18: Vile, *The Declaration of Independence,* esp. 38–39, 94–95, 117–19, 164–65, 193, 226–27, 276–78, 295–96, 308–9. The Royal Navy/Admiralty: Fisher, "The Twenty-Eight Charges Against the King in the Declaration of Independence." Congress issued a similar set of objections in September 1774. See Pennsylvania *Packet,* Oct. 31, 1774, 4. Customs ports: Barrow, *Trade and Empire,* appendix D, 269–72.
5. Grievances 4 and 5: Vile, *The Declaration of Independence,* 30–31, 82–83. Fleeing royal governors: reference is to John Murray, Earl of Dunmore (Virginia, June 1775), Josiah Martin (North Carolina, July 1775), and William Tryon (New York, October 1775).
6. Grievance 20 (Quebec Act): 14 George III, cap. 83, "An Act for making more effectual Provision for the Government of the Province of Quebec in North America," June 22, 1774, preamble and clause 1; Whiteley, "Newfoundland, Quebec, and the Administration of the Coast of Labrador"; Lennox, "Seeing Red."
7. Pincus, *The Heart of the Declaration,* 114–15, q. on 114. See also Perl-Rosenthal, *Citizen Sailors,* 46–54, and Lynd and Waldstreicher, "Free Trade, Sovereignty, and Slavery."
8. Jarvis, *In the Eye of All Trade, 1680–1783,* q. on 1.
9. Breen, *The Will of the People,* esp. 3–6, q. on 5; Nash, *The Unknown American Revolution,* esp. xiii–xiv, xx–xvii.
10. Lemisch, "Jack Tar in the Streets"; Rediker, *Between the Devil and the Deep Blue Sea;* Linebaugh and Rediker, *The Many-Headed Hydra;* Gilje, *Liberty on the Waterfront;* Perl-Rosenthal, *Citizen Sailors,* esp. chap. 2.
11. Sailors of African descent: Bolster, *Black Jacks;* Farr, *Black Odyssey;* Cecelski, *The Waterman's Song,* esp. chaps. 1–3; Harris, *Patroons and Periaguas;* Nash, *Forging Freedom,* 134–71.
12. Settler women in ports: Creighton and Norling, *Iron Men, Wooden Women;* Crane, *Ebb Tide in New England;* Norling, *Captain Ahab Had a Wife;* Cleary and Murray, *Elizabeth Murray,* chap. 2; Wulf, *Not All Wives,* chap. 4; Vickers and Walsh, *Young Men and the*

Sea, chap. 5; Catterall and Campbell, "Introduction: Mother Courage and Her Sisters," 1–36; Main, "Women on the Edge." An applicable nineteenth-century study is Doe, *Enterprising Women and Shipping in the Nineteenth Century*, chap. 2.

13. For example, Price, "What Did Merchants Do?"; Doerflinger, "Philadelphia Merchants," and Doerflinger, *A Vigorous Spirit of Enterprise;* Matson, *Merchants & Empire;* Hart and Matson, "Situating Merchants in Late Eighteenth-Century British Atlantic Port Cities"; Goloboy, *Charleston and the Emergence of Middle-Class Culture;* Land, *Colonial Ports, Global Trade;* Truxes, *Overseas Trade*. Commodities and enslavement: for example, Hancock, *Oceans of Wine;* DuPlessis, *The Material Atlantic;* Smith, "Gedney Clarke of Salem and Barbados"; Clark-Pujara, *Dark Work;* Kelley, *The Voyage of the Slave Ship Hare*, chaps. 1 and 9.
14. For example, Fowler, *Rebels Under Sail;* Norton, *Captains Contentious;* Nelson, *George Washington's Secret Navy;* McGrath, *Give Me a Fast Ship;* Dolin, *Rebels at Sea;* Hulbert, *The Untold War at Sea*.
15. Especially useful Atlantic World or oceanic studies include Bailyn, *Atlantic History;* Burnard and Vidal, "Location and Conceptualization of Historical Frameworks"; Bolster, "Putting the Ocean in Atlantic History"; Flayhart, "Oceanic Historiography"; Bentley, "Sea and Ocean Basins as Frameworks of Historical Analysis"; Wigen, "Introduction"; Polónia, "Maritime History"; Jarvis, *In the Eye of All Trade*, 1–7.
16. Pares, *War and Trade in the West Indies;* Anderson, *The Crucible of War*, xvii–xxii; Kimball, "What Have We to Do with Slavery?," and Kimball, "An Essential Link in a Vast Chain," esp. 11–17; O'Shaughnessy, *An Empire Divided*, xi–xvi, 238–44; O'Malley, "Beyond the Middle Passage," 157–58; Kelley, *American Slavers*, 123–34. Caribbean Basin overview: Morgan, "The Caribbean Environment to 1850," 19–129.
17. Rediker, *Between the Devil and the Deep Blue Sea*, 1–9, 84, 101–6, 207–20; q. on 212. See also Linebaugh and Rediker, *The Many-Headed Hydra*, 160–62, 168–69; Vickers, "An Honest Tar"; Norton, "Temporality, Isolation, and Violence"; Perl-Rosenthal, *Citizen Sailors*, esp. chap. 3; Magra, *Poseidon's Curse*, esp. chap. 10.
18. Vickers and Walsh, *Young Men and the Sea*, 221–26, 241–46; Vickers, *Farmers & Fishermen*, 152n12; Jarvis, *In the Eye of All Trade*, esp. chap. 5; Gilje, *Liberty on the Waterfront*, 14–19; Heyrman, *Commerce and Culture*, 161–72, 254–59. French and Dutch Caribbean ports: Moore, *Louisbourg Portaits*, chap. 3; Cabantous, *Les citoyens du large*, esp. chap. 3; Rupert, *Creolization and Contraband*, 141–64.
19. Vickers and Walsh, "Young Men and the Sea," q. on 21. Seaborne capital sources: Doerflinger, *A Vigorous Spirit*, 50–55, 116–18; McCusker and Menard, *The Economy of British America*, esp. 72, 75–76, 80–84 (esp. 80n15), 109–11, 155–56, 321, 334–37; compare with Lamoreaux, "Rethinking the Transition to Capitalism."
20. Overviews of contraband: for example, Klooster, "Inter-Imperial Smuggling"; Karras, *Smuggling*, esp. chaps. 1 and 2; Rupert, *Creolization and Contraband;* Kwass, *Contraband;* Schmitt, "Virtue in Corruption"; Banks, "Contraband."
21. Smith, *The Wealth of Nations*, 1138–40, q. on 1139. See also Harper, *The English Navigation Laws*, esp. chaps. 13–17; Dickerson, *The Navigation Acts and the American Revolution*, esp. chaps 1 and 9; Southwick, "The Molasses Act"; Sawers, "The Navigation Acts Revisited"; Frese, "Smuggling, the Navy, and the Customs Service,"199–212; Tyler, *Smugglers and Patriots*, 8–20; Truxes, *Defying Empire*, "Introduction"; Chet, *The Ocean Is a Wilderness*, chap. 4; Reeder, *Smugglers, Pirates, and Patriots*, 13–16, 37–45. Critiques

of Mercantilism: for example, Barth, "Reconstructing Mercantilism"; Pincus, "Rethinking Mercantilism."

22. Hunt, *The Middling Sort,* esp. 12–20, q. on 20. See also Matson, *Merchants & Empire,* 203–14, 270–74, 301–8; Dierks, "Middle-Class Formation in Eighteenth-Century North America," 99–108; Gilje, *The Road to Mobocracy,* 28–32, 176–78, 242–46, 303–15; Hemphill, "Manners and Class in the Revolutionary Era"; Goloboy, "The Early American Middle Class," 537–45. Connecticut: Main, *Connecticut Society in the Era of the American Revolution,* 39–42, and Main, *Society and Economy in Colonial Connecticut,* 290–94.
23. Franklin: for example, Morgan, *Benjamin Franklin,* 104–28, 145–85; 242–51; Houston, *Benjamin Franklin and the Politics of Improvement,* chap. 1; Wood, *The Americanization of Benjamin Franklin,* 104–51, 183–209; Gallagher, "The Rhetorical Strategy of Franklin's 'Way to Wealth,'" esp. 475–85. "Self-made men": Weber, *The Protestant Ethic and the Spirit of Capitalism,* esp. 14–16, 27–28, 103–4; Wyllie, *The Self-Made Man in America,* 13–20, 40–45; Landsman, *From Colonials to Provincials,* 52–54; Zakim, "The Business Clerk as Social Revolutionary," esp. 600–603; Paul, *Myths That Made America,* 369–73.
24. "Rogue": Oxford English Dictionary Online; Mentz and Dionne, *Rogues and Early Modern English Culture,* esp. 1–10; Basdeo, https://reynolds-news.com/2016/01/25/rogues-in-early-modern-england/, q.; Liberman, "Old Slang: Rogue," https://blog.oup.com/2010/05/old-slang-rogue/.
25. Horatio Gates: Nelson, *General Horatio Gates,* 6–34 passim. Robert Morris: Rappleye, *Robert Morris,* 7–15. Christopher Gadsden: McDonough, *Christopher Gadsden and Henry Laurens,* 16–17. Francis Marion: Bass, *Swamp Fox,* 6–7. Paul Cuffe: Harris, *Paul Cuffee,* 17; Thomas, *Paul Cuffe.* 3; Farr, *Black Odyssey,* 176–78. Carter Braxton: Dill, *Carter Braxton,* 10, 20, 22–23. Benedict Arnold: Brandt, *The Man in the Mirror,* 7–18; Martin, *Benedict Arnold,* 33–51 passim.
26. Taylor, *American Revolutions,* 4–6, 61–62; DuVal, *Independence Lost,* xiii–xxi; McDonnell and Waldstreicher, "Revolution in the *Quarterly?,*" esp. 662–63; Gould and Zagarri, "Situating the United States in Vast Early America," esp. 192–96.
27. Wolfe, *Settler Colonialism,* 1–6; Ostler and Shoemaker, "Settler Colonialism in Early American History"; Greer, "Settler Colonialism and Empire in Early America"; Smallwood, "Reflections on Settler Colonialism."

Prologue

1. General Description of Westminster and London based on Edward Ward, *London Spy Compleat in Eighteen parts* (London, 4th ed., 1709) 29–31, 47–49, 149–51, 281–83 (https://archive.org/details/bim_eighteenth-century_the-london-spy-compleat-_ward-edward_1709_1); FGD, entries for Jan. 31, 1747–Apr. 24, 1747 inclusive and Dec. 21, 1750–Apr. 30, 1751; Porter, *English Society in the Eighteenth Century,* 39–47; George, *London Life in the Eighteenth Century,* 1–11, 63–85; Greig, *The Beau Mónde,* 7–12, 66–94; Almeroth-Williams, *City of Beasts,* esp. 40–61, 160–62; White, *A Great and Monstrous Thing,* 4–9, 36–43. Illustrated sources used in description: Nathaniel Buck, "Panorama of London: Drawing taken from Mr. Watson's Summer House opposite to Somerset House," c. 1749 (https://www.londonmuseum.org.uk/collections/v/object-101940/panorama-of-london-drawing-taken-from-mr-watsons-summer-house-opposite-to-somerset-house/); Thomas Jefferys, "A new and exact plan of the city's

of London and Westminster, the borough of Southwark, and the additional new buildings churches &c. to the present year 1735 . . ." (https://collections.leventhalmap.org/search/commonwealth:4m90fn31g); John Rocque, "A Plan of the cities of London and Westminster, and borough of Southwark, with the contiguous buildings," 1746 (https://www.loc.gov/item/76696823/).

2. Armitage, *The Ideological Origins of the British Empire,* 170–81, q. on 173.
3. Westminster: Ward, *London Spy Compleat,* 47–49, 149–55; Greig, *The Beau Monde,* 137–40. Illustrated source used in description: Giovanni Antonio Canal (Canaletto), "View of London and Whitehall from the Privy Garden,"1747 (https://commons.wikimedia.org/wiki/File:Giovanni_Antonio_Canal,_il_Canaletto_-_London_-_Whitehall_and_the_Privy_Garden_from_Richmond_House_-_WGA03943.jpg).
4. Baugh, *British Naval Administration in the Age of Walpole,* 29–38, 61–66; Brewer, *The Sinews of Power,* 66–85; Kinkel, *Disciplining the Empire,* 10–12, 54–56, 65–75; Wilkinson, *The British Navy and the State in the Eighteenth Century,* 19–27; Morriss, *The Foundations of British Maritime Ascendancy,* 34–46. Illustrated source used in description: John Bowles, "The Admiralty Office," 1731 (https://www.londonmuseum.org.uk/collections/v/object-92879/the-admiralty-office/).
5. Henretta, *"Salutary Neglect,"* esp. chaps. 1–3, q. on 145; Olson, *Making the Empire Work,* 104–5, 110–25; Steele, *Politics of Colonial Policy,* 25–28, 152–65; Brewer, "The Myth of 'Salutary Neglect'"; Land, *Colonial Ports, Global Trade,* 6–7, chap. 6.
6. Brewer, *The Sinews of Power,* 231–43. French colonial administration: Banks, *Chasing Empire Across the Sea,* esp. chap. 1; Pritchard, *In Search of Empire,* 241–63.
7. 6 George II, cap. 13, "The Molasses Act"; Southwick, "The Molasses Act"; Sheridan, "The Molasses Act."
8. FGD, entry for Jan. 30, 1747, and note of same date; White, *A Great and Monstrous Thing,* 224–26. Illustrated source used in description: F. H. W. Sheppard, "Piccadilly, South Side," British History Online (https://www.british-history.ac.uk/survey-london/vols29-30/pt1/pp251-270).
9. Olson, *Making the Empire Work,* 99–104, 219n.
10. Bowen, "The Bank of England During the Log Eighteenth Century"; Brewer, *The Sinews of Power,* 114–26, 132–34.
11. Flavell, *When London Was Capital of America,* 85–93. London coffeehouses: Ward, *London Spy Compleat,* 209–11, 297–98; FGD, entries of Feb. 15–28, 1746/47, and Dec. 10–25, 1750, q. from entry for Dec. 20, 1750; Rudé, *Hanoverian London,* 77–79; Lillywhite, *London Coffee Houses,* 21–22, 216–21 (Garraway's), 330–32 (Lloyd's); White, *A Great and Monstrous Thing,* 181–82.
12. Lillywhite, *London Coffee Houses,* 282–84 (Jamaica), 387–88 (New England), also 147–48, 407–8, 444–45, 622–23; George, *London Life in the Eighteenth Century,* 134–38; Shyllon, *Black People in Britain,* 84–88, 94–97; Sheridan, *Sugar and Slavery,* 60–66, 294–305; Gerzina, *Black London,* 13–24 passim, 76–77; White, *A Great and Monstrous Thing,* 127–37.
13. Hancock, *Citizens of the World,* 88–94, q. on 90; Pares, *A West-India Fortune,* 175, 357; Olson, "The London Mercantile Lobby," 22–26; White, *A Great and Monstrous Thing,* 137–49.
14. Illustrated source used in description: T. Simpson, "Engraving of East India House," 1766 (https://commons.wikimedia.org/wiki/File:E_India_House.jpg); Robins, *The*

Corporation That Changed the World, 8–9; Sutton, *East India Company's Maritime Service,* 19–20.

15. Hayes, *Rules for the Port of London;* Hoon, *The Organization of the English Customs System,* esp. chap. 3; Brewer, *The Sinews of Power,* 91–101, 215–16; Ashworth, *Customs and Excise,* esp. chap. 1.
16. Description of dock district: Rediker, *Between the Devil and the Deep Blue Sea,* 21–31, q. on 21; Ward, *London Spy Compleat,* 281–83; JCB, A Citizen of London, *New and Compleat Survey of London* (London, 1742), 113–15; George, *London Life in the Eighteenth Century,* 138–40; Rudé, *Hanoverian London,* 21–25, 58–60; Shyllon, *Black People in Britain,* 122–28; White, *A Great and Monstrous Thing,* 32, 167–69. Illustrated source used in description: Louis-Philippe Boitard, "Imports of Great Britain from France," 1757 (https://collections.vam.ac.uk/item/O1240590/the-imports-of-great-britain-engraving-louis-philippe-boitard/?carousel-image=2012FE6270).
17. Robins, *The Corporation That Changed the World,* 20–21; Sutton, *The East India Company's Maritime Service,* 4, 21, 36–38.
18. Frénée, "Pirates and Gallows at Execution Dock."

1. The Apprentice

1. Phinney, *A Brief History of Lewis Allen,* 4–5, q. on 5; Steele, *The English Atlantic,* 182–88; Aggarwala, "I want a Packet to Arrive"; McCusker, "New York City and the Bristol Packet."
2. Games, "Migration," 31–50; Fogleman, "Migrations to the Thirteen British North American Colonies," table 1 (698); Bailyn and DeWolfe, *Voyagers to the West,* 24–28, 208–11; Fischer, *Albions's Seed,* 605–15; Richards, *Britannia's Children,* 67–90; Wokeck, *Trade in Strangers,* 37–54.
3. Data derived from https://www.slavevoyages.org/; Inikori, "Introduction"; Morton-Williams, "The Oyo Yoruba and the Atlantic Trade"; Eltis, *The Rise of African Slavery in the Americas,* chaps. 2 and 9; and Thornton, *Africa and Africans in the Making of the Atlantic World,* chap. 4. Backcountry: Rindfleisch, "Family, Linen, and Emigration in Ulster," esp. 140–43; Wokeck, *Trade in Strangers,* chap. 4.
4. Peterson, *The City-State of Boston,* 250–55; DeLucia, *Memory Lands,* 33–38. Fishing and whaling: Cumming, "Colonial Charting of the Massachusetts Coast"; Vickers, *Farmers & Fishermen,* 116–24, 145–57, 192–94, 276–79; Magra, *The Fisherman's Cause,* 6–8, 19–25. Illustrated sources used in description of Boston Harbor: John Bonner, "The Town of Boston in New England, 1722" (3rd printing, 1725) (https://www.masshist.org/database/viewer.php?old=1&item_id=1783); Cyprian Southack, "A correct map of the coast of New England," 1758–1760 (https://collections.leventhalmap.org/search/commonwealth:cj82m0337).
5. Description of Boston town ca. 1730s based largely on Hamilton, "Itinerarium of Dr. Alexander Hamilton," 256–63; FGD, entries of Nov. 7–8, 1750; Nash, *The Urban Crucible,* 65–74; Griffin, *Old Brick,* chap. 1; Warden, *Boston, 1689–1776,* chap. 2; Rediker, *Between the Devil and the Deep Blue Sea,* 62–66; Lemay, *The Life of Benjamin Franklin,* vol. 1, chap. 1; Kamensky, *A Revolution in Color,* 11–17; Peterson, *The City-State of Boston,* chap. 5; Kornwolf and Kornwolf, *Architecture and Town Planning,* 2:959–63, 975–78. Illustrated source used in this description: John Carwitham, "A south east view of

the great city of Boston in America," c.1730–1760 (https://www.loc.gov/resource/pga.04612/). With apologies to Anne Rice.

6. Abenaki delegations: for example, Boston *Gazette,* July 29, 1734, 3; Housatonic Indians, Boston *Evening Post,* Nov. 29, 1736; as Christian converts, New England *Weekly Journal,* Aug. 3, 1736, 2; sailors: Weekly Rehearsal, Mar. 26, 1733, 2; "Indian" servant women: Boston *News-Letter,* Aug. 9, 1733, 2. Mohawk visit in Hamilton, "Itinerarium of Dr. Alexander Hamilton," 260. Enslaved Africans: for example, "Sale of Negroes," Boston *Gazette,* Apr. 2, 1733, 4; New England *Weekly Journal,* May 13, 1734, 2; Boston *Gazette,* Jan. 6, 1735, 4. Runaways: Boston *Gazette,* Oct. 21, 1734, 4; New England *Weekly Journal,* Nov. 4, 1735, 2; "Give away" of a "Negro child," New England *Weekly Journal,* Feb. 25, 1734, 2.
7. "Disorderly houses": for example, Boston *Gazette,* Aug. 2, 1733, 2, and Sept. 17, 1733, 2. Mobs: Warden, *Boston, 1689–1776,* chap. 6; Nash, *The Urban Crucible,* 70–74, 80–87.
8. Art of conversation in settler Boston: Hamilton, "Itinerarium of Dr. Alexander Hamilton," 258–62; Maier, "Boston and New York in the Eighteenth Century," esp. 189–92; Franklin, *Short Account,* cited in Huang, "Franklin's Father Josiah," 109.
9. Allen Sr.'s voyages: for example, AFC, fol. 1, "Disbursements . . . for the Sloop *Three Friends,*" Feb. 1734–May 1736, images nos. 6–8, 10, 12–28, 88; voyage examples in Boston *Weekly News-Letter,* May 9, 1734, 2, and June 19, 1735, 2; New England *Weekly Journal,* June 15, 1736, 2; Boston *Evening-Post,* Oct. 10, 1737, 2; New England *Weekly Journal,* Jan. 15, 1740, 2. Similar sea captain: Cumming, "The Turbulent Life of Captain James Wimble." Chesapeake grain exports: for example, Klingaman, "The Development of the Coastwise Trade of Virginia"; Kulikoff, "The Economic Growth of the Eighteenth-Century Chesapeake Colonies."
10. War: Harding, *The Emergence of Britain's Global Naval Supremacy,* 39–86; Black, *Fighting for America,* chap. 4. Eighteenth-century shopkeeping: for example, Mui and Mui, *Shops and Shopkeeping;* Cleary and Murray, *Elizabeth Murray,* esp. 45–65; Hartigan-O'Connor, *The Ties That Buy,* 151–56. Shop advertisement examples: Boston *Evening-Post,* May 9, 1743, 3, and Nov. 5, 1744, 4; Boston *Post-Boy,* Dec. 31, 1744, 4.
11. Textiles: DuPlessis, *The Material Atlantic,* esp. 215–24; Lucas and Campbell, "Economic Significance of Cloth and Apparel," 213–26, 235–47; Hood, "The Material World of Cloth." AFC, fol. 2A, Nathaniel Allen to Henry Allen (no relation), Mar. 11, 1748, q.; Nathaniel Allen to William Wellbank, May 21, 1747; Nathaniel Allen to Thomas Lane, Oct. 26, 1748. Advertisement examples: Boston *Evening-Post,* Sept. 26, 1743, 4, and Nov. 19, 1744, 4; Boston *Post-Boy,* Dec. 31, 1744, 4.
12. Hart and Matson, "Situating Merchants in Late Eighteenth-Century British Atlantic Port Cities," q. on 660; Gould, "Entangled Atlantic Histories." Correspondents: AFC, fol. 2A, Nathaniel Allen Letterbook, Daybook, 1744–1754: Gardener and Shaw, 27; James Browne, numerous entries starting Aug. 17, 1748; and Tillinghast, Oct. 6, 1749. AFC, B1F1, John Shackmaple to Nathaniel Allen, Dec. 25, 1737.
13. AFC, fol. 2A, Nathaniel Allen Letterbook, 1747–1754, Nathaniel Allen to Lane and Caswell, Nov. 17, 1747; Nathaniel Allen to William Wellbank, Nov. 23, 1747, 1st and 2nd qq; Nathaniel Allen to William Wellbank, Dec. 24, 1748; Nathaniel Allen to Thomas Lane, May 3, 1749, 3rd q. Dry goods: Doerflinger, A *Vigorous Spirit of Enterprise,* 88–96, 138; Matson, *Merchants & Empire,* 130–31.

14. Axtell, *The School Upon a Hill,* 175–78, 282–88, 1st q. on 286; Cremin, *American Education,* 180–91, 387–95, 479–509, 521–47 passim, 2nd q. on 394. See also Lockridge, *Literacy in Colonial New England,* 52–57; Monaghan, "Literacy Instruction and Gender in Colonial New England"; Middlekauff, *Ancients and Axioms,* 63–102; Vinovskis, *Education, Society, and Economic Opportunity,* 5–9.
15. Rough articulation: RIHS, *The Letter Book of James Browne of Providence, merchant, 1735–1738,* vii, 17–60; Beekman and Beekman, *Beekman Mercantile Papers,* 1:3–175. Penmanship practicing: examples AFC, B7F1, Accounts of C. Christophers, inside cover, Oct. 1763; AFC, fol. 5, inside front and back covers, and fol. 6, back cover, 1758. Literacy essential for maritime advancement: Earle, "The Origins and Careers of English Merchant Seamen," esp. 131–33.
16. Rise of numeracy: Tollnek and Baten, "Farmers at the Heart of the 'Human Capital Revolution'?"; Edwards, "A Business Education for 'the Middling Sort of People.'" In settler schools: for example, Cremin, *American Education,* 362, 376, 501–3; Holmes et al., *Three Centuries of Accounting in Massachusetts,* chap. 4; Cohen, *Calculating People,* 39–42, 118–25.
17. History of double-entry bookkeeping: for example, De Roover, "New Perspectives on Medieval Accounting"; Yamey, "Notes on the Origins of Double-Entry bookkeeping"; Yamey et al., *Accounting in England and Scotland, 1543–1800;* Edwards and Walker, *The Routledge Companion to Accounting History,* 52–59, 95–119. The Enlightenment and accounting: John Mair, *Book-Keeping Methodiz'd, or a methodical treatment of merchant-accompts . . . ,* 3rd ed. (Edinburgh, 1749), vi–xi, 1st q. on viii; May, *The Enlightenment in America,* 2nd q. on 2.
18. Mair, *Bookkeeping Methodiz'd,* 5–20; JCB, Thomas Crosby, *The Book-keeper's Guide . . .* (London, 1749), 49–85; JCB, Alexander Malcolm, *A Treatise on Book-Keeping* (London, 1731), esp. 3–33. Book credit: Baxter, "Credit, Bills, and Bookkeeping"; Coleman et al., "Accounting in Colonial Virginia"; Smith, "The Account Book of Richard Poor." French equivalent: JCB, Aulnais, *Guide de Commerce,* Seconde partie (Paris, 1771), esp. 43–154. Accounting across cultures: for example, Braudel, *Civilization & Capitalism,* 2:572–75; Roche, *France in the Enlightenment,* 161–67; Gervais, "A Merchant or a French Atlantic?"
19. Ditz, "Formative Ventures," 1st q. on 63. British Atlantic mercantile networks: for example, Price, "What Did Merchants Do?"; Smith, "Gedney Clarke of Salem and Barbados"; Grassby, *Kinship and Capitalism,* 297–305; Hart and Matson, "Situating Merchants in Late Eighteenth-Century British Atlantic Port Cities," 670–74; Dierks, *In My Power,* chap. 2. AFC, B8F4, Jabez Huntington (Norwich) to Allen, Sept. 12, 1789, 2nd q.
20. Martin, "Merchants and Trade of the Connecticut River Valley": on Jeremiah Wadsworth, 75–76; on Charles Bull, 102–4, 107–8. Clerk apprentices: Hart and Matson, "Situating Merchants in Late Eighteenth-Century British Atlantic Port Cities," esp. 665–70; di Bonaventura, *For Adam's Sake,* 66–73.
21. Cited in Roche, *France in the Enlightenment,* q. on 167.
22. Shipping: for example, Davis, *The Rise of the English Shipping Industry,* esp. 63–65, 374–75; Shepherd and Walton, *Shipping, Maritime Trade,* appendix 6, 241–45; McCusker and Menard, *The Economy of British America,* 318–21, esp. 319n15. Contemporary account

of vessel ownership: Morgan, "Robert Dinwiddie's Reports on the British American Colonies," 319–23, 339–44 (for 1748). Navigation: Middlekauff, *Ancients and Axioms,* 66–67, 96–98; Thornton, "The 'Intelligent Mariner,'" 613–17; Levy-Eichel, "Suitable to the Meanest Capacity."

23. JCB, Thomas Crosby, *Mariner's Guide, being a complete Treatise . . .* (London, 1751), 23–137, 158–63, 176–83; Reid, *The Merchant Ship in the British Atlantic,* 27–29. Contemporary sailing basics: for example, Cort, *The Blue Book of Sailing,* 4–51. Equivalents in France: for example, Monsieur Bouguer, *Nouveau Traité de Navigation . . .* (Paris, 1753), basic navigation, 326–78, and sailing methods, 379–423. Shoals and islets: CANARI, *The Caribbean Islands,* 3.
24. JCB, Crosby, *Mariner's Guide,* 184–279; Thornton, "The 'Intelligent Mariner'"; Kelley, *The Voyage of the Slave Ship Hare,* 53–55.
25. Sobel, *Longitude,* esp. 2–8; Withers, *Zero Degrees,* 7–12, 39–57.
26. See Jaffee, "The Village Enlightenment in New England," q. on 339; Jaffee, *A New Nation of Goods,* chap. 2; Bertucci, apparently unaware of Jaffee, *Artisanal Enlightenment,* esp. "Introduction." Maritime Enlightenment concepts: Laloë, *Geography of the Ocean,* chap. 4; Manning and Cogliano, "Introduction"; Withers, "Where Was the Atlantic Enlightenment?"; Gilje, "The Enlightenment at Sea in the Atlantic World."
27. Mariner guides: for example, JCB, John Thornton and William Fisher, *The English Pilot, The Fourth Book: The West India Navigation* (London, 1760 ed.); manuscript logbooks: for example, AAS, Logbooks, fol. 1, Logbook of Capt. Thaddeus Maccarty, 1718–1719, and vol. 2F, Logbook of James Blakeney, 1757–1758; RIHS, James Browne, "Navigational Exercises"; RIHIS, "Logbook of the Brig Hope, 1747/48."
28. Dafoe, *Robinson Crusoe,* 12–24; Vickers, *Farmers & Fishermen,* esp. 156–88; Vickers and Walsh, *Young Men and the Sea;* 105–9, 136–41.
29. Walsh, "Recruitment and Promotion," q. on 33.

2. The Widow and the Young Captain

1. War between 1739 and 1748: Black, *Fighting for America,* chap. 4; Scott, The Birth of a *Great Power System,* chap. 2. Boston hardship: Baxter, *The House of Hancock,* esp. 193–95; Warden, *Boston, 1689–1776,* 135–41; Huang, "Financing Poor Relief," Allen père's shipping woes: AFC, fol. 2A, Nathaniel Allen to William Wellbank, Feb. 25, 1747, and Sept. 15, 1747; Nathaniel Allen to Richard Wilson, Nov. 18, 1748.
2. AFC, fol. 2A, Nathaniel Allen to Richard Wilson, Oct. 20, 1747; Nathaniel Allen to William Wellbank, Sept. 12, 1748, 1st q.; AFC, B1F1, Nathaniel Allen to Thomas Allen, Sept. 24, 1750, 2nd q. Capture of Louisbourg: Rawlyk, *Nova Scotia's Massachusetts,* chap. 9 and 177–78, 190–91; Peterson, *The City-State of Boston,* 265–77.
3. Description based on Pastore, *Between Land and Sea,* 17–27, 46–49, 53–61; Andersen, *This Fine Piece of Water,* 2–22; Meinig, *The Shaping of America,* 42–43, 92–93, 100–109; NDAR 11:616, Samuel Wolcott to Nathaniel Shaw Jr., Mar. 12, 1778, q.
4. Pequot War: Oberg, *Dominion and Civility,* 103–12; Bailyn, *The Barbarous Years,* 443–49; Cave, *The Pequot War,* chap. 4; Reflecting nineteenth-century racial biases but with additional details: Caulkins, *History of New London,* 19–38, 30–35, 118–20. Allen's arrival: AFC, B4F1, Thomas Allen to Lewis Allen, Jan. 15, 1779.

5. Caulkins, *History of New London,* 6–9, 76, 81, 95, 122–23, q. on 122; Daniels, *The Connecticut Town,* 15–17, 186–90. Norwich: Caulkins, *History of Norwich,* 18–25, 60–72; Daniels, *The Connecticut Town,* 20–27, 186–90.
6. Physical description of New London: Caulkins, *History of New London,* 62–65, 258–63, 401–2, 440–48; di Bonaventura, *For Adam's Sake,* maps xi–xii, 51–52, 109–12, 235–36, 285–306 passim; Kornwolf and Kornwolf, *Architecture and Town Planning,* 2:1015–17.
7. Hamilton, "The Itinerarium of Dr. Alexander Hamilton," 248–49, q. on 248.
8. Di Bonaventura, *For Adam's Sake,* 1st q. on 111, 2nd q. on 91, 3rd q. on 208–9; Caulkins, *History of New London,* 14–15, 253; Rev. Matthew Stewart, cited in Hallam, *Annals of St. James's,* 4th q. on 35.
9. Polónia, "Seaports as Centres of Economic Growth," q. on 388, and Polónia, "The European Seaport System"; Bolster, *The Mortal Sea,* 51–52. Compare with more expansive "foreland": Land, *Colonial Ports, Global Trade,* 15–24. Roney, "Introduction," esp. 649–52; Morgan, "Building British Atlantic Port Cities," esp. 214–17; Jackson, *The History and Archaeology of Ports,* 36–41, q. on 39.
10. Caulkins, *History of New London,* 1st q. on 229, and 235–42, 390; Daniels, *The Connecticut Town,* 146–48; Van Dusen, "The Trade of Revolutionary Connecticut," 2nd q. on 7; Avitable, "The Atlantic World Economy," 103, 273–78.
11. Cronon, *Changes in the Land,* 22–46, and citing Thomas Morton, *New English Canaan,* both qq. on 30–31. Coastal fish and shellfish: Caulkins, *History of New London,* 118, 124, 212, 287, 610–11, 687; Pastore, *Between Land and Sea,* 24–30, 148–53, 206–8; Andersen, *This Fine Piece of Water,* 82–87; 134–38; DeLucia, *Memory Lands,* 32–34. "Salt hay" fertilizer: Caulkins, *History of New London,* 82; examples, AFC, fol. 37, Farm Accounts 1782, entries for work completed Apr. 13, Apr. 20–27, and Aug. 26, 1782.
12. Classic hinterland description: Sargent, *Seaports & Hinterlands,* 4–14; Polónia, "The European Seaport System," esp. 152; Jackson, *Hull in the Eighteenth Century,* chap. 2; Meinig, *The Shaping of America,* 257–67. Livestock: Lemon, *The Best Poor Man's Country,* 152–55, 161–68; Cronon, *Changes in the Land,* 128–51; Pastore, *Between Land and Sea,* 64–75; Anderson, *Creatures of Empire,* 2004, chap. 5; Hart, "From Field to Plate." New London and livestock trade: Caulkins, *History of New London,* 81–82, 230–34, 270–87 passim, 306–7; Avitable, "The Atlantic World Economy," 103–7, 119–20; di Bonaventura, *For Adam's Sake,* 240–48.
13. AFC, fol. 2A, "Account of Mr. Thomas Allen of New London," Sept. 10–18, 1750; CSL, NLCC, B89, F8, no. 8, Writ of Summons by Thomas Allen ("Late of Boston, now residing in New London"), Feb. 27, 1749/1750; ibid., F1, no. 47, Writ of Summons by Thomas Allen, May 25, 1750. Connections with father: AFC, fol. 2, "Thomas Allen of New London," Sept. 18, 1750. Early voyages: AFC, B1F1, Nathaniel Allen to Thomas Allen, Sept. 24, 1750; AFC, B4F1, Thomas Allen to Lewis Allen, Jan. 15, 1779; New York *Gazette,* Dec. 2, 1751, 2. Currency in 1750s: £1 in Massachusetts currency was worth roughly three quarters of £1 sterling (i.e., fifteen English shillings). See Allen's accounts in AFC, fols. 4–18, and McCusker, *Money and Exchange in Europe and America,* 131–37 and tables 3.1 and 3.2.
14. Governor Saltonstall: ANB, "Gurdon Saltonstall"; Caulkins, *History of New London,* 196–98, 214–17; Bushman, *From Puritan to Yankee,* 91–102, 164–169; di Bonaventura, *For Adam's Sake,* 45–51, 98–99; Poteet, "The Lordly Prelate." Customs director Shackmaple: Nutting, "John Shackmaple," and Nutting, "Charter and Crown," 143–65; AFC,

B7F1, London Custom House commission for John Shackmaple, May 27, 1718. Family: Elizabeth, born Sept. 13, 1714; her children with John Jr. were Sarah (born July 4, 1733), Elizabeth (born Dec. 5, 1734), Lydia (born July 2, 1736), John Shackmaple Jr. (the third so named; born May 11, 1738), and Richard (born July 17, 1741); Caulkins, *History of New London,* 239, 278–79; Totten, *Christophers Genealogy,* 62–63, 90–93; Stoddard, *Genealogical History of the Allen Family,* 30–32; Hallam, *Annals of St. James's,* 17–18, 26–32.

15. Contributors to St. James included "Nathan and Abraham (Jews)." CSL, Minutes of St. James Church, 1:30–31. Economic growth: for example, Daniels, "Economic Development," 434–40; Avitable, "The Atlantic World Economy," table 2.2 (116), table 2.3 (119), 183–90, table 4.1 (277), 211, 277–84. New London Society: Davis, "A Connecticut Land Bank"; Stark, "New London Society and Connecticut Politics"; Newell, *From Dependency to Independence,* q. on 184. New Lights: For example, Bushman, *From Puritan to Yankee,* chaps. 12 and 13; Hempstead, *Diary,* 360, 377, 380, 406–7; Stout and Onuf, "James Davenport"; di Bonaventura, *For Adam's Sake,* 307–15.
16. Caulkins, *History of New London,* 388. Local epidemics: di Bonaventura, *For Adam's Sake,* 177–81, 215–18.
17. Settler women as shoreside maritime community: for example, Creighton and Norling, "Introduction," in *Iron Men, Wooden Women;* Herndon, "The Domestic Cost of Seafaring"; Vickers and Walsh, *Young Men and the Sea,* chap. 5; Crane, *Ebb Tide in New England,* 9–21; Norling, *Captain Ahab Had a Wife,* chap. 1; Jarvis, *In the Eye of All Trade,* chap. 5; Catterall and Campbell, "Introduction: Mother Courage and Her Sisters," esp. 7–9; Foy, "Maritime Populations"; Main, "Women on the Edge." "Deputy husbands": Ulrich, citing seventeenth-century author Thomas Fuller, *Good Wives,* 35–38, q. on 36.
18. Salmon, *Women and the Law of Property,* 140–47, 160–62, 168–69; Crane, *Ebb Tide in New England,* 182–87; Herndon, "The Domestic Cost of Seafaring," 63–68; di Bonaventura, *For Adam's Sake,* 189–94, 261–62, 318. Salem: Vickers and Walsh, *Young Men and the Sea,* 151.
19. Widow dowers: Geddes and Zak, "The Rule of One-Third." Beach property: New London Town Clerk's Office, Plat Book 13, 172–73, 241–42, 244–45; AFC, B8F1, "Judgement of Jesse Root & Samuel Parsons, Beach Rights of the heirs of John Shackmaple, Esq.," Mar. 26, 1783. Church pew: CSL, Minutes of St. James Church, vol. 1, 1st q. on 36. Tax rate: CSL, RG 062.95, B21, tax rates for years 1733–52, 2nd q.
20. Hempstead, *Diary,* July 27, 1754, q. on 634. Charivaris: for example, Davis, "The Reasons of Misrule"; Thompson, "Rough Music"; Stewart, "Skimmington." July 27, 1754, q. on 634; CSL, RG3, NLCC, B98F7, no. 80, Appleton v. Shackmaple, Nov. 14, 1753.
21. AFC, fol. 2, Nathaniel Allen Accounts 1747–1754, transactions from Aug. 17, 1748, to Feb. 6, 1751, inclusive; JCB, BFBR, B707, F. 1, James Brown, *Dolphin* receipts, Aug. 12, 1748, to Oct. 12, 1748, inclusive. Brown's death: JCB, Capt. Brown(e)'s copy of the *English Pilot,* 1745; Hedges, *The Browns of Providence Plantations,* 11–12; Rappleye, *Sons of Providence,* 21–22.
22. AFC, B1F1, Nathaniel Allen to Thomas Allen, Sept. 24, 1750, q.; AFC, B7F1, "Fortune in Accts Currt w/Thomas Allen."
23. AFC, fol. 4, Account of the Schooner *Dispatch,* Mar. 19, 1755, voyage from New London to Nevis; AFC, B4F1, Thomas Allen to Lewis Allen, Jan. 15, 1779, q.

3. Partners of the Caribbean

1. RIHS, James Brown(e), mss. 828, "Jornal of a voige from Rhoadisland to Sincristohers," 1747–1748, observations of Feb. 24, 1747, q.; New York *Mercury*, Jan. 28, 1754, 2; Naylor, "Logbooks," esp. 775–80. Sea and wind conditions examples: Goelet, *The Voyages and Travels of Francis Goelet*, entries for Sept. 3–Oct. 19, 1754; AFC, B1F3, Willson to Allen, Oct. 8, 1768; RIHS, Darius Sessions, "Smithfield Logbook," observations of Nov. 28, 1749–Jan. 14, 1750.
2. Ibid., Brown(e), "Jornal of a voige," observations of Feb. 20–28, 1748, 1st and 2nd qq.; AFC, B1F1, Youngs Ledyard to Thomas Allen, Oct. 31, 1755, 3rd q.
3. Hempstead, *Diary*, 38; Caulkins, *History of New London*, 651–52; RIHS, Brown(e), "'Jornal of a voige,' 1747–48"; Crosby, *Mariner's Guide*, 142–43, 323; Franklin, *Autobiography*, 32–33.
4. Landmarks examples: RIHS, James Brown(e), "Journal of a Voyage in the Snoe Nonesuch . . . to the island of Barbadoes," observation of Apr. 7, 1742; Goelet, *The Voyages and Travels of Francis Goelet*, observation of Nov. 2, 1758; Fisher and Thornton, *The English Pilot* (1760), 25–34. Illicit papers: Pitman, *The Development of the British West Indies*, 298–301; Pares, *War and Trade in the West Indies*, 397; McCusker, *Rum and the American Revolution*, 1:161–62.
5. For example, Pitman, *The Development of the British West Indies*, 231–32; Pares, *Yankees and Creoles*, 105–7; Sheridan, *Sugar and Slavery*, esp. chaps. 12 and 13. Overview of Caribbean plantations: Curtin, *The Rise and Fall of the Plantation Complex*.
6. Overview of capitalization: Truxes, *Overseas Trade*, 149–60. See also Pares, *Yankees and Creoles*, 65–74.
7. Donnadieu "Boisson de rustres"; McCusker, *Rum and the American Revolution*, 1:55–58, 318–21, and McCusker, "Business of Distilling"; Hrodèj, "L'interlope à Saint-Domingue"; Sheridan, *Sugar and Slavery*, 352–57; Pritchard, *In Search of Empire*, 124–38, 162–88; Smith, *Caribbean Rum*, 61–71; Mandelblatt, "Atlantic Consumption of French Rum."
8. France and French Island trade: for example, ANOM, Série C8[A] 47, de Givry au Ministre, May 25, 1736, fol. pp. 305–8; ibid., 60, Bompar and Hurson au Ministre, May 9, 1754, fol. pp. 240–240v.; Saintard, *Essai sur les intérêts du commerce national . . .* ; May, *Histoire économique*, 136–46; Tarrade, *Le commerce colonial*, 1:95–101; Bouëdec, *Activités maritimes*, 47–73; Lafleur, "Liens commerciaux." New France: Mathieu, *Le commerce entre la Nouvelle-France et les Antilles*, esp. chap. 3; Miquelon, *New France, 1701–1744*, chap. 7. French Island customs patrols: Banks, "Official Duplicity," 232–33, 242–44.
9. For example, Mulich, *In a Sea of Empires*, 15–26, 31–42, q. on 15; Mintz, "The Caribbean as a Socio-Cultural Area," esp. 19–21, and Mintz, *Sweetness and Power*, xv–xvii; Palmié and Scarano, "Introduction"; Moya Pons, *History of the Caribbean*, esp. chaps. 8 and 9; Blérald, *Histoire économique*, esp. chap. 1; Hauser and Kelly, "Colonies Without Frontiers," 47, 50–52; Schnurmann, "Atlantic Trade and American Identities"; Schnakenbourg, "Neutres et neutralité."
10. McCusker, *Rum and the American Revolution*, 535–39, and McCusker, "Rum Trade and the Balance of Payments"; McCusker and Menard, *The Economy of British America*, 36–37, 71–85, 155. Origins: Truxes, *Overseas Trade*, 142–45, 164–76, 200–213.
11. ADLA, *Lettres Patents . . . concernant le commerce Ētranger*, octobre 1727. See also Tarrade, *Le commerce colonial*, 1:83–95; Pritchard, *In Search of Empire*, 192, 203–8, 221–22;

Boer, "Imperfect Strangers"; Lesueur and Guibert, "Introduction: L'Exclusif"; summarized in Banks, *Chasing Empire Across the Sea,* 177–78.

12. 6 George II, Cap. 13. "Molasses Act"; Pittman, *The Development of the British West Indies,* 242–70; Southwick, "The Molasses Act"; Sheridan, *Sugar and Slavery,* 58–74, 348–57; Matson, *Merchants & Empire,* 192–96, 204–5. Reactions in support of the act: for example, *Boston News-Letter,* Apr. 5, 1734, 1st q. on 1; July 4, 1734, 2nd q. on 1; *New-England Weekly Journal,* May 22, 1732, 1.
13. Pares, *War and Trade in the West Indies,* 78–82, esp. 80n1 and 396–98. Price of molasses: AFC, B1F1, Nathaniel Allyn to Thomas Allen, Aug. 24, 1755. Traditional views: Dickerson, *The Navigation Acts and the American Revolution,* 82–84; Barrow, *Trade and Empire,* 134–37, 142–43. Compare with Matson, *Merchants & Empire,* 211–13; Land, *Colonial Ports, Global Trade,* esp. 111–17.
14. AFC, fol. 4, Accounts with Nathan Allyn, Groton; B1F1, Thomas Allen to Nathaniel Allyn, letters of Mar. 23, 1755; Apr. 4, 1755, May 24, 1755; July 24, 1755; Sept. 17, 1755.
15. Scott, "Introduction," 1st q. on 1, and "Jacob Goelet." 1–8; Goelet, *The Voyages and Travels of Francis Goelet,* entries of Oct. 21–22, 1754, and Jan. 5, 1756 [sic, 1755]; New York *Mercury,* Sept. 30, 1754, 4. AFC, B1F1, Thomas Allen to Nathaniel Allyn, Apr. 24, 1755, 2nd q.
16. Sheridan, *Sugar and Slavery,* 442–45, q. on 442. Foreign merchant communities, examples: Haagensen, *Description of the Island of St. Croix,* 43–44; Westergaard, *The Danish West Indies Under Company Rule,* 130–31, 247–48; Willis, "The Trade Between North America and the Danish West Indies," esp. 88–89, 94–103; Koot, "Anglo-Dutch Trade"; Jordaan and Wilson, "The Eighteenth-Century Dutch, Danish, and Swedish Free Ports"; Lafleur, "Familles hollandaises en Guadeloupe." Jewish Sephardim merchants: Emmanuel and Emmanuel, *History of the Jews,* esp. 213–52; Lafleur, "Les Juifs aux îles francaises du vent"; Stiefel, "Experimenting with Acceptance."
17. Delle, "Settlement Pattern of Sugar Plantations," 41–44, 54–55, q. on 55. Rise of Statia: Knappert, "Geschiedenis van de Nederlandsche Bovenwindsche Eilanden," chap. 2, pt. 2; chap. 6, pt. 2, esp. 257–61; and chap. 7, pt. 1, esp. 547–50; Hartog, History of St. Eustatius, 34–42; Goslinga, *The Dutch in the Caribbean,* chaps. 4 and 6; Klooster, Illicit Riches, 89–101; Emmer, "Jesus Christ Was Good"; Enthoven, "That Abominable Nest of Pirates," 259–71. Settler merchants called the transfer trade *Overscheppen;* see New York *Mercury,* July 30, 1759, 1.
18. De Windt: Hoff and Barta, "De Windt Families of the West Indies."
19. Oranjestad description: Hartog, *History of St. Eustatius,* 43–47, 56–59, 126; Attema, *St. Eustatius,* 5–16, 22–25, 33–37; Delle, "Settlement Pattern of Sugar Plantations," esp. 41–45; Barka, "Citizens of St. Eustatius," 224–29; Enthoven, "That Abominable Nest of Pirates," 245–52.
20. Enslaved port labor: Rupert, *Creolization and Contraband,* 129, 141–45, 155–62; Jarvis, *In the Eye of All Trade,* 106–9, 129, 145–47, 257–59; Geggus, "Major Port Towns of Saint-Domingue," 99–100, 108–10; Pérotin-Dumon, *La ville aux iles,* 547–52, 556–73.
21. Goslinga, *The Dutch in the Caribbean,* 198–212; Klooster, *Illicit Riches,* chap. 5; de Vries, "Dutch Economic Growth in Comparative-Historical Perspective," 460, table 2.
22. Goelet, *The Voyages and Travels of Francis Goelet,* entries of Oct. 22, 1754, and Jan. 5, 1755. Sea captain business: AFC, B1F1, Thomas Allen to Nathaniel Allyn, July 24, 1755; AFC, fol. 5, entries, 1–26 passim. Hammelton/Hamilton: AFC, fol. 4, James

Hammelton to Nathaniel Allyn, Mar. 20, 1755; Thomas Allen to Nathaniel Allyn, July 24, 1755. De Windt: ibid., fol. 5, 1–21, 31–35.

23. AFC, fol. 5, mahogany furniture, 3–4; hammocks, 4; cot, 4; kenting, 4; key, 6; accounting house, 1st and 2nd qq, 8 and 9, blank book and paper, 21; pistols, 12; stationery and sign, 14. French books and map: AFC, B1F1, Thomas Allen to Samuel Allen, Sept. 2, 1755, 3rd q.
24. Sloops: AFC, fol. 5, entries 3 and 9, respectively. Number of "Adventures": French Guadeloupe, six; British Georgia, two; French Grenada, one, Saint-Martin, one, and Martinique, one; Danish St. Croix, one; British New York, one; British St. Kitts, one.
25. Overview of French *Îles du Vent:* Chateau-Degat and Barfluer, "Structures et évolution," 65–120. Guadeloupe: for example, Hoy, "Changing Agricultural Land Use on Guadeloupe"; Schnakenbourg, "Statistiques pour l'histoire de l'économie de plantation en Guadeloupe et Martinique," and Schnakenbourg, "Recherche sur l'histoire du coton en Guadeloupe"; Abenon, *La Guadeloupe,* 2:79–132; Røge, *Economists and the Reinvention of Empire,* 24–38.
26. AFC, fol. 5, "Adventure to Grand Terre," entries of July 16, 1755, 16; purchase of *Charming Peggy,* July 22, 1755, 9; July 27, 1755, 10; various voyage accounts, July 30, 1755, 10–11, July 30, 1755, 12, Aug. 1, 1755, 12, Aug. 7, 1755, 12, Aug. 10, 1755, 12–13, part repayment for *Charming Peggy;* omitted entries, July 28–31, 1755, 15; Aug. 12, 1755, 13; paying sailor's wages, Sept. 14, 1755, 22; Sept. 9, 1755, 23.
27. Pennsylvania *Gazette,* Sept. 4, 1755, 2.
28. AFC, B1F1, Nathaniel Allyn to Thomas Allen, Aug. 24, 1755.
29. AFC, B1F1, Gurdon Saltonstall to Thomas Allen, Oct. 6, 1755, q.; Stein, *The French Sugar Business,* 70–73.
30. McCusker, "Business of Distilling."
31. Rumors of war: AFC, B1F1, Thomas Allen to Nathaniel Allyn, Aug. 24, 1755, and Youngs Ledyard to Thomas Allen, Oct. 31, 1755. Declarations: JCB, Broadsides, no. 7738, "His Majesty's Declaration," dated May 17, 1756; New York *Mercury,* July 26, 1756, 2.

4. In the Shadow of Statia Rock

1. Allen's return: AFC, fol. 4, Nathan Allyn, his Account with Thomas Allen of St Eustatius (Aug. 8, 1755–July 31, 1756); fol. 6, entry of Dec. 3, 1756. Initial views on smuggling: Morgan, "Robert Dinwiddie's Reports on the British American Colonies," q. on 333. JCB, Anonymous, *A Short View of the Encroachments of the French* (London, 1750), esp. 12–14; JCB, Postlethwayt and Augustus, *A Short State of the Progress of French Trade* (London, 1756), 1–16, 52–57.
2. AFC, B4F2, Charles Arding to Allen, Nov. 18, 1783.
3. AFC, B4F2, insert in fol. 7, Estate of Richard Shackmaple Jr., May 29, 1758.
4. Enslaved lodging: Dunn, *Sugar and Slaves,* 248–49; Isaac, *The Transformation of Virginia,* 30–32; di Bonaventura, *For Adam's Sake,* 113, 228. Ship captain examples: AFC, fol. 5, 72, 93.
5. Embargoes: Connecticut: AFC, B1F1, Nathaniel Allyn to Thomas Allen, Aug. 24, 1755; CCR 9: Embargo of March 1758, 105–7; NLCHS, New London *Summary,* June 6, 1760, 2. Massachusetts: AFC, B1F1, Samuel Allen to Allen, Dec. 6, 1755. Overviews of trade

embargoes include Pares, *War and Trade in the West Indies,* 426–46, and Truxes, *Defying Empire,* 67–68.

6. AFC, fol. 5, 142–43; New York *Mercury,* Feb. 5, 1759, suppl. 1; Truxes, *Defying Empire,* 69, 91–92, 104.
7. Gramarye, "Finite Variety," and "1758 St. Eustatius Census Transcript."
8. First shipment of December 1756, designated "Sales no. 1"; second shipment of February 1757, designated "Sales no. 2." Dutch-Spanish cloth trade: Klooster, *Illicit Riches,* 178–81. New capital: AFC, fol. 5, 65; Goelet, *The Voyages and Travels of Francis Goelet,* entry Amsterdam [January] 1757; Baxter, *The House of Hancock,* 84, 113–15; Barrow, *Trade and Empire,* 48, 151; Enthoven, "That Abominable Nest of Pirates," 264–65, 286–87, 287n56; Hope Brothers: Buist, *At Spes Non Fracta,* esp. chaps. 1–2. Cannon: AFC, fol. 5, 67, 86, 88.
9. Ship arrival no. 2: AFC, fol. 5, Sales no. 2 entries, 74–139 passim; Sales no. 1 entries, 65–98 passim, diapers, 72, 78, 80.
10. AFC, fol. 5, 109, q. Currency: 1 piece of eight (pc) = 8 Spanish reals or 48 Dutch stuivers. Allen's conversions based on AFC, fol. 5: 1 piece of eight = 3 shillings, 9 pence, or 5⅓ pcs (5 pcs/2 reals/4 stuivers) = £1 sterling. See also McCusker, *Money and Exchange in Europe and America,* 95–98.
11. Saint-Domingue: Debien, *Une plantation du Saint-Domingue,* 58–66. Bompar: Banks, *Chasing Empire Across the Sea,* 203–4.
12. De Windt: AFC, fol. 5, gunpowder: 77, 79, 80, 95, 99; cutlasses, 79; swivel guns, 86; cannon, 88. Other merchants: AFC, fol. 5, 5–143 passim, and compared with Gramarye, "1758 St. Eustatius Census Transcript"; French Caribbean Jews: Lafleur, "Les juifs aux îles françaises du vent."
13. Pierre Desmonts: Parisis and Parisis, "Le siècle du sucre à Saint-Martin français," 3–208, esp. 37–39.
14. Examples: AFC, fol. 5, Elena Dunewell, Mary Mathews, both 69; Elizabeth Peterson, 70; Mrs. Lawrence, 75, 143, 145; Widow Leverick, 75 (twice), 124; Widow Bennett, 129; Mrs. Barnard, 134; pork sold, 142; "Johaner," 151. AFC, fol. 6, account for "Negro Peggy."
15. AFC, fol. 5, clothing, 118; schooling, 128; investments, 123; and AFC, fol. 6, "Richard Shackmaple Estate," insert.
16. AFC, fol. 6, "Women & Gaming," insert; AFC, fol. 5: entertainment, 74; pineapples, 114, 117, 121; parrot, 129; wine, eggs, 92, 150; enslaved woman, 152.
17. AFC, fol. 5, 5, 14, 67–69, 75, 77, 79, 81, 99–100, 119, 123 (London), 128, 129, 132, 137–38.
18. AFC, fol. 5, 125–26, 130, 144–45.
19. AFC, B1F1, Thomas Allen to Nathaniel Allyn, May 26, 1755, q.; AFC, fol. 5, 99.
20. AFC, fol. 5, 70–101 passim. Flour Act: also Exportation Act, 30 George II, cap. 9.
21. Klooster, *Illicit Riches,* 191–93. ANOM C^8 B 22, *États du Commerce,* no. 11–27, 1758. Dutch sugar trade: de Vries, "Dutch Economic Growth in Comparative-Historical Perspective," 460, table 2.
22. AFC, fol. 5, 73–127 passim; for molasses, 100–107, 110–13, 140–48; rum, 79, 92, 141, 148.
23. AFC, fol. 5, *Polly,* 86–92 passim; *Dove,* 104–6 passim; *Triumph,* 140–42 passim; *Charming Hannah,* 143–46 passim.

24. AFC, fol. 5, 70–117 passim. Caribbean coffee: for example, JCB, John Ellis, An *Historical Account of Coffee with an Engraving and Botanical Description of the Tree . . .* (London, 1774), 17, 30, 43–44; Smith, "Sugar's Poor Relation"; McDonald, "The Chance of the Moment"; Klooster, *Illicit Riches*, 193–94.
25. May, *Histoire économique de la Martinique*, 92–99 and table 2 (307). French coffee trade: for example, Mauro, *Histoire du café*, 21–26; Troulliot, "Motion in the System"; Doerflinger, "The Antilles Trade," 397–415, esp. table 2 (404); Schnakenbourg, "Statistiques pour l'histoire de l'économie de plantation en Guadeloupe et Martinique," 3–121 passim; Lafleur, "La culture du café en Guadeloupe." Settler views of French coffee, examples: Pennsylvania *Gazette*, Jan. 13, 1757, 4; New York *Gazette*, June 7, 1762, 3; Georgia *Gazette*, July 26, 1764, 4. Also noted in JCB, Ellis, *Historical Account of Coffee*, 30.
26. For example, Pares, *Yankees and Creoles*, 89–92, 139–47, and Pares, *Merchants & Planters*, 38–39; Daudin, "Profitability of Slave and Long-Distance Trading"; Butel, *The Atlantic*, 160–63; Smith, "The Account Book of Richard Poor," table 1; Miquelon, *Dugard of Rouen*, table 33 (210–13).
27. Overall profits: AFC, fol. 5, 76. Specific commodities: AFC, fol. 5, sugar: 86, 100, 130, 132; coffee: 94, 117, 130, 133; rum, 76, 124; molasses: 73, 80, 110, 112; flour: 120, 147; beef: 117, 118. 120, 147.
28. AFC, fol. 5, pp. 113–14; See also O'Brien, "Mercantilism and Imperialism," 469–501.
29. AFC, B1F1, Thomas Mumford to Thomas Allen, Jan. 27, 1758; Joseph Chew to Thomas Allen, Jan. 28, 1758, both qq.
30. Truxes, *Defying Empire*, 58, 69, 77; also New London *Summary*, Oct. 2, 1758, 1; New York *Gazette*, Mar. 20, 1758, 2.
31. AFC, fol. 6, "Richard Shackmaple Estate," insert.

5. The "Fair Trader" and the "Deputy First Mate"

1. Louisbourg Siege: Rawlyk, *Nova Scotia's Massachusetts*, 217–219; Johnston, *Endgame 1758*, chap. 6. Recent Seven Years' War overviews in English: Anderson, *Crucible of War*, 297–316; Searing, "The Seven Years' War in West Africa," 263–91; Bryant, "The War in Bengal," 399–427; Baugh, *The Global Seven Years War.*
2. Seven Years' War privateering: for example, Gipson, *The Great War for the Empire*, 8:67–72; Lydon, *Pirates, Privateers, and Profits;* Truxes, *Defying Empire*, 53–71; Moats, *Navigating Neutrality*, 12–18; Rediker, *Villains of All Nations*, 1st q. Advantages: Boston *Post Boy*, Aug. 27, 1759, 2nd q. on 2; see also New London *Summary*, Oct. 27, 1758, 2, and New York *Gazette*, Nov. 26, 1759, 1.
3. *Royal Defiance:* many entries; for example, AFC, fol. 7, "St. Eustatius Daybook," May 1, 1758; AFC, fol. 9, "Ship Account Books, 1758–59"; AFC, fol. 10, "Thomas Allen, Ship Account Book," 1758–59, and fol. 14, "Ship Book, Commenced for Brig[e] *Defiance*," and entries on *de Vrouw Ursula*, July 26, 1758. News in Boston *Post-Boy*, July 10, 1758, 1; New York *Mercury*, July 10, 1758, 4; New Hampshire *Gazette*, July 13, 1758, 2. Settling debts: AFC, fol. 15 (debt totaling £2,626/11/5).
4. Description of property based on AFC, B7F1, Thomas Allen Conveyance to Gabriel Ludlow, Aug. 13, 1761, q.; Interior furnishings: AFC, fol. 12, Thomas Allen, "Inventory of Sundry Household Furniture." "Middling sort" home furnishings: Bushman, *The*

Refinement of America, 110–25; Kornwolf and Kornwolf, *Architecture and Town Planning,* 2:1015–7, 1092–13.

5. CSL, RG062.95, box 2, New London Tax Assessments for 1753, 1759, and 1760. Enslaved: AFC, fol. 11, Sale of "1 negro boy called Jack" (for £40), June 21, 59, 233; AFC, fol. 14, "Inventory of House Hold Furniture," 1761.
6. Trade: for example, Avitable, "The Atlantic World Economy," 104–13, fig. 3.1 (190) and fig. 3.2 (191); McCusker and Menard, *The Economy of British America,* table 9.2 (196). Shipping based on inventories in AFC, fols. 9, 11, 12, 14, 15. British conquest of Guadeloupe: Smelser, *The Campaign for the Sugar Islands, 1759;* Barreau, "La campagne de 1759."
7. Truxes, *Defying Empire,* chaps. 3, 4, and 5, respectively; illicit landing sites in Greater New York area, 40–48; Pares, *War and Trade in the West Indies,* esp. 454–68; Tyler, *Smugglers and Patriots,* 25–36.
8. Use of "fair trader": EEB, Anonymous, *The Case of the Fair-Trader* (London?, 1748); Johnson, "Fair Traders and Smugglers in Philadelphia"; Carp, "Did Dutch Smugglers Provoke the Boston Tea Party?," 347, 357. Objections to smugglers: for example, New Hampshire *Gazette,* Feb. 2, 1759, 2; Boston *Gazette,* "Allegory," Sept. 12, 1757, both qq. on 1–2; New York *Mercury,* Sept. 26, 1757, 1, and June 5, 1758, 3; New York *Weymouth Gazette,* July 23, 1759, 3.
9. New London *Summary,* Feb. 2, 1759, 1st q. on 3. Selfish merchants: New York *Gazette,* Nov. 24, 1760, 2nd and 3rd qq. on 3. Overviews of debate: for example, Truxes, *Defying Empire,* 39–51, 99–105, 125–30; Barrow, *Trade and Empire,* 60–68; Stout, *The Royal Navy in America,* chap. 2; Tyler, *Smugglers and Patriots,* 25–30.
10. New London *Summary,* Aug. 3, 1759, 2–3, both qq. on 3; reprinted Boston *Gazette,* Aug. 13, 1759, 1.
11. New London *Summary,* June 6, 1760, 1–2; all qq. from this essay. Similar view: JCB, "Merchant of London," in *A State of the Trade Carried on by the French* (London, 1760).
12. British selling French sugar: Postlethwayt and Augustus, *A Short State of the Progress of French Trade.* See also Cavignac, *Jean Pellet,* 211–42; Butel, *Les négociants bordelais,* 47–82; Stein, *The French Sugar Business,* 108–17. Smuggling not aiding French: for example, Boston *Gazette,* July 23, 1759, 2.
13. New York *Gazette,* Oct. 13, 1761, 3, q. Other examples: New Hampshire *Gazette,* May 12, 1758, 3; New London *Summary,* July 17, 1761, 2.
14. "Fair Trader": Boston *Gazette,* Dec. 7, 1761, 1, q. Writs of Assistance Trial: for example, Smith, *The Writs of Assistance Case,* chaps. 9 and 16; Tyler, *Smugglers and Patriots,* 36–56 passim, Adams q. on 53.
15. Willson: Boston *Evening Post,* Aug. 27, 1759, 1, and New York *Gazette,* Sept. 3, 1759, 2. Store: AFC, fols. 9, 11, 12, 14, 15 passim. Connecticut shipping losses: Avitable, "The Atlantic World Economy," appendix 1, 151–54.
16. Mann, *Republic of Debtors,* 17,19, 32, 43, and 275n50; McCleskey and Squire, "Knowing When to Fold," 519–24. Disturbance: CSL, NLCC, Trials, vol. 23, no. 41. *Dominus Rex* [King's Law] *v. Thomas Allen & Nathaniel Shaw Jr,* June 24, 1760.
17. AFC, B1F2, Thomas Allen to Elizabeth Allen, including letters of Nov. 7, 1760, Jan. 9, 1761 (from Allen in "Mont[e] Christo"), Mar. 16, 1761, and July 27, 1761; see also New London *Summary,* Feb. 6, 1761, 3, and June 26, 1761. Enslaved sale: AFC, B7F1, "Deed of Sale of Three Slaves," Dec. 16, 1760 (total of £160).

18. Loss: AFC, B7F1, Inventory no. 1, ship *Loyalty;* also New London *Summary,* Dec. 26, 1760, 3; Boston *Evening Post,* Dec. 29, 1760, 2; AFC, B1F2, Thomas Allen to Elizabeth Allen, Jan. 9, 1761, q.
19. AFC, B1F1, for example, Samuel Allen to Nathaniel Allen, letters of Aug. 29, 1758, June 14, 1759, and Oct. 4, 1759, q. Death notice: Boston *News-Letter,* Sept. 11, 1760, 2; Warden, *Boston 1689–1776,* 152, 161. Jolley Allen: Boston *News-Letter,* Dec. 17, 1761, 1.
20. Elizabeth and accounts: AFC, fol. 13, General Store Daybook, 1759–1761; Allen also employed a young clerk. Women and business in ports: Creighton and Norling, "Introduction," in *Iron Men, Wooden Women;* Herndon, "The Domestic Cost of Seafaring"; Vickers and Walsh, *Young Men and the Sea,* chap. 5; Crane, *Ebb Tide in New England,* 9–21; Norling, *Captain Ahab Had a Wife,* chap. 1; Jarvis, *In the Eye of All Trade,* chap. 5; Catterall and Campbell, "Introduction: Mother Courage and Her Sisters," esp. 7–9, Matson, "Women's Economies in North America Before 1820"; Wulf, *Not All Wives,* chap. 4, esp. 130–43; Hartigan-O'Connor, "She Said She did not Know Money"; Cleary and Murray, *Elizabeth Murray,* chap. 2; Zabin, *Dangerous Economies,* chap. 2.
21. AFC, B1F2, Thomas Allen (New York) to Elizabeth Allen, Mar. 27, 1761, 1st q.; ibid., Thomas Allen to Elizabeth Allen, May 12, 1761, 2nd q.
22. AFC, B1F2, Nov. 27, 1761, q. See also letters of May 17, 1761, and Dec. 1, 1761.
23. AFC, B1F2, Mar. 27, 1761, 1st q.; ibid., Nov. 5, 1761, 2nd, 3rd, and 4th qq.
24. AFC, B1F2, Deed "to Gabriel Ludlow & Co. of NY, for House, lot, warehouse, and wharf," to Joshua Chandlar, Aug. 13,1761. Sale to Capt. John Shackmaple: AFC, B7F1, "Invoice of Sundry Goods sold at Vendue, Oct. 26, 1761"; CSL, New London Land Records, 3237.v190000, Deed of Thomas Allen to Gabriel Ludlow & Co., New York, Aug. 10, 1761. Thomas Mumford of Groton: Mumford, *Mumford Memoirs.*
25. AFC, B1F2, Thomas Allen to Elizabeth Allen, Nov. 27, 1761, 1st q.; AFC., B7F1, Thomas Allen to Samuel Loudon, Jan. 10, 1762, 2nd q.
26. North Province: JCB, Moreau de St-Méry, *Description topographiqe, physique, civile, politique et historique de la partie française de l'isle St-Domingue* . . . (Paris, 1796), 1:117–23; summarized in Dubois, *Avengers of the New World,* 25–26. Land calculations based on Bibliothèque Nationale, "Carte de la partie Nord-est des possessions françoises de l'île St. Domingue . . . ," 1750. Following Moreau's usage of "Le Cap François." African enslavement in Saint-Domingue/Haiti: for example, Geggus, "Slave and Free Colored Women in Saint Domingue," and Geggus, "The Slaves and Free People of Color of Cap Français"; Fick, *The Making of Haiti,* chaps. 1 and 4; Socolow, "Economic Roles of the Free Women of Color"; Garrigus, *Before Haiti,* chaps. 1, 2, and 4; Ghachem, *The Old Regime,* chap. 1.
27. AFC, B7F1, Thomas Allen to Elizabeth Allen, Dec. 3, 1761, 1st q. Description of Le Cap ca. 1761 based largely on JCB, Moreau de St-Méry, *Description topographique,* 1:350–59, 369–82, 2nd q. on 376–77 translation by the author; ibid., 2:120–30, 143–46; McClellan, *Colonialism and Science,* esp. 81–102; Geggus, "Major Port Towns," tables and figures on 105–8; Pinon, "Villes fondées à Saint-Domingue." Packwood: AFC, B7F1, Thomas Allen to Elizabeth Allen, Dec. 8, 1761.
28. AFC, B7F1, Thomas Allen to Elizabeth Allen, Jan. 9, 1762, q.; Thomas Allen to Samuel Loudon, Jan. 10, 1762. Losses: AFC, B7F1, Thomas Allen to Samuel Loudon, Jan. 10, 1762, enclosed letter of Thomas Allen to William Cobham, also Jan. 10, 1762; Thomas

Allen to James Mumford, Feb. 15, 1762; expenses, AFC, B7F1, Inventory no. 1, "Account for *Hawk,*" Jan. 6, 1762.

29. AFC, B7F1, copy of Inventory no. 1, "Fortune in Acct^{s} Curr^{t}" 1758–1762; Inventory no. 2, "Summary of Voyages," July 1758—May 1762, continued on Inventory no. 3. CSL, RG1.10, no. 2, Petition of Thomas Allen for bankruptcy, June 30, 1762, all qq.; also Mann, *Republic of Debtors,* 72 and 283n63 [not 285 as stated].

6. The Insolvent Debtor

1. "New Gaol": Mann, *Republic of Debtors,* 86–88, and 289n21; Hall, *The Old Martyrs' Prison;* Abbott, "The Neighborhoods of New York," 41–51; Loorya, "Deconstructing City Hall Park." Stamp Act: for example, Maier, *From Resistance to Revolution,* 55–59, 67–70; Hattem, "As Serves Our Interest Best," 40–70; Tiedemann, *Reluctant Revolutionaries,* 72–80.
2. Description of Allen and escape: New York *Gazette,* Dec. 23, 1765, 3.
3. AFC, fol. 18, "Accounts of Adventure of Brig *Hope,*" Dec. 7, 1762. Grenada: for example, Gipson, *The Great War for the Empire,* vol. 9, 236–45; Murdoch, "Land Policy"; Quintanilla, "Mercantile Communities in the Ceded Islands."
4. AFC, B1F2, Thomas Allen to Nathaniel Allen, Nov. 23, 1763, q.; Edmund Kingdon to Thomas Allen, Jan. 29, 1764; AFC, "Fortune of Thom^{s} Allen," Inventory no. 4, "West India Accounts", Oct. 31, 1765; Boston *News-Letter,* Aug. 9, 1764, 3 (dissolution of Allen & Kingdon); CSL, NLCC, Trials no. 87, *Allen* (executor for William Kingdon) *v. Scovell,* Nov. 13, 1764.
5. AFC, B5F2, John Evans to Thomas Allen, July 10, 1789; Portsmouth Athenaeum, John Evans Papers, S1176, Diary entries mentioning Allen's theft include May 28, 1788 (39) and Jan. 25, 1789 (55).
6. Return: New Hampshire *Gazette,* Sloop *Hope,* Allen master, from Barbados, Oct. 4, 1764, 3. Rhode Island as debtor's asylum: JCB, Anonymous, *The Ill Policy and Inhumanity of Imprisoning Insolvent Debtors* (Newport, 1754); Mann, *Republic of Debtors,* 50–60, q. on 51.
7. Rappleye, *Sons of Providence,* 46–52, q. on 51; Withey, *Urban Growth in Colonial Rhode Island,* 33–35; Coleman, "The Insolvent Debtor in Rhode Island," 413–34.
8. Economic depression ca. 1761–1766: Truxes, *Overseas Trade,* 236–40; Breen, *The Marketplace of Revolution,* 204–10. Nova Scotia: Rawlyk, *Nova Scotia's Massachusetts,* 220–23; Fischer "Revolution Without Independence," 106–19; Boston: Nash, *The Urban Crucible,* 155–59, 1st q. on 154; Tyler, *Smugglers and Patriots,* 65–75; Blake, *Public Health in the Town of Boston,* 88–96. Connecticut: Zeichner, *Connecticut's Years of Controversy,* 44–48, 78–82, 2nd q. on 47; Avitable, "The Atlantic World Economy," 111–13. New York: Harrington, *The New York Merchant,* 316–51; Matson, *Merchants & Empire,* 276–98, 3rd q. on 282. Philadelphia: Jensen, *Maritime Commerce of Philadelphia,* 118–29; Smith, "Material Lives," 185–88, and table 3; Doerflinger, *Vigorous Spirit of Enterprise,* 168–80.
9. Lee, *Essay* (1764), cited in Holton, *Forced Founders,* q. on 49; 4 George III, cap. 15, "An Act for granting certain duties in the British Colonies and plantations. . . ." See also Morgan and Morgan, *The Stamp Act Crisis,* 37–40.

10. Mann, *Republic of Debtors,* 55–60; Coleman, *Debtors and Creditors in America,* 74–93, table on 420, q. on 76; Hoppit, *Risk and Failure in English Business,* 35–37. Original law: JCB, 28 George II, cap. 13, "Act of the Relief of Insolvent Debtors," 1754. Petition: AFC, B7F1, Thomas Allen Petition to Rhode Island Assembly, Feb. 20, 1765.
11. Coleman, *Debtors and Creditors in America,* 1st q. on 12; Mann, *Republic of Debtors,* 34–47, 2nd q. on 37. Overviews: De Roover, *Money, Banking, and Credit,* 331–337; Sgard, "Do Legal Origins Matter?"
12. Thomas Dekker (1606), cited in Hoppit, *Risk and Failure in English Business,* 19–35, 1st q. on 20; Mann, *Republic of Debtors,* 2nd q. on 56–57.
13. Trumbull: Weaver, *Jonathan Trumbull,* 97–129; Roth, *Connecticut's War Governor,* 10–24.
14. Act: CCR 12, "An Act for preventing Fraud in Debtors and for securing the Effects of Insolvent Debtors . . ." [1765], 357–66, q. on 358; ibid., [1763], 127–33. Ibid., q. on 362–363; Coleman, *Debtors and Creditors in America,* 76–79.
15. AFC, fol. 15, Inventories, all quotes.
16. Description of New York: based largely on Pownall, *A topographical description,* 42–45, 1st q. on 45; Hamilton, "The Itinerarium of Dr. Alexander Hamilton," 206–12; Kalm, *Travels in North America,* 1:30–36, "Journal of a French Traveller," 2:81–84. Stamp Act advertisements: New York *Mercury,* July 15, 22, and Aug. 5, 1765, 2nd q.
17. Fictional account of Allen's arrest based on Mann, *Republic of Debtors,* 86–88, 289n21, qq. on 87. Serving writs: ibid., 24–29.
18. Coleman, *Debtors and Creditors in America,* 105–14, 1st q. on 107–8; *Beekman Papers,* 1:515, Gerard Beekman to Samuel Fowler, Jan. 11, 1768, 2nd and 3rd qq., partly cited in Mann, *Republic of Debtors,* 60. New York Bankruptcy Law of 1765: *Colonial Laws of New York,* 4:10.
19. Providence *Gazette,* Aug. 24, 1765, 1, cited in du Rivage, *Revolution Against Empire,* q. on 112. Act: JCB, 5 George III, cap. 12, "An Act for granting and applying certain Stamp Duties, . . ." Stamp Act crisis: the classic study is Morgan and Morgan, *The Stamp Act Crisis,* chap. 9; see also Maier, *From Resistance to Revolution,* chap. 3; Stout, *The Royal Navy in America,* 91–109; O'Shaughnessy, *An Empire Divided,* chap. 4; Gould, *The Persistence of Empire,* 110–36. Isle of Man "Revestment Act": JCB, 5 George III, cap. 39; "An Act for more effectually preventing Mischiefs arising . . . from the Illicit and Clandestine Trade"; Mhurchadha, "Chasing the Smugglers"; Truxes, *Overseas Trade,* 215–19.
20. Calculation stamp costs based on New York *Mercury,* Sept. 2, 1765, 3; also Dickerson, *The Navigation Acts and the American Revolution,* 191–92.
21. Maier, *From Resistance to Revolution,* qq. on 56.
22. Allen: AFC, B7F1, "Sundry Voyages Registered by Thos Allen . . . from July 1758 to May 1762" and "Fortune in Acc^{t} Curr^{t} with Thos Allen," both dated Oct. 31, 1765; and AFC, B7F1, Allen to Doughty, Dec. 3, 1765. Stamp Act violence: For example, Maier, *From Resistance to Revolution,* 67–69, 78–82; Matson, *Merchants & Empire,* 291–94; Tiedemann, *Reluctant Revolutionaries,* chap. 3, esp. 73–81.
23. Thomas Doughty: for example, New York *Mercury,* Jan. 5, 1756, 3; New York *Gazette,* Dec, 5, 1757, 2, and Feb. 19, 1763, 2. William Cobham: for example, New York *Mercury,* Mar. 8, 1762, 2; Jan. 17, 1763, 3; and May 23, 1763, 3.
24. Merchant profiles from Matson, *Merchants & Empire,* 77, 90, 138, 147, 150, 158, 163, 253, 259, 266–68, 276–80, 298–99, 307, 419n8, 424n38, 436–37n148, 1st q. on 276; Truxes,

Defying Empire, 24, 43, 59–60, 94, 153, 181–82, 190–94, 215, 220, 247n13, 269n39; 2nd q. on 181; Minty *Unfriendly to Liberty,* 126–28, 233.

25. Smith, *An Empire of Print,* 6–11, q. on 8; ANB, 13:940–41.
26. ANB, 13:941; Wall, *Samuel Loudon,* 75–78; Brennan, "Shaped by Revolution." Advertisements: for example, New York *Mercury,* Sept. 19, 1757, q. on 3; Oct. 22, 1759, 3; July 7, 1760, 6; Aug. 13, 1764, 3; Aug. 12, 1765, 4; and New York *Gazette,* Dec. 25, 1762, 4, and Dec. 3, 1764, 3.
27. AFC, fols. 12 and 15, both dated July 20, 1765, passim; AFC, B7F1, Inventory dated Oct. 31, 1765, insert, quote.
28. AFC, B7F1, Thomas Allen circular letter "To His Creditors," Nov. 28, 1765, all quotes. Licenses: Coleman, *Debtors and Creditors in America,* 79, 109; Mann, *Republic of Debtors,* 67–72; Hoppit, *Risk and Failure in English Business,* 29–32. US bankruptcy law: Congressional Research Service, *Bankruptcy Basics: A Primer* (https://www.uscourts.gov/services-forms/bankruptcy/bankruptcy-basics).
29. AFC, B1F2, Thomas Allen to Thomas Doughty, Dec. 3, 1765, 1st q.; Hoppit, *Risk and Failure in English Business,* 2nd q. on 34.
30. *Colonial Laws of New York,* "An Act more Effectually to Secure to Creditors the Benefits Intended by the Acts . . . ," 862–66.
31. New York *Gazette,* December 23, 1765, q. on 3; AFC, B5F2, Jonathan Bull to Thomas Allen, Oct. 2, 1789.
32. AFC, B1F2, Samuel Loudon to Thomas Allen, Feb. 13, 1766, 1st q., and Feb. 26, 1766, 2nd and 3rd qq.
33. See AFC, B7F1, Thomas Allen, "Copia, to the Hon'ble Hezekiah Huntington, Esq., Chief Judge of the County Court . . . ," stitched manuscript booklet July 22, 1766–Sept. 30, 1766; ibid., "Schedule of Houshold [*sic*] & Materials Reserved to Mr. Thom.[s] Allen for his use," Sept. 2, 1766.

7. The Smuggler

1. Classic studies of the political ideals and turmoil animating the settler mainland, 1763–1774: see, for example, Bailyn, *The Ideological Origins of the American Revolution;* Maier, *From Resistance to Revolution;* Nash, *The Urban Crucible;* Greene, *Peripheries and Center;* Wood, *The Radicalism of the American Revolution;* Beeman, *Varieties of Political Experience.*
2. Ceded Islands: Dominica, St. Vincent, Tobago, and Grenada. See Doerflinger, "The Antilles Trade," fig. 1 (400); Boulle, "Patterns of French Colonial Trade," 50, 57, 60. Richardson, "The Slave Trade," calculations based on table 1, 746; O'Shaughnessy, *An Empire Divided,* 58–65. Rum: for example, Smith, *Caribbean Rum,* 75–76, 81–84, 90–93; McCusker, *Rum and the American Revolution,* 1:6–9, 352–53, and esp. tables D-35, D-38, D-45, and table V-3C, 358; Mandelblatt, "Atlantic Consumption of French Rum." Cotton and cocoa: Schnakenbourg, "Recherche sur l'histoire du coton en Guadeloupe." Coffee and cocoa: Niddrie, "Eighteenth-Century Settlement in the British Caribbean"; McDonald, "The Chance of the Moment"; Bivar Marquese "A Tale of Two Coffee Colonies," esp. 738–45; Aizpura, *Curazao y la costa de Caracas,* 24–52. Cassava and bananas: JCB, Moreau de St-Méry, *Description topographique,* 1:123–24, 252, 264; 2:346, 463; Garcia-Álvarez, "Santo, Seña, y Ruta Histórica del Plátano Hasta Cuba," esp. 152–53;

O'Shaughnessy, *An Empire Divided,* 60–72 passim. Logwoods: Rossano, "Down to the Bay"; Camille and Espejo-Saavedra, "Historical Geography of the Belizean Logwood Trade."

3. Estimates from https://www.slavevoyages.org/assessment/estimates. Overview of enslaved migration: for example, Berlin, *Many Thousands Gone,* chap. 6 passim and chap. 7, esp. 180–86; Thornton, *Africa and Africans in the Making of the Atlantic World,* xxvi–xxxii, 305–14; Hall, *Slavery and African Ethnicities in the Americas,* chaps. 6 and 7, esp. 148–53. French migration and *gens de couleur:* Frostin, "Angevins de modeste condition," q. on 449, translation by the author; Garrigus, "Buccaneers Became Ballet Masters," and Garrigus, *Before Haiti,* esp. 117–19, 142–49; Léon, *Marchands et spéculateurs dauphinois,* 23–32. Jamaican Maroons: Campbell, *The Maroons of Jamaica 1655–1796,* 153–61, 181–95; Burnard, *Jamaica in the Age of Revolution,* chap. 4. Scots in Grenada: Quintanilla, "The World of Alexander Campbell," and Quintanilla, "Mercantile Communities in the Ceded Islands"; Hamilton, *Scotland, the Caribbean, and the Atlantic World,* 23–24, 66–69, 152–59. Amelioration and Early Abolition: for example, Ward, *British West Indian slavery, 1750–1834;* Morrissey, *Slave Women,* chaps. 4 and 7; Eltis, *Economic Growth and the Ending of the Transatlantic Slave Trade,* chap. 1; Richardson, *Principles and Agents,* chap. 5; Drescher, "Revolution in England?"
4. Reforms: for example, Kaplan, *Bread, Politics and Political Economy,* chap. 3; Marshall, *Making and Unmaking Empires,* chap. 6; Mokyr, *The Enlightened Economy,* chap. 2; Faccarello, "Pierre de Boisguilbert"; Moats, *Navigating Neutrality,* chap. 2. Overviews of revolts: Louisiana: Brasseaux, *Denis-Nicolas Foucault,* 65–90; Dawdy, *Building the Devil's Empire,* 220–25; Kolb, "New Orleans Revolt of 1768." Saint-Domingue: Frostin, *Les révoltes blanches,* chap. 6; Garrigus, *Before Haiti,* 122–37. St. Vincent: Taylor, *The Black Carib Wars,* chap. 3.
5. Early free ports: for example, Armytage, *The Free Port System in the British West Indies,* 24–26, 36–37; Goebel, "The 'New England Trade,'" esp. 335–42; Tarrade, *Le commerce colonial,* 1:74–79, 106–9, 153–55; Schnakenbourg, "La Guadeloupe pendant la première administration britannique"; Kleiser, "An Empire of Free Ports." Dubuc: for example, Tarrade, *Le commerce colonial,* 1:186–223; Azimi, "Premiers Commis de la marine"; Houllemare, "Les Bureaus des colonies"; Røge, *Economists and the Reinvention of Empire,* 109–21. Often signed as "Dubuq."
6. Tarrade, *Le commerce colonial* 1:156–62, 223–67, 287–327; Røge, *Economists and the Reinvention of Empire* 121–33; Goebel, "The 'New England Trade,'" 356–64.
7. Danish free ports: for example, Connecticut *Courant,* Dec. 31, 1764, 1; Newport *Mercury,* Mar. 4, 1765, 2; Pennsylvania *Chronicle,* Aug. 24, 1767, 1–2; Willis, "The Trade Between North America and the Danish West Indies," 73–78. Acts: JCB, 6 George III, cap. 52, "An Act for repealing certain duties . . ." (Revenue Act of 1766); JCB, 6 George III, cap. 49, "An Act for opening and establishing certain Ports in the islands of Jamaica and Dominica . . . ," 1766; Munro, *Acts of the Privy Council of England,* vol. 5, June 6, 1766, q. on 13.
8. Monte Cristi: Newport *Mercury,* June 27, 1763, 3. Bermuda: Connecticut *Gazette,* Dec. 19, 1766, 1, and New York *Gazette,* May 28, 1767, 3. St. John's: New York *Mercury,* Apr. 13, 1767, 2; Dominica: Providence *Gazette,* July 2, 1763, 1, and New York *Gazette,* June 30, 1766, 2. Pensacola: Boston *Evening Post,* Aug. 25, 1766, 1. "French Hispaniola": Newport *Mercury,* Jan. 19, 1767, 2.

9. Boston *Evening Post,* Aug. 25, 1766, q. on 1, emphasis added. See also "A friend to the Northern Colonies," Newport *Mercury,* Nov. 21, 1763, 2; Boston *Evening-Post,* May 26, 1766, q. on 2; Matson, *Merchants & Empire,* 294–295.
10. Guadeloupe: AFC, fol. 19, "Accounts of the Brigantine *Mansfield,*" 1767. Danish St. Croix: Haagensen, *Description of the Island of St. Croix,* x–xx, 43–45; Willis, "The Trade Between North America and the Danish West Indies," 26–29, 42–50, 92–106. British merchants: JCB, Parliament, *The Case of a Considerable Number of British and American Merchants. . . . of the Island of Santa Cruz* (London, 1766).
11. AFC, fol. 22, St. Croix Accounts Diary, February–April 1768.
12. Twelve voyages, December 1768–April 1771.
13. New London *Summary,* Sept. 21, 1759, 4; Totten, *Christophers Genealogy,* 163–64; AFC, B7F3, Allen, Statement of hardship in petition to court; New London Town Clerk's office, Book 16, Aug. 10, 1758, 206; June 19, 1759, 233–34.
14. AFC, B1F2, Thomas Willson to Thomas Allen, Oct. 4, 1767, 1st q. Friendship: AFC, B1F3, Thomas Willson to Thomas Allen, Oct. 29, 1768, 2nd q. Not so friendly examples: AFC, B1F3, Thomas Willson to Thomas Allen, March 19, 1769, 3rd q.; Thomas Willson to Thomas Allen, Oct. 29, 1768, 4th q. Charges of drinking: AFC, B2F3, Nathan Hinman to Thomas Allen, Mar. 20, 1773; B3F1, Richard Alsop to Thomas Allen, June 8, 1774.
15. Examples: AFC, B1F3, Thomas Willson to Thomas Allen, May 16, 1768, and Oct. 26, 1768, q.; Thomas Allen to Thomas Willson, Nov. 20, 1768.
16. *Sally I* voyage: AFC, B1F3, Thomas Allen to Thomas Willson, Nov. 20, 1768, q.; AFC, fol. 21, Individual Accounts, 1767–1773, "Thomas Willson"; AFC, fol. 23, Account Book, 1768–1770. "Horse Jockeys": Caulkins, *History of New London,* 241, 254. Settler livestock trade: Lemon, *The Best Poor Man's Country,* table 27 (152), table 28 (155), 194–97; Postma, "Suriname and Its Atlantic Connections," 301–3; Wu, "Jamaican Trade, 1688–1769," 243–86 passim and table 6.36; Hart, "From Field to Plate"; Anderson, *Creatures of Empire,* chap. 5.
17. AFC, B1F3, Thomas Allen to Thomas Willson, Jan. 6, 1769, q. Horse prices: AFC, fol. 22, "Memorand^{m} Book"; Avitable, "The Atlantic World Economy," 49–61, fig. 2.4 (156).
18. Avitable, "The Atlantic World Economy," 50–51, 97–98, table 2.3 (119), 120–33, 155–56, q. on 97. Comparable figures from McCusker and Menard, *The Economy of British America,* tables 5.2, 108, and 6.1, 130.
19. Based on Anderson, "Animals into the Wilderness," esp. 388.
20. Postma, "Suriname and Its Atlantic Connections," 302; Avitable, "The Atlantic World Economy," 60–61, 97; AFC, B2F1, Thomas Willson to Thomas Allen, Nov. 8, 1770.
21. AFC, B1F3, Thomas Allen to Thomas Willson, Nov. 20, 1768, q., and Jan. 6, 1769.
22. See AFC, B7F2, "Charter Party . . . between Zadock Brewster Owner of the Sloop *Sally* . . . and Thomas Allen," Dec. 20, 1768; ibid., Capt. Brewster to Thomas Allen, Mar. 22, 1769; AFC, fol. 23, Jan. 1769.
23. *Sally II* cargo: AFC, B1F3, Thomas Allen to Thomas Willson, Jan. 6, 1769. Manufactured items: for example, Hedges, *The Browns of Providence Plantations,* chaps. 5 and 6; Matson, *Merchants & Empire,* 248–62; Smith, "The Market for Manufactures." Willson's innovation: AFC, B7F2, "Agreement," Jan. 5, 1769; AFC, B1F3, Thomas Allen to Thomas Willson, Jan. 6, 1769.

24. AFC, B1F3, "Portledge Bill" for the *Sally,* Dec. 20, 1768, to Jan. 10, 1769, and Partial invoice for Sloop *Sally,* Jan. 12, 1769. Connecticut *Gazette,* Jan. 13, 1769, 3; AFC, B1F3, Sailing orders for Capt. Champlin, Jan. 9, 1769.
25. Connecticut *Gazette,* Feb. 24, 1769, q. on 3.
26. AFC, B1F3, Thomas Willson to Thomas Allen, Jan. 24, 1769, qq., and Feb. 18, 1769.
27. AFC, B1F3, Thomas Allen to Thomas Willson, Mar. 7, 69, qq.; ibid., Thomas Willson to Thomas Allen, Apr. 16, 1769.
28. AFC, B1F3, Thomas Willson to Thomas Allen, Mar. 19, 1769.
29. Customs patrols: Barrow, *Trade and Empire,* chap. 10; Stout, *The Royal Navy in America,* 130–35. AFC, B1F3, Thomas Allen to Thomas Willson, Jan. 6, 1769; Boston *Evening Post,* Sept. 10, 1764, 3. Fishers Island: Saint and Krimsky, *Making Freedom,* 26–37 passim.
30. AFC, B1F3, Thomas Allen to Thomas Willson, Jan. 6, 1769, original instructions; AFC, B7F2, "Bill of Clearance" issued by Abraham Chaliwwell, "president" of Tortola, May 15, 1769.
31. AFC, B1F3, Thomas Allen to Thomas Willson, Mar. 7, 1769, 1st q.; Thomas Willson to Thomas Allen, Apr. 27, 1769, 2nd q.
32. AFC, fol. 23, Accounts, "Contents of Sloop Sally"; AFC, B1F3, Thomas Willson to Thomas Allen, May 16, 1769, q.
33. Some other examples: AFC, fol. 23, Accounts for *Hannah* (Blakslee), *Hector* (Mellaly), "*New Sally*" (Richards); AFC, B1F3, Thomas Allen to Joseph Christophers, May 2, 1769; AFC, B2F1, Capt. Thomas Willson (Antigua) to Thomas Allen, Nov. 8, 1770. Examples of sailing discrepancies: Connecticut *Gazette,* Jan. 13, 1769, 3, *Sally* ("Champlain"), and Feb. 9, 1770, 3, *Hannah* (Blakslee).
34. AFC, B7F3, "Indenture of Lease for House and Wharf," Mar. 16, 1770, both quotes.
35. Two accounts, Connecticut *Gazette,* Mar. 16, 1770, both qq. on 2.

8. The Rogue Merchants

1. Fitch, *A History of the Fitch Family,* 100–101; Bayles, *History of Windham County,* 64, 133–34; Willingham, "Windham, Connecticut," 47, 52, 138–39, and 322nn24–25.
2. AFC, B2F4, Eleazer Fitch to Thomas Allen, June 3, 1773, all quotes. Often spelled "Ebenezer" in the correspondence.
3. *Gentleman's Magazine,* "American News," Aug. 1772; Stout, *The Royal Navy in America,* 141–43; DeVaro, "The Impact of the Gaspee Affair," 65–95, esp. 92.
4. New London *Gazette,* June 25, 1773, 3, and Aug. 7, 1772, 3; Connecticut *Journal,* Dec. 18, 1772, 3.
5. Van Dusen, "The Trade of Revolutionary Connecticut," 127–56; Saladino, "The Economic Revolution," 1–42; Kimball, "An Essential Link in a Vast Chain," esp. 83–87, and q. on 113; Avitable, "The Atlantic World Economy," esp. 109–13.
6. British financial crisis: Sheridan, "The British Credit Crisis of 1772 and the American Colonies," esp. 165–70; Goodspeed, *Legislating Instability,* chap. 1, esp. 13–19; Truxes, *Overseas Trade,* 256–63. Nonimportation movement: Breen, *Marketplace of Revolution,* esp. 244–89, q. on 248; other works include Nash, *The Unknown American Revolution,* 89–103; Maier, *From Resistance to Revolution,* 115–38; Carp, *Defiance of the Patriots,* 66–82; Griffin, *The Townshend Moment,* 118–35, 142–51.

7. Description of New London ca. 1770: Caulkins, *History of New London*, 440–49, 462–85, 494–98 (fire pump, 475); Van Dusen, "The Trade of Revolutionary Connecticut," 20–37. Lighthouse: CSL, RG10, Trade & Maritime, "Memorial" for a Lighthouse, 1760. Wharves: Hemsptead, *Diary*, 553, 569, 582, 594, 611, 626, 639, 687. Town center: Connecticut *Gazette*, Oct. 12, 1781, "List of Dwelling Houses, Stores, etc. that were set on fire . . . ," 1; CSL, RG 70, St. James Church Records, 1:40, 44, 63–67; CSL, RG3, NLCCC, B94, fol. 17 (1771) and fol. 22 (1772) (taverns).
8. AFC, fol. 24, "Housebook" for 1770, Mar. 3, 1770; AFC, B7F3, "Indenture of Lease of Land" Duncan Stewart to Thomas Allen, Mar. 16, 1770. Advertisements, examples: Boston *Gazette*, Apr. 30, 1770, 4; Pennsylvania *Chronicle*, May 14, 1770, 4.
9. Hancock, *Oceans of Wine*, 242–45, 1st q. on 244; Klein, "Coffeehouse Civility," 2nd q. on 31. Coffee as new Atlantic World commodity in English: Troulliot, "Motion in the System"; Smith, "Accounting for Taste," and Smith, "Sugar's Poor Relation"; McDonald, "Sea Change," esp. 3–9. Coffeehouses as Enlightened "space": for example, Habermas, *Structural Transformation*, 34–40, 82–85; Roche, *France in the Enlightenment*, 626–32; Brinkman-Schwartz, "The Heart of the Maritime World"; Staloff, "Secular Culture."
10. Allen's wharf: for example, AFC, fol. 26, Ship Book, 1771; New London *Gazette*, May 14, 1773, 2.
11. Description of Allen's London Coffee House: AFC, fol. 24, "Housebook" for 1770; AFC, B2F4, Thomas Allen to John Ewing, Apr. 19, 1773; AFC, B7F3, "Indenture of Lease for House and Wharf," Mar. 16, 1770, and "Appraisal of Coffee House Fixtures," Sept. 15, 1775. Coffeehouse descriptions: for example, Rice, *Early American Taverns*, 38–41; Conroy, *In Public Houses*, 89–96. Alcohol: for example, AFC, Accounts in fols. 24, 25, 29, 32; Hirsch, *Forgotten Drinks of Colonial New England;* Hancock and McDonald, *Public Drinking*, 4:390–92, 403–10; Salinger, *Taverns and Drinking in Early America*, 54–59, 65–67.
12. Turtle clubs, examples: AFC, fol. 27, "Account of James Chapman," May 4, 1771, and "Account of Mons. Constant," Aug. 16, 1771. Social clubs: for example, Bridenbaugh, *Cities in Revolt*, 162–68; Rice, *Early American Taverns*, 118–21; Salinger, *Taverns and Drinking in Early America*, 76–82.
13. Examples: AFC, B7F3, Eleazer Fitch Account with Thomas Allen, Oct. 12, 1774, and Miscellaneous Accounts with ship captains, October 1774; AFC, fol. 21, Account of Nathaniel Shaw Jr. with Thomas Allen, June 19, 1770–July 26,1772; AFC, fol. 26, "Wharfebook" accounts Apr. 24, 1770–May 3, 1771. Outfitting ships: Matson, "Putting the *Lydia* to Sea," esp. 312–20.
14. AFC, fol. 29, Day Book, 1772. Voltaire, *Candide*, 68–69.
15. Stewart: for example, Boston *Evening Post*, Sept. 10, 1764, 2; New London *Gazette*, July 3, 1767, 2, Apr. 7, 1769, 3, and Apr. 9, 1773, 2; CSL, RG 3, St. James Records, 55, 57, 60; Caulkins, *History of New London*, 477–78. Moffatt: see Morgan and Morgan, *The Stamp Act Crisis*, 150–54. AFC, B2F3, William Coit to Thomas Allen, Aug. 17, 1773, q.
16. Norwich Region: Jabez Huntington, Eleazer Fitch, William Coit. Hartford: John Chenevard and Samuel Olcott (both related by marriage). Wethersfield: the brothers Barnabas and Silas Deane and their in-law, Joseph Webb, Jr. Middletown: Richard Alsop, Jacob Sebor, and Comfort Sage.
17. Information on Allen's cronies, ads and correspondence examples; inns/distilling: Norwich *Packet*, Dec. 8, 1774, 4; AFC, B2F1, Ebenezer Fitch to Thomas Allen,

June 5,1770. Dry goods: AFC, B2F3, Richard Alsop to Thomas Allen, Mar. 16, 73; Connecticut *Courant,* Aug. 26, 1765, 3; Connecticut *Gazette,* Sept. 19, 1766, 1 (Fitch and future Gov. Trumbull), and Mar. 4, 1768, 4. Lotteries: New London *Summary,* Sept. 28, 1759, 4; Connecticut *Courant* July 21, 1772, 4, and July 19, 1774. Insurance: AFC, B2F3, Comfort Sage to Thomas Allen, Mar. 9, 1773; AFC, B2F4, Richard Alsop to Thomas Allen, Sept. 8, 1773. Printed sources: for example, Love, *The Colonial History of Hartford,* 178, 236; Martin, "Merchants and Trade of the Connecticut River Valley," 8–9, 88–93, 115–16; Kimball, "An Essential Link in a Vast Chain," 79–80.

18. Sea captains: for example, SlaveVoyages.org (https://www.slavevoyages.org/voyage/database), Voyage ID no. 25343 and New York *Mercury,* Feb. 18, 1760, 3 (Chenevard); Case, *Freemasonry in Connecticut,* 48 (Coit); Stiles, *History of Ancient Wethersfield,* 1:497, 566 (B. Deane); Connecticut *Courant,* Nov. 3, 1766, 4; NTSP, B24, Ledger 36, Ship Premiums, 1756–1767, 4 (Sage). Owned enslaved people: Sage and Sage, *Genealogical record of the descendants of David Sage,* 113. Freemasons: for example, Lipson, *Freemasonry in Federalist Connecticut,* 51–57, 68n47; Beers, *History of Middlesex County,* 110–12; Murray, *St. Johns Lodge No. 4,* 4–20, 32–33. On New London, see Case, *Freemasonry in Connecticut,* 3 (Duncan Stewart and Thomas Moffatt), 48, 54. On eighteenth-century settler freemasonry, see Bullock, *Revolutionary Brotherhood,* chaps. 2 and 3, esp. 59–61 and 91; and Harland-Jacobs, "'Hands Across the Sea.'"
19. Political office: for example, Windham Connecticut *Journal,* May 22, 1772, 3; Norwich *Packet,* Dec. 16, 1773, 3; Beers, *History of Middlesex County,* 73; Love, *The Colonial History of Hartford,* 352; Martin, "Merchants and Trade of the Connecticut River Valley," 146, 241n35, 243n3, 243; James, *Silas Deane,* 3–5. "The Company": New York *Journal,* Dec. 17, 1772, 6. Committees of Inspection: Alsop, the Deane Brothers, Coit, Huntington, Mumford, and Sage.
20. Madeira: Hancock, "Markets, Merchants," 69–78, and Hancock, *Oceans of Wine,* chaps. 7–9, esp. 115–20, 133–56. Chenevard: see note 18, and Hinman, *A Catalogue of the Names of the Puritan Settlers,* 565.
21. AFC, B2F2, John Chenevard to Thomas Allen, Oct. 15, 1772, all qq. *Abigail:* Connecticut *Gazette,* June 12, 1772, 3.
22. AFC, B2F2, John Chenevard to Thomas Allen, Dec. 15, 1772, verso. Christopher Champlin and Robert Lawton had stores in Newport. Duties: Full duties amounted to £3/1/3 in New York currency/hhd, which should have amounted to £131/13/9. Including the clerk's fees and bond redemption, Chenevard paid an actual duty of only £11/13/4 in New York currency. AFC, B2F4, John Chenevard to "Mr. Allin," Oct. 22, 1773.
23. Remuneration examples (of at least fourteen documented): AFC, B2F1, Eleazer Fitch to Thomas Allen, "Saturday morning" 1771; AFC, B2F4, William Coit to Thomas Allen, Aug. 17, 1773; AFC, B3F2, Joseph Webb to Thomas Allen, Aug. 4, 1774. Similar instructions, Brown Brothers of Providence, JCB, BFBR, B674, F6, Moses Brown to Nathan Arnold, Dec. 31, 1767.
24. William Allen (no relation), *The American Crisis . . . ,* cited in Lynd and Waldstreicher, "Free Trade, Sovereignty, and Slavery," q. on 604.
25. For example, Lanctôt, *Canada and the American Revolution,* 17–42; Gilje, *The Road to Mobocracy,* 25–30, 39–40; Lawson, *The Imperial Challenge,* chap. 7; Cogliano, "Deliverance from Luxury;" McConville, "Pope's Day Revisited"; Carté, *Religion and the American Revolution,* 139–47. New London 1760s: Caulkins, *History of New London,* 481–82.

26. Political decision: Middlekauff, *The Glorious Cause*, 407–8; Jones, "Displaying the Ensigns of Harmony'" esp. 431–34; Carté, *Religion and the American Revolution*, 247–49, q. on 248. French education: Spurlin, *The French Enlightenment in America*, 14–18, 29–40. Elite French visitors: for example, Monaghan and Marino, *French Travellers in the United States;* du Pont, *Life of Eleuthère Irénée du Pont;* Anonymous, "Journal of a French Traveller in the Colonies, 1765," pts. 1 and 2; Kapp, *The Life of John Kalb;* St. John de Crèvecoeur, *Letters of An American Farmer;* Furstenberg, *When the United States Spoke French.*
27. Huguenots: for example, Butler, *Huguenots in America;* Van Ruymbeke and Sparks, *Memory and Identity;* Van Ruymbeke, *From New Babylon to Eden.* Acadians: Hodson, *The Acadian Diaspora*, esp. chap. 2; q. on 47.
28. Trade with Catholics: for example, Hedges, *The Browns of Providence Plantations*, chap. 2; Doerflinger, *A Vigorous Spirit of Enterprise*, 108–16, 173–77; Hancock, *Oceans of Wine*, esp. 135–63; Jones, "Displaying the Ensigns of Harmony," 434–39.
29. AFC, fol. 25, "Inn Accounts,"1770–71, fol. 27, "Inn Accounts," 1771–72, and fol. 29, "Inn Accounts," 1772–73; NTSP, B23, ledger 28, Accounts, including several merchants with French names. Poorer French emigrants: for example, Léon, *Marchands et spéculateurs dauphinois*, 23–32, 46–50; Frostin, *Les révoltes blanches*, 338–340; Garrigus, *Before Haiti*, 118–119.
30. AFC, fol. 25, "Inn Accounts," Dec. 12, 1771; NTSP, B25, ledger 1, Nathaniel Shaw Account with Thomas Allen, 1773–1783. Sistare: for example, NTSP, B21, P146.9313, Account of Gabriel Sistare with Thomas Shaw; Caulkins, *History of New London*, 483n2.
31. Frostin, *Les révoltes blanches*, 282–295, 306–9, q. on 289, translation by the author; Frostin, "Les colons de Saint-Domingue"; Røge, *Economists and the Reinvention of Empire*, 109–19.
32. AFC, B2F2, Thomas Willson (Le Cap) to Thomas Allen, Aug. 16, 1772, and Thomas Willson (Philadelphia) to Thomas Allen, Dec. 24, 1772. Other examples: AFC, B2F2, Gaspar Boissière to Thomas Allen, May 2, 1772; Farribault d'Émoulins to Thomas Allen, May 26, 1772; AFC, B2F3, Capt. Noble Hinman to Thomas Allen, Mar. 20, 1773; AFC, B2F4, John Biddle to Thomas Willson, July 24, 1773; Isaac Wharton to Thomas Allen, Sept. 21, 1773. Biddle Family: Biddle, "Owen Biddle," esp. 299–308.
33. CSL, RG 62.95, B21, "Grand Levy for the First Society of . . . New London," for 1768, 1770, 1772, and 1774. Jones, *Wealth of a Nation to Be*, 51, 37, 164 165, 177.
34. NLTC, Town Meeting Minutes for Dec. 23, 1771, Dec. 24, 1772, Dec. 21, 1773, Apr. 20, 1774, and Jan. 27, 1775, q.
35. CSL, St. James Church Records, vol. 1, Apr. 16, 1770, 60; Apr. 19, 1772, 62; Apr. 4, 1774, 65. Union School: Anderson, *The Martyr and the Traitor*, 102–4, 147–48; Caulkins, *History of New London*, 619–22; CCR 14: 382–84. Basic curriculum: Frost, *Connecticut Education*, 29–41.
36. Examples: Connecticut *Gazette*, July 9, 1773, 3; Nov. 19, 1773, 3; and Apr. 8, 1774, 3. Marine List reprinted: for example, Boston *Evening Post*, Mar. 13, 1775, 3; Essex *Gazette*, Mar. 14, 1775, 2; New York *Gazette*, Mar. 20, 1775, 6.
37. Labaree, *The Boston Tea Party*, chap. 7; Young, *The Shoemaker and the Tea Party*, chap. 6; Carp, *Defiance of the Patriots*, esp. chap. 6; Norton, "The Seventh Tea Ship."
38. 14 George III, cap. 19, "Boston Port Act"; Perry, *British Politics*, 27–29. Hundred Years' War: Saul, *Richard II*, 190–91.

9. The Inimical

1. Ammerman, *In the Common Cause*, 5–7, 19–20; Breen, *The Marketplace of Revolution*, 1–20, q. on 2; Marston, *King and Congress*, 41–44, 69–75.
2. Early Loyalists: for example, Marston, *King and Congress*, 16–22, 39; Gould, *The Persistence of Empire*, 136–38. Wilkes: Maier, "John Wilkes"; Cash, *John Wilkes;* Alpaugh, *Friends of Freedom*, chap. 3. Loyalists: Maier, *From Resistance to Revolution*, 162–78; Bannister and Riordan, "Loyalism and the British Atlantic."
3. Maier, *From Resistance to Revolution*, 278–83; Minty, *Unfriendly to Liberty*, chap. 4; Peters, *General History of Connecticut*, appendix, 246–55; Buel, *Dear Liberty*, 25–32; Breen, *American Insurgents, American Patriots*, 177–84. AFC, B3F2, Joseph Webb to Thomas Allen, Sept. 5, 1774, q.
4. Connecticut *Gazette*, Nov. 11, 1774, 1–3, q. on 1; Feb. 10, 1775, 3; Nash, *The Urban Crucible*, 212–16, 218–21, 224–40; Raphael, *The First American Revolution*, 64–89 passim, 135–37. Windham: Willingham, "Windham, Connecticut," 126–51.
5. Nash, *The Unknown American Revolution*, 178–89, 1st q. on 178, and chap. 3, 2nd and 3rd qq. on 94; Eustace, *Passion Is the Gale*, 171–84; Breen, *American Insurgents, American Patriots*, 177–84, and Breen, *The Will of the People*, 9–15.
6. Connecticut *Gazette*, Sept. 30, 74, 3, q.; Ammerman, *In the Common Cause*, 20–34, 42–47, 78–85; Carp, *Defiance of the Patriots*, 196–200. New London Committee: for example, Connecticut *Gazette*, Dec. 2, 1774, 1, and Apr. 20, 1775, 3.
7. AFC, B7F3, "Great Neck Lease," Mar. 20, 1775, and "Mt. Pleasant Lease," Sept. 1, 1775; latter renewed by Lewis Allen, AFC, B7F4, Mar. 30, 1776; AFC, B3F4, Stephen Gorton deed of land sale to Thomas Allen, Dec. 11, 1776.
8. Naval patrols example: Connecticut *Gazette*, Feb. 3, 1775, 3. Dumaresq: Connecticut *Gazette*, Dec. 2, 1774, q. on 1; Newport *Mercury*, Dec. 19, 1774, 1.
9. Lynd and Walstreicher, "Free Trade, Sovereignty, and Slavery," q. on 609; Carp, *Defiance of the Patriots*, 17–21.
10. AFC, B3F2, Thomas Willson to Thomas Allen, Sept. 1774; AFC, B3F2., Noble Hinman to Thomas Allen, Aug. 18, 1774; AFC, B3F3, Barnabas Deane to Thomas Allen, Feb. 7, 1775, q.
11. Richard: May 1758 (see chap. 4). Samuel: August 1760 (see chap. 5). John Shackmaple Jr.: for example, NTSP, B26, ledger 5, Capt. John Shackmaple Accounts, 1765–1767; AFC, B1F3, William Wanton to Thomas Allen, June 27, 1768; New London Town Clerk's Office, Book 18, 266, Deed of Land, Widow Phebe Shackmaple, Nov. 25, 1771. Nathaniel Allen: Boston *News-Letter*, Nov. 8, 1770, q. on 3; Ward, *History of the Town of Shrewsbury*, 216.
12. Nathaniel Allen Will: Massachusetts. Probate Court, Worcester County, FamilySearch .org (https://www.familysearch.org/ark:/61903/3:1:3Q9M-C9YT-H8F?view=fullText), Image Group Number: 007704434. Jolley Allen: for example, AFC, fol. 36, "An Account . . . of the Sufferings and Losses of Mr. Jolley Allen," 30–32, and AFC, B2F3, Lewis Allen to Thomas Allen, Jan. 14, 1773. Advertisement examples: Boston *News-Letter*, July 28, 1763, 4; Boston *Gazette*, June 13, 1768, 3; Boston *Evening Post*, Jan. 24, 1774, 4. Inheritance: for example, Haskins, "The Beginnings of Partible Inheritance"; Ditz, *Property and Kinship*, chap. 7; Damiano, "To Well and Truly Administer."

13. William: AFC, B2F2, Lewis Allen to Thomas Allen, Sept. 11, 1772, 1st q.; Dorcas Allen Will, AFC., B7F3, Jan. 12, 1775, 2nd q.
14. Lewis: Ward, "History of the Town of Shrewsbury," 31–32; Washburn, *Historical Sketches of Leicester,* 163–64, 343; Lewis and Mary married Sept. 26, 1770, in Worcester; Rice, *Vital Records of the Town of Shrewsbury,* 193. Caleb: for example, AFC, B2F4, Caleb Allen to Thomas Allen, May 22, 1773; AFC, B3F1, Thomas Willson to Thomas Allen, Mar. 3, 1774; AFC, fol. 31, "Stock and Expense Book for 1774 . . . debt of Caleb Allen."
15. AFC, B4F1, Thomas Allen to Lewis Allen, Jan. 15, 1779, 2–3.
16. For example, AFC., B2F1, James Stewart to Thomas Allen, May 27, 1771; AFC, B2F2, James Stewart to Thomas Allen, Feb. 9, 1772 (apprenticeship terms); AFC, B2F3, Noble Hinman to Thomas Allen, Feb. 18, 1773; AFC, B3F2, James and Alexander Stewart to Thomas Allen, Dec. 16, 1774, q.; New York *Gazette,* May 3, 1773, 3. Clerkships: Axtell, *The School Upon a Hill,* 112–20.
17. AFC, B3F2, Thomas Junior to Thomas Allen, Nov. 14, 1774, 1st and 2nd qq., and Nov. 30, 1774, 3rd q.
18. Raphael, *The First American Revolution;* Connecticut *Gazette,* Apr. 21, 1775, 3; Nichols, *A History of Freetown,* 18–20 (enslaved men not mentioned). Dunmore's Proclamation: David, *Dunmore's New World,* esp. 103–10.
19. AFC, B3F3, Lewis Allen to Thomas Allen, Apr. 13, 1775; Norwich *Packet,* Apr. 22, 1775, 2; Connecticut *Gazette,* Apr. 28, 1775, 1; Buel, *Dear Liberty,* 35–36.
20. AFC, B3F3, Lewis Allen to Thomas Allen, July 13, 1775; Christopher Christophers to Thomas Allen, Aug. 15, 1775; Amasa Keyes to Thomas Allen, Aug. 24, 1775. Overviews of events include Gross, *The Minutemen and Their World,* 104–41; Taylor, *American Revolutions,* 123–44; and Holton, *Liberty Is Sweet,* 155–91, 209–14.
21. Overviews: Anderson, *The Martyr and the Traitor,* 82–96; also Zeichner, *Connecticut's Years of Controversy,* 200–207; East, *Connecticut's Loyalists,* 23–36; Parkinson, *The Common Cause,* chap.1. Vilification: New London *Gazette,* Sept. 29, 1775, 1st q. on 3; Connecticut *Courant,* Oct. 2, 1775, 2nd q. on 1.
22. Connecticut *Journal,* May 21, 1773, 2, reporting Boston Town Hall meeting of May 17, 1773, both qq.; Breen, *The Will of the People,* 86–97; Zeichner, *Connecticut's Years of Controversy,* 204.
23. Ibid., 233–35; Smith, "The American Loyalists"; Jasanoff, *Liberty's Exiles,* 364–65, 365n16.
24. British movements: Connecticut *Gazette,* Aug. 4, 1775, 3, Sept. 1, 1775, 3, and Sept. 8, 1775, 3. Allen's Marine List: Connecticut *Gazette,* Apr. 28, 1775, 3; June 23, 1775, 3; Aug. 4, 1775, 3, q.
25. AFC, B3F3, John Chenevard to Thomas Allen, Apr. 23, 1775 (Hartford); AFC, B3F3, James Stewart to Thomas Allen, May 21, 1775 (New York); Richard Alsop to Thomas Allen (in New Haven), Aug. 25, 1775. Adams cited in Lynd and Waldstreicher, "Free Trade, Sovereignty, and Slavery," q. on 626.
26. AFC, B3F3, Thomas Allen Sr. to Thomas Allen Jr., Aug. 16, 1775.
27. Ibid., Thomas Allen Jr. to Thomas Allen Sr., Sept. 6, 1775, q., and Sept. 26, 1775.
28. 16 George III, cap. 5, "Prohibitory Act." Thomas Jr. may have been briefly imprisoned by the British. AFC, B1F1, Hiram Holt to the AAS, Apr. 8, 1857.

29. APDC, vol. 4, James Warren to John Adams, Apr. 3, 1776, 97. See also Stoddard, "An Account of Part of the Sufferings and Losses of Jolley Allen," 67–72.
30. AFC, fol. 36, Jolley Allen, "An Account of Part of the Sufferings and Losses of Jolley Allen," 32–39, q. on 34.
31. Ibid., 40–42, q. on 42.
32. Ibid., 43–47, q. on 43; AFC, B3F4, Lewis Allen Petition, June 10, 1776; Lewis Allen to Thomas Allen, June 16, 1776.
33. AFC, fol. 36, Jolley Allen, "An Account of Part of the Sufferings and Losses of Jolley Allen," 47–48, q. on 48. Stone: Boston *Gazette,* July 24, 1775, 4; Boston *Continental Journal,* June 5, 1777, 2. Ward, *History of the Town of Shrewsbury,* 73–74, 183, 201, 424–25. Names "Josiah" and "Jonas" are used interchangeably; unclear if two different men.
34. AFC, fol. 36, Jolley Allen, "An Account of Part of the Sufferings and Losses of Jolley Allen," 49–51, q. on 50.
35. Ibid., 51–53, q. on 52.
36. Ibid.
37. Ibid., 53–58; AFC, B3F4, Lewis Allen to Thomas Allen, July 12, 1776, and Sept. 27, 1776.
38. AFC, fol. 36, Jolley Allen, "An Account of Part of the Sufferings and Losses of Jolley Allen," 59–60, q. on 59.
39. Ibid.
40. Ibid., q. on 59.
41. Ibid., Lewis Allen to Thomas Allen, letters of Apr. 22, 1777, July 16, 1777, and Dec. 7, 1777.
42. AFC, fol. 31, "Stock and Expense Book for 1774 (to 1778)," debt of Capt. Thomas Willson, January 1, 1774, and entry for Willson, January 1, 1777; AFC, fol. 31, lawsuit background, Thomas Allen v. Thomas Willson, B8F3, Mar. 3, 1786.
43. AFC, B3F4, Thomas Allen, Stitched Petition for Liberty, Feb. 17, 1777.

10. The Prisoner and the Privateer Port

1. Arrest described in AFC, B3F4, stitched petition of Thomas Allen to Committee of Safety, Feb. 17, 1777, fol. 1–1v. Arrest and imprisonment of Loyalists: Compeau, *Dishonored Americans,* chap. 2; Breen, *The Will of the People,* 101–20; Godbeer, *A World of Trouble,* 139–47.
2. AFC, B3F4, stitched petition of Thomas Allen, fols. 1v.–2v., Feb. 17–Feb. 23, 1777; both qq. fol. 3v.
3. AFC, fol. 5, copy of Thomas Allen to Col. Dyar Throop, Feb. 26, 1777, q.
4. AFC, fol. 5, form letter by Thomas Allen, Petition for liberty, Mar. 3, 1777, q.
5. Connecticut *Courant,* July 8, 1776, 1st q. on 2; Rogers and Shaw, *Connecticut's Naval Office,* Nathaniel Shaw to Robert Morris, Feb. 4, 1777, 2nd q on 296, Connecticut *Gazette,* Mar. 8, 1776, 2, and Apr. 6, 1776, 2. Long Island Sound: Radune, *Sound Rising,* chap. 9; Middlebrook, *History of Maritime Connecticut,* esp. 2:47–251 passim.
6. Skemp, *William Franklin,* 213–225; Jones, "The Rage of Tory-Hunting," esp. 733–36.
7. AFC, B3F4, copy of form letter by Thomas Allen; Petition for liberty, Mar. 3, 1777; CSR 1, Thomas Allen of New London sentenced, 189. Lebanon: Roth, *Connecticut's War Governor,* 13–16; Willingham, "Windham, Connecticut," 156–61, 187–88, 316–17. Inimical laws: CSR 1:226–27, "An Act for prescribing and enjoining an Oath of Fidelity

to this State"; Cuddihy, *The Fourth Amendment*, chap. 23. Interior exile: compare with Godbeer, *A World of Trouble*, 147–53.

8. Van Dusen, "The Trade of Revolutionary Connecticut," chap. 14, q. on 187; Walsh, *Connecticut Industry*, 18–41.
9. Destler, *Connecticut*, 15–43; Huston, *Logistics of Liberty*, chap. 5; Horgan, *Forged in War*, 44–52.
10. AFC, B7F4, Thomas Allen Journal, Apr. 2, 1777; Van Dusen, "The Trade of Revolutionary Connecticut," 218–23.
11. AFC, B3F4, Thomas Allen Journal, Mar. 10, 1777, 1st and 2nd qq.; ibid., Petition for liberty, Mar. 30, 1777, 3rd and 4th qq. Seneca: most likely the 1718 edition of L'Estrange, *Seneca's Moral*. "Foundation of true joy is the conscience" is found on p. 107 of the 1775 edition, cited here.
12. AFC, B3F4, Petition for liberty, Mar. 30, 1777, 1st and 2nd qq.
13. AFC, B3F4, entry evening of Apr. 3, 1777; q. CSR 1: Freedom granted by Assembly, Apr. 3, 1777, 202.
14. Sources for war events discussed in this and the next paragraph include Taylor, *American Revolutions*, 176–90; Weddle, *The Compleat Victory*, Introduction, chaps. 18–20 and 23; Dull, *A Diplomatic History of the American Revolution*, chaps. 11 and 12.
15. War fatigue: for example, Taylor, *American Revolutions*, 194–209, 287–93, q. on 209; Henretta, "The War for Independence and American Economic Development"; Buel, *Dear Liberty*, chap. 5; Holton, *Liberty Is Sweet*, chap. 27; Godbeer, *A World of Trouble*.
16. JCC, 4:229–32, 247–48, and 251–54. Privateering overviews: for example, Van Dusen, "The Trade of Revolutionary Connecticut," 236–45; Roland et al., *The Way of the Ship*, chap. 10; Willis, *The Struggle for Sea Power*, 93–100; McGrath, *Give Me a Fast Ship*, chap. 11; Hulbert, *The Untold War at Sea*, chap. 1. Courts and Naval Boards: Bourguignon, *The First Federal Court*, 43–57; Fowler, *Rebels Under Sail*, chaps. 3–5.
17. Rogers and Shaw, *Connecticut's Naval Office*, 16–22, 45–53.
18. *General Putnam:* Rogers and Shaw, *Connecticut's Naval Office*, 54–65; Allen, *A Naval History of the American Revolution*, 296–98; Horgan, *Forged in War*, 110. Captain Allon: for example, NTSP, B20, P141.9051, Thomas Allon to Nathaniel Shaw, May 22, 1778, q.; NTSP., B12, 79.4663, Thomas Allon Sailing Orders for *General Putnam*, May 24, 1778; NTSP, B21, P149.5565, Bond for Privateer *Nancy*, Sept. 28, 1778; NTSP, B13, P86.4946, 1783. Clark and Biddle, "Letters," 381–84; Pennsylvania *Packet*, Apr. 8, 1780, 3; *Clarendon Courier*, 4, no. (3), 1992, 9 (https://cdm16072.contentdm.oclc.org/digital/collection/p16072coll11/id/537/rec/44 or http://www.carolana.com/NC/Counties/Clarendon_Courier_Volume_4_Number_3_1992.pdf); CSRNC, "Minutes . . . Wilmington/New-Hanover Committee of Safety," https://docsouth.unc.edu/csr/index.php/document/csr10-0012#p10-24. His handwriting style differed from Thomas Allen's, including a distinct "o," and without the usual flourish and age.
19. Norwich *Packet*, Sept. 21, 1778, 3; NTSP, B25, ledger 3, *General Putnam* prizes (*Princess Royale* [captured June 24, 1778], *Thomas* [May 5, 1778], *Dispatch* [July 5, 1778], *Elizabeth* [July 6, 1778], *Surprize* [July 9, 1778], and *Carolina* [Sept. 14, 1778]). Prizes as source of naval supply: for example, NTSP, B20, P141.9044, John Lamb to Nathaniel Shaw, May 23, 1778; NTSP, B6, 30.3169, Admiralty Office to Nathaniel Shaw, May 9, 1780.
20. NTSP, B14, P92.5434, Isaac Sears Protest, July 3, 1779; ibid., B23, ledger 28, I. Sears Account (1778), 57.

21. NTSP, B5, F26, 1629, Court Deposition 1784, dispute over *General Putnam* prizes, Sept. 1778; Grubb, *The Continental Dollar,* chap. 13.
22. Author's database culled from court libels printed in the Connecticut *Gazette,* 1776–1783.
23. News in the next three paragraphs from Connecticut *Gazette* of Apr. 29, 1779, May 5, 1779, May 3, 1779, May 20, 1779, and May 27, 1779.
24. CSR 2:224–27, "An Act for Ascertaining the Quantity of Grain, Flour and Meal . . .", April 7, 1779, q., 225; Connecticut *Gazette,* Apr. 29, 1779, 3.
25. Smallpox: for example, Connecticut *Gazette,* Jan. 29, 1779, 3, and Feb. 19, 1779; Rogers, Nathaniel Shaw to Marine Committee, Mar. 14, 1779, q. on 322; Fenn, *Pox Americana,* 85–94, 108–10; Wehrman, *The Contagion of Liberty,* 3–11, 213–36. "Laying": keeping anchored at wharfside.
26. Connecticut *Gazette,* May 5, 1779, q. on 3.
27. Connecticut *Gazette,* Feb. 10, 1779, 3; Apr. 29, 1779, 1–3, q. on 1.
28. Connecticut Gazette, May 13, 1779, q. on 5; also, Connecticut *Journal,* May 19, 1779, 3; Middlebrook, *History of Maritime Connecticut,* 73, 160.
29. Connecticut *Gazette,* May 27, 1779, q. on 3; Minty, *Unfriendly to Liberty,* 126.
30. CSR, 1:333, 335–37, both qq. on 333; Connecticut *Gazette,* July 4, 1777, 3; Caulkins, *History of New London,* 551; genealogical reference, https://www.stewartsociety.org/history-of-the-stewarts.cfm?section=famous-stewarts&subcatid=19&histid=176.
31. Caulkins, *History of New London,* 445–48; Connecticut *Gazette,* Sept. 8, 1779, 3; AFC, fol. 36, Thomas Allen to Jolley Allen, Aug. 29, 1780, 77.
32. Army, Connecticut *Gazette,* Apr. 29, 1779, 3; Navy, ibid., May 27, 1779, 3.
33. Pomp: Connecticut *Gazette,* Apr. 15, 1779, q. on 4. Other examples: Connecticut *Gazette,* Apr. 8, 1779, 4 (Ferrow), and May 13, 1779, 3 (Prince) and 4 (Warwick).
34. Post office: Connecticut *Gazette,* June 16, 1775, 4.
35. Clandestine sheep droving: AFC, B4F1, Thomas Allen to Lewis Allen, Jan. 15, 1779. Possible Bigelow-Allen partnership: for example, AFC, B4F1, J[ohn] Bigelow to Thomas Allen, Apr. 26, 1779, May 14, 1779, and May 28, 1779; Buel, *Dear Liberty,* 257–67. Bigelow: Howe, *Genealogy of the Bigelow Family,* 88.
36. Opened mail: for example, AFC, B4F1, Jolley Allen to Thomas Allen, July 30, 1779, and May 20, 1780; AFC, fol. 36, "Sufferings of Jolley Allen," Lewis Allen to Jolley Allen, May 12, 1778, and Nov. 20, 1779; q. on 13. Censorship: Gilbert, "The Connecticut Loyalists," 273–91; Adelman, "A Constitutional Conveyance of Intelligence"; Grasso, *A Speaking Aristocracy,* chap. 8.
37. AFC, B4F1, Jolley Allen to Eleanor Allen, July 30, 1779; AFC, fol. 36, "Sufferings of Jolley Allen," copy of Thomas Allen to Jolley Allen, Apr. 10, 1780, 77.

11. "Unhappy New London"

1. This paragraph and the next are based on Nash, *The Unknown American Revolution,* chap. 7; Taylor, *American Revolutions,* 194–99, 203–8, 226–38; Holton, *Liberty Is Sweet,* chap. 27 and 400–415, 422–26; and Ellis, *The Cause,* 210–33.
2. Callahan, *Flight from the Republic,* 90; Conway, "British Governments and the Conduct of the American War," esp. 159–66; Bickham, *Making Headlines,* 97–102, q. on 99.

3. Description of London ca. 1779–1781 for this paragraph and the next are based on George, "London and the Life of the Town," 160–96; Rudé, *Hanoverian London, 1714–1808,* 9–14, 21–25, 60–83, 174–82; and Norton, *The British-Americans,* 63–72.
4. AFC, fol. 36 "Sufferings of Jolley Allen," 1st q. on 60; 2nd q. on 61.
5. Pepperell: Jones, *The Loyalists of Massachusetts,* 232–33; Norton, *The British-Americans,* 72–73. AFC, fol. 36, Jolley Allen to William Pepperell, Nov. 22, 1779, 23. Germain: Bickham, *Making Headlines,* q. on 145; O'Shaughnessy, *Men Who Lost America,* chap. 5.
6. AFC, fol. 36, "Sufferings of Jolley Allen," Mar. 26, 1777, 61. Callahan, *Flight from the Republic,* 124; Berkin, *Jonathan Sewall,* 119.
7. Callahan, *Flight from the Republic,* 90.
8. Berkin, *Jonathan Sewall,* 117–19, q. on 118; Norton, *The British-Americans,* 79–92; George, "London and the Life of the Town."
9. Norton, *The British-Americans,* 121–22; AFC, B4F2, William Allen to Thomas Allen, June 3, 1783, q.
10. Quintus Fabius Maximus Verrucosus (280–203 BCE). London *Chronicle,* July 22, 1780, cited in Bickham, *Making Headlines,* 2009, q. on 198.
11. AFC, fol. 36, Inventory of clothing, 8–9; ibid., Jolley Allen to Thomas Allen, 69–70, 1st q. on 69; 2nd q. on 17; 3rd q. on 70; 4th q. on 62. See also B4F1, Jolley Allen to Thomas Allen, Oct. 31, 1780.
12. See, for example, Connecticut *Gazette,* 4/7/1781, privateer news/British depredations, 3–4; Connecticut *Courant,* June 29, 1781, privateer news dateline New London, 3; Connecticut *Journal,* Aug. 9, 1781, 4; Caulkins, *History of New London,* 540–44. Saltsonstall and the Penobscot Expedition: for example, Allen, *A Naval History of the American Revolution,* vol. 2, chap. 12; Burbank, "Want of Proper Spirit and Energy"; Norton, "Dudley Saltonstall," and Norton, "The Penobscot Expedition." *Hannah* prize: Connecticut *Journal,* Aug. 9, 1781, 4; Connecticut *Gazette,* Aug. 24, 1781, 3.
13. Irish Pale: Hinderaker and Mancall, *At the Edge of Empire,* 1–9; Ellis, *Ireland's English Pale,* chaps. 7 and 8. Lord William Barrington in Peckham, *Sources of American Independence,* 1:121, q.
14. Arnold at Richmond: Georgia *Royal Gazette,* Supplement, Mar. 8, 1781, 4; Wallace, *Traitorous Hero,* 271–77; Lender and Martin, "A Traitor's Epiphany," 329–36. Amphibious operations: for example, Carpenter et al., *The War of American Independence,* 160–62, 241–46; Willis, *The Struggle for Sea Power,* 110–11, 123–26, 343–52; Syrett, "British Amphibious Operations," and Syrett, "The Methodology of British Amphibious Operations."
15. MacKenzie, *Diary of Frederick Mackenzie,* 2:546–47, 564–57, 580–84; Clinton, *The American Rebellion,* 313–27, q. on 320. Reports on the French squadron at Newport: for example, MacKenzie, *Diary of Frederick Mackenzie* 2:469–540 passim; also Willcox, "Rhode Island in British Strategy." Washington cited in Mackesy, *The War for America,* 411–14, q. on 413; O'Shaughnessy, *Men Who Lost America,* chap. 6.
16. Clinton, *The American Rebellion,* 198–99, 330–31, 443–44; New York *Gazette & Weekly Mercury,* Feb. 25, 1782, reprinting letter Clinton to Lord Germain in London *Gazette* dated Nov. 6, 1781, 2. Command officially assigned to Arnold Sept. 1, MacKenzie, *Diary of Frederick Mackenzie,* 2:603–10. Syrett, *The Royal Navy in American Waters,* 144–51.

17. Caulkins, *History of New London,* 1st q. on 544; MacKenzie, *Diary of Frederick Mackenzie,* 2:597–601, 2nd q. on 598; Mackesy, *The War for America, 1775–1783,* 421–23.
18. Caulkins, *History of New London,* 546–47.
19. Landing: likely Pequot Beach on the west, and Eastern and Avery beaches on the east. See Daniel Lyman, "A sketch of New London & Groton . . . ," [1781], Library of Congress (https://www.loc.gov/item/gm71000695/). Summary of attack: Patriot based on NLCHS, D.H151r, Affidavit of Robert Hallam, 9/6/1781; Rogers and Mumford, *Groton Heights,* Zabdiel Rogers to Thomas Mumford, Sept. 8, 1781; Rathbun, *Narrative of Jonathan Rathbun,* including "Narrative of Rufus Avery," 17–40; Connecticut *Journal,* Sept. 13, 1781, 1. British, all variations of Arnold's official report: for example, *Royal Gazette* (New York), Sept. 19, 1781, 3–4; Clinton, *The American Rebellion,* "Extract from Brigadier General Arnold's report to Sir Henry Clinton," 565–70.
20. Connecticut *Gazette,* Sept. 7, 1781, 3.
21. Rogers and Mumford, *Groton Heights and New London,* Rogers to Thomas Mumford, Sept. 8, 1781; Connecticut *Gazette,* Sept. 28, 1781, 3.
22. Battle of Fort Griswold based on Rogers and Mumford, *Groton Heights and New London,* Rogers to Thomas Mumford, Sept. 8, 1781; Caulkins, *History of New London,* 557–72.
23. AAS Digital Sources "Copy of a letter from Brigadier General Arnold to his Excellency the Commander in Chief," (dated Sept. 8, 1781), *Political Magazine,* Nov. 1, 1781, 1st q. on 665–66; Wallace, *Connecticut's Dark Star of the Revolution,* 2nd q. on 61.
24. News of attack: for example, Providence *Gazette,* Sept. 8, 1781, 3; Worcester *Gazette,* Sept. 13, 1781, 3; Boston *Independent Ledger,* Sept. 17, 1781, 4. Retribution: *Freeman's Journal,* Sept. 26, 1781, 1st on 2. "Unhappy New London": APDC, Abigail Adams to John Adams, Sept. 29, 1781, 2nd q.
25. Rathbun et al., *Narrative of Jonathan Rathbun,* q. on 9–10.
26. Connecticut *Gazette,* Oct. 12, 1781, 1. Prisoners: Connecticut *Journal,* Nov. 15, 1781, 3; Worcester *Spy,* Jan. 10, 1782, 3; Pennsylvania *Packet,* Jan. 26, 1782, 3.
27. Connecticut *Gazette,* Sept. 14, 1781, 1; Sept. 21, 1781, 2; Sept. 28, 1781, 3–4; Oct. 5, 1781, 3–4; Oct. 12, 1781, 2; New York *Royal Gazette,* Nov. 28, 1781, q. on 3. Privateering: Author database of prize libels printed in the Connecticut *Gazette,* Nov. 4, 1781–June 11, 1783.
28. Franco-American wartime trade: for example, Van Dusen, "The Trade of Revolutionary Connecticut," chap. 22; Godechot, "Les relations économiques," q. on 30, translation by author; Marzagalli, *Bordeaux et les États-Unis,* 29–33, 51–56, 71–82. Growth of interior: for example, Nettels, *The Emergence of a National Economy,* 69–75, 251–55; Jensen, *The New Nation,* 219–27; McCusker and Menard, *The Economy of British America,* 363–74. Connecticut: Saladino, "The Economic Revolution," chaps. 2, 10; Walsh, *Connecticut Industry,* 48–64; Buel, *In Irons,* 168–73.
29. Examples: Connecticut *Gazette,* Sept. 8, 1780, 4; Mar. 8, 1781, 4; Sept. 28, 1781, 4; Connecticut *Journal,* Nov. 29, 1781, 3; CSL, RG3, NLCC Files, B176/F19, no. 4, Barnes v. Rogers, 1782; Rogers and Shaw, *Connecticut's Naval Office,* Thomas Shaw to Gov. Jonathan Trumbull, Aug. 10, 1780, 106–9; Buel, *Dear Liberty,* 257–72, 283–93, q. on 285.
30. Libels in Connecticut *Gazette,* issues of Apr. 5, 12, 19, and 26, 1782, all p. 3; overall, Connecticut *Gazette,* Oct. 1781–May 1783 (last notice of prize ships libeled). "Cottage and cove" smuggling: for example, Kwass, *Contraband,* chap. 11; Heebøll-Holm, *Ports,*

Piracy and Maritime War, "Introduction" and chap. 3; Rule, "Social Crime"; Farrell, "Smuggling Silks," esp. 286–93. Elite involvement: Buel, *Dear Liberty,* 268–69, 295; Roth, *Connecticut's War Governor;* Rogers and Shaw, *Connecticut's Naval Office,* Thomas Shaw to Jonathan Trumbull, Aug. 10, 1780, 106–9.

31. East, *Connecticut's Loyalists,* 45–49; Zeichner, "The Rehabilitation of Loyalists," and Zeichner, "The Loyalist Problem"; McKito, *From Loyalists to Loyal Citizens,* 4.
32. Allen: NLTC, Town Meeting Minutes, Dec. 3, 1781. Taber: Connecticut *Gazette,* Feb. 8, 1782, 4. Elizabeth: AFC, B4F1, Lewis Allen to Thomas Allen, Mar. 29, 1782.
33. Allen Land transferals: B8F1, copies of deeds for six separate land parcels, Thomas Allen to Thomas Allen Jr., all dated Feb. 8, 1782. Refugee land sales: for example, State Acts CSR 2:9–12 (Oct. 1778), 267 (May 1779); 472–73 (July 1781); Buel, *Dear Liberty,* 146–47, 256, 370, 396. Retirement quip: AFC, fol. 36, copy of Thomas Allen to Jolley Allen, May 15, 1780, 74–75.
34. Heated exchanges: for example, AFC, B3F4, Lewis Allen to Thomas Allen, Dec. 7, 1777; AFC, B4F1, Thomas Allen to Lewis Allen, Jan. 15, 1779; ibid., Thomas Allen to Jolley Allen, Apr. 22, 1780. Harboring Loyalists: ibid., Lewis Allen to Thomas Allen, Nov. 30, 1781, 1st q.; ibid., Lewis Allen to Thomas Allen, Jan. 25, 1782, 2nd and 3rd qq.
35. AFC, B4F1, Rev. Thomas Waight (of Shrewsbury) to Thomas Allen, Nov. 8, 1782; AFC, fol. 36, an inserted letter by John Stock to A. H. Pickering, dated June 10, 1892, noted that Jolley Allen was buried at St. John of Wapping cemetery on June 7, 1782. Obituary: Massachusetts *Spy,* Nov. 17, 1782, 3.
36. AFC, fol. 36, copy of Lewis Allen's Account with Jolley Allen, May 10, 1780, 73–74.
37. AFC, B4F2, "An inventory of the Estate Real and personal whereof Lewis Allen, about 1783," n.d.
38. AFC, B4F2, Thomas Allen to "Sister" Mary Allen, Apr. 20, 1783; Elijah Dix to Thomas Allen, Mar. 1, 1783; AFC, B4F1, Elijah Dix to Thomas Allen, Nov. 27, 1782, q. on 2.
39. AFC, B4F2, Thomas Allen to Mary "Polley" Allen, June 4, 1783, qq.

12. The Born-Again Yankee

1. Imagined scenario; advertisement for City Coffee House, Connecticut *Gazette,* Jan. 14, 1785, 4.
2. Gould, *Among the Powers of the Earth,* 119–30; Taylor, *American Revolutions,* 302–11.
3. AFC, B8F1, Petition of Thomas Allen to Common Council of New London, Mar. 30, 1784, and Petition, Oct, 13, 1784, qq.
4. Estate and Marriage: Mt. Pleasant: Washburn, *Historical Sketches of the Town of Leicester,* 164; Rice, *Vital Records of the Town of Leicester,* Marriage notation July 7, 1784, 116; AFC, B4F4, Thomas Allen to Mary Allen, July 12, 1787. Compliment examples: AFC, B4F2, John Chenevard to Thomas Allen, July 7, 1785; AFC, B4F4, William Constant (Guadeloupe) to Thomas Allen, Feb. 5, 1787. Coffee House: AFC, B5F1, Isaac Jones to Thomas Allen, signing over of lease by "Mr. Bloors" (Blowers) in 1784, Nov. 14, 1788.
5. Advertisement: Connecticut *Gazette,* Jan. 14, 1785, quotes, 4; Massachusetts *Spy,* Feb. 17, 1785, 4; American *Herald,* Mar. 28, 1785, 3; Maryland *Journal,* June 10, 1785, 2.
6. AFC, B5F2, Sally Allen to "Aunt Allen" (Mary Allen), May 7, 1789; AFC, B5F3, Sally Allen to Mary Allen, May 19, 1790, qq.; AFC, BF61, Sally Allen to Mary Allen, Oct. 19, 1792.

Nancy: AFC, B4F2, death also by consumption, Thomas Allen to Thomas Whaight, Feb. 15, 1784.

7. Jolley Jr.: AFC, B5F3, Nathaniel Allen Jr. to Thomas Allen, July 30, 1790. Nathaniel: AFC, B4F4, Berry and Sage to Thomas Allen, Apr. 30, 1787, 1st and 2nd qq.; AFC, B5F3, Nathaniel Allen Jr. to Thomas Allen, Nov. 14, 1790, 3rd q.
8. AFC, B5F1, Nehemiah Waterman to Thomas Allen, Apr. 4, 1788, and June 26, 1788, q. Currency and loan problems in Connecticut: Buel, *Dear Liberty,* 144–52, 198–207, 215–22, 316–20. Confederation financial crisis: Chu, *Stumbling Toward the Constitution,* chap. 4; Holton, *Unruly Americans,* chap. 4 and 134–37.
9. CSL, RG001, Revolutionary War Series 1, Chappel Petition, Jan. 12, 1778, 192–93; ibid., fol. 31, "Stock and Expense Book for 1774 (to 1778)," debt of Capt. Thomas Willson, Jan. 1, 1774, and entry for Willson, Jan. 1, 1777.
10. AFC, B8F1, copy of "Court Opinion issued by General Samuel Parsons & Lyle Moot, Esq.," Mar. 26, 1783, with notes by Thomas Allen appended, q.
11. CSL, RG003, vol. 26, no. 2, Thomas Allen v. Thomas Willson, Feb. 1786; ibid., vol. 26, no. 145, *Thomas Allen v. Thomas Willson,* Sept. 1787.
12. AFC, B4F4, Thomas Allen, copy of oath given to Connecticut State Superior Court, Oct. 9, 1787, 1st q.; AFC, B5F2: Thomas Willson to Thomas Allen, Mar. 27, 1789, 2nd q.
13. Examples: AFC, B4F2, Giles Sage to Thomas Allen, Oct. 20, 1783; Thomas Mumford to Thomas Allen, May 2, 1784; and George Burr to same, May 3, 1785; AFC, B8F3, Jacob Sebor account with Thomas Allen, Apr. 14, 1786.
14. AFC, B4F3, John Shaw (New York) to Thomas Allen, May 8, 1786; AFC, B5F2, Nathan Sage to Thomas Allen, Oct. 19, 1789.
15. AFC, B5F2, Oliver Bowen to Thomas Allen, Apr. 20, 1789. Bowen: Founders Online, Oliver Bowen to George Washington, Apr. 1789; Beeman, *Plain, Honest Men,* 324–29; Sparks, *Africans in the Old South,* 85; Clark-Pujara, *Dark Work,* 80–85; Kelley, *American Slavers,* 167–84. Numbers of Greater New England slave ship ventures to Atlantic Africa, 1789–1808: Massachusetts, thirty-one; Rhode Island, fifteen; New York, nine; and one each from Connecticut and New Hampshire, from SlaveryVoyages.org (https://www.slavevoyages.org). My thanks to Traci Picard, Brown University, for leads on Bowen.
16. Tench Coxe cited in Bjork, "The Weaning of the American Economy," q. on 541. Mid-1780s depression: Nettels, *The Emergence of a National Economy,* 45–49, 60–69; Hedges, *The Browns of Providence Plantations,* 292–300; Bjork, *Stagnation and Growth,* appendices and tables, 48–76 passim, 104–9; Chu, *Stumbling Toward the Constitution,* 43–61; summarized in Taylor, *American Revolutions,* 362–70. Contrasting view: Jensen, *The New Nation,* 184–92, 246–55.
17. Harlow and Madden, *British Colonial Developments,* "American Intercourse Act, March, 1783," 249–51; Norwich *Packet,* July 15, 1784, q. on 3; *State Gazette of South Carolina,* Jan. 12, 1786, 2. Postwar British trade regulation: For example, Jensen, *The New Nation,* 157–63; Wright, "The British Objectives"; McCusker, "Growth, Stagnation, or Decline?," esp. 291–301.
18. Nelson cited in Bjork, "The Weaning of the American Economy:" q. on 551. British views of trade: for example, Harlow and Madden, *British Colonial Developments,* Captain Horatio Nelson to Lord Sydney, Mar. 20, 1785, 265–67; Ritcheson, *Aftermath of Revolution,* 6–30.

19. Massachusetts *Spy*, French Trade Laws on Martinique, Sept. 11, 1783, 3; Connecticut *Gazette*, July 7, 1786, 3. Franco-American trade: Jensen, *The New Nation*, 166–68, 200–205; Ritcheson, *Aftermath of Revolution*, 24–27, q. on 26, author's translation; Godechot, "Les relations économiques"; Tarrade, *Le commerce colonial* 1:502–6, 531–55; Meyer, "Les difficultés du commerce franco-américain"; Stover, "French-American Trade"; Cheney, *Revolutionary Commerce*, 177–91; Marzagalli, "The Failure of a Transatlantic Alliance?," 456–58, and Marzagalli, *Bordeaux et les États-Unis*, 31–50, 56–76, 82–88; Chu, *Stumbling Toward the Constitution*, 5–10; Covo, *Entrepôt of Revolutions*, 28–39.
20. AFC, fol. 37, Journal of Farm Work at Mt. Pleasant, Thomas Allen Jr., entries of Apr. 1782 to Mar. 1785.
21. AFC, B8F2, Contract between Thomas Allen Jr. and Ebenezer Ledyard & Sons (Groton) to build a sloop, Nov. 12, 1784; ibid., Deed of sale of 1/3 sloop "*Renown* now *Resolution*," Randall, Son and Stewart to Thomas Allen Junior, July 25, 1785. Allen Jr.'s first voyage: AFC, B8F2, Account of "Shirley Bangor" (Shirley, Banger & Co., Madeira) with Capt. Thomas Allen [Jr.], Sept. 7, 1785 There may have been another voyage to Ireland. See New York *Daily Advertiser*, Nov. 28, 1785, 2.
22. AFC, B4F3, Thomas Allen Jr. to Thomas Allen Sr., May 19, 1786; ibid., Allen Sr. to Allen Jr., May 21, 1786, both quotes. Rumors of new trade bill: for example, New York *Independent Journal*, Apr. 19, 1786, 2; Pennsylvania *Packet*, May 12, 1786, 3; Connecticut *Gazette*, May 26, 1786, 3; Charleston *Morning Post*, June 12, 1786, 2.
23. 1786 Shipping Act: JCB, Sherwin, "Compendium of Acts" (London, 1786), 26 George III, cap. 60, 1786, "Shipping Act of 1786," q. on 1166. News reports: Connecticut *Journal*, 7/26/1786, 2; New York *Daily Advertiser*, "Abstract from the British Navigation Act," dateline London, June 21, Sept. 6, 1786, 2; Harlow, *The Founding of the Second British Empire*, 1:235–41, 254–73. Reaction: for example, APDC, vol. 18, Stephen Higginson to Adams, July 1786, 408–16; New Jersey *Gazette*, Apr. 24, 1786, 3; Connecticut *Gazette*, June 30, 1786, 3.
24. AFC, B4F3, Thomas Allen Jr. to Allen Sr., July 21, 1786.
25. AFC, B4F4, James Stewart to Thomas Allen Sr., Apr. 14, 87. Ship "pedigree" examples: AFC, B4F4, Samuel Dana to Thomas Allen Sr., Nov. 13, 1787; AFC, B5F2, Daniel Smith to Thomas Allen Sr., Sept. 22, 1789.
26. State tariffs: for example, Crowley, *The Privileges of Independence*, 75–87, 103–6; Chew, "Neo-Mercantilism, American Style"; Chu, *Stumbling Toward the Constitution*, 159–66. Annapolis Convention: for example, Whealy, "The Revolution Is Not Over"; Onuf, "It Is Not a Union," esp. 101–4.
27. AFC, B5F2, Edmund Thayer to Thomas Allen (Jr.), Oct. 6,1791; AFC, B6F1, "Account of a Journey on Horse-back," June 5–13, 1792, qq. on 5–6; AFC, B8F3, Thomas Allen Jr., "Fishers Is. Account," Mar. 19, 1787.
28. Loyalist diaspora overviews: Jasanoff, *Liberty's Exiles*, 48–52, 85–110, 276–309, qq. on 11; Ritcheson, *Aftermath of Revolution*, 59–64; 85–95; Breen, *The Will of the People*, 201–18. New York evacuation: for example, *Royal Gazette*, Aug. 13, 1783, 1, and Nov. 5, 1783; Connecticut *Journal*, Dec. 3, 1783, 1. "Black Loyalists": Frey, *Water from the Rock*, 192–201; Egerton, *Death or Liberty*, 194–220; Gilbert, *Black Patriots and Loyalists*, chap. 8. Lower Canada: for example, Fitch, *A History of the Fitch family*, 100–101; Hackett, *Eleazer Fitch*, 2–6; Jasanoff, *Liberty's Exiles*, 198–209.

29. For example, Buel, *Dear Liberty,* 290–97; Zeichner, "The Rehabilitation of Loyalists"; McKito, *From Loyalists to Loyal Citizens,* 26–32.
30. AFC, B4F2, Charles Arding to Thomas Allen, Oct. 18, 1783, qq.; Nov. 18, 1783; and May 19, 1784; New York *Packet,* Jan. 22, 1784, 1.
31. AFC, B4F3, Philip Jarvis to Thomas Allen, Mar. 8, 1786; George Andrews to Thomas Allen, May 5, 1786; Connecticut *Gazette,* July 25, 1785, 3; Jarvis et al., *The Jarvis Family,* 38–39. Early Shelburne and Loyalist Nova Scotia: for example, *Freeman's Journal* (Philadelphia), Sept. 24, 1783, 3; New York *Daily Advertiser,* Oct. 18, 1785, 3; Huskins, "Shelburnian Manners."
32. AFC, B4F3, Thayer & Jarvis to Capt. George Andrews, Mar. 30, 1786, q.; ibid., Philip Jarvis to Thomas Allen, Aug. 18, 1786. *Dolphin* movements: Connecticut *Gazette,* Nov. 11, 1785, 3; Apr. 7, 1786, 3; July 13,1787, 3 (*Dolphin* seized for smuggling).
33. Viets: AFC, B4F3, Roger Viets to Thomas Allen, June 26, 1786; MacKinnon, *This Unfriendly Soil,* 169–70, 173, 176–78; Anderson, *The Martyr and the Traitor,* 170–171, 176–177; DCB, "Roger Viets." Seabury: Connecticut *Gazette,* May 26, 1786, 3; AFC, B4F4, Samuel Seabury to Thomas Allen, two separate notes, 1787; Columbian *Herald* (new St. James), Nov. 5, 1787, 2; Steiner, *Samuel Seabury,* 222–32, 316–18; McBride, *Pulpit and Nation,* 70–80.

13. "Brethren in Navigation"

1. AFC, B5F2, Mary Buiesson to Thomas Allen, Nov. 25, 1789.
2. Similar concepts: Griffin, *The Age of Atlantic Revolution,* 52–55, q. 55; Laloë, *The Geography of the Ocean,* chap. 4; Withers, "Where was the Atlantic Enlightenment?"; Gilje, "The Enlightenment at Sea in the Atlantic World"; Benton and Perl-Rosenthal, "Afterword."
3. Based on Readex, "America's Historical Newspapers" Database; Thomas, *History of Printing in America,* vol. 1; Library of Congress, "Checklist of 18th-c American newspapers"; North, *History and Present Condition . . .,* esp. table 47.
4. Numbers: based on Readex, "America's Historical Newspapers" Database, and Thomas, *The History of Printing in America,* vol. 1; Library of Congress, "Checklist of 18th-c American newspapers"; North, *History and Present Condition . . . ,* table 47. Circulation: Clark, "Early American Journalism," 354–55; Tucher, "Newspapers and Periodicals," 390–97.
5. Clark, "Early American Journalism," 356–62; Raven, *Publishing Business,* chap. 8; Slauter, "Forward-Looking Statements"; Warner, "Communicating Liberty."
6. AFC, B4F3, Nathaniel Gardiner to Thomas Allen, May 16, 1786.
7. Connecticut *Gazette,* May 26, 1786, 3; Caulkins, *History of New London,* 640.
8. New London whaling: Caulkins, *History of New London,* chap. 37; Decker, *Whaling Industry of New London,* 19–29, 117–18, and appendix 1, 120–45; Stackpole, *The Sea-Hunters,* 96, 452–57.
9. Connecticut *Gazette,* Apr. 14, 1785, 3; Dear and Kemp, "By (the wind)," in *Oxford Companion to Ships and the Sea.*
10. Examples in Connecticut *Gazette:* Jan. 2, 1789, 2 (Baron Hupsch's experiments to reanimate the dead with electric shocks); Jan. 30, 1789, 3 (dangerous mid-Atlantic reef); Apr. 17, 1789, 1 (raising hemp for ship's rope and other uses).

11. Connecticut *Gazette,* Apr. 17, 1789, 3; AFC, fol. 4, "Account book of Th. Allen, 1755–56"—reverse pagination, "Remarks Extract^{d} from Captn Peter Marshall (Mashet) of the Brig *Experiment,*" q. Examples: Pennsylvania *Packet* (Philadelphia), Apr. 29, 1789, 3; Berkshire *Chronicle,* May 1, 1789, 3; New York *Daily Gazette,* May 2, 1789, 2.
12. Examples—Independence Day: Connecticut *Gazette,* July 8, 1785, 2; July 7, 1786, 1st q. on 3; July 10, 1789, 3; Washington's Birthday: Connecticut *Gazette,* Jan. 23, 1789, 3; Feb. 17, 1790. Ratification of Constitution: Connecticut *Gazette,* Aug. 29, 1788, 3. Customs: Connecticut *Gazette,* July 31, 1789, 2–4, 2nd q. on 2; Collier, "Sovereignty Finessed."
13. Example: *Independent Gazette* (Philadelphia), Aug. 26, 1789, 3.
14. New-York *Packet,* Mar. 30, 1786, 4; New York *Daily Advertiser,* Apr. 6, 1786, 2. McDonald, *Novus Ordo Seclorum,* 98–115, 131–42, 1st q. on 100; John Jay, cited in Gould, *Among the Powers of the Earth,* 130–34, 2nd q. on 131. Navigation and the Constitution: for example, Ritcheson, *Aftermath of Revolution,* chap. 7; Chu, *Stumbling Toward the Constitution,* esp. chap. 8; Mallon, "Negotiated Federalism," esp. 696–701.
15. Connecticut *Gazette,* Jan. 30, 1789, q. 3.
16. Connecticut *Gazette,* Nov. 6, 1789, 1st q. on 3. Respectively, Connecticut *Gazette,* Nov. 27, 89, 3 (first two incidents); Dec. 18, 1789, 2nd q. on 3.
17. AFC, B4F3, Jabez Perkins to Thomas Allen, May 21, 1786, 1st q.; AFC, B5F1, Joseph Caldwell to Thomas Allen, Sept. 9, 1788, 2nd q.; AFC, B5F2, William Seymour to Thomas Allen, Jan. 29, 1789, 3rd q.; AFC, B5F3, Le Gay and Evans (Barbados) to Thomas Allen, June 22, 1790, 4th q.
18. AFC, B4F3, Amos Palmer to Thomas Allen, Jan. 28, 1786; see also AFC, B5F4, Sam Mealy to Thomas Allen May 1, 1791.
19. Connecticut *Gazette,* Apr. 19, 1792, 3. Examples: New York *Daily Advertiser,* Apr. 12, 1792, 2; New Hampshire *Spy,* June 12, 1792, 4. "Gale Town" appears to have been New London's nickname at this time.
20. AFC, B5F2, John Evans to Thomas Allen, July 10, 1789, q.; also ibid., Ichabod Wheeler to Thomas Allen, July 23, 1789.
21. See Bolster, *Black Jacks,* 23–28, 133–40; Cecelski, *The Waterman's Song,* 16–18; Gilje, *Liberty on the Waterfront,* 25–31, 107–9, 135–38.
22. AFC, B3F3, William Bull to Thomas Allen, 1790, q.; AFC, B5F4, Asa Benton to same, May 30, 1791. African American sailors and the early Republic: for example, Bolster, *Black Jacks,* 23–28, 133–40; Gilje, *Liberty on the Waterfront,* 25–31, 107–9, 135–38.
23. Alpaugh, *Friends of Freedom,* chap. 7, q. on 188; Examples: Connecticut *Gazette,* Mar. 13, 1789, 2, 3; ibid., Dec. 25, 1789, 2, 3. Allen's Marine List reprinted in Spooner's Vermont *Journal,* Dec. 27, 1791, 3.
24. AFC, fol. 50, entry, Sept. 13, 1791 (first news brought by "M. Fustan of Cape Francis"); ibid., entry Dec. 9, 1791.
25. AFC, B5F1, Elijah Babcock to Thomas Allen, Apr. 8, 1788, and Sept. 9, 1788.
26. AFC, B5F1, Elijah Babcock to Thomas Allen, Sept. 9, 1788, q.
27. AFC, B5F1, Woodward and Green to Thomas Allen, Oct. 1, 1788, qq.
28. AFC, B5F2, Clement Biddle to Thomas Allen, June 24, 1789, q; Brown and Francis to Thomas Allen, July 31, 1793.
29. AFC, B5F2, John Trumbull to Thomas Allen, Aug. 26, 1789, Aug. 28, 1789, and Sept. 4, 1789.

30. AFC, B5F2, John Trumbull to Thomas Allen, Oct. 18, 1789, qq.
31. AFC, B5F2, Sept. 5, 89, Daniel Rodman to Thomas Allen, Sept. 5, 1789; AFC, B6F2, John Williams to Thomas Allen, May 27, 1793; Allen's Marine List, Philadelphia *Independent Gazette,* Sept, 10, 1789, q. on 4.
32. AFC, B5F3, Jacob Sebor to Thomas Allen, 4/8/1790; Connecticut *Gazette,* May 19, 1791, 3.
33. New York *Daily Advertiser,* May 8, 1793, q. on 2; Middlesex *Gazette,* Sept. 14, 1793, 3; Connecticut *Gazette,* Sept. 26, 1793, 3.
34. Examples: Middlesex *Gazette,* Nov. 23, 1793; Boston *Independent,* Nov. 25, 1793; *The Diary, or Loudon's Register* (New York), Dec. 12, 1793; Catskill *Packet,* Dec. 17, 1793, 3. Polly Allen: Connecticut *Gazette,* Dec. 19, 1793, 4. Pool: advertisement for store, Connecticut *Gazette,* May 29, 1789, 3. Pool's Marine List examples: Connecticut *Gazette,* Sept. 26, 1793, 3; American *Mercury,* Apr. 20, 1795, 3. Caulkins, *History of New London,* 579.
35. CSL, Probate Records, 1794: "A List of Balances Found Against the Estate of Thomas Allen of New London Decs'd," Aug. 9, 1794; ibid., "Sundry Notes Inventoried but thought not Worth carrying out," Jan. 13, 1794.
36. CSL, Probate Records, 1794: "Inventory and Appraisal of the Estate of Capt. Thomas Allen, Dec'd," Jan. 13, 1794; ibid., "Return of Sales of Thoms. Allen's Estate," Nov. 10, 1794.

Epilogue

1. For example, AFC, B6F2, Francis Winthrop to Thomas Allen Jr., letters of June 21, 1793, Dec. 17, 1793, July 13, 1794; AFC, B9F3, Thomas Allen Account with Francis Winthrop, Apr. 6, 1798; AFC, fol. 57, "Fishers Island Farm Accounts," 1794–1800. Wool accounts: examples, AFC, fol. 57, Thomas Allen Account with Francis Winthrop, May 24, 1800, and Dec. 25, 1800; AFC, fol. 54, Thomas Allen Farm Journal, 1792–1800.
2. Early cloth manufacturing: for example, Cole, *The American Wool Manufacture,* esp. 61–97; Saladino, "The Economic Revolution," 306–36; Prude, *The Coming of Industrial Order,* 34–46; Dublin, *Transforming Women's Work,* 39–49; Cappon et al., *Atlas of Early American History,* 106–7.
3. For example, AFC, B6F3, Thomas Allen Jr. to Francis Bayard Winthrop, Feb. 26, 1796; Winthrop to Allen, Mar. 5, 1796; John Franks to Thomas Allen Jr., May 19, 1797; AFC, fol. 57, "Fishers Island Farm Accounts," Oct. 1796.
4. AFC, B6F2, Nathaniel Allen to Thomas Allen, May 4, 1795, private letter, 1st quote; ibid., general letter, 2nd q.
5. Overviews of early republic eastward oceanic trade: Kimball, *The East India Trade of Providence, 1787–1807;* Bhagat, *Americans in India,* 8–26; Fichter, *So Great a Proffit,* 35–55 and chap. 8; Van, "Cents and Sensibilities"; Norwood, *Trading Freedom,* chap. 1; Chu, *Stumbling Toward the Constitution,* chap. 2.
6. Providence *Gazette,* May 22, 1790, q. on 3. In addition to preceding note, see Verney, "An Eye for Prices," esp. 403–9, and Bean, *Yankee India,* 16–22, 33–43, 67–70.
7. AFC, B6F2, Nathaniel Allen to Thomas Allen, May 4, 1795, private letter, q.
8. Ibid., B1F1, Hiram Holt to the American Antiquarian Society, Apr. 8, 1857.

9. Post-1789 republican society: Wood, *Empire of Liberty,* 315–29, 347–56; Frymer, *Building an American Empire,* 35–37, 47–50.
10. Early republic expansion by land: for example, White, *The Middle Ground,* chap. 11; Blackhawk, *Violence over the Land,* chap. 5; Gilje, *Free Trade and Sailors' Rights,* 128–36; Frymer, *Building an American Empire,* chaps. 2–3. Expansion by sea: in addition to notes 5 and 6 this chapter, see also Lambert, *The Barbary Wars,* chap. 3; Rouleau. *With Sails Whitening Every Sea;* and Blackhawk, *Rediscovery of America,* chap. 8.

SELECTED BIBLIOGRAPHY

Archives

American Antiquarian Society, Worcester, Massachusetts

Allen Family Collection, 1718–1838

Digital Collection: Allen Family Collection. https://gigi.mwa.org/imagearchive/filename/361733

Logbook Collection, 1716–1874

Archives Départementales de Loire-Atlantique, Nantes, France

Chambre de Commerce, Box C

Archives Nationales d'Outre-mers (ANOM), Aix-en-Province, France

Série C8[A], Correspondence Générale de la Martinique; Série C8[B], Correspondence envoyé au Martinique

Bibibliothèque Nationale de France, Paris

Digital resources (https://gallica.bnf.fr)

Connecticut State Library and Archives

RG (Record Group) 001 (Deceased Estates, 1693/94–1820; Insolvent Debtors, 1762–1787; Revolutionary War, 1st and 3rd Series; Trade and Maritime Affairs, 1668–1789; Travel: Highways, Ferries, Bridges, and Taverns, 1700–1788)

RG003: New London County Superior Court (NLCSC) Dockets and Files

RG003.4A: NLCSC Native Americans Collection, 1698–1855

RG003.95: New London Justice of the Peace Records, 1755–1903

RG010: Maritime and Trade

RG 062.95: Local Government Records. Town of New London

RG070: Minutes of St. James Church

New London Land Records (microfilm)

John Carter Brown Library, Providence, Rhode Island

Brown Family Business Records: Records of James Browne d. 1750 and *English Pilot* (1745); Obadiah Brown; Nicholas Brown & Co.; Brown and Benson (1783–1792)

Rare Books Collection Americana
Broadside Collection

New London County Historical Society, New London, Connecticut

Newspapers: New London *Summary* 1758–1763
Printed: B.C76, 1774 Census
Manuscript Collections: Chew Correspondence; Anglican Church correspondence; Ebenezer Huntington Correspondence; Aaron Lopez, Sailing Instructions; Charles Bulkley Correspondence; Samuel Belden Correspondence; New London Auctions; Nathaniel Shaw—Jonathan Trumbull Correspondence; New London Rate Books, 1750 and 1759; Windham Chamber of Commerce Minutes; Israel Putnam and Taverns; Road Surveys, 1770–1774; Wagoneers; White Beach Lots; Fort Trumbull description; British Blockade Meeting; Zabdial Rogers, Account of New London Attack, Sept. 7, 1781; New London Beach survey, 1784
Cartography: Niantick Map; Great Neck Map

New London Town Clerk's Office, New London, Connecticut

Land Grantees Books; New London Town Marriages Book; New London Town Meeting Minutes.

Portsmouth Athenaeum, Portsmouth, New Hampshire

John Evans Papers, John Evans Diary

Rhode Island Historical Society, Providence, Rhode Island

The Letter Book of James Browne of Providence, merchant, 1735–1738, Introduction by George Philip Krapp. Providence: Rhode Island Historical Society, 1929
Manuscripts: Mss. 948, Records of James Browne Mss. 828, The Ships' Logs Collection

Yale University, Manuscripts and Archives, New Haven, Connecticut

Nathaniel and Thomas Shaw Papers, Manuscript Collection no. 445 (cited in notes as box (B), folder (F), piece or box (B), ledger (L))

Newspapers and Magazines

From Early American Newspapers, Series 1. https://www.readex.com/products/early-american-newspapers-series-01-1690-1876-colonies-nation

Digital Archives and Sources

Colonial Laws of New York from the Year 1664, James B. Lyon, 1894. https://babel.hathitrust.org/cgi/pt?id=hvd.32044018719872&view=1up&seq=13&skin=2021
Congressional Research Service, *Bankruptcy Basics: A Primer.* https://www.uscourts.gov/services-forms/bankruptcy/bankruptcy-basics
Dictionary of Canadian Biography. https://www.biographi.ca/en
Gaspee Virtual Archives. https://gaspee.org/GentlemensMag.html

Library of Congress, *Journals of the Continental Congress*, vols. 2–7. https://www.loc.gov/collections/century-of-lawmaking/articles-and-essays/continental-congress/journals-of-the-continental-congress/

Massachusetts Historical Society, Adams Papers Digital Collection, vols. 2–4. https://www.masshist.org/publications/adams-papers/

National Archives, *Founders Online*. https://founders.archives.gov

Political Magazine & Parliamentary, Naval, Military & Literary Journal (London). https://babel.hathitrust.org/cgi/pt?id=mdp.39015067321748&seq=1

Slave Voyages, Trans-Atlantic Slave Trade-Database. https://www.slavevoyages.org/voyage/database.

Statutes UK. https://statutes.org.uk/site/ (Acts of Parliament, unless noted otherwise)

Secondary and Printed Primary Sources Cited

Abbott, Carl. "The Neighborhoods of New York, 1760–1775." *New York History* 55, no. 1 (1974): 35–54.

Abénon, Lucien-René. *La Guadeloupe de 1671 à 1759: Étude politique, économique et sociale.* 2 vols. L'Harmattan, 1987.

Adelman, Joseph M. "'A Constitutional Conveyance of Intelligence, Public and Private': The Post Office, the Business of Printing, and the American Revolution." *Enterprise & Society* 11, no. 4 (2010): 711–54.

Aggarwala, Rohit T. "'I Want a Packet to Arrive': Making New York City the Headquarters of British America, 1696–1783." *New York History* 98, no. 1 (2017): 7–39.

Aizpura, Ramon. *Curazao y la costa de Caracas: Introducción al estudio del contrabando en la provincia de Venezuela en tiempos de la Compañia Guipuzcoana, 1730–1780*. Academia Nacional dela Historia, 1993.

Allen, Gardner Weld. *A Naval History of the American Revolution*. 2 vols. 1913. Russell & Russell, 1962.

Almeroth-Williams, Thomas. *City of Beasts: How Animals Shaped Georgian London*. Manchester University Press, 2019.

Alpaugh, Micah. *Friends of Freedom: The Rise of Social Movements in the Age of Atlantic Revolutions*. Cambridge University Press, 2022.

Ammerman, David L. *In the Common Cause: American Response to the Coercive Acts of 1774*. University of Virginia Press, 1974.

Anastaplo, George. *Reflections on Constitutional Law*. University Press of Kentucky, 2006.

Andersen, Tom. *This Fine Piece of Water: An Environmental History of Long Island Sound*. Yale University Press, 2002.

Anderson, Fred. *Crucible of War: The Seven Years' War and the Fate of Empire in British North America, 1754–1766*. Vintage Books, 2001.

Anderson, Virginia DeJohn. "Animals into the Wilderness: The Development of Livestock Husbandry in the Seventeenth-Century Chesapeake." *William and Mary Quarterly* 59, no. 2 (2002): 377–408.

Anderson, Virginia DeJohn. *Creatures of Empire: How Domestic Animals Transformed Early America*. Oxford University Press, 2004.

Anderson, Virginia DeJohn. *The Martyr and the Traitor: Nathan Hale, Moses Dunbar, and the American Revolution*. Oxford University Press, 2017.

Anonymous. "Journal of a French Traveller in the Colonies, 1765, I." *American Historical Review* 26, no. 4 (1921): 726–47.

Anonymous. "Journal of a French Traveller in the Colonies, 1765, II." *American Historical Review* 27, no. 1 (1921): 70–89.

Armitage, David. *The Declaration of Independence: A Global History.* Harvard University Press, 2007.

Armitage, David. *The Ideological Origins of the British Empire.* Cambridge University Press, 2000

Armytage, Frances. *The Free Port System in the British West Indies: A Study in Commercial Policy, 1766–1822.* Longmans, Green, 1953.

Ashworth, William J. *Customs and Excise: Trade, Production, and Consumption in England, 1640–1845.* Oxford University Press, 2003.

Attema, Y. *St. Eustatius: A Short History of the Island and Its Monuments.* Walburg Pers, 1976.

Avitable, Joseph. "The Atlantic World Economy and Colonial Connecticut." PhD diss., University of Rochester, 2009.

Axtell, James. *The School Upon a Hill: Education and Society in Colonial New England.* Yale University Press, 1974.

Azimi, Vida. "Les premiers commis de la marine au XVIIIe siècle." *Revue historique de droit français et étranger* 81, no. 4 (2003): 503–25.

Bailyn, Bernard. *Atlantic History: Concept and Contours.* Harvard University Press, 2005.

Bailyn, Bernard. *The Barbarous Years: The Peopling of British North America: The Conflict of Civilizations, 1600–1675.* Knopf, 2012.

Bailyn, Bernard. *The Ideological Origins of the American Revolution.* 1967. Belknap Press of Harvard University Press, 1992.

Bailyn, Bernard, and Barbara DeWolfe. *Voyagers to the West: A Passage in the Peopling of America on the Eve of the Revolution.* Vintage Books, 1988.

Banks, Kenneth J. *Chasing Empire Across the Sea: Communications and the State in the French Atlantic, 1713–1763.* McGill–Queen's University Press, 2002.

Banks, Kenneth J. "Contraband." In *The Princeton Companion to the Atlantic World,* ed. Joseph C. Miller et al., 119–23. Princeton University Press, 2015.

Banks, Kenneth J. "Official Duplicity: The Illicit Slave Trade of Martinique, 1713–1763." In *The Atlantic Economy during the Seventeenth and Eighteenth Centuries: Organization, Operation, Practice, and Personnel,* ed. Peter A. Coclanis, 229–51. University of South Carolina Press, 2005.

Bannister, Jerry, and Liam Riordan. "Loyalism and the British Atlantic, 1660–1840." In *The Loyal Atlantic: Remaking the British Atlantic in the Revolutionary Era,* ed. Jerry Bannister and Liam Riordan, 3–36. University of Toronto Press, 2012.

Barka, Norman F. "Citizens of St. Eustatius, 1781: A Historical and Archaeological Study." In *The Lesser Antilles in the Age of European Expansion,* ed. Robert L. Paquette and Stanely L. Engerman, 223–38. University Press of Florida, 1996.

Barreau, Jean. "La campagne de 1759." *Bulletin de la Société d'Histoire de la Guadeloupe* 27 (1976): 3–57.

Barrow, Thomas C. *Trade and Empire: The British Customs Service in Colonial America, 1660–1775.* Harvard University Press, 1967.

Barth, Jonathan. "Reconstructing Mercantilism: Consensus and Conflict in British Imperial Economy in the Seventeenth and Eighteenth Centuries." *William and Mary Quarterly* 73, no. 2 (2016): 257–90.

Bass, Robert D. *Swamp Fox: The Life and Campaigns of General Francis Marion*. Holt, 1959.

Baugh, Daniel A. *British Naval Administration in the Age of Walpole*. Princeton University Press, 1965.

Baugh, Daniel A. *The Global Seven Years War, 1754–1763: Britain and France in a Great Power Contest*. Taylor and Francis, 2021.

Baxter, William T. "Credit, Bills, and Bookkeeping in a Simple Economy." *The Accounting Review* 21, no. 2 (1946): 154–66.

Baxter, William T. *The House of Hancock; Business in Boston, 1724–1775*. Harvard University Press, 1945.

Bayles, Richard. M. *History of Windham County, Connecticut*. W. Preston, 1889.

Bean, Susan S. *Yankee India: American Commercial and Cultural Encounters with India in the Age of Sail, 1784–1860*. Peabody Essex Museum, 2001.

Becker, Carl. *The Declaration of Independence: A Study in the History of Political Ideas*. Harcourt, Brace, 1922.

Beekman, Gerard, and James Beekman. *The Beekman Mercantile Papers, 1746–1799*, vol. 1. Edited by Philip L. White. New-York Historical Society, 1956.

Beeman, Richard R. *Plain, Honest Men: The Making of the American Constitution*. Random House, 2010.

Beeman, Richard R. *The Varieties of Political Experience in Eighteenth-Century America*. University of Pennsylvania Press, 2004.

Beers, J. B. *History of Middlesex County, Connecticut, with Biographical Sketches of Its Prominent Men*. J. B. Beers, 1884.

Bentley, Jerry H. "Sea and Ocean Basins as Frameworks of Historical Analysis." *Geographical Review* 89, no. 2 (1999): 215–24.

Benton, Lauren A., and Nathan Perl-Rosenthal. "Afterward: Land-Sea Regimes in World History." In *A World at Sea: Maritime Practices and Global History*, edited by Lauren A. Benton and Nathan Perl-Rosenthal, 186–92. University of Pennsylvania Press, 2020.

Berkin, Carol. *Jonathan Sewall: Odyssey of an American Loyalist*. Columbia University Press, 1974.

Berlin, Ira. *Many Thousands Gone: The First Two Centuries of Slavery in North America*. Belknap Press of Harvard University Press, 1998.

Bertucci, Paola. *Artisanal Enlightenment: Science and the Mechanical Arts in Old Regime France*. Yale University Press, 2017.

Bhagat, G. *Americans in India, 1784–1860*. New York University Press, 1970.

Bickham, Troy O. *Making Headlines: The American Revolution as Seen Through the British Press*. Northern Illinois University Press, 2009.

Biddle, Henry D. "Owen Biddle." *Pennsylvania Magazine of History and Biography* 16, no. 3 (1892): 299–329.

Bivar Marquese, Rafael de. "A Tale of Two Coffee Colonies: Environment and Slavery in Suriname and Saint-Domingue, ca. 1750–1790." *Comparative Studies in Society and History* 64, no. 3 (2022): 722–55.

Bjork, Gordon C. *Stagnation and Growth in the American Economy, 1784–1792*. Garland, 1985.

Bjork, Gordon C. "The Weaning of the American Economy: Independence, Market Changes, and Economic Development." *Journal of Economic History* 24, no. 4 (1964): 541–60.

Black, Jeremy. *Fighting for America: The Struggle for Mastery in North America, 1519–1871*. Indiana University Press, 2011.

Blackhawk, Ned. *Rediscovery of America: Native Peoples and the Unmaking of U.S. History*. Yale University Press, 2023.

Blackhawk, Ned. *Violence over the Land: Indians and Empires in the Early American West*. Harvard University Press, 2006.

Blake, John Ballard. *Public Health in the Town of Boston, 1630–1822*. Harvard University Press, 1959.

Blérald, Alain P. *Histoire économique de la Guadeloupe et de la Martinique: Du XVIIe siècle à nos jours*. Karthala, 1986.

Boer, Tessa de. "Imperfect Strangers: Frenchmen, Foreigners, and Illegality in Eighteenth-Century Guadeloupe." In *Diversity and Empires: Negotiating Plurality in European Imperial Projects from Early Modernity*, edited by Elisabeth Heijmans and Sophie Rose, 155–77. Taylor & Francis, 2023.

Bolster, W. Jeffrey. *Black Jacks: African American Seamen in the Age of Sail*. Harvard University Press, 1997.

Bolster, W. Jeffrey. *The Mortal Sea: Fishing the Atlantic in the Age of Sail*. Belknap Press of Harvard University Press, 2012.

Bolster, W. Jeffrey. "Putting the Ocean in Atlantic History: Maritime Communities and Marine Ecology in the Northwest Atlantic, 1500–1800." *American Historical Review* 113, no. 1 (2008): 19–47.

Boulle, Pierre H. "Patterns of French Colonial Trade and the Seven Years' War." *Histoire Sociale/Social History* 7, no. 13 (1974): 48–86.

Bourguignon, Henry J. *The First Federal Court: The Federal Appellate Prize Court of the American Revolution, 1775–1787*. American Philosophical Society, 1977.

Bowen, H. V. "The Bank of England During the Long Eighteenth Century, 1694–1820." In *The Bank of England: Money, Power and Influence, 1694–1994*, edited by Richard Roberts and David Kynaston, 1–18. Oxford University Press, 1995.

Brandt, Clare. *The Man in the Mirror: A Life of Benedict Arnold*. Random House, 1994.

Brasseaux, Carl A. *Denis-Nicolas Foucault and the New Orleans Rebellion of 1768*. McGinty Publications, Louisiana Tech University, 1987.

Braudel, Fernand. *Civilization and Capitalism, 15th–18th Century*. Vol. 2, *The Wheels of Commerce*. Vol. 3, *The Perspective of the World*. Translated by Siân Reynolds. Harper & Row, 1986.

Breen, T. H. *American Insurgents, American Patriots: The Revolution of the People*. Hill and Wang, 2010.

Breen, T. H. *The Marketplace of Revolution: How Consumer Politics Shaped American Independence*. Oxford University Press, 2004.

Breen, T. H. *The Will of the People: The Revolutionary Birth of America*. Harvard University Press, 2019.

Brennan, Denis P. "Shaped by Revolution: Samuel Loudon and the New-York Packet, 1776–1783." PhD diss., State University of New York at Albany, 1992.

Brewer, Holly. "The Myth of 'Salutary Neglect': Empire and Revolution in the Long Eighteenth Century." In *The Cambridge History of the Age of the Atlantic Revolutions*. Vol. 1,

The Enlightenment and the British Colonies, edited by Wim Klooster, 189–206. Cambridge University Press, 2023.

Brewer, John. *The Sinews of Power: War, Money, and the English State, 1688–1783*. Harvard University Press, 1990.

Bridenbaugh, Carl. *Cities in Revolt: Urban Life in America, 1743–1776*. Knopf, 1955.

Brinkman-Schwartz, Anna. "The Heart of the Maritime World: London's 'Mercantile' Coffee Houses in the Seven Years' War and the American War of Independence, 1756–83." *Historical Research* 94, no. 265 (2021): 508–31.

Brunsman, Denver. *The Evil Necessity: British Naval Impressment in the Eighteenth-Century Atlantic World*. University of Virginia Press, 2013.

Bryant G. J. "The War in Bengal." In *The Seven Years' War: Global Views*, edited by Mark H. Danley and Patrick J. Speelman, 399–427. Brill, 2012.

Buel, Richard. *Dear Liberty: Connecticut's Mobilization for the Revolutionary War*. Wesleyan University Press, 1980.

Buel, Richard. *In Irons: Britain's Naval Supremacy and the American Revolutionary Economy*. Yale University Press, 1998.

Buist, Marten G. *At Spes Non Fracta: Hope & Co. 1770–1815: Merchant Bankers and Diplomats at Work*. Martinus Nijhoff, 1974.

Bullock, Steven C. *Revolutionary Brotherhood: Freemasonry and the Transformation of the American Social Order, 1730–1840*. University of North Carolina Press, 1996.

Burbank, Dale W. "Want of Proper Spirit and Energy: The Penobscot Expedition, 1779." Master's thesis, United States Military Academy, 1995.

Burnard, Trevor. *Jamaica in the Age of Revolution*. University of Pennsylvania Press, 2020.

Burnard, Trevor, and Cécile Vidal, "Location and Conceptualization of Historical Frameworks: Early American History and Its Multiple Reconfigurations in the United States and Europe." In *Historians across Borders: Writing American History in a Global Age*, edited by Nicolas Barreyre et al., 141–62. University of California Press, 2014.

Bushman, Richard L. *From Puritan to Yankee: Character and the Social Order in Connecticut, 1690–1765*. Harvard University Press, 1967.

Bushman, Richard L. *The Refinement of America: Persons, Houses, Cities*. Vintage Books, 1993.

Butel, Paul. *The Atlantic*. Routledge, 1999.

Butel, Paul. *Les négociants bordelais: L'Europe et les îles au XVIIIe siècle*. Aubier, 1974.

Butler, Jon. *The Huguenots in America: A Refugee People in New World Society*. Harvard University Press, 1983.

Cabantous, Alain. *Les citoyens du large: Les identités maritimes en France (XVIIe–XIXe siècle)*. Aubier, 1995.

Callahan, North. *Flight from the Republic: The Tories of the American Revolution*. Bobbs-Merrill, 1967.

Camille, Michael J., and Rafael Espejo-Saavedra. "Historical Geography of the Belizean Logwood Trade." *Yearbook (Conference of Latin Americanist Geographers)* 22 (1996): 77–85.

Campbell, Mavis C. *The Maroons of Jamaica, 1655–1796: A History of Resistance, Collaboration & Betrayal*. Bergin & Garvey, 1988.

CANARI. *The Caribbean Islands: Biodiversity Hotspot. Final Technical Report*. Caribbean Natural Resources Institute, 2019. https://www.cepf.net/sites/default/files/cepf-caribbean-islands-ecosystem-profile-summary-2020-english.pdf.

Cappon, Lester Jesse, et al. *Atlas of Early American History: The Revolutionary Era, 1760–1790*. Princeton University Press, 1976.

Carp, Benjamin L. *Defiance of the Patriots: The Boston Tea Party & the Making of America*. Yale University Press, 2010.

Carp, Benjamin L. "Did Dutch Smugglers Provoke the Boston Tea Party?" *Early American Studies* 10, no. 2 (2012): 335–59.

Carpenter, Stanley D. M., Kevin J. Delamer, James R. McIntyre, and Andrew T. Zwilling. *The War of American Independence, 1763–1783: Falling Dominoes*. Routledge, 2023.

Carté, Katherine. *Religion and the American Revolution: An Imperial History*. University of North Carolina Press, 2021.

Case, James R. *Freemasonry in Connecticut: Connecticut Freemasons in the Revolution*. Committee on the Bicentennial of the American Revolution Grand Lodge, 1974.

Cash, Arthur H. *John Wilkes: The Scandalous Father of Civil Liberty*. Yale University Press, 2006.

Catterall, Douglas, and Jodi Campbell. "Introduction: Mother Courage and Her Sisters. Women's Worlds in the Premodern Atlantic." In *Women in Port: Gendering Communities, Economies, and Social Networks in Atlantic Port Cities, 1500–1800*. Brill, 2012.

Caulkins, Francis Manwaring. *History of New London, Connecticut, from the First Survey of the Coast in 1612 to 1860*. H. D. Utley, 1895.

Caulkins, Francis Manwaring. *History of Norwich, Connecticut, from Its Settlement in 1660 to January 1845*. T. Robinson, 1845.

Cave, Alfred A. *The Pequot War*. University of Massachusetts Press, 1996.

Cavignac, Jean. *Jean Pellet, Commerçant de Gros, 1694–1772*. S.E.V.P.E.N., 1967.

Cecelski, David S. *The Waterman's Song: Slavery and Freedom in Maritime North Carolina*. University of North Carolina Press, 2001.

Chateau-Degat, Richard, and Jean B. Barfluer. "Structures et évolution de l'économie colonial esclavagiste." In *Histoire et civilisation de la Caraîbe (Guadeloupe, Martinique, Petites Antilles): Économie et cadres sociaux du long XVIIIe siècle*. Vol. 2, *Le temps des matrices*, edited by Jean-Pierre Sainton, 65–120. Karthala, 2012.

Cheney, Paul. *Revolutionary Commerce: Globalization and the French Monarchy*. Harvard University Press, 2010.

Chet, Guy. *The Ocean Is a Wilderness: Atlantic Piracy and the Limits of State Authority, 1688–1856*. University of Massachusetts Press, 2014.

Chew, Richard S. "Neo-Mercantilism, American Style: The Virginia Port Bill of 1784 and the Madisonian Origins of U.S. Fair Trade Ideology." *Virginia Magazine of History and Biography* 127, no. 2 (2019): 98–127.

Chu, Jonathan M. *Stumbling Toward the Constitution: The Economic Consequences of Freedom in the Atlantic World*. Palgrave Macmillan, 2012.

Clark, Charles E. "Early American Journalism: News and Opinion in the Popular Press." In *A History of the Book in America*. Vol. 1, *The Colonial Book in the Atlantic World*, edited by Hugh Amory, David D. Hall, and Scott E. Casper, 347–66. University of North Carolina Press, 2007.

Clark, William Bell, and Nichoals Biddle. "The Letters of Captain Nicholas Biddle." *Pennsylvania Magazine of History and Biography* 74, no. 3 (1950): 348–405.

Clark-Pujara, Christy. *Dark Work: The Business of Slavery in Rhode Island*. New York University Press, 2016.

Cleary, Patricia, and Elizabeth Murray. *Elizabeth Murray: A Woman's Pursuit of Independence in Eighteenth-Century America*. University of Massachusetts Press, 2000.

Clinton, Henry. *The American Rebellion: Sir Henry Clinton's Narrative of His Campaigns, 1775–1782, with an Appendix of Original Documents*. Edited by William B. Willcox. Yale University Press, 1954.

Cogliano, Francis D. "Deliverance from Luxury: Pope's Day, Conflict and Consensus in Colonial Boston, 1745–1765." *Studies in Popular Culture* 15, no. 2 (1993): 15–28.

Cohen, Patricia Cline. *Calculating People: The Spread of Numeracy in Early America*. Routledge, 1982.

Cole, Arthur Harrison. *The American Wool Manufacture*. Harvard University Press, 1926.

Coleman, Armand R., William G. Shenkir, and Williard E. Stone, "Accounting in Colonial Virginia: A Case Study." *Journal of Accountancy*, July (1974), 32–43.

Coleman, Peter J. *Debtors and Creditors in America: Insolvency, Imprisonment for Debt, and Bankruptcy, 1607–1900*. State Historical Society of Wisconsin, 1974.

Coleman, Peter J. "The Insolvent Debtor in Rhode Island 1745–1828." *William and Mary Quarterly* 22, no. 3 (1965): 413–34.

Collier, Christopher. "Sovereignty Finessed: Roger Sherman, Oliver Ellsworth, and the Ratification of the Constitution in Connecticut." In *The Constitution and the States: The Role of the Original Thirteen in the Framing and Adoption of the Federal Constitution*, edited by Patrick T. Conley and John P. Kaminski, 93–112. Madison House, 1988.

Compeau, Timothy. *Dishonored Americans: The Political Death of Loyalists in Revolutionary America*. University of Virginia Press, 2023.

Congressional Research Service. "Bankruptcy Basics: A Primer." United States Congress, updated Oct. 12, 2022.

Conroy, David W. *In Public Houses Drink and the Revolution of Authority in Colonial Massachusetts*. University of North Carolina Press, 2001.

Conway, Stephen. "British Governments and the Conduct of the American War." In *Britain and the American Revolution*, edited by H. T. Dickinson, 155–79. Addison Wesley Longman, 1998.

Cort, Adam. *The Blue Book of Sailing: The 22 Keys to Sailing Mastery*. McGraw-Hill, 2009.

Covo, Manuel. *Entrepôt of Revolutions: Saint-Domingue, Commercial Sovereignty, and the French-American Alliance*. Oxford University Press, 2022.

Crane, Elaine Forman. *Ebb Tide in New England: Women, Seaports, and Social Change, 1630–1800*. Northeastern University Press, 1998.

Creighton, Margaret S., and Lisa Norling. *Iron Men, Wooden Women: Gender and Seafaring in the Atlantic World, 1700–1920*. Johns Hopkins University Press, 1996.

Cremin, Lawrence A. *American Education, the Colonial Experience, 1607–1783*. Harper & Row, 1970.

Cronon, William. *Changes in the Land: Indians, Colonists, and the Ecology of New England*. Hill and Wang, 1983.

Crowley, John E. *The Privileges of Independence: Neomercantilism and the American Revolution*. Johns Hopkins University Press, 1993.

Cuddihy, William J. *The Fourth Amendment: Origins and Original Meaning, 602–1791*. Oxford University Press, 2009.

Cumming, William P. "Colonial Charting of the Massachusetts Coast." In *Seafaring in Colonial Massachusetts*, 67–116. Colonial Society of Massachusetts, 1980.

Cumming, William P. "The Turbulent Life of Captain James Wimble." *North Carolina Historical Review* 46, no. 1 (1969): 1–18.

Curtin, Philip D. *The Rise and Fall of the Plantation Complex: Essays in Atlantic History.* Cambridge University Press, 1998.

Defoe, Daniel. *The Life and strange adventures of Robinson Crusoe, of York, mariner.* Houghton-Mifflin, 1885.

Damiano, Sara T. "'To Well and Truly Administer': Female Administrators and Estate Settlement in Newport, Rhode Island, 1730–1776." *New England Quarterly* 86, no. 1 (2013): 89–124.

Daniels, Bruce C. *The Connecticut Town: Growth and Development, 1635–1790.* Wesleyan University Press, 1979.

Daniels, Bruce C. "Economic Development in Colonial and Revolutionary Connecticut: An Overview." *William and Mary Quarterly* 37, no. 3 (1980): 429–50.

Daudin, Guillaume. "Profitability of Slave and Long-Distance Trading in Context: The Case of Eighteenth-Century France." *Journal of Economic History* 64, no. 1 (2004): 144–71.

David, James Corbett. *Dunmore's New World: The Extraordinary Life of a Royal Governor in Revolutionary America—with Jacobites, Counterfeiters, Land Schemes, Shipwrecks, Scalping, Indian Politics, Runaway Slaves, and Two Illegal Royal Weddings.* University of Virginia Press, 2013.

Davis, Andrew MacFarland. "A Connecticut Land Bank of the Eighteenth Century." *Quarterly Journal of Economics* 13, no. 1 (1898): 70–84.

Davis, Natalie Zemon. "The Reasons of Misrule: Youth Groups and Charivaris in Sixteenth-Century France." *Past & Present* 50 (1971): 41–75.

Davis, Ralph. *The Rise of the English Shipping Industry in the Seventeenth and Eighteenth Centuries.* 1962. International Maritime Economic History Association, 2012.

Dawdy, Shannon Lee. *Building the Devil's Empire: French Colonial New Orleans.* University of Chicago Press, 2008.

De Roover, Raymond. *Money, Banking and Credit in Mediaeval Bruges; Italian Merchant Bankers, Lombards and Money-Changers.* Mediaeval Academy of America, 1948.

De Roover, Raymond. "New Perspectives on Medieval Accounting." *Accounting Review* 30, no. 3 (1955): 405–20.

de Vries, Jan. "Dutch Economic Growth in Comparative-Historical Perspective, 1500–2000." *The Economist: Quarterly Review of the Royal Netherlands Economic Association* 148, no. 4 (2000): 443–67.

Dear, Ian C. B., and Peter Kemp, eds. "By (the Wind)." In *The Oxford Companion to Ships and the Sea,* 2nd ed. Oxford University Press, 2006. https://www.oxfordreference.com/display/10.1093/acref/9780199205684.001.0001/acref-9780199205684.

Debien, Gabriel. *Une Plantation de Saint-Domingue: La Sucrerie Galbaud Du Fort (1690–1802).* Les Presses de l'Institut français d'archéologie orientale du Caire, 1976.

Decker, Robert Owen. *Whaling Industry of New London.* Liberty Cap Books, 1974.

Delle, James A. "Settlement pattern of Sugar Plantations on St. Eustatius, Netherlands Antilles." In *Spatial Patterning in Historical Archaeology: Selected Studies of Settlement,* edited Donald W. Linebaugh and Gary G. Robinson, 33–61. King and Queen Press, 1994.

DeLucia, Christine M. *Memory Lands: King Philip's War and the Place of Violence in the Northeast.* Yale University Press, 2018.

Destler, Chester McArthur. *Connecticut: The Provisions State.* Pequot Press, 1973.

DeVaro, Lawrence J. "The Impact of the Gaspee Affair on the Coming of the American Revolution, 1772–1773." PhD diss., Case Western Reserve University, 1973.

di Bonaventura, Allegra. *For Adam's Sake: A Family Saga in Colonial New England.* Liveright, 2013.

Dickerson, Oliver M. *The Navigation Acts and the American Revolution.* 1951. A. S. Barnes, 1963.

Dierks, Konstantin. *In My Power: Letter Writing and Communications in Early America.* University of Pennsylvania Press, 2009.

Dierks, Konstantin. "Middle-Class Formation in Eighteenth-Century North America." In *Class Matters: Early North America and the Atlantic World,* edited by Simon Middleton and Billy G. Smith, 99–108. University of Pennsylvania Press, 2008.

Dill, Alonzo Thomas. *Carter Braxton, Virginia Signer: A Conservative in Revolt.* University Press of America, 1983.

Ditz, Toby L. "Formative Ventures: Mercantile Letters and the Articulation of Experience." In *Epistolary Selves: Letters and Letter-Writers, 1600–1945,* edited by Rebecca Earle, 59–78. Ashgate, 1999.

Ditz, Toby L. *Property and Kinship: Inheritance in Early Connecticut, 1750–1820.* Princeton University Press, 1986.

Doe, Helen. *Enterprising Women and Shipping in the Nineteenth Century.* Boydell & Brewer, 2009.

Doerflinger, Thomas M. "The Antilles Trade of the Old Regime: A Statistical Overview." *Journal of Interdisciplinary History* 6, no. 3 (1976): 397–415.

Doerflinger, Thomas M. "Philadelphia Merchants and the Logic of Moderation, 1760–1775." *William and Mary Quarterly* 40, no. 2 (1983): 197–226.

Doerflinger, Thomas M. *A Vigorous Spirit of Enterprise: Merchants and Economic Development in Revolutionary Philadelphia.* University of North Carolina Press, 1986.

Dolin, Eric Jay. *Rebels at Sea: Privateering in the American Revolution.* Liveright, 2022.

Donnadieu, Jean-Louis. "Boisson de rustres, nectar d'esthètes: Le long chemin du 'brûle-ventre' au 'rhum' (XVIe–XVIIIe siècles)." *Bulletin de la Société d'Histoire de la Guadeloupe*188 (2021): 77–131.

Drescher, Seymour. "Revolution in England? Abolitionism." In *The Cambridge History of the Age of the Atlantic Revolutions.* Vol. 2, *France, Europe, and Haiti,* edited by Wim Klooster, 396–420. Cambridge University Press, 2023.

du Pont, Bessie Gardner. *Life of Eleuthère Irénée du Pont from Contemporary Correspondence.* University of Delaware Press, 1923.

du Rivage, Justin. *Revolution Against Empire: Taxes, Politics, and the Origins of American Independence.* Yale University Press, 2018.

Dublin, Thomas. *Transforming Women's Work: New England Lives in the Industrial Revolution.* Cornell University Press, 1994.

Dubois, Laurent. *Avengers of the New World: The Story of the Haitian Revolution.* Belknap Press of Harvard University Press, 2004.

Dubois, Laurent. *Haiti: The Aftershocks of History.* Picador, 2012.

Dull, Jonathan R. *A Diplomatic History of the American Revolution.* Yale University Press, 1985.

Dunn, Richard S. *Sugar and Slaves: The Rise of the Planter Class in the English West Indies, 1624–1713.* University of North Carolina Press, 1972.

DuPlessis, Robert S. "Cloth and the Emergence of the Atlantic Economy." In *The Atlantic Economy during the Seventeenth and Eighteenth Centuries: Organization, Operation, Practice, and Personnel,* edited by Peter A. Coclanis, 72–94. University of South Carolina Press, 2005.

DuPlessis, Robert S. *The Material Atlantic: Clothing, Commerce, and Colonization in the Atlantic World, 1650–1800.* Cambridge University Press, 2016.

DuVal, Kathleen. *Independence Lost: Lives on the Edge of the American Revolution.* Random House, 2016.

Earle, Peter. "The Origins and Careers of English Merchant Seamen in the Late Seventeenth and Early Eighteenth Centuries." In *The Social History of English Seamen, 1650–1815,* edited by Cheryl A. Fury, 129–46. Boydell & Brewer, 2017.

East, Robert A. *Connecticut's Loyalists.* Pequot Press, 1974.

Edwards, John Richard. "A Business Education for 'the Middling Sort of People' in Mercantilist Britain." *British Accounting Review* 41 (2009): 240–55.

Edwards, John Richard, and Stephen P. Walker, eds. *The Routledge Companion to Accounting History.* Routledge Taylor & Francis Group, 2020.

Egerton, Douglas R. *Death or Liberty: African Americans and Revolutionary America.* Oxford University Press, 2009.

Ellis, John. *An Historical Account of Coffee with an Engraving, and Botanical Description of the Tree; to which are added Sundry Papers relative to its Culture and Use, as an article of Diet and Commerce.* London, 1774.

Ellis, Joseph J. *The Cause: The American Revolution and Its Discontents, 1773–1783.* Liveright, 2021.

Ellis, Steven G. *Ireland's English Pale, 1470–1550: The Making of a Tudor Region.* Boydell Press, 2021.

Eltis, David. *Economic Growth and the Ending of the Transatlantic Slave Trade.* Oxford University Press, 1987.

Eltis, David. *The Rise of African Slavery in the Americas.* Cambridge University Press, 2000.

Emmanuel, I. S., and Suzanne A. Emmanuel. *History of the Jews of the Netherlands Antilles.* Vol. 1. American Jewish Archives, 1970.

Emmer, Pieter C. "'Jesus Christ Was Good, But the Trade Was Better': An Overview of the Transit Trade of the Dutch Antilles, 1634–1795." In *The Lesser Antilles in the Age of European Expansion,* edited by Robert L. Paquette and Stanely L. Engerman, 206–22. University Press of Florida, 1996.

Enthoven, Victor. "'That Abominable Nest of Pirates': St. Eustatius and the North Americans, 1680–1780." *Early American Studies* 10, no. 2 (2012): 239–301.

Eustace, Nicole. *Passion Is the Gale: Emotion, Power, and the Coming of the American Revolution.* University of North Carolina Press, 2008.

Faccarello, Gilbert. "Pierre de Boisguilbert and the Foundations of Laissez-Faire." In *A History of Economic Thought in France: Political Economy in the Age of Enlightenment,* ed. by Gilbert Faccarello and Claire Silvant, 31–44. Routledge, 2024.

Farr, James. *Black Odyssey: The Seafaring Traditions of Afro-Americans.* Peter Lang, 1991.

Farrell, William. "Smuggling Silks into Eighteenth-Century Britain: Geography, Perpetrators, and Consumers." *Journal of British Studies* 55, no. 2 (2016): 268–94.

Fenn, Elizabeth A. *Pox Americana: The Great Smallpox Epidemic of 1775–82.* Hill and Wang, 2001.

Fichter, James R. *So Great a Proffit: How the East Indies Trade Transformed Anglo-American Capitalism*. Harvard University Press, 2010.

Fick, Carolyn E. *The Making of Haiti: The Saint Domingue Revolution from Below*. University of Tennessee Press, 1990.

Fischer, David Hackett. *Albion's Seed: Four British Folkways in America*. Oxford University Press, 1989.

Fischer, Lewis R. "Revolution Without Independence: The Canadian Colonies, 1749–1775." In *The Economy of Early America: The Revolutionary Period, 1763–1790*, edited by Ronald Hoffman et al., 88–123. University of Virginia Press, 1988.

Fisher, Sydney George. "The Twenty-Eight Charges Against the King in the Declaration of Independence." *Pennsylvania Magazine of History and Biography* 31, no. 3 (1907): 257–303.

Fitch, Roscoe Conkling. *A History of the Fitch Family A.D. 1400–1930*. Vol. 2. Privately published, 1930.

Flavell, Julie. *When London Was Capital of America*. Yale University Press, 2010.

Flayhart, William Henry. "Oceanic Historiography: The American Dimension." In *Maritime History at the Crossroads: A Critical Review of Recent Historiography*, edited by Frank Broeze, 249–76. Liverpool University Press, 1995.

Fogleman, Aaron S. "Migrations to the Thirteen British North American Colonies, 1700–1775: New Estimates." *Journal of Interdisciplinary History* 22, no. 4 (1992): 691–709.

Fowler, William M. *Rebels Under Sail: The American Navy During the Revolution*. Scribner, 1976.

Foy, Charles R. "Maritime Populations." In *The Princeton Companion to Atlantic History*, edited by Joseph C. Miller, 324–26. Princeton University Press, 2015.

Franklin, Benjamin. *The Autobiography & Other Writings*, with an introduction by Peter Shaw. Bantam, 1982.

Frénée, Samantha. "Pirates and Gallows at Execution Dock: Nautical Justice in Early Modern England." *Criminocorpus*, 2015.

Frese, Joseph R. "Smuggling, the Navy, and the Customs Service, 1763–1772." In *Seafaring in Colonial Massachusetts*, 199–212. Colonial Society of Massachusetts, 1980.

Frey, Sylvia R. *Water from the Rock: Black Resistance in a Revolutionary Age*. Princeton University Press, 1991.

Frost, J. Wiliam. *Connecticut Education in the Revolutionary Era: "For God and Country."* Pequot Press, 1974.

Frostin, Charles. "Angevins de modeste condition établis à Saint-Domingue (Correspondance Labry, 1752–1778)." *Revue française d'histoire d'outre-mer* 57, no. 209 (1970): 447–68.

Frostin, Charles. *Les révoltes blanches à Saint-Domingue aux XVII*[e] *et XVIII*[e] *siècles*. 1975. Presses Universitaires de Rennes, 2015.

Frymer, Paul. *Building an American Empire: The Era of Territorial and Political Expansion*. Princeton University Press, 2017.

Furstenberg, François. *When the United States Spoke French: Five Refugees Who Shaped a Nation*. Penguin Press, 2014.

Gallagher, Edward J. "The Rhetorical Strategy of Franklin's 'Way to Wealth.'" *Eighteenth-Century Studies* 6, no. 4 (1973): 475–85.

Games, Alison. "Migration." In *The British Atlantic World, 1500–1800*, ed. David Armitage and Michael J. Braddick, 31–50. Palgrave Macmillan, 2002.

García-Álvarez, Alejandro. "Santo, Seña, y Ruta Histórica del Plátano Hasta Cuba." *Revista de Indias* 61, no. 221 (2001): 141–66.

Garrigus, John D. *Before Haiti: Race and Citizenship in French Saint-Domingue*. Palgrave Macmillan, 2006.

Garrigus, John D. "'Buccaneers Became Ballet Masters': The Emergence of New Racial Identities in Saint-Domingue, 1763–1777." Paper presented at the 2008 Historical Society meeting, Fort Worth, Texas, June 7, 2008.

Geddes, Rick, and Paul J. Zak. "The Rule of One-Third." *Journal of Legal Studies* 31, no. 1 (2002): 119–37.

Geggus, David. "Major Port Towns of Saint Domingue in the Later Eighteenth Century." In *Atlantic Port Cities: Economy, Culture, and Society in the Atlantic World, 1650–1850*, edited by Franklin W. Knight and Peggy K. Liss, 87–116. University of Tennessee Press, 1991.

Geggus, David. "Slave and Free Colored Women in Saint Domingue." In *More Than Chattel: Black Women and Slavery in the Americas*, edited by David Barry Gaspar and Darlene Clark Hine, 259–78. Indiana University Press, 1996.

Geggus, David. "The Slaves and Free People of Color of Cap Français." In *The Black Urban Atlantic in the Age of the Slave Trade*, edited by Jorge Cañizares-Esguerra, Matt D. Childs, and James Sidbury, 101–21. University of Pennsylvania Press, 2013.

George, M. Dorothy. *London Life in the Eighteenth Century*. 1925. Capricorn Books, 1965.

George, M. Dorothy. "London and the Life of the Town." In *Johnson's England*. Vol. 1, edited by Arthur Stanley Turberville, 160–196. Clarendon Press of Oxford University Press, 1952.

Gervais, Pierre. "A Merchant or a French Atlantic? Eighteenth-Century Account Books as Narratives of a Transnational Merchant Political Economy." *French History* 25, no. 1 (2011): 28–47.

Gerzina, Gretchen. *Black London: Life before Emancipation*. Rutgers University Press, 1995.

Ghachem, Malick W. *The Old Regime and the Haitian Revolution*. Cambridge University Press, 2012.

Gilbert, Alan. *Black Patriots and Loyalists: Fighting for Emancipation in the War for Independence*. University of Chicago Press, 2012.

Gilbert, G. A. "The Connecticut Loyalists." *American Historical Review* 4, no. 2 (1899): 273–91.

Gilje, Paul A. "The Enlightenment at Sea in the Atlantic World." In *The Atlantic Enlightenment*, edited by Susan Manning and Francis D. Cogliano, 281–306. Ashgate, 2008.

Gilje, Paul A. *Free Trade and Sailors' Rights in the War of 1812*. Cambridge University Press, 2012.

Gilje, Paul A. *Liberty on the Waterfront: American Maritime Culture in the Age of Revolution*. University of Pennsylvania Press, 2004.

Gilje, Paul A. *The Road to Mobocracy: Popular Disorder in New York City, 1763–1834*. University of North Carolina Press, 1987.

Gipson, Lawrence Henry. *The Great War for the Empire*. Vol. 8, *The Culmination, 1760–1763*. Knopf, 1970.

Gipson, Lawrence Henry. *The Great War for the Empire*. Vol. 9, *The Triumphant Empire: New Responsibilities within the Enlarged Empire, 1763–1766*. Knopf, 1968.

Godbeer, Richard. *A World of Trouble: A Philadelphia Quaker Family's Journey through the American Revolution*. Yale University Press, 2020.

Godechot, Jacques. "Les relations économiques entre la France et les États-Unis de 1778 à 1789." *French Historical Studies* 1, no. 1 (1958): 26–39.

Goebel, Dorothy Burne. "The 'New England Trade' and the French West Indies, 1763–1774: A Study in Trade Policies." *William and Mary Quarterly* 20, no. 3 (1963): 332–72.

Goelet, Francis. *The Voyages and Travels of Francis Goelet, 1746–1758*. Edited by Kenneth Scott. Queen's College Press, 1970.

Goloboy, Jennifer L. *Charleston and the Emergence of Middle-Class Culture in the Revolutionary Era*. University of Georgia Press, 2016.

Goloboy, Jennifer L. "The Early American Middle Class." *Journal of the Early Republic* 25, no. 4 (2005): 537–45.

Goodspeed, Tyler Beck. *Legislating Instability: Adam Smith, Free Banking, and the Financial Crisis of 1772*. Harvard University Press, 2016.

Goslinga, Cornelis C. *The Dutch in the Caribbean and on the Wild Coast 1580–1680*. University of Florida Press, 1971.

Gould, Eliga H. *Among the Powers of the Earth: The American Revolution and the Making of a New World Empire*. Harvard University Press, 2012.

Gould, Eliga H. "Entangled Atlantic Histories: A Response from the Anglo-American Periphery." *The American Historical Review* 112, no. 5 (2007): 1415–22.

Gould, Eliga H. *The Persistence of Empire: British Political Culture in the Age of the American Revolution*. University of North Carolina Press, 2000.

Gould, Eliga H., and Rosemarie Zagarri, "Situating the United States in Vast Early America: Introduction." *William and Mary Quarterly* 78, no. 2 (2021): 189–200.

Gramarye, Eliza. "1758 St. Eustatius Census Transcript." Department of History, University of Rochester, 2015.

Gramarye, Eliza. "Finite Variety: A Demographic Analysis of 18th Century St. Eustatius' Transformation into the 'Golden Rock.'" Department of History, University of Rochester, 2017.

Grassby, Richard. *Kinship and Capitalism: Marriage, Family, and Business in the English-Speaking World, 1580–1740*. Cambridge University Press, 2001.

Grasso, Christopher. *A Speaking Aristocracy: Transforming Public Discourse in Eighteenth-Century Connecticut*. University of North Carolina Press, 1999.

Greene, Jack P. *Peripheries and Center: Constitutional Development in the Extended Polities of the British Empire and the United States, 1607–1788*. University of Georgia Press, 1986.

Greer, Alan. "Settler Colonialism an Empire in Early America." *William and Mary Quarterly* 76, no. 3 (2019): 383–90.

Greig, Hannah. *The Beau Monde: Fashionable Society in Georgian London*. Oxford University Press, 2013.

Griffin, Edward M. *Old Brick: Charles Chauncy of Boston, 1705–1787*. University of Minnesota Press, 1980.

Griffin, Patrick. *The Age of Atlantic Revolution: The Fall and Rise of a Connected World*. Yale University Press, 2023.

Griffin, Patrick. *The Townshend Moment: The Making of Empire and Revolution in the Eighteenth Century*. Yale University Press, 2017.

Gross, Robert A. *The Minutemen and Their World*. 1976. Hill and Wang, 2001.

Grubb, Farley. *The Continental Dollar: How the American Revolution Was Financed with Paper Money*. University of Chicago Press, 2023.

Haagensen, Reimert. *Description of the Island of St. Croix in America in the West Indies*. Translated and edited by Arnold R. Highfield. Virgin Islands Humanities Council, 1995.

Habermas, Jürgen. *The Structural Transformation of the Public Sphere: An Inquiry into a Category of Bourgeois Society*. MIT Press, 1991.

Hackett, Linda H. *Eleazer Fitch: The First Leader of Stanstead Township*. Stanstead Historical Society, 1941.

Hall, Edward H. *The Old Martyrs' Prison, New York*. American Scenic and Historic Preservation Society, 1902.

Hall, Gwendolyn Midlo. *Slavery and African Ethnicities in the Americas: Restoring the Links*. University of North Carolina Press, 2005.

Hallam, Robert A. *Annals of St. James's, New London, For One Hundred and Fifty Years*. M. H. Mallory, 1873.

Hamilton, Douglas. *Scotland, the Caribbean, and the Atlantic World, 1750–1820*. Manchester University Press, 2016.

Hamilton, Dr. Alexander. "The Itinerarium of Dr. Alexander Hamilton." In *Colonial American Travel Narratives*, edited by Wendy Martin, 173–326. Penguin Books, 1994.

Hancock, David J. *Citizens of the World: London Merchants and the Integration of the British Atlantic Community, 1735–1785*. Cambridge University Press, 1995.

Hancock, David J. "Markets, Merchants, and the Wider World of Boston Wine, 1700–1775." In *Entrepreneurs: The Boston Business Community, 1700–1850*, edited by Conrad Edick Wright and Katheryn P. Viens, 63–95. Northeastern University Press, 1997.

Hancock, David J. *Oceans of Wine: Madeira and the Emergence of American Trade and Taste*. Yale University Press, 2009.

Hancock, David J., and Michelle McDonald, eds. *Public Drinking in the Early Modern World: Voices from the Tavern, 1500–1800*. Vol. 4, *America*. Pickering & Chatto, 2011.

Harding, Richard. *The Emergence of Britain's Global Naval Supremacy: The War of 1739–1748*. Boydell Press, 2010.

Harland-Jacobs, Jessica. "'Hands Across the Sea': The Masonic Network, British Imperialism, and the North Atlantic World." *Geographical Review* 89, no. 2 (1999): 237–53.

Harlow, Vincent T. *The Founding of the Second British Empire, 1763–1793*. Vol. 1. Longmans, Green, 1952.

Harlow, Vincent T., and A. F. Madden. *British Colonial Developments, 1774–1834: Select Documents*. Clarendon Press of Oxford University Press, 1953.

Harper, Lawrence A. *The English Navigation Laws: A Seventeenth-Century Experiment in Social Engineering*. 1939. Octagon Books, 1973.

Harrington, Virginia D. *The New York Merchant on the Eve of the Revolution*. 1935. Peter Smith, 1964.

Harris, Lynn B. *Patroons and Periaguas: Enslaved Watermen and Watercraft of the Lowcountry*. University of South Carolina Press, 2014.

Harris, Sheldon H. *Paul Cuffe: Black America and the African Return*. Simon & Schuster, 1972.

Hart, Emma. "From Field to Plate: The Colonial Livestock Trade and the Development of an American Economic Culture." *William and Mary Quarterly* 73, no. 1 (2016): 107–40.

Hart, Emma, and Cathy Matson. "Situating Merchants in Late Eighteenth-Century British Atlantic Port Cities." *Early American Studies* 15, no. 4 (2017): 660–82.

Hartigan-O'Connor, Ellen. "'She Said She Did Not Know Money': Urban Women and Atlantic Markets in the Revolutionary Era." *Early American Studies* 4, no. 2 (2006): 322–52.

Hartigan-O'Connor, Ellen. *The Ties That Buy: Women and Commerce in Revolutionary America.* University of Pennsylvania Press, 2009.

Hartog, John (Johannes). *History of St. Eustatius.* De Wit NV, 1976.

Haskins, George L. "The Beginnings of Partible Inheritance in the American Colonies." *Yale Law Journal* 51, no. 8 (1942): 1280–315.

Hattem, Michael D. "'As Serves Our Interest Best': Political Economy and the Logic of Popular Resistance in New York City, 1765–1776." *New York History* 98, no. 1 (2017): 40–70.

Hauser, Mark W., and Kenneth G. Kelley. "Colonies Without Frontiers: Inter-Island Trade in the Eighteenth and Nineteenth-Century Caribbean." In *Islands at the Crossroads: Migration, Seafaring, and Interaction in the Caribbean,* edited by Mark W. Hauser et al., 41–56. University of Alabama Press, 2011.

Hayes, Richard. *Rules for the Port of London.* London, 1722.

Heebøll-Holm, Thomas K. *Ports, Piracy and Maritime War: Piracy in the English Channel and the Atlantic, c. 1280–c. 1330.* Brill, 2013.

Hedges, J. B. *The Browns of Providence Plantations.* Vol. 1, *Colonial Years.* Harvard University Press, 1952.

Hemphill, C. Dallett. "Manners and Class in the Revolutionary Era: A Transatlantic Comparison." *William and Mary Quarterly* 63, no. 2 (2006): 345–72.

Hempstead, Joshua. *Diary of Joshua Hempstead of New London, Connecticut: Covering a Period of Forty- Seven Years from September, 1711, to November, 1758.* Facsimile. New London County Historical Society, 1901; repr. 1970.

Henretta, James A. *"Salutary Neglect": Colonial Administration under the Duke of Newcastle.* Princeton University Press, 1972.

Henretta, James A. "The War for Independence and American Economic Development." In *The Economy of Early America: The Revolutionary Period, 1763–1790,* edited by Ronald Hoffman et al., 45–87. University of Virginia Press, 1988.

Herndon, Ruth Wallis. "The Domestic Cost of Seafaring: Town Leaders and Seaman's Families in Eighteenth-Century Rhode Island." In *Iron Men, Wooden Women: Gender and Seafaring in the Atlantic World, 1700–1920,* edited by Margaret S. Creighton and Lisa Norling, 55–69. Johns Hopkins University Press, 1996.

Heyrman, Christine Leigh. *Commerce and Culture: The Maritime Communities of Colonial Massachusetts, 1690–1750.* W. W. Norton, 1984.

Hinderaker, Eric, and Peter C. Mancall. *At the Edge of Empire: The Backcountry in British North America.* Johns Hopkins University Press, 2003.

Hinman, Royal R. *A Catalogue of the Names of the Puritan Settlers of the Colony of Connecticut.* Case, Tiffany, 1852.

Hirsch, Corin. *Forgotten Drinks of Colonial New England: From Flips & Rattle-Skulls to Switchell & Spruce Beer.* Arcadia Press, 2014.

Hoadly, Charles J., ed. *The Public Records of the Colony of Connecticut.* Vols. 7–15. Lockwood and Brainard, 1873–1890. [Cited as CCR]

Hoadly, Charles J., ed. *The Public Records of the State of Connecticut.* Vols. 1–3. Lockwood and Brainard, 1894–1922. [Cited as CSR]

Hodson, Christopher. *The Acadian Diaspora: An Eighteenth-Century History.* Oxford University Press, 2012.

Hoff, Henry B., and F. Kenneth Barta. "De Windt Families of the West Indies." *Genealogist* 3 (1982): 106–27.

Holmes, William, et al. *Three Centuries of Accounting in Massachusetts*. Arno Press, 1978.

Holton, Woody. *Forced Founders: Indians, Debtors, Slaves, and the Making of the American Revolution in Virginia*. University of North Carolina Press, 1999.

Holton, Woody. *Liberty Is Sweet: The Hidden History of the American Revolution*. Simon & Schuster, 2021.

Holton, Woody. *Unruly Americans and the Origins of the Constitution*. Hill and Wang, 2008.

Hood, Adrienne D. "The Material World of Cloth: Production and Use in Eighteenth-Century Rural Pennsylvania." *William and Mary Quarterly* 53, no. 1 (1996): 43–66.

Hoon, Elizabeth Evelynola. *The Organization of the English Customs System, 1696–1786*. 1938; Greenwood Press, 1968.

Hoppit, Julian. *Risk and Failure in English Business, 1700–1800*. Cambridge University Press, 1987.

Horgan, Lucille E. *Forged in War: The Continental Congress and the Origin of Military Supply and Acquisition Policy*. Greenwood Press, 2002.

Houllemare, Marie. "Le Bureau des colonies et ses commis." In *La liasse et la plume: Les bureaux du Sécretariat d'État de la Marine (1699–1792)*, edited by Jörg Ulbert and Sylviane Llinares, 99–109. Presses Universitaires de Rennes, 2022.

Houston, Alan Craig. *Benjamin Franklin and the Politics of Improvement*. Yale University Press, 2008.

Howe, Gilman Bigelow. *Genealogy of the Bigelow Family of America, from the Marriage in 1642 of John Biglo and Mary Warren to the Year 1890*. C. Hamilton, 1890.

Hoy, Don R. "Changing Agricultural Land Use on Guadeloupe, French West Indies." *Annals of the Association of American Geographers* 52, no. 4 (1962): 441–54.

Hrodèj, Philippe. "L'interlope à Saint-Domingue comme un moyen de survie d'une colonie dans les fondemonts." In *Entre exclusif et contrebande: Les navigations commerciales aux Antilles (1600–1830)*, ed. Jean-Sébastien Guibert and Boris Lesueur, 43–58. L'Harmattan, 2022.

Huang, Nian-Sheng. "Franklin's Father Josiah: Life of a Colonial Boston Tallow Chandler, 1657–1745." *Transactions of the American Philosophical Society, New Series*, 90, no. 3 (2000): i–viii, 1–155.

Huang, Nian-Sheng. "Financing Poor Relief: In Colonial Boston." *Massachusetts Historical Review* 8 (2006): 72–103.

Hulbert, Kylie A. *The Untold War at Sea: America's Revolutionary Privateers*. University of Georgia Press, 2022.

Hunt, Margaret R. *The Middling Sort: Commerce, Gender, and the Family in England, 1680–1780*. 1996. University of California Press, 2020.

Huskins, Bonnie. "'Shelburnian Manners': Gentility and the Loyalists of Shelburne, Nova Scotia." *Early American Studies* 13, no. 1 (2015): 151–88.

Huston, James A. *Logistics of Liberty: American Services of Supply in the Revolutionary War and After*. University of Delaware Press, 1991.

Inikori, J. E. "Introduction." In *Forced Migration: The Impact of the Export Slave Trade on African Societies*, ed. J. E. Inikori, 13–60. Africana, 1982.

Isaac, Rhys. *The Transformation of Virginia, 1740–1790*. University of North Carolina Press, 1982.

Jackson, Gordon. *Hull in the Eighteenth Century: A Study in Economic and Social History.* Oxford University Press, 1971.

Jackson, Gordon. *The History and Archaeology of Ports.* World's Work, 1983.

Jaffee, David. *A New Nation of Goods: The Material Culture of Early America.* University of Pennsylvania Press, 2010.

Jaffee, David. "The Village Enlightenment in New England, 1760–1820." *William and Mary Quarterly* 47, no. 3 (1990): 327–46.

James, Coy Hilton. *Silas Deane, Patriot or Traitor?* Michigan State University Press, 1975.

Jarvis, George Atwater, et al. *The Jarvis family: or, The descendants of the first settlers of the name in Massachusetts and Long Island, and those who have more recently settled in other parts of the United States and British America.* Case, 1879.

Jarvis, Michael J. *In the Eye of All Trade: Bermuda, Bermudians, and the Maritime Atlantic World, 1680–1783.* University of North Carolina Press, 2010.

Jasanoff, Maya. *Liberty's Exiles: American Loyalists in the Revolutionary World.* Vintage Books, 2012.

Jensen, A. L. *The Maritime Commerce of Colonial Philadelphia.* State Historical Society of Wisconsin, 1963.

Jensen, Merrill. *The New Nation: A History of the United States During the Confederation, 1781–1789.* Knopf, 1950.

Johnson, Victor L. "Fair Traders and Smugglers in Philadelphia, 1754–1763." *Pennsylvania Magazine of History and Biography* 83, no. 2 (1959): 125–49.

Johnston, A. J. B. *Endgame 1758: The Promise, the Glory, and the Despair of Louisbourg's Last Decade.* University of Nebraska Press, 2007.

Jones, Alice Hanson. *Wealth of a Nation to Be: The American Colonies on the Eve of the Revolution.* New York: Columbia University Press, 1980.

Jones, E. Alfred. *The Loyalists of Massachusetts; Their Memorials, Petitions and Claims.* 1930; Genealogical Publishing, 1969.

Jones, T. Cole. "'Displaying the Ensigns of Harmony': The French Army in Newport, Rhode Island, 1780–1781." *New England Quarterly* 85, no. 3 (2012): 430–67.

Jones, T. Cole. "'The Rage of Tory-Hunting': Loyalist Prisoners, Civil War, and the Violence of American Independence." *Journal of Military History* 81, no. 2 (2017): 719–46.

Jordaan, Han, and Victor Wilson. "The Eighteenth-Century Danish, Dutch, and Swedish Free Ports in the Northeastern Caribbean: Continuity and Change." In *Dutch Atlantic Connections, 1680–1800: Linking Empires, Bridging Borders,* ed. Gert Oostindie and Jessica V. Roitman, 275–308. Brill, 2014.

Kalm, Peter. *Peter Kalm's Travels in North America: The English Version of 1770,* edited by Adolph B. Benson. 2 vols. Dover, 1964

Kamensky, Jane. *A Revolution in Color: The World of John Singleton Copley.* W. W. Norton, 2016.

Kaplan, Steven L. *Bread, Politics and Political Economy in the Reign of Louis XV.* Martinus Nijhoff, 1976.

Kapp, Friedrich. *The Life of John Kalb, Major-General in the Revolutionary Army.* Holt, 1884.

Karras, Alan L. *Smuggling: Contraband and Corruption in World History.* Rowman and Littlefield, 2010.

Kelley, Sean M. *American Slavers: Merchants, Mariners, and the Transatlantic Commerce in Captives, 1644–1865.* Yale University Press, 2023.

Kelley, Sean M. *The Voyage of the Slave Ship Hare: A Journey into Captivity from Sierra Leone to South Carolina*. University of North Carolina Press, 2016.

Kimball, Eric. "An Essential Link in a Vast Chain: New England and the West Indies, 1700–1775." PhD diss., University of Pittsburgh, 2009.

Kimball, Eric. "'What Have We to Do with Slavery?': New Englanders and the Slave Economies of the West Indies." In *Slavery's Capitalism: A New History of American Economic Development*, edited by Sven Beckert and Seth Rockman, 181–94. University of Pennsylvania Press, 2016.

Kimball, Gertrude Selwyn. *The East-India Trade of Providence from 1787 to 1807*. Preston and Rounds, 1896.

Kinkel, Sarah. *Disciplining the Empire: Politics, Governance, and the Rise of the British Navy*. Harvard University Press, 2018.

Kleiser, R. Grant. "An Empire of Free Ports: British Commercial Imperialism in the 1766 Free Port Act." *Journal of British Studies* 60 (2021): 334–61.

Klingaman, David C. "The Development of the Coastwise Trade of Virginia in the Late Colonial Period." *Virginia Magazine of History and Biography* 77, no. 1 (1969): 26–45.

Klooster, Wim. *Illicit Riches: Dutch Trade in the Caribbean, 1648–1795*. KITLV Press, 1998.

Klooster, Wim. "Inter-Imperial Smuggling in the Americas, 1600–1800." In *Soundings in Atlantic History: Latent Structures and Intellectual Currents, 1500–1830*, ed. Bernard Bailyn and Patricia L. Denault, 141–80. Harvard University Press, 2009.

Knappert, Laurentius. "Geschiedenis van de Nederlandsche Bovenwindsche Eilanden im de 18de Eeuw: Hoofdstuk VI (Vervolg)." *De West-Indische Gids* 13 (1931/1932): 249–68.

Knappert, Laurentius. "Geschiedenis van de Nederlandsche Bovenwindsche Eilanden im de 18de Eeuw: Hoofdstuk II (Vervolg)." *De West-Indische Gids* 11 (1929/1930): 513–41.

Knappert, Laurentius. "Geschiedenis van de Nederlandsche Bovenwindsche Eilanden im de 18de Eeuw: Hoofdstuk VII." *De West-Indische Gids* 13 (1931/1932): 545–68.

Kolb, Frances. "The New Orleans Revolt of 1768: Uniting against Real and Perceived Threats of Empire." *Louisiana History* 59, no. 1 (2018): 5–39.

Koot, Christian J. "Anglo-Dutch Trade in the Chesapeake and the British Caribbean, 1621–1733." In *Dutch Atlantic Connections, 1680–1800: Linking Empires, Bridging Borders*, edited by Gert Oostindie and Jessica V. Roitman, 72–100. Brill, 2014.

Kornwolf, James D., and Georgiana W. Kornwolf. *Architecture and Town Planning in Colonial North America*. 2 vols. Johns Hopkins University Press, 2002.

Kulikoff, Allan. "The Economic Growth of the Eighteenth-Century Chesapeake Colonies." *Journal of Economic History* 39, no. 1 (1979): 275–88.

Kwass, Michael. *Contraband: Louis Mandrin and the Making of a Global Underground*. Harvard University Press, 2014.

Labaree, Benjamin W. *The Boston Tea Party*. Northeastern University Press, 1979.

Labaree, Leonard Woods, ed. *The Public Records of the State of Connecticut*. Vols. 4–6. Connecticut State Printing Office, 1942–45. [Cited as CSR]

Lafleur, Gérard. "Familles hollandaises en Guadeloupe aux XVIIe et XVIIIe siècles." *Bulletin de la Société d'Histoire de la Guadeloupe* 163 (2012): 59–75.

Lafleur, Gérard. "La culture du café en Guadeloupe, de son introduction à sa quasi disparition." *Bulletin de la Société d'Histoire de la Guadeloupe* 145 (2006): 59–120.

Lafleur, Gérard. "Les juifs aux îles françaises du vent (XVIIe–XVIIIe siècles)." *Bulletin de la Société d'Histoire de la Guadeloupe* 65–66 (1985): 77–131.

Lafleur, Gérard. "Liens commerciaux entres les Petites Antilles et l'Amérique du Nord sous l'Ancien régime." *Cahiers d'histoire* 32, no. 2 (2013): 13–39.

Laloë, Anne-Flore. *The Geography of the Ocean: Knowing the Ocean as a Space.* Routledge, 2016.

Lambert, Frank. *The Barbary Wars: American Independence in the Atlantic World.* Hill and Wang, 2005.

Lamoreaux, Naomi R. "Rethinking the Transition to Capitalism in the Early American Northeast." *Journal of American History* 90, no. 2 (2003): 437–61.

Lanctôt, Gustave. *Canada and the American Revolution, 1774–1783.* George G. Harrap, 1967.

Land, Jeremy. *Colonial Ports, Global Trade, and the Roots of the American Revolution (1700–1776).* Koninklijke Brill, 2023.

Landsman, Ned C. *From Colonials to Provincials: American Thought and Culture, 1680–1760.* Cornell University Press, 1997.

Law, Michael S. *The Founder's Revolution: The Forgotten History and Principles of the Declaration of Independence.* Morgan James, 2018.

Lawson, Philip. *The Imperial Challenge: Quebec and Britain in the Age of the American Revolution.* McGill–Queen's University Press, 1990.

Lemay, J. A. Leo. *The Life of Benjamin Franklin.* Vol. 1. University of Pennsylvania Press, 2006.

Lemisch, Jesse. "Jack Tar in the Streets: Merchant Seamen in the Politics of Revolutionary America." *William and Mary Quarterly* 25, no. 3 (July 1968): 371–407.

Lemon, James T. *The Best Poor Man's Country: A Geographical Study of Early Southeastern Pennsylvania.* Johns Hopkins University Press, 1972.

Lender, Mark Edward, and James Kirby Martin. "A Traitor's Epiphany: Benedict Arnold in Virginia and His Quest for Reconciliation." *Virginia Magazine of History and Biography* 125, no. 4 (2017): 314–37.

Lennox, Jeffers. "Seeing Red: The Quebec Act and Its Geographic Implications." In *Entangling the Quebec Act: Transnational Contexts, Meanings, and Legacies in North America and the British Empire,* ed. Ollivier Hubert and François Furstenberg, 267–303. McGill-Queen's University Press, 2020.

Léon, Pierre. *Marchands et spéculateurs dauphinois dans le monde antillais du XVIIIe siècle: Les Dolle et les Raby.* Les belles lettres, 1963.

L'Estrange, Sir Roger. *Seneca's morals by way of abstract: To which is added, a discourse under the title of An after-thought: adorned with cuts.* London, 1775. https://babel.hathitrust.org/cgi/pt?id=njp.32101068310349.

Lesueur, Boris, and Jean-Sébastien Guibert. "Introduction: L'Exclusif, un simple monopole national." In *Entre exclusif et contrebande: Les navigations commerciales aux Antilles (1600–1830),* edited by Jean-Sébastien Guibert and Boris Lesueur, 13–40. L'Harmattan, 2022.

Levy-Eichel, Mordechai. "Suitable to the Meanest Capacity': Mathematics, Navigation and Self-Education in the Early Modern British Atlantic." *Mariner's Mirror* 103, no. 4 (2017): 450–65.

Liberman, Anatoly. "Old Slang: *Rogue.*" *OUP Blog,* May 12, 2010.

Library of Congress. *Checklist of American Eighteenth-Century Newspapers in the Library of Congress.* Edited by John Van Ness Ingram. U.S. Government Printing Office, 1912.

Lillywhite, Bryant. *London Coffee Houses: A Reference Book of Coffee Houses of the Seventeenth, Eighteenth, and Nineteenth Centuries.* Allen and Unwin, 1963.

Linebaugh, Peter, and Marcus Rediker. *The Many-Headed Hydra: Sailors, Slaves, Commoners, and the Hidden History of the Revolutionary Atlantic*. Beacon Press, 2000.

Lipson, Dorothy Ann. *Freemasonry in Federalist Connecticut*. Princeton University Press, 1977.

Lockridge, Kenneth A. *Literacy in Colonial New England: An Enquiry into the Social Context of Literacy in the Early Modern West*. W. W. Norton, 1974.

Loorya, Alyssa. "Deconstructing City Hall Park: The Development and Archaeology of the Common." PhD diss., City University of New York, 2018.

Love, William DeLoss. *The Colonial History of Hartford Gathered from Original Records*. Privately published, 1914.

Lucas, Wendy, and Noel Campbell. "Economic Significance of Cloth and Apparel: An Analysis of George Washington's Shipping Receipts 1754–1772." *Essays in Economic & Business History* 34 (2016): 208–57.

Lydon, James G. *Pirates, Privateers, and Profits*. Gregg Press, 1970.

Lynd, Staughton, and David Waldstreicher. "Free Trade, Sovereignty, and Slavery: Toward an Economic Interpretation of American Independence." *William and Mary Quarterly* 68, no. 4 (2011): 597–630.

Mackenzie, Frederick. *Diary of Frederick Mackenzie: Giving a Daily Narrative of His Military Service as an Officer of the Regiment of Royal Welch Fusiliers. . . .* 2 vols. Harvard University Press, 1930.

Mackesy, Piers. *The War for America, 1775–1783*. Harvard University Press, 1964.

MacKinnon, Neil. *This Unfriendly Soil: The Loyalist Experience in Nova Scotia, 1783–1791*. McGill–Queen's University Press, 1986.

Magra, Christopher P. *The Fisherman's Cause: Atlantic Commerce and Maritime Dimensions of the American Revolution*. Cambridge University Press, 2009.

Magra, Christopher P. *Poseidon's Curse: British Naval Impressment and the Atlantic Origins of the American Revolution*. Cambridge University Press, 2016.

Maier, Pauline. *American Scripture: Making the Declaration of Independence*. Vintage Books, 1998.

Maier, Pauline. "Boston and New York in the Eighteenth Century." *Proceedings of the American Antiquarian Society* 91 (1982): 177–95.

Maier, Pauline. *From Resistance to Revolution: Colonial Radicals and the Development of American Opposition to Britain, 1765–1776*. Vintage Books, 1974.

Maier, Pauline. "John Wilkes and American Disillusionment with Britain." *William and Mary Quarterly* 20, no. 3 (1963): 373–95.

Main, Gloria L. "Women on the Edge: Life at Street Level in the Early Republic." *Journal of the Early Republic* 32, no. 3 (2012): 331–47.

Main, Gloria L., and Jackson T. Main. "The Red Queen in New England?" *William and Mary Quarterly* 56, no. 1 (1999): 121–50.

Main, Jackson T. *Connecticut Society in the Era of the American Revolution*. Bicentennial Commission of Connecticut, 1977.

Main, Jackson T. *Society and Economy in Colonial Connecticut*. Princeton University Press, 1985.

Mallon, Grace E. "Negotiated Federalism: Intergovernmental Relations on the Maritime Frontier, 1789–1815." *William and Mary Quarterly* 81, no. 4 (2024): 687–720.

Mandelblatt, Bertie. "Atlantic Consumption of French Rum and Brandy and Economic Growth in the Seventeenth- and Eighteenth-century Caribbean." *French History* 25, no. 1 (2011): 9–27.

Mann, Bruce H. *Republic of Debtors: Bankruptcy in the Age of American Independence.* Harvard University Press, 2002.

Manning, Susan, and Francis D. Cogliano. "Introduction." In *The Atlantic Enlightenment,* ed. Susan Manning and Fracis D. Cogliano, 1–31. Ashgate, 2008.

Marshall, P. J. *The Making and Unmaking of Empires: Britain, India, and America c. 1750–1783.* Oxford University Press, 2007.

Marston, Jerrilyn Greene. *King and Congress: The Transfer of Political Legitimacy, 1774–1776.* Princeton University Press, 1987.

Martin, James Kirby. *Benedict Arnold, Revolutionary Hero: An American Warrior Reconsidered.* New York University Press, 1997.

Martin, Margaret E. "Merchants and Trade of the Connecticut River Valley, 1750–1820." *Smith College Studies in History* 24, nos. 1–4 (1938–39): 1–284.

Marzagalli, Silvia. *Bordeaux et les États-Unis, 1776–1815: Politique et stratégies négociantes dans la genèse d'un réseau commercial.* Librairie Droz, 2015.

Marzagalli, Silvia. "The Failure of a Transatlantic Alliance? Franco-American Trade, 1783–1815." *History of European Ideas* 34, no. 4 (2008): 456–64.

Mathieu, Jacques. *Le commerce entre a Nouvelle-France et les Antilles au XVIIIe siècle.* Fides, 1981.

Matson, Cathy D. *Merchants & Empire: Trading in Colonial New York.* Johns Hopkins University Press, 1998.

Matson, Cathy D. "Putting the *Lydia* to Sea: The Material Economy of Shipping in Colonial Philadelphia." *William and Mary Quarterly* 74, no. 2 (2017): 303–32.

Matson, Cathy D. "Women's Economies in North America before 1820: Special Forum Introduction." *Early American Studies* 4, no. 2 (2006): 271–90.

Mauro, Frédéric. *Histoire du café.* Éditions Desjonquères, 1991.

May, Henry F. *The Enlightenment in America.* Oxford University Press, 1976.

May, Louis Philippe. *Histoire économique de la Martinique (1635–1763).* 1930. Société de distribution et de culture de Martinique, 1972.

McBride, Spencer W. *Pulpit and Nation: Clergymen and the Politics of Revolutionary America.* University of Virginia Press, 2017.

McClellan, James E. *Colonialism and Science: Saint Domingue in the Old Regime.* 1992. University of Chicago Press, 2010.

McCleskey, Turk, and James C. Squire. "Knowing When to Fold: Litigation on a Writ of Debt in Mid-Eighteenth-Century Virginia." *William and Mary Quarterly* 76, no. 3 (2019): 509–44.

McConville, Brendan. "Pope's Day Revisited, 'Popular' Culture Reconsidered." *Explorations in Early American Culture* 4 (2000): 258–80.

McCusker, John J. "The Business of Distilling in the Old World and the New in the Seventeenth and Eighteenth Centuries: The Rise of a New Enterprise and Its Connection with Colonial America." In *The Early Modern Atlantic Economy,* edited by John J. McCusker and Kenneth Morgan, 186–224. Cambridge University Press, 2000.

McCusker, John J. "Growth, Stagnation, or Decline? The Economy of the British West Indies, 1763–1790." In *The Economy of Early America: The Revolutionary Period, 1763–1790,* edited by Ronald Hoffman et al., 275–302. University of Virginia Press, 1988.

McCusker, John J. *Money and Exchange in Europe and America, 1600–1775: A Handbook.* University of North Carolina Press, 1978.

McCusker, John J. "New York City and the Bristol Packet: A Chapter in Early Eighteenth Century Postal History." In *Essays in the Economic History of the Atlantic World,* 177–89. Routledge, 1997.

McCusker, John J. *Rum and the American Revolution: The Rum Trade and the Balance of Payments of the Thirteen Continental Colonies.* 2 vols. Garland, 1989.

McCusker, John J. "The Rum Trade and the Balance of Payments of the Thirteen Continental Colonies, 1650–1775." *Journal of Economic History* 30, no. 1 (1970): 244–47.

McCusker, John J., and Russell R. Menard. *The Economy of British America, 1607–1789.* University of North Carolina Press, 1985.

McDonald, Forrest. *Novus Ordo Seclorum: The Intellectual Origins of the Constitution.* University Press of Kansas, 1985.

McDonald, Michelle Craig. "The Chance of the Moment: Coffee and the New West Indies Commodities Trade." *William and Mary Quarterly* 62, no. 3 (2005): 441–72.

McDonald, Michelle Craig. "Sea Change: Coffee and 'Plantations for the Poorer Sort.'" Paper presented at the Fourteenth Annual Conference of the Early American Economy and Society, Philadelphia, October 24–25, 2014.

McDonnell, Michael A., and David Waldstreicher. "Revolution in the *Quarterly?* A Historiographical Analysis." *William and Mary Quarterly* 74, no. 4 (2017): 633–66.

McDonough, Daniel J. *Christopher Gadsden and Henry Laurens: The Parallel Lives of Two American Patriots.* Susquehanna University Press, 2000.

McGrath, Tim. *Give Me a Fast Ship: The Continental Navy and America's Revolution at Sea.* NAL Caliber, 2014.

McKito, Valerie H. *From Loyalists to Loyal Citizens: The DePeyster Family of New York.* State University of New York Press, 2015.

Meinig, D. W. *The Shaping of America: A Geographical Perspective on 500 Years of History.* Vol. 1, *Atlantic America 1492–1800.* Yale University Press, 1986.

Mentz, Steve, and Craig Dionne. *Rogues and Early Modern English Culture.* University of Michigan Press, 2004.

Meyer, Jean. "Les difficultés du commerce Franco-Américain vues de Nantes (1776–1790)." *French Historical Studies* 11, no. 2 (1979): 159–83.

Mhurchadha, Maighréad Ní. "Chasing the Smugglers: The Customs Service in Rush 1674–1765." *Dublin Historical Record* 69, no. 1 (2016): 102–16.

Middlebrook, Louis F. *History of Maritime Connecticut during the American Revolution, 1775–1783.* Essex Institute, 1925.

Middlekauff, Robert. *Ancients and Axioms: Secondary Education in Eighteenth-Century New England.* Yale University Press, 1963.

Middlekauff, Robert. *The Glorious Cause: The American Revolution, 1763–1789.* 1982. Oxford University Press, 2007.

Minty, Christopher F. *Unfriendly to Liberty: Loyalist Networks and the Coming of the American Revolution in New York City.* Cornell University Press, 2023.

Mintz, Sidney W. "The Caribbean as a Socio-Cultural Area." In *Peoples and Cultures of the Caribbean: An Anthropological Reader,* edited by Michael M. Horowitz, 17–46. Natural History Press, 1971.

Mintz, Sidney W. *Sweetness and Power: The Place of Sugar in Modern History.* Penguin Books, 1986.

Miquelon, Dale. *Dugard of Rouen, French Trade to Canada and the West Indies, 1729–1770.* McGill–Queen's University Press, 1978.

Miquelon, Dale. *New France, 1701–1744: A Supplement to Europe.* McClelland and Stewart, 1987.

Moats, Sandra. *Navigating Neutrality: Early American Governance in the Turbulent Atlantic.* University of Virginia Press, 2021.

Mokyr, Joel. *The Enlightened Economy: An Economic History of Britain, 1700–1850.* Yale University Press, 2009.

Monaghan, E. Jennifer. "Literacy Instruction and Gender in Colonial New England." *American Quarterly* 40, no. 1 (1988): 18–41.

Monaghan, Frank, and Samuel J. Marino. *French Travellers in the United States, 1765–1932: A Bibliography.* Antiquarian Press, 1961.

Moore, Christopher. *Louisbourg Portraits: Life in an Eighteenth-Century Garrison Town.* Macmillan, 1982.

Morgan, Edmund S. *Benjamin Franklin.* Yale University Press, 2003.

Morgan, Edmund S., and Helen M. Morgan. *The Stamp Act Crisis: Prologue to Revolution.* 1963. University of North Carolina Press, 2011.

Morgan, Kenneth. "Building British Atlantic Port Cities: Bristol and Liverpool in the Eighteenth Century." In *Building the British Atlantic World Book: Spaces, Places, and Material Culture, 1600–1850,* edited by Daniel Maudlin and Bernard L. Herman, 212–28. University of North Carolina Press, 2016.

Morgan, Kenneth. "Robert Dinwiddie's Reports on the British American Colonies." *The William and Mary Quarterly* 65:2 (2008), 305–46.

Morgan, Philip D. "The Caribbean Environment to 1850." In *Sea and Land: An Environmental History of the Caribbean,* edited by Philip D. Morgan et al., 19–129. Oxford University Press, 2022.

Morrissey, Marietta. *Slave Women in the New World: Gender Stratification in the Caribbean.* University Press of Kansas, 2021.

Morriss, Roger. *The Foundations of British Maritime Ascendancy: Resources, Logistics and the State, 1755–1815.* Cambridge University Press, 2010.

Morton-Williams, Peter. "The Oyo Yoruba and the Atlantic Trade, 1670–1830." In *Forced Migration: The Impact of the Export Slave Trade on African Societies,* edited by J. E. Inikori, 167–86. Africana, 1982.

Moya Pons, Frank. *History of the Caribbean: Plantations, Trade, and War in the Atlantic World.* Markus Wiener, 2007.

Mui, Hoh-cheung, and Lorna H. Mui. *Shops and Shopkeeping in Eighteenth Century England.* McGill–Queen's University Press, 1989.

Mulich, Jeppe. *In a Sea of Empires: Networks and Crossings in the Revolutionary Caribbean.* Cambridge University Press, 2020.

Mumford, James Gregory. *Mumford Memoirs, being the story of the New England Mumfords from the Year 1655 to the present time.* Updike, 1900.

Munro, James, ed. *Acts of the Privy Council of England.* Vol. 5, *1766–1783. Hereford Times,* 1912. https://babel.hathitrust.org/cgi/pt?id=coo.31924026356331&seq=1.

Murdoch, D. H. "Land Policy in the Eighteenth-Century British Empire: The Sale of Crown Lands in the Ceded Islands, 1763–1783." *Historical Journal* 27, no. 3 (1984): 549–74.

Murray, William C. *St. John's Lodge no. 4, 1762–1962*. Forgotten Books, 2018.

Nash, Gary B. *Forging Freedom: The Formation of Philadelphia's Black Community, 1720–1840*. Harvard University Press, 1988.

Nash, Gary B. *The Unknown American Revolution: The Unruly Birth of Democracy and the Struggle to Create America*. Penguin Books, 2006.

Nash, Gary B. *The Urban Crucible: The Northern Seaports and the Origins of the American Revolution*. Abridged edition. Harvard University Press, 1986.

Naylor, Simon. "Logbooks and the Law of Storms: Maritime Meteorology and the British Admiralty in the Nineteenth Century." *Isis* 106, no. 4 (2015): 771–97.

Nelson, James L. *George Washington's Secret Navy: How the American Revolution Went to Sea*. McGraw-Hill, 2008.

Nelson, Paul David. *General Horatio Gates: A Biography*. Louisiana State University Press, 1976.

Nettels, Curtis P. *The Emergence of a National Economy, 1775–1815*. 1962. M. E. Sharpe, 1989.

Newell, Margaret Ellen. *From Dependency to Independence: Economic Revolution in Colonial New England*. Cornell University Press, 1998.

Nichols, Gilbert M. *A History of the Town of Freetown, Massachusetts*. J. H. Franklin, 1902.

Niddrie, D. L. "Eighteenth-Century Settlement in the British Caribbean." *Transactions of the Institute of British Geographers* 40 (1966): 67–80.

Norling, Lisa. *Captain Ahab Had a Wife: New England Women & the Whalefishery, 1720–1870*. University of North Carolina Press, 2000.

Norton, Louis Arthur. *Captains Contentious: The Dysfunctional Sons of the Brine*. University of South Carolina Press, 2009.

Norton, Louis Arthur. "Dudley Saltonstall and the Penobscot Expedition, 1779." *Connecticut History Review* 42, no. 1 (2003): 19–39.

Norton, Louis Arthur. "The Penobscot Expedition: A Tale of Two Indicted Patriots." *The Northern Mariner / Le marin du nord* 16, no. 4 (2006): 1–28.

Norton, Matthew. "Temporality, Isolation, and Violence in the Early Modern English Maritime World." *Eighteenth-Century Studies* 48, no. 1 (2014): 37–66.

Norton, Mary Beth. *The British-Americans: The Loyalist Exiles in England, 1774–1789*. Little, Brown, 1972.

Norton, Mary Beth. "The Seventh Tea Ship." *William and Mary Quarterly* 73, no. 4 (2016): 681–710.

Norwood, Dael A. *Trading Freedom: How Trade with China Defined Early America*. University of Chicago Press, 2022.

Nutting, Bradley. "Charter and Crown: Relations of Connecticut with the English Government, 1662–1776." PhD diss. University of North Carolina, 1972.

Nutting, Bradley. "John Shackmaple and the Connecticut Ports Controversy." *Connecticut Historical Society Bulletin* 38 (1973): 33–40.

Oberg, Michael L. *Dominion and Civility: English Imperialism and Native America, 1585–1685*. Cornell University Press, 1999.

O'Brien, Patrick. "Mercantilism and Imperialism in the Rise and Decline of the Dutch and British Economies 1585–1815." *De Economist: Quarterly Review of the Royal Netherlands Economic Association* 148, no. 4 (2000): 469–501.

O'Malley, Gregory E. "Beyond the Middle Passage: Slave Migration from the Caribbean to North America, 1619–1807." *William and Mary Quarterly* 66, no. 1 (2009): 125–72.

Olson, Alison G. "The London Mercantile Lobby and the Coming of the American Revolution." *Journal of American History* 69, no. 1 (1982): 21–41.

Olson, Alison G. *Making the Empire Work: London and American Interest Groups, 1690–1790*. Harvard University Press, 1992.

Onuf, Peter. "'It Is Not a Union.'" *Wilson Quarterly* 11, no. 2 (1987): 96–104.

O'Shaughnessy, Andrew Jackson. *An Empire Divided: The American Revolution and the British Caribbean*. University of Pennsylvania Press, 2000.

O'Shaughnessy, Andrew Jackson. *The Men Who Lost America: British Leadership, the American Revolution, and the Fate of the Empire*. Yale University Press, 2013.

Ostler Jeffrey, and Nancy Shoemaker. "Settler Colonialism in Early American History: Introduction." *William and Mary Quarterly* 76, no. 3 (2019): 361–68.

Palmié, Stephan, and Francisco A. Scarano. "Introduction: Caribbean Counterpoints." In *The Caribbean: A History of the Region and Its Peoples*, edited by Stephan Palmié and Francisco A. Scarano, 1–21. University of Chicago Press, 2011.

Pares, Richard. *Colonial Blockade and Neutral Rights, 1739–1763*. 1938. Porcupine Press, 1975.

Pares, Richard. *Merchants and Planters*. Cambridge University Press, 1960.

Pares, Richard. *War and Trade in the West Indies, 1739–1763*. 1939. Repr. Frank Cass, 1963.

Pares, Richard. *A West-India Fortune*. Archon Books, 1968.

Pares, Richard. *Yankees and Creoles*. 1956. Archon Books, 1968.

Parisis, Denise, and Henri Parisis. "Le siècle du sucre à Saint-Martin français." *Bulletin de la Société d'Histoire de la Guadeloupe*, 99–102 (1994): 3–208.

Parkinson, Robert G. *The Common Cause: Creating Race and Nation in the American Revolution*. University of North Carolina Press, 2016.

Pastore, Christopher L. *Between Land and Sea: The Atlantic Coast and the Transformation of New England*. Harvard University Press, 2014.

Paul, Heike. *Myths That Made America: An Introduction to American Studies*. Transcript Verlag, 2014.

Peckham, Howard H. *Sources of American Independence: Selected Manuscripts from the Collections of the William L. Clements Library*. Vol. 1. University of Chicago Press, 1978.

Pencak, William. "The Declaration of Independence: Changing Interpretations and a New Hypothesis." *Pennsylvania History: A Journal of Mid-Atlantic Studies* 57, no. 3 (1990): 225–35.

Perl-Rosenthal, Nathan. *Citizen Sailors: Becoming American in the Age of Sail*. Harvard University Press, 2015.

Pérotin-Dumon, Anne. *La Ville aux iles, la ville dans l'île: Basse-Terre et Point-à-Pitre, Guadeloupe, 1650–1820*. Karthala, 2000.

Perry, K. R. *British Politics and the American Revolution*. St. Martin's Press, 1990.

Peters, Reverend Samuel. *General History of Connecticut: From Its First Settlement Under George Fenwick to Its Latest Period of Amity with Great Britain Prior to the Revolution . . .* Edited by Samuel Jarvis McCormick. 1782. Books for Libraries Press, 1969.

Peterson, Mark A. *The City-State of Boston: The Rise and Fall of an Atlantic Power, 1630–1865*. Princeton University Press, 2019.

Phinney, Mary Allen. *A Brief History of Lewis Allen (of Fisher's Island and New London Conn.) and His Descendants (from 1699–1954)*. Tuttle Publishing, 1954.

Pincus, Steve C. A. "Rethinking Mercantilism: Political Economy, the British Empire, and the Atlantic World in the Seventeenth and Eighteenth Centuries." *William and Mary Quarterly* 69, no. 1 (2012): 3–34.

Pincus, Steve C. A. *The Heart of the Declaration: The Founders' Case for an Activist Government.* Yale University Press, 2016.

Pinon, Pierre. "Villes fondées à Saint-Domingue au XVIIIe siècle: Une régularité sans concession." In *La ville régulière: Modèles et tracés,* ed. Xavier Malverti and Pierre Pinon, 123–45. Picard, 1997.

Pitman, Frank Wesley. *The Development of the British West Indies, 1700–1763.* 1917. Routledge, 2018.

Polónia, Amélia. "The European Seaport System at the Beginning of the Early Modern Age." In *The Sea in History: The Early Modern World,* ed. Christian Buchet and Gérard Le Bouëdec, 148–57. Boydell & Brewer, 2017.

Polónia, Amélia. "Maritime History: A Gateway to Global History?" In *Maritime History as Global History,* edited by Amélia Polónia and Maria Fusaro, 1–20. Liverpool University Press, 2010.

Polónia, Amélia. "Seaports as Centres of Economic Growth: The Portuguese Case, 1500–1800." In *Shipping and Economic Growth 1350–1850,* edited by Richard W. Unger, 379–409. Brill, 2011.

Porter, Roy. *English Society in the Eighteenth Century.* Allen Lane, 1982.

Postma, Johannes. *The Dutch in the Atlantic Slave Trade, 1600–1815.* Cambridge University Press, 1990.

Postma, Johannes. "Suriname and Its Atlantic Connections, 1667–1795." In *Riches from Atlantic Commerce: Dutch Transatlantic Trade and Shipping, 1585–1817,* edited by Johannes Postma and Victor Enthoven, 287–321. Brill, 2003.

Poteet, J. M. "The Lordly Prelate: Gurdon Saltonstall Against His Times." *New England Quarterly* 53, no. 4 (1980): 483–507.

Pownall, Thomas. *A topographical description of the Dominions of the Unites States of America. . . .* London, 1776. University of Pittsburgh, 1949, Lois Mulkearn, editor.

Price, Jacob M. "What Did Merchants Do? Reflections on British Overseas Trade, 1660–1790." *Journal of Economic History* 49, no. 2 (1989): 267–84.

Pritchard, James S. *In Search of Empire: The French in the Americas, 1670–1730.* Cambridge University Press, 2004.

Prude, Jonathan. *The Coming of Industrial Order: Town and Factory Life in Rural Massachusetts, 1810–1860.* Cambridge University Press, 1983.

Quintanilla, Mark. "Mercantile Communities in the Ceded Islands: The Alexander Baartlett & George Campbell Company." *International Social Science Review* 79, no. 1–2 (2004): 14–26.

Quintanilla, Mark. "The World of Alexander Campbell: An Eighteenth-Century Grenadian Planter." *Albion: A Quarterly Journal Concerned with British Studies* 35, no. 2 (2003): 229–56.

Radune, Richard A. *Sound Rising: Long Island Sound at the Forefront of America's Struggle for Independence.* Research in Time Publications, 2011.

Raphael, Ray. *The First American Revolution: Before Lexington and Concord.* New Press, 2002.

Rappleye, Charles. *Robert Morris: Financier of the American Revolution.* Simon & Schuster, 2010.

Rappleye, Charles. *Sons of Providence: The Brown Brothers, the Slave Trade, and the American Revolution.* Simon & Schuster, 2006.

Rathbun, Jonathan, et al. *Narrative of Jonathan Rathbun: With the Narratives of Rufus Avery and Stephen Hempstead, Eye Witnesses, Including the Narrative of Thomas Herttell.* New York Times/Arno Press, 1971.

Raven, James. *Publishing Business in Eighteenth-Century England.* Boydell & Brewer, 2014.

Rawlyk, George A. *Nova Scotia's Massachusetts: A Study of Massachusetts–Nova Scotia Relations 1630 to 1784.* McGill–Queen's University Press, 1973.

Rediker, Marcus. *Between the Devil and the Deep Blue Sea: Merchant Seamen, Pirates, and the Anglo-American Maritime World, 1700–1750.* Cambridge University Press, 1987.

Rediker, Marcus. *Villains of All Nations: Atlantic Pirates in the Golden Age.* Beacon Press, 2004.

Reeder, Tyson. *Smugglers, Pirates, and Patriots: Free Trade in the Age of Revolution.* University of Pennsylvania Press, 2019.

Reid, Phillip. *The Merchant Ship in the British Atlantic, 1600–1800: Continuity and Innovation in a Key Technology.* Brill, 2020.

Rice, Franklin P. *Vital Records of the Town of Leicester, Massachusetts, to the End of 1849.* F. P. Rice, 1903.

Rice, Franklin P. *Vital Records of the Town of Shrewsbury, Massachusetts, to the End of 1849.* Franklin P. Rice, 1904.

Rice, Kym S. *Early American Taverns: For the Enlightenment of Friends and Strangers,* Fraunces Tavern Museum and Regnery Gateway, 1983.

Richards, Eric. *Britannia's Children: Emigration from England, Scotland, Wales and Ireland since 1600.* Hambledon & London, 2005.

Richardson, David. *Principles and Agents: The British Slave Trade and Its Abolition.* Yale University Press, 2022.

Richardson, David. "The Slave Trade, Sugar, and British Economic Growth, 1748–1776." *Journal of Interdisciplinary History* 17, no. 4 (1987): 739–69.

Rindfleisch, Bryan C. "Family, Linen, and Emigration in Ulster, 1700–1740: The Galphin Family in Two Worlds." *New Hibernia Review/Iris Éireannach Nua* 20, no. 4 (2016): 128–43.

Ritcheson, Charles R. *Aftermath of Revolution: British Policy Toward the United States, 1783–1795.* Southern Methodist University Press, 1969.

Robins, Nick. *The Corporation That Changed the World: How the East India Company Shaped the Modern Multinational.* Pluto, 2012.

Roche, Daniel. *France in the Enlightenment.* Translated by Arthur Goldhammer. Harvard University Press, 1998.

Røge, Pernille. *Economists and the Reinvention of Empire: France in the Americas and Africa, c. 1750–c. 1815.* Cambridge University Press, 2019.

Rogers, Ernest E., ed., and Nathaniel Shaw. *Connecticut's Naval Office at New London during the War of the American Revolution.* 1933. Repr. Heritage Books, 2008.

Rogers, Zabdiel, and Thomas Mumford, *Groton Heights and New London.* Privately printed, 1881. https://archive.org/details/1781grotonheightooroge/page/n1/mode/2up.

Roland, Alex, W. Jeffrey Bolster, and Alexander Keyssar. *The Way of the Ship: America's Maritime History Reenvisioned, 1600–2000.* John Wiley & Sons, 2008.

Roney, Jessica Choppin. "Introduction: Distinguishing Port Cities, 1500–1800." *Early American Studies* 15, no. 4 (2017): 649–59.

Rossano, Geoffrey L. "Down to the Bay: New York Shippers and the Central American Logwood Trade, 1748–1761." *New York History* 70, no. 3 (1989): 229–50.

Roth, David M. *Connecticut's War Governor, Jonathan Trumbull.* Pequot Press, 1974.

Rouleau, Brian. *With Sails Whitening Every Sea: Mariners and the Making of an American Maritime Empire*. Cornell University Press, 2014.

Rudé, George. *Hanoverian London, 1714–1808*. University of California Press, 1971.

Rule, J. G. "Social Crime in the Rural South in the Eighteenth and Early Nineteenth Centuries." *Southern History* 1 (1979): 135–53.

Rupert, Linda M. *Creolization and Contraband: Curaçao in the Early Modern Atlantic World*. University of Georgia Press, 2012.

Sage, Elisha L., and Charles D. Sage. *Genealogical record of the descendants of David Sage; A Native of Wales, born in 1639, and one of the first settlers of Middletown, Connecticut in 1652*. Charles Sage, 1919.

Saint, Chandler B., and George A. Krimsky. *Making Freedom: The Extraordinary Life of Venture Smith*. Wesleyan University Press, 2009.

Saintard, Pierre-Louis. *Essai sur les intérêts du commerce national pendant la guerre, ou Lettres d'un citoyen sur la permission de commercer dans les colonies, annoncée pour les puissances neutres*. 1756.

Saladino, Gaspare J. "The Economic Revolution in Late Eighteenth Century Connecticut." PhD diss., University of Wisconsin, 1964.

Salinger, Sharon V. *Taverns and Drinking in Early America*. Johns Hopkins University Press, 2002.

Salmon, Marylynn. *Women and the Law of Property in Early America*. University of North Carolina Press, 1986.

Sargent, A. J. *Seaports & Hinterlands*. A. and C. Black, 1938.

Saul, Nigel. *Richard II*. Yale University Press, 2008.

Sawers, Larry. "The Navigation Acts Revisited." *Economic History Review* 45, no. 2 (1992): 262–84.

Schmitt, Casey S. "Virtue in Corruption: Privateers, Smugglers, and the Shape of Empire in the Eighteenth-Century Caribbean." *Early American Studies* 13, no. 1 (2015): 80–110.

Schnakenbourg, Christian. "La Guadeloupe pendant la première administration britannique: Le mémoire du gouverneur Dalrymple du 16 février 1762." *Bulletin de la Société d'Histoire de la Guadeloupe* 174 (2016): 51–72.

Schnakenbourg, Christian. "Neutres et neutralité dans le monde antillais du XVIIIe siècle." *Bulletin de la Société d'Histoire de la Guadeloupe* 174 (2016): 5–19.

Schnakenbourg, Christian. "Recherche sur l'histoire du coton en Guadeloupe (XVIIe–XIXe siècles)." *Bulletin de la Société d'Histoire de la Guadeloupe* 152 (2009): 79–118.

Schnakenbourg, Christian. "Statistiques pour l'histoire de l'économie de plantation en Guadeloupe et Martinique (1635–1835)." *Bulletin de la Société d'Histoire de la Guadeloupe* 31 (1977): 3–121.

Schnurmann, Claudia. "Atlantic Trade and American Identities: The Correlations of Supranational Commerce, Political Opposition, and Colonial Regionalism." In *The Atlantic Economy During the Seventeenth and Eighteenth Centuries: Organization, Operation, Practice, and Personnel*, ed. Peter A. Coclanis, 186–204. University of South Carolina Press, 2005.

Scott, H. M. *The Birth of a Great Power System, 1740–1815*. Pearson/Longman, 2006.

Scott, Kenneth. "Introduction." In Francis Goelet, *The Voyages and Travels of Francis Goelet, 1746–1758*. Edited by Kenneth Scott. Queen's College Press, 1970.

Scott, Kenneth. "Jacob Goelet: Translator of Dutch." *Halve Maen* 55, no. 4 (1981): 1–8.

Searing, James F. "The Seven Years' War in West Africa: The End of Company Rule and the Emergence of the Habitants." In *The Seven Years' War: Global Views*, ed. Mark H. Danley and Patrick J. Speelman, 263–91. Brill, 2012

Sgard, Jérôme. "Do Legal Origins Matter? The Case of Bankruptcy Laws in Europe 1808–1914." *European Review of Economic History* 10, no. 3 (2006): 389–419.

Shepherd, James F., and Gary M. Walton. *Shipping, Maritime Trade, and the Economic Development of Colonial North America.* Cambridge University Press, 1972.

Sheridan, Richard B. "The British Credit Crisis of 1772 and The American Colonies." *Journal of Economic History* 20, no. 2 (1960): 161–86.

Sheridan, Richard B. "The Molasses Act and the Market Strategy of the British Sugar Planters." *Journal of Economic History* 17, no. 1 (1957): 62–83.

Sheridan, Richard B. *Sugar and Slavery: An Economic History of the British West Indies, 1623–1775.* Johns Hopkins University Press, 1974.

Shyllon, F. O. *Black People in Britain 1555–1833.* Oxford University Press, 1977.

Skemp, Sheila L. *William Franklin: Son of a Patriot, Servant of a King.* Oxford University Press, 1990.

Slauter, Will. "Forward-Looking Statements: News and Speculation in the Age of the American Revolution." *Journal of Modern History* 81, no. 4 (2009): 759–92.

Smallwood, Stephanie E. "Reflections on Settler Colonialism, the Hemispheric Americas, and Chattel Slavery." *William and Mary Quarterly* 76, no. 3 (2019): 407–16.

Smelser, Marshall. *The Campaign for the Sugar Islands, 1759: A Study of Amphibious Warfare.* University of North Carolina Press, 1955.

Smith, Adam. *The Wealth of Nations.* 1776. Repr. Bantam Classics, 2003; Edwin Cannan, editor.

Smith, Billy G. "The Material Lives of Laboring Philadelphians, 1750 to 1800." *William and Mary Quarterly* 38, no. 2 (1981): 164–202.

Smith, Frederick H. *Caribbean Rum: A Social and Economic History.* University Press of Florida, 2005.

Smith, Paul H. "The American Loyalists: Notes on Their Organization and Numerical Strength." *William and Mary Quarterly* 25, no. 2 (1968): 259–77.

Smith, M. H. *The Writs of Assistance Case.* University of California Press, 1978.

Smith, S. D. "The Account Book of Richard Poor, Quaker Merchant of Barbados." *William and Mary Quarterly* 66, no. 3 (2009): 605–28.

Smith, S. D. "Accounting for Taste: British Coffee Consumption in Historical Perspective." *Journal of Interdisciplinary History* 27, no. 2 (1996): 183–214.

Smith, S. D. "Gedney Clarke of Salem and Barbados: Transatlantic Super-Merchant." *New England Quarterly* 76, no. 4 (2003): 499–549.

Smith, S. D. "The Market for Manufactures in the Thirteen Continental Colonies, 1698–1776." *Economic History Review* 51, no. 4 (1998): 676–708.

Smith, S. D. "Sugar's Poor Relation: Coffee Planting in the British West Indies, 1720–1833." In *The Slavery Reader*, ed. Gad Hueman and James Walvin, 175–93. Routledge, 2003.

Smith, Steven Carl. *An Empire of Print: The New York Publishing Trade in the Early American Republic.* Pennsylvania State University Press, 2017.

Sobel, Dava. *Longitude: The True Story of the Lone Genius Who Solved the Greatest Scientific Problem of His Time.* 1995. Penguin, 1996.

Socolow, Susan M. "Economic Roles of the Free Women of Color of Cap Français." In *More Than Chattel: Black Women and Slavery in the Americas*, ed. David Barry Gaspar and Darlene Clark Hine, 279–97. Indiana University Press, 1996.

Southwick, Albert B. "The Molasses Act—Source of Precedents." *William and Mary Quarterly* 8, no. 3 (1951): 389–405.

Sparks, Randy J. *Africans in the Old South: Mapping Exceptional Lives Across the Atlantic World*. Harvard University Press, 2016.

Spurlin, Paul Merrill. *The French Enlightenment in America: Essays on the Times of the Founding Fathers*. 1984. University of Georgia Press, 2021.

Stackpole, Edouard A. *The Sea-Hunters: The New England Whalemen During Two Centuries, 1635–1835*. 1953; Greenwood Press, 1972.

Staloff, Darren. "Secular Culture in Search of an American Enlightenment." In *A Companion to Colonial America*, edited by Daniel Vickers, 389–407. John Wiley & Sons, 2006.

Stark, Bruce. "New London Society and Connecticut Politics." *Connecticut History* 25 (1984): 1–21.

Steele, Ian K. *The English Atlantic, 1675–1740: An Exploration of Communication and Community*. Oxford University Press, 1986.

Steele, Ian K. *Politics of Colonial Policy: The Board of Trade in Colonial Administration 1696–1720*. Clarendon Press of Oxford University Press, 1968.

Stein, Robert Louis. *The French Sugar Business in the Eighteenth Century*. Louisiana State University Press, 1988.

Steiner, Bruce E. *Samuel Seabury, 1729–1796: A Study in the High Church Tradition*. Ohio University Press, 1971.

Stelten, Ruud. *From Golden Rock to Historic Gem: A Historical Archaeological Analysis of the Maritime Cultural Landscape of St. Eustatius, Dutch Caribbean*. Sidestone Press, 2019.

Stewart, Steven J. "Skimmington in the Middle and New England Colonies." In *Riot and Revelry in Early America*, edited by William Pencak, Matthew Dennis, and Simon P. Newman, 41–86. Pennsylvania State University Press, 2002.

Stiefel, Barry L. "Experimenting with Acceptance, Caribbean-Style: Jews as Aliens in the Anglophone Torrid Zone." In *The Torrid Zone: Caribbean Colonization and Cultural Interaction in the Long Seventeenth Century*, edited by L. H. Roper, 162–75. University of South Carolina Press, 2018.

St. John de Crèvecoeur, J. Hector. *Letters from an American Farmer*. Edited and with an introduction by Susan Manning. 1782. Oxford University Press, 2009.

Stiles, Henry Reed. *History of Ancient Wethersfield, Connecticut*. Facsimile of 1904 edition, 2 vols. New Hampshire Publishing, 1974.

Stoddard, Frances M. *Genealogical history of the Allen family and some of their connections*. Boston: Privately printed, 1891. https://archive.org/details/genealogicalhistoostod/page/n5/mode/2up.

Stoddard, Frances M. "An Account of Part of the Sufferings and Losses of Jolley Allen." *Proceedings of the Massachusetts Historical Society* 16 (1878): 67–99.

Stout, Harry S., and Peter Onuf. "James Davenport and the Great Awakening in New London." *Journal of American History* 70, no. 3 (1983): 556–78.

Stout, Neil R. *The Royal Navy in America, 1760–1775: A Study of Enforcement of British Colonial Policy in the Era of the American Revolution*. Naval Institute Press, 1973.

Stover, John F. "French-American Trade During the Confederation, 1781–1789." *North Carolina Historical Review* 35, no. 4 (1958): 399–414.

Sutton, Jean. *The East India Company's Maritime Service, 1746–1834: Masters of the Eastern Seas*. Boydell Press, 2010.

Syrett, David. "British Amphibious Operations during the Seven Years and American Wars." In *Assault from the Sea: Essays on the History of Amphibious Warfare*, edited by Merrill L. Bartlett, 51–59. Naval Institute Press, 1983.

Syrett, David. "The Methodology of British Amphibious Operations during the Seven Years and American Wars." *Mariner's Mirror* 58, no. 3 (1972): 269–80.

Syrett, David. *The Royal Navy in American Waters, 1775–1783*. Scolar Press, 1989.

Tarrade, Jean. *Le commerce colonial de la France à la fin de l'Ancien Régime: L'Évolution du régime de l'Exclusif de 1763 à 1789*. 2 vols. Presses Universitaires de France, 1972.

Taylor, Alan. *American Revolutions: A Continental History, 1750–1804*. W. W. Norton, 2016.

Taylor, Alan. "Introduction: Expand or Die: The Revolution's New Empire." *William and Mary Quarterly* 74, no. 4 (2017): 619–32.

Taylor, Christopher. *The Black Carib Wars: Freedom, Survival and the Making of the Garifuna*. Signal Books, 2012.

Thomas, Isaiah. *The History of Printing in America, with a Biography of Printers, and an Account of Newspapers*. 2nd ed., vol. 1. Munsell, 1874.

Thomas, Lamont D. *Paul Cuffe: Black Entrepreneur and Pan-Africanist*. University of Illinois Press, 1988.

Thompson, E. P. "'Rough Music': Le charivari anglais." *Annales. Histoire, Sciences Sociales* 27, no. 2 (1972): 285–312.

Thornton, John K. *Africa and Africans in the Making of the Atlantic World, 1400–1800*. 2nd ed. Cambridge University Press, 1998.

Thornton, Tamara Plakins. "The 'Intelligent Mariner': Nathaniel Bowditch, the Science of Navigation, and the Art of Upward Mobility in the Maritime World." *New England Quarterly* 79, no. 4 (2006): 609–35.

Tiedemann, Joseph S. *Reluctant Revolutionaries: New York City and the Road to Independence, 1763–1776*. Cornell University Press, 1997.

Tollnek, Franziska, and Joerg Baten. "Farmers at the Heart of the 'Human Capital Revolution'? Decomposing the Numeracy Increase in Early Modern Europe." *Economic History Review* 70, no. 3 (2017): 779–809.

Totten, John R. 1919. *Christophers Genealogy. Jeffrey and Christopher Christophers of New London, Conn., and Their Descendants*. Tuttle Publishing, 1921.

Troulliot, Michel-Rolph. "Motion in the System: Coffee, Color, and Slavery in Eighteenth-Century Saint-Domingue." *Review (Fernand Braudel Center)* 5, no. 3 (1982): 331–88.

Truxes, Thomas M. *Defying Empire: Trading with the Enemy in Colonial New York*. Yale University Press, 2008.

Truxes, Thomas M. *The Overseas Trade of British America: A Narrative History*. Yale University Press, 2021.

Tucher, Andie. "Newspapers and Periodicals." In *A History of the Book in America*. Vol. 2, *An Extensive Republic: Print, Culture, and Society in the New Nation*, edited by Robert A. Gross and Mary Kelley, 389–408. University of North Carolina Press, 2007.

Tyler, John W. *Smugglers and Patriots: Boston Merchants and the Advent of the American Revolution*. 1986; Northeastern University Press, 2019.

Ulrich, Laurel Thatcher. *Good Wives: Image and Reality in the Lives of Women in Northern New England, 1650–1750*. Oxford University Press, 1983.

Van, Rachel Tamar. "Cents and Sensibilities: Fairness and Free Trade in the Early Nineteenth Century." *Diplomatic History* 42, no. 1 (2018): 72–89.

Van Ruymbeke, Bertrand, and Randy J. Sparks. *Memory and Identity: The Huguenots in France and the Atlantic Diaspora*. University of South Carolina Press, 2003.

Van Ruymbeke, Bertrand. *From New Babylon to Eden: The Huguenots and Their Migration to Colonial South Carolina*. University of South Carolina Press, 2006.

Van Dusen, Albert E. "The Trade of Revolutionary Connecticut." PhD diss., University of Pennsylvania, 1948.

Verney, Michael A. "An Eye for Prices, an Eye for Souls: Americans in the Indian Subcontinent, 1784–1838." *Journal of the Early Republic* 33, no. 3 (2013): 397–431.

Vickers, Daniel. *Farmers & Fishermen: Two Centuries of Work in Essex County, Massachusetts, 1630–1850*. University of North Carolina Press, 1994.

Vickers, Daniel. "An Honest Tar: Ashley Bowen of Marblehead." *New England Quarterly* 69, no. 4 (1996): 531–53.

Vickers, Daniel, and Vince Walsh. "Young Men and the Sea: The Sociology of Seafaring in Eighteenth-Century Salem, Massachusetts." *Social History* 24, no. 1 (1999): 17–38.

Vickers, Daniel, and Vince Walsh. *Young Men and the Sea: Yankee Seafarers in the Age of Sail*. Yale University Press, 2005.

Vile, John R. *The Declaration of Independence: America's First Founding Document in U.S. History and Culture*. ABC-CLIO, 2019.

Vinovskis, Maris A. *Education, Society, and Economic Opportunity: A Historical Perspective on Persistent Issues*. Yale University Press, 1995.

Voltaire, *Candide; or Optimism*. 1759; Yale University Press, 2017.

Wall, Alexander J. "Samuel Loudon (1727–1813) (Merchant, Printer, and Patriot)." *New-York Historical Society Quarterly Bulletin* 6, no. 3 (1922): 75–92.

Wallace, Willard Mosher. *Connecticut's Dark Star of the Revolution, General Benedict Arnold*. Bicentennial Commission of Connecticut, 1978.

Wallace, Willard Mosher. *Traitorous Hero: The Life and Fortunes of Benedict Arnold*. Harper, 1954.

Walsh, James P. *Connecticut Industry and the Revolution*. Bicentennial Commission of Connecticut, 1978.

Walsh, Vince. "Recruitment and Promotion: The Merchant Fleet of Salem, Massachusetts, 1670–1765." In *The Market for Seamen in the Age of Sail*, edited by Lewis R. Fischer, 27–46. Liverpool University Press, 1994.

Walton, Gary M., and James F. Shepherd. *The Economic Rise of Early America*. Cambridge University Press, 1979.

Ward, Andrew H. "History of the Town of Shrewsbury." *Worcester Magazine and Historical Journal* 2, no. 1 (1825–1826): 1–36.

Ward, J. R. *British West Indian Slavery, 1750–1834: The Process of Amelioration*. Clarendon Press of Oxford University Press, 1988.

Warden, G. B. *Boston, 1689–1776*. Little, Brown & Co., 1970.

Warner, William B. "Communicating Liberty: The Newspapers of the British Empire as a Matrix for the American Revolution." *English Literary History* 72, no. 2 (2005): 339–61.

Washburn, Emory. *Historical Sketches of the Town of Leicester, Massachusetts, During the First Century from Its Settlement.* John Wilson and Son, 1860.

Weaver, Glenn. *Jonathan Trumbull, Connecticut's Merchant Magistrate, 1710–1785.* Connecticut Historical Society, 1956.

Weber, Max. *The Protestant Ethic and the Spirit of Capitalism.* 1916; Routledge, 2001.

Weddle, Kevin J. *The Compleat Victory: Saratoga and the American Revolution.* Oxford University Press, 2021.

Wehrman, Andrew M. *The Contagion of Liberty: The Politics of Smallpox in the American Revolution.* Johns Hopkins University Press, 2022.

Westergaard, Waldemar C. *The Danish West Indies Under Company Rule (1671–1754) with a Supplementary Chapter 1755–1917.* Translated and with an introduction by H. Morse Stephens. Macmillan, 1917.

Whealy, Mervin B. "'The Revolution Is Not Over': The Annapolis Convention of 1786." *Maryland Historical Magazine* 81, no. 3 (1986): 228–40.

White, Jerry. *A Great and Monstrous Thing: London in the Eighteenth Century.* Harvard University Press, 2013.

White, Richard. *The Middle Ground: Indians, Empires, and Republics in the Great Lakes Region, 1650–1815.* Cambridge University Press, 1991.

Whiteley, W. H. "Newfoundland, Quebec, and the Administration of the Coast of Labrador, 1774–1783." *Acadiensis* 6, no. 1 (1976): 92–112.

Wigen, Kären. "Introduction." In *Seascapes: Maritime Histories, Littoral Cultures, and Transoceanic Exchanges,* edited by Jerry H. Bentley et al., 1–18. University of Hawaii Press, 2007.

Wilkinson, Clive. *The British Navy and the State in the Eighteenth Century.* Boydell Press in association with the National Maritime Museum, 2004.

Willcox, William B. "Rhode Island in British Strategy, 1780–1781." *Journal of Modern History* 17, no. 4 (1945): 304–31.

Willingham, William Floyd. "Windham, Connecticut: Profile of a Revolutionary Community, 1755–1818." PhD diss., Northwestern University, 1972.

Willis, Jean Louise. "The Trade Between North America and the Danish West Indies, 1756–1807, with Special Reference to St. Croix." PhD diss., Columbia University, 1963.

Willis, Sam. *The Struggle for Sea Power: A Naval History of the American Revolution.* Norton, 2016.

Withers, Charles W. J. "Where Was the Atlantic Enlightenment? Questions of Geography." In *The Atlantic Enlightenment,* edited by Susan Manning and Francis D. Cogliano, 61–95. Ashgate, 2008.

Withers, Charles W. J. *Zero Degrees: Geographies of the Prime Meridian.* Harvard University Press, 2017.

Withey, Lynne. *Urban Growth in Colonial Rhode Island: Newport and Providence in the Eighteenth Century.* State University of New York Press, 1984.

Wokeck, Marianne S. *Trade in Strangers: The Beginnings of Mass Migration to North America.* Pennsylvania State University Press, 1999.

Wolfe, Patrick. *Settler Colonialism and the Transformation of Anthropology: The Politics and Poetics of an Ethnographic Event.* Cassell, 1999.

Wood, Gordon S. *The Americanization of Benjamin Franklin.* Penguin, 2004.

Wood, Gordon S. *Empire of Liberty: A History of the Early Republic, 1789–1815*. Oxford University Press, 2009.

Wood, Gordon S. *The Radicalism of the American Revolution*. Vintage Books, 1993.

Wright, Esmond. "The British Objectives, 1780–1783: 'If Not Dominion, Then Trade.'" In *Peace and the Peacemakers: The Treaty of 1783*, edited by Ronald Hoffman and Peter J. Albert, 3–29. University Press of Virginia, 1986.

Wu, Yu. "Jamaican Trade, 1688–1769: A Quantitative Study." PhD diss., Johns Hopkins University, 1995.

Wulf, Karin. *Not All Wives: Women of Colonial Philadelphia*. Cornell University Press, 2000.

Wyllie, Irving G. *The Self-Made Man in America: The Myth of Rags to Riches*. Rutgers University Press, 1966.

Yamey, Basil S. "Notes on the Origin of Double-Entry Bookkeeping." *Accounting Review* 22, no. 3 (1947): 263–72.

Yamey, Basil S., et al. *Accounting in England and Scotland, 1543–1800: Double Entry in Exposition and Practice*. Sweet & Maxwell, 1963.

Young, Alfred F. *The Shoemaker and the Tea Party: Memory and the American Revolution*. Beacon Press, 1999.

Zabin, Serena R. *Dangerous Economies: Status and Commerce in Imperial New York*. University of Pennsylvania Press, 2009.

Zakim, Michael. "The Business Clerk as Social Revolutionary; or, a Labor History of the Nonproducing Classes." *Journal of the Early Republic* 26, no. 4 (2006): 563–603.

Zeichner, Oscar. *Connecticut's Years of Controversy, 1750–1776*. University of North Carolina Press, 1949.

Zeichner, Oscar. "The Loyalist Problem in New York After the Revolution." *New York History* 21, no. 3 (1940): 284–302.

Zeichner, Oscar. "The Rehabilitation of Loyalists in Connecticut." *New England Quarterly* 11, no. 2 (1938): 308–30.

INDEX

Italicized page numbers refer to illustrations; the letter t *following a page number refers to a table.*

The Revolutionary Age

A Great Revolution in Church and State: Religion, Government, and Property in the Chesapeake, 1700–1830
ALYSSA PENICK

Suffering for the Crown: The Hudson Valley Loyalists and the Violence of Revolution
KIERAN J. O'KEEFE

The American Revolution on Trial: A New Nation Confronts the Burden of Independence
T. H. BREEN

The American Revolution at 250: Twenty-Four Historians Reflect on the Founding
FRANCIS D. COGLIANO, EDITOR

The Global Age of Revolutions: A History from 1650 to Today
BRYAN A. BANKS AND CINDY ERMUS, EDITORS

Barbary Entanglements: Realizing American Independence on the World Stage
JOHN M. CHAMBERLIN

The Course of Human Events: The Declaration of Independence and the Historical Origins of the United States
STEVEN SARSON

Napoleon in America: Bonaparte and the Rhetoric of US Empire
MARK F. EHLERS

Before Manifest Destiny: The Contested Expansion of the Early United States
NICHOLAS G. DIPUCCHIO

Revolutionary Diplomacy: Spanish Connections and the Birth of the United States
THOMAS E. CHÁVEZ

Declarations of Independence: Indigenous Resilience, Colonial Rivalries, and the Cost of Revolution
CHRISTOPHER R. PEARL

Dishonored Americans: The Political Death of Loyalists in Revolutionary America
TIMOTHY COMPEAU

The American Liberty Pole: Popular Politics and the Struggle for Democracy in the Early Republic
SHIRA LURIE

European Friends of the American Revolution
ANDREW J. O'SHAUGHNESSY, JOHN A. RAGOSTA, AND MARIE-JEANNE ROSSIGNOL, EDITORS

The Tory's Wife: A Woman and Her Family in Revolutionary America
CYNTHIA A. KIERNER

Writing Early America: From Empire to Revolution
TREVOR BURNARD

Spain and the American Revolution: New Approaches and Perspectives
GABRIEL PAQUETTE AND GONZALO M. QUINTERO SARAVIA, EDITORS

The American Revolution and the Habsburg Monarchy
JONATHAN SINGERTON

Navigating Neutrality: Early American Governance in the Turbulent Atlantic
SANDRA MOATS

Ireland and America: Empire, Revolution, and Sovereignty
PATRICK GRIFFIN AND FRANCIS D. COGLIANO, EDITORS